Microsoft

How We Test Software at Microsoft®

D1335650

Alan Page
Ken Johnston
Bj Rollison

PUBLISHED BY
Microsoft Press
A Division of Microsoft Corporation
One Microsoft Way
Redmond, Washington 98052-6399

Library of Congress Control Number: 2008940534

Printed and bound in the United States of America.

1 2 3 4 5 6 7 8 9   QWT   3 2 1 0 9 8

Distributed in Canada by H.B. Fenn and Company Ltd.

A CIP catalogue record for this book is available from the British Library.

Microsoft Press books are available through booksellers and distributors worldwide. For further information about international editions, contact your local Microsoft Corporation office or contact Microsoft Press International directly at fax (425) 936-7329. Visit our Web site at www.microsoft.com/mspress. Send comments to mspinput@microsoft.com.

Microsoft, Microsoft Press, Access, Active Accessibility, Active Directory, ActiveX, Aero, Excel, Expression, Halo, Hotmail, Hyper-V, Internet Explorer, Microsoft Surface, MS, MSDN, MS-DOS, MSN, OneNote, Outlook, PowerPoint, SharePoint, SQL Server, Virtual Earth, Visio, Visual Basic, Visual Studio, Voodoo Vince, Win32, Windows, Windows Live, Windows Media, Windows Mobile, Windows NT, Windows Server, Windows Vista, Xbox, Xbox 360, and Zune are either registered trademarks or trademarks of the Microsoft group of companies. Other product and company names mentioned herein may be the trademarks of their respective owners.

The example companies, organizations, products, domain names, e-mail addresses, logos, people, places, and events depicted herein are fictitious. No association with any real company, organization, product, domain name, e-mail address, logo, person, place, or event is intended or should be inferred.

This book expresses the author's views and opinions. The information contained in this book is provided without any express, statutory, or implied warranties. Neither the authors, Microsoft Corporation, nor its resellers, or distributors will be held liable for any damages caused or alleged to be caused either directly or indirectly by this book.

Acquisitions Editor: Ben Ryan
Project Editor: Lynn Finnel
Editorial Production: Waypoint Press
Cover Illustration: John Hersey

Body Part No. X14-71546

To my wife, Christina, and our children, Cole and Winona, who sacrificed their time with me so I could write this book; and for my parents, Don and Arlene, for their constant support, and for giving me a sanctuary to write.

—Alan Page

To my children, David and Grace, for allowing their dad the time to write; and to my wife, Karen, who while I was working on a presentation for a testing conference first suggested, "Why don't you just call it 'How we test at Microsoft.'" Without those words (and Alan leading the way), we would not have started or finished this project.

—Ken Johnston

To my mother and father for their unending love, sage wisdom, and especially their patience. I also want to thank my 6-year-old daughter Elizabeth whose incessant curiosity to learn new things and persistent determination to conquer diverse challenges has taught me that the only problems we cannot overcome are those for which we have not yet found a solution.

—Bj Rollison

This book is dedicated to the test engineers at Microsoft who devote themselves to the most challenging endeavor in the software process, and who continue to mature the discipline by breaking through traditional barriers and roles in order to help ship leading-edge, high-quality software to our customers. For us, it is truly a privilege to mentor and work alongside so many professional testers at Microsoft, because through our interactions with them we also continue to learn more about software testing.

Contents at a Glance

Table of Contents

What do you think of this book? We want to hear from you!

Microsoft is interested in hearing your feedback so we can continually improve our books and learning resources for you. To participate in a brief online survey, please visit:

www.microsoft.com/learning/booksurvey

What do you think of this book? We want to hear from you!

Microsoft is interested in hearing your feedback so we can continually improve our books and learning resources for you. To participate in a brief online survey, please visit:

www.microsoft.com/learning/booksurvey

Acknowledgments

This book never would have happened without the help of every single tester at Microsoft. Many helped directly by reviewing chapters or writing about their experiences in testing. Others helped by creating the legacy of software testing at Microsoft, or by continuing to innovate in the way we test software.

Including the names of all 9,000 testers at Microsoft would be impractical (especially when many former employees, people from other disciplines, and even external reviewers contributed to the completion of this book). On the other hand, we do want to call out the names of several people who have contributed substantially to the creation of this book.

This book grew out of the opinions, suggestions, and feedback of many current and former Microsoft employees. Some of the most prominent contributors include Michael Corning, Ed Triou, Amol Kher, Scott Wadsworth, Geoff Staneff, Dan Travison, Brian Rogers, John Lambert, Sanjeev Verma, Shawn McFarland, Grant George, Tara Roth, Karen Carter-Schwendler, Jean Hartman, James Whittaker, Irada Sadykhova, Alex Kim, Darrin Hatakeda, Marty Riley, Venkat Narayanan, Karen Johnston, Jim Pierson, Ibrahim El Far, Carl Tostevin, Nachi Nagappan, Keith Stobie, Mark Davis, Mike Blaylock, Wayne Roseberry, Carole Cancler, Andy Tischaefer, Lori Ada-Kilty, Matt Heusser, Jeff Raikes, Microsoft Research (especially Amy Stevenson), the Microsoft Test Excellence Team, the Microsoft Test Leadership Team, and the Microsoft Test Architect Group.

We'd also like to thank Lynn Finnel, the Project Editor for this book, who continued to give us encouragement and support throughout the creation of this book.

Introduction

I still remember the morning, sometime late in the fall of 2007, when my manager at the time, Ken Johnston, uttered these five words, "You should write a book."

He had just come back from delivering a talk at an industry test conference (not coincidentally titled, "How We Test Software at Microsoft,") and was excited by the audience reception. Ken loves to give presentations, but he somehow thought I should be the one to write the book.

I humored him and said, "Sure, why not." I went on to say that the book could cover a lot of the things that we teach in our software testing courses, as well as a smattering of other popular test approaches used at Microsoft. It could be interesting, but there are a ton of books on testing—I know, I've probably read a few dozen of them—and some of them are really good. What value to the testing community could yet another book provide?

I was about to talk the nonsense out of Ken when I realized something critical: At Microsoft, we have some of the best software test training in the world. The material and structure of the courses are fantastic, but that's not what makes it so great. The way our instructors tie in anecdotes, success stories, and cool little bits of trivia throughout our courses is what makes them impactful and memorable. I thought that if we could include some stories and bits of information on how Microsoft has used some of these approaches, the book might be interesting. I began to think beyond what we teach, of more test ideas and stories that would be fun to share with testers everywhere. I realized that some of my favorite programming books were filled with stories embedded with all of the "techie" stuff.

The next thing I knew, I was writing a proposal. An outline began to come together, and the form of the book began to take shape, with four main themes emerging. It made sense to set some context by talking about Microsoft's general approaches to people and engineering. The next two sections would focus on how we do testing inside Microsoft, and the tools we use; and the final section would look at the future of testing inside Microsoft. I sent the proposal to Microsoft Press, and although I remained excited about the potential for the book, part of me secretly hoped that Microsoft Press would tell me the idea was silly, and that I should go away. Alas, that didn't happen, and shortly thereafter, I found myself staring at a computer screen wondering what the first sentences would look like.

From the very beginning, I knew that I wanted Ken to write the first two chapters. Ken has been a manager at Microsoft for years, and the people stuff was right up his alley. About the time I submitted the proposal, Ken left our group to manage the Office Online group. Soon after, it became apparent that Ken should also write the chapter on how we test Software plus Services. He's since become a leader at the company in defining how we test Web services, and it would have been silly not to have him write Chapter 14, "Testing Software

Plus Services". Later on, I approached BJ Rollison, one of Microsoft's most prominent testers, to write the chapters about functional and structural test techniques. Bj Rollison designed our core software testing course, and he knows more about these areas of testing than anyone I know. He's also one of the only people I know who has read more books on testing than I have. Ken, Bj and I make quite a trio of authors. We all approach the task and produce our material quite differently, but in the end, we feel like we have a mix of both material and writing styles that reflects the diversity of the Microsoft testing population. We often joke that Bj is the professor, Ken tries to be the historian and storyteller, and I just absorb information and state the facts. Although we all took the lead on several chapters, we each edited and contributed to the others' work, so there is definitely a melding of styles throughout the book.

I cannot begin to describe how every little setback in life becomes gigantic when the task of "writing a book" is always on your plate. Since starting this book, I took over Ken's old job as Director of Test Excellence at Microsoft. Why in the world I decided to take on a job with entirely new challenges in the middle of writing a book I'll never know. In hindsight, however, taking on this role forced me to gain some insight into test leadership at Microsoft that benefitted this book tremendously.

My biggest fear in writing this book was how much I knew I'd have to leave out. There are over 9,000 testers at Microsoft. The test approaches discussed in this book cover what most testers at Microsoft do, but there are tons of fantastically cool things that Microsoft testers do that couldn't be covered in this book. On top of that, there are variations on just about every topic covered in this book. We tried to capture as many different ideas as we could, while telling stories about what parts of testing we think are most important. I also have to admit that I'm slightly nervous about the title of this book. "How We Test Software at Microsoft" could imply that everything in this book is done by every single tester at Microsoft, and that's simply not true. With such a large population of testers and such a massive product portfolio, there's just no way to write about testing in a way that exactly represents every single tester at Microsoft. So, we compromised. This book simply covers the most popular testing practices, tools, and techniques used by Microsoft testers. Not every team does everything we write about, but most do. Everything we chose to write about in this book has been successful in testing Microsoft products, so the topics in this book are a collection of some of the things we know work.

In the end, I think we succeeded, but as testers, we know it could be better. Sadly, it's time to ship, but we do have a support plan in place! If you are interested in discussing anything from this book with the authors, you can visit our web site, *www.hwtsam.com*. We would all love to hear what you think.

—*Alan Page*

Who This Book Is For

This book is for anyone who is interested in the role of test at Microsoft or for those who want to know more about how Microsoft approaches testing. This book isn't a replacement for any of the numerous other great texts on software testing. Instead, it describes how Microsoft applies a number of testing techniques and methods of evaluation to improve our software.

Microsoft testers themselves will likely find the book to be interesting as it includes techniques and approaches used across the company. Even nontesters may find it interesting to know about the role of test at Microsoft

What This Book Is About

This book starts by familiarizing the reader with Microsoft products, Microsoft engineers, Microsoft testers, the role of test, and general approaches to engineering software. The second part of the book discusses many of the test approaches and tools commonly used at Microsoft. The third part of the book discusses some of the tools and systems we use in our work. The final section of the book discusses future directions in testing and quality at Microsoft and how we intend to create that future.

Part I, "About Microsoft"

    Chapter 1, "Software Engineering at Microsoft,"

    Chapter 2, "Software Test Engineers at Microsoft"

    Chapter 3, "Engineering Life Cycles"

Part II, "About Testing"

    Chapter 4, "A Practical Approach to Test Case Design"

    Chapter 5, "Functional Testing Techniques"

    Chapter 6, "Structural Testing Techniques"

    Chapter 7, "Analyzing Risk with Code Complexity"

    Chapter 8, "Model-Based Testing"

Part III, "Test Tools and Systems"

    Chapter 9, "Managing Bugs and Test Cases"

    Chapter 10, "Test Automation"

    Chapter 11, "Non-Functional Testing"

    Chapter 12, "Other Tools"

    Chapter 13, "Customer Feedback Systems"

    Chapter 14, "Testing Software Plus Services"

Find Additional Content Online

As new or updated material becomes available that complements this book, it will be posted online on the Microsoft Press Online Developer Tools Web site. The type of material you might find includes updates to book content, articles, links to companion content, errata, sample chapters, and more. This Web site is available at *www.microsoft.com/learning/books/ online/developer*, and is updated periodically.

More stories and tidbits about testing at Microsoft will be posted on *www.hwtsam.com*.

Support for This Book

If you have comments, questions, or ideas regarding the book, or questions that are not answered by visiting the sites above, please send them to Microsoft Press via e-mail to

mspinput@microsoft.com.

Or via postal mail to

Microsoft Press
Attn: *How We Test Software at Microsoft* Editor
One Microsoft Way
Redmond, WA 98052-6399.

Please note that Microsoft software product support is not offered through the above addresses.

Part I
About Microsoft

Chapter 1
Software Engineering at Microsoft

Ken Johnston

Part I of this book, Chapters 1 through 3, provides a lot of information about Microsoft, what our goals are, how we are organized to engineer products, and how we ship products. A lot of the information in this chapter has been shared publicly, but we have pulled a few strings to share some new details of Microsoft internals.

There are many books, articles, and Web sites that cover Microsoft's history in detail, but we felt that a brief overview within this book that focused on Microsoft engineering would help readers better understand the why behind how we test software at Microsoft. All the methods and tools we discuss in the rest of the book are influenced by our history, vision, and business objectives.

The Microsoft Vision, Values and Why We "Love This Company!"

It is actually pretty hard to get engineers to show a lot of exuberance, unless perhaps for the finals of the World Cup championships for football (soccer) or cricket. Microsoft engineers are no different, except for maybe one other event.

Each year, in early October, dozens of busses bring thousands of Microsoft employees from our Redmond, Washington campus to Safeco field, where the Seattle Mariners play baseball, for the annual company meeting. Something shy of 20 thousand employees usually attend in person with tens of thousands more tuning in online.

The last speaker is always Steve Ballmer. He always bursts on stage to thunderous cheers and loud, rocking music, such as "Eye of the Tiger," from the "Rocky" movies. Steve then storms around the stage pumping up the crowd even more before he dashes down the steps and takes a lap around the infield. As he moves along through the crowd he hands out victorious high fives and receives many hearty pats on the back. At points along his path he pauses to pump up the attendees in the stadium seats before finally running back up onto the huge stage. He usually takes a moment to catch his breath, and then lead us through several rounds of my favorite chorus, "I LOVE THIS COMPANY." The videos are easy to find, just try the video search at *www.live.com* and enter "Steve Ballmer company meeting."

It's true; Microsoft is a really cool company and, as the rest of this book will show, the best company in the world at which to be a software tester. Our rich history, great products and geeky traditions, like the company meeting and a pumped up CEO, help make Microsoft a great place to be an engineer.

For the first 24 years of Microsoft's existence, the company vision was "A PC on every desk and in every home." In many ways, Microsoft has succeeded in achieving that mission. But, with the rapid growth of the Internet, the need to deliver devices such as the Xbox, and a shifting focus to services, the company vision had to be updated. From 1999 to 2002, we used "Empowering people through great software—any time, any place, and on any device." It was certainly a bigger and bolder vision than just focusing on PCs, but it was still not big enough. In 2002, we released a new mission statement, "To enable people and businesses throughout the world to realize their full potential." Figure 1-1 shows the 2008 Microsoft corporate logo, which reflects this vision.

Microsoft®
Your potential. Our passion.®

FIGURE 1-1 Corporate logo in 2008, updated to reflect the company vision.

During the company meeting in September of 2008, our CEO, Steve Ballmer, announced the new company mission statement, "Create experiences that combine the magic of software with the power of Internet services across a world of devices." Projected alongside on the screen were images of PCs, servers, rich browser applications, and devices from cell phones to gaming consoles and others in between. The mission really is to bring software plus services to every powerful Internet connected device. The mission statement is in addition to the vision we released in 2002, and so we now have a vision and a mission statement. Interestingly, during the launch of the new mission statement, Steve paused for a moment to answer a question I found myself asking. What about the old vision of your potential is our passion? Steve commented that the original goal of "a PC on every desk and in every home," had served for many years as both a vision and a mission statement for the company. He went on to say that we may never again have a single clear statement like that one to guide the company, but that is a reflection of our success and broad impact on the world. While I like the vision that focuses on helping others realize their potential, as an engineer I like the concreteness of software, the Internet, and a world of devices. As a tester this scares me because now my test matrix has once again been expanded.

Supporting the mission, we have six company values: Integrity and Honesty, Open and Respectful, Big Challenges, Passion, Accountable, and Self-Critical. Out of this list the one value that engineers most often reference is Big Challenges. This value is the one engineers use when they talk about the next big thing and why we need to do it now. Big Challenges also includes taking smart risks, being persistent but not inflexible, and being courageous but not reckless.

Upholding our mission and taking on big challenges are common bonds that drive the engineers at Microsoft. These values are what drive testers at Microsoft to keep working hard to find that next bug, and the next one after that, so that our customers can have great products.

When asked why he joined Microsoft to replace the retiring Jeff Raikes as president of the Business Division, Stephen Elop covered several points that contributed to his decision, but focused on a single word that clearly resonated with the audience: impact. "Joining the Microsoft team represents an opportunity to positively impact the life and work of millions of people around the world. There is nothing more gratifying than having someone come up to you in an airport and saying 'Look at what I have been able to do with your software' "

Changing the world through software requires great products and the organizations to deliver those products. Microsoft is notorious for reorganizing our engineering workforce. Although this notoriety is well founded, for several years at the top level we have had the following three divisions of product engineering:

- **Platform Products and Services Division (PSD)**   Includes the Client Group, the Server & Tools Group, and the Online Services Group

- **Business Division (MBD)**   Includes the Information Worker Group, the Microsoft Business Solutions Group, and the Unified Communications Group

- **Entertainment and Devices Division (E&D)**   Includes the Home & Entertainment Group and the Mobile & Embedded Devices Group

> **Tip** Internally, the Business Division is known as the MBD, which stands for Microsoft Business Division; this is because BD is not a TLA (three-letter acronym) and the use of TLAs to refer to every single product and team is hard-wired into the culture.

Essentially, all software development is managed by these three divisions. Each division is run by a president that reports to our CEO Steve Ballmer, who also has many other direct reports. By the time this book ships, Bill Gates will have retired from full-time work at Microsoft, but he will probably show up in organization charts for many years to come. Figure 1-2 shows a simplified organization chart for Microsoft.

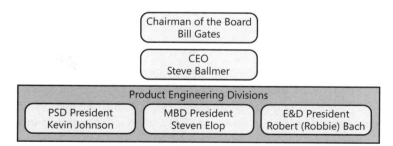

FIGURE 1-2 How the three product engineering divisions fit into the organization.

Each division generates billions of dollars in profit on $10 billion to $20 billion in revenue, making each division bigger than many Fortune 500 companies. In each division there are dozens of products. Some of the products generate a lot of revenue and profit, others are investments and don't turn a profit for many years.

What holds a division together is its focus on its market segment and customers: E&D is about entertainment, MBD is about software for businesses, and PSD builds the platforms on which our partners and other teams at Microsoft build to provide solutions for their companies or customers.

Our chief software architect, Ray Ozzie, reports directly to Steve Ballmer, as do many other senior leaders, such as Kevin Turner, Chief Operating Officer (COO), and Brad Smith, senior VP of our Legal and Corporate Affairs team (LCA). There are some software engineers in all parts of the company, even human resources, but the vast majority of engineers and testers work in these three divisions.

Time to order new T-shirts again

It was a hot and sunny day in 1998. Steve Ballmer wasn't yet CEO or president of Microsoft when they called all the Project Atlas engineers together to meet with him in one of the big lecture rooms. Just the day before, the Project Atlas T-shirts had been handed out, and I had mine on. I should have known we were in trouble when we were given T-shirts of a man holding the world on his shoulders—Project Atlas was about delivering software and services on any device, any place, and at any time. We were a small group of about 200 engineers and were given that task. This vision eventually became the Microsoft corporate mission, so we were clearly underresourced.

As we were walking from our building to the meeting room, one of our testers came up next to me and said, "Time to order new shirts." Then, he proceeded to run ahead.

I called to him, "What do you mean?"

"It's simple, man," he said, turning to face me as he walked backward with the crowd of engineers. "We have the project T-shirts in hand. We're on our way to meet with Steve Ballmer. Don't you see? We're being re-orged."

"This is the third project shirt I've been given this year," I said. "We can't be getting re-orged again."

Well, my friend was right, and I was wrong—our team was reorganized, and from then on the phrase "time to order new shirts" has always elicited a mixed response from me. On the one hand it could mean time to drop everything and start over on a new project, but on the other hand it could mean a chance to get one of those great t-shirts that you wear into the office on rare occasions that always generate a long, "Oh, I remember that project…" conversation. I have two such t-shirts.

One time we actually had a t-shirt made for all the testers in the division that had a comic strip on it from Doonesbury. If you want to see the strip, it was published on 3/19/1996, and included a phrase that is a favorite among tester circles, "Bug checking is brutally cool." Garry Trudeau, the creator of Doonesbury, actually autographed one of the shirts and we proudly displayed the shirt in the lobby of our building for many years.

In reality, getting reset so many times turned out to be a good experience. Over the next several years, I was able to test on several server products and several services without having to change teams or managers. I actually shipped a couple of the projects and those ship parties were a lot of fun.

Microsoft Is a Big Software Engineering Company

The fact that Microsoft is a big company is no surprise to anyone: In January 2008, Microsoft employed more than 90,000 people worldwide. The impact this size has on how things are done at Microsoft is important to understand.

For Microsoft, *big* is really about *breadth*—the breadth of the product portfolio that ships to market every year, the breadth of the markets Microsoft sells and competes in, and the breadth of the engineering challenges the company takes on to meet all of these demands.

For example, the breadth of the software product offerings from Microsoft is vast. In fiscal year 2007 (July 1 through June 30), Microsoft shipped more than 100 major products such as the Microsoft Office system, the Windows operating system, games and game consoles, home entertainment products, business solutions such as customer relationship management (CRM) software, mobile embedded devices, consumer Web services such as Live Mail and Search, and small business Web services. Microsoft is beginning to invest in services in the business-to-business (B2B) space and is continuing to expand in other emerging software markets. Microsoft continues to invest in robotics, Internet Protocol–based Television (IPTV), and in automotive PCs.

Equally stunning are the number of markets Microsoft ships products to. When Microsoft releases a new software product or service, we typically simultaneously ship, or "sim-ship," it worldwide. This requires almost every product to have content translated into more than 80 languages and dialects. Table 1-1 shows the breadth of some products in the Microsoft portfolio.

TABLE 1-1 Microsoft Product Factoids

Product	Factoid
Windows operating system	Microsoft Windows has more than 90 percent market share for desktop PCs and is expected to be installed on more than 1 billion PCs by mid-2008 (around the time this book is published).
Microsoft Office	Office 95 supported 27 different languages. Office 2007 supports more than four times as many languages and the list continues to grow as the worldwide market for software grows.
Windows Mobile	Windows Mobile is now the number one operating system for PDA phones with more than 20 million units sold in 2007.
Xbox 360	More than 14 million units were sold worldwide before the end of 2007.
Halo 3 game	*Halo 3* (exclusive for the Xbox 360) sales topped $170 million in the first 24 hours of its release, making it the fastest-selling video game in history.
Windows Live Mail	This is the largest e-mail service in the world with more than 425 million active mail accounts.
Virtual Earth	Virtual Earth serves up more than 600 million map tiles a day. (A map tile is a section of a map that users can zoom in and out.)

The size of the company and the diversity of the portfolio explain why there is no one way to build and ship products at Microsoft. At its very heart, Microsoft is a software company powered by the innovations of its employees. Even across diverse products and processes, product groups share many of the same best practices and tools used for testing software. Part 1 of this book focuses on the people side of Microsoft: how we organize teams, and how teams approach challenges in testing the breadth of software Microsoft offers. Parts 2 through 4 explain and demonstrate how our best practices and tools work.

Developing Big and Efficient Businesses

We have two major organizational models for the engineering workforce. As a business goes from incubation to maturity, it may evolve from one model to another. When Office first started, it wasn't even Office. It was Word and Excel, and then PowerPoint and Access. For several releases each product was developed and shipped independently. This model for greater independence to ship is often referred to as the PUM (Product Unit Manager) model, and is the most common across Microsoft.

With the PUM model a team manages all the engineering assets they need (or at least can get) in one single organization. They typically do not have to take dependencies on other teams unless it's for some technology another team is close to shipping. The PUM model is ideal for rapid shipping and adjusting to competitors, but it does not allow for the centralization of common functions, such as build or test automation tools. With this approach, duplication of effort is higher, as is communications overhead. Almost every product, no matter how mature, still has some of these smaller teams within it. Both Microsoft Office and Windows still use the PUM model for incubation features while trying to ship major versions.

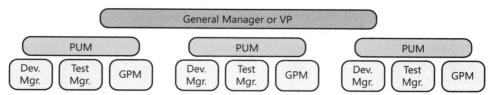

FIGURE 1-3 The common PUM model for engineering teams.

The Shared Team Model

As products and product categories mature, teams usually get much bigger, and centralization to improve efficiencies and reduce costs starts to happen naturally. This model has many names, but the shared team approach is probably the best. With the shared team approach, common features and tasks are placed into a central shared team, and the other product teams must take dependencies on this team or they won't be able to ship successfully with the right feature set.

Microsoft Office is a great example. From the day someone had the brilliant idea that we should bundle our productivity applications and sell them as a suite, the Office team has been headed down the path of a shared team. In fact, Office calls this the Office Shared Services team (OSS).

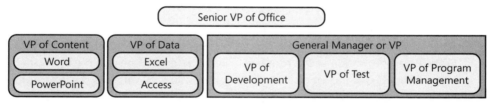

FIGURE 1-4 Typical Office organizational structure.

Within the Office organization there are product teams (Word, Excel, and Sharepoint) that focus on a particular applications and the user base that relies heavily on them, and then there are shared teams (User Interface, Build, and Document Lifecycle) that focus on shared technologies and scenarios. The product teams tend to focus on their specific customer base (Excel cares about what's best for the spreadsheet user), but they do that in the context of shared initiatives (what's the best way to convey our user interface consistently such that someone learning Office only needs to learn one approach). By doing this they enable innovation in each product category while still maintaining consistency. Those goals can be at odds with each other, but having teams that represent each constituency working together results in a comprehensive vision for the design, development, and testing of the overall Office product release.

The same thing happens in Microsoft engineering, and test, specifically. Each product team has a test team focused on innovative ways to verify the functionality of its products, but there are great gains to be had by innovating on a consistent set of test tools and approaches whenever possible. Because of this, Office is able to create innovative approaches to specific products, such as Feature Crews (covered in chapter 3), OASYS (Office Automation System) for automated testing, and Big Button for pre-checking tests.

The shared model not only produces efficiencies it forces creative contention. A shared team may have unique insights for common look and feel but the needs of a particular user segment might not be met by the initial designs. Shared infrastructure that isn't of high enough quality will slow down the other teams and if quality isn't improved they will work around the share team.

There are many variations between the full PUM model and a full Shared Team model. In fact there are probably no instances within Microsoft where any two teams have the exact same org structure and approach to engineering their products. Many people have used the metaphor that from the outside Microsoft looks like a battleship, but when you look at it from inside we are more like a bunch of speed boats rushing about to get to a common end point, but all in our own way. A friend of mine came up with a much better analogy for Microsoft product engineering teams.

Shipping a Software Product Is Like Producing a Play

When I started at Microsoft, I struggled to rationalize all the different processes, practices and engineering roles, which led me to think about how things get done around here. On one hand, we need creativity and innovation. On another, we are a big company. Somehow, it would not reconcile; what makes a large company successful rarely drives innovation at the root level. The analogy that helped me understand the environment was with a performing arts organization. As with any theatre company, we have directors, producers, actors (engineers, naturally!), A-list and B-list stars, stage producers, and other enabling folks. The idea is that while everything in performing arts is about creativity, make no mistake, a theatre production has to sell tickets, that is, find its customer. Trendsetting and having foresight about what will be popular is just as important in performing arts as it is in software development, especially in the current experience-driven world.

Marketing, sales, legal positioning of edgy subjects, and such play their role as well. The way I connected it with Microsoft was that executives and finance are producers, GMs are directors, and engineers are actors. Everyone else has a role that's parallel to a role in theatre production. Innovation is a driver of the product similar to creativity in theatre. Trendsetting is the same as introducing a breakthrough product. Once I built that connection, I felt like I did when I stood in the wings of my beloved Kirov Ballet, watching my good friend and neighbor dance; I felt I had arrived and made sense of this weird, fascinating, oh-so-treasured Microsoft Wonderland. The Alice in me felt as though she had reached the bottom of the Rabbit Hole.

The key to the whole analogy is balancing the contradictions of a large software company that has to produce big profits with high margins and be dynamic and creative at the very same time. There is some inherent conflict between large production scale and creativity; balancing them successfully is a core of the success of Microsoft. No Google, or Apple, or Sun has quite yet mastered this challenge at scale. Only the likes of Cirque du Soleil and Microsoft have proven they can do it.

—*Irada Sadykhova (Director, Engineering Learning & Organization Effectiveness – Engineering Excellence)*

Working Small in a Big Company

Microsoft isn't just about big businesses. We start many small businesses in the process of looking for that next big thing.

I once heard Bill Gates compare Microsoft product development to the movie industry. He made the analogy that every big movie studio places bets in different categories. One category is the blockbuster movie such as the latest remake of *King Kong*. Typically, these are very expensive movies to produce and come with a great deal of risk—they are either a box office bomb, such as the 2002 Eddie Murphy movie *The Adventures of Pluto Nash,* which is considered the biggest flop ever with a budget close to $100 million and box office receipts of only $4.4 million, or they are a breakthrough winner, like the reigning box office champ *Titanic*, which earned $1.8 billion worldwide, or *Napoleon Dynamite*, which turned a $400,000 investment into more than $46 million at the box office (not counting DVD and other sales). Another category includes the second or third installment of franchise movies such as *Spiderman II* and *Spiderman III* or any of the sequels in the Star Wars series. Big box office receipts are expected from these franchise movies.

All movies have a goal of being profitable, but risk is often mitigated by reducing the level of investment. Bill's point was that there will always be unexpected hits and successful franchises, but the key to long-term success is to spread the risk across a large portfolio and to try to find that next big franchise movie. The predictable long-term profits from a franchise can then be used to fund other projects that might yield the next big movie series. Peter Jackson's "Lord of the Rings" series and the Harry Potter movies, which have had multiple directors but are all based on the books by J. K. Rowling, are examples of big bets that paid off with multiple highly profitable releases. In fact, both of these franchises have more movies in the works. Peter Jackson is developing two movies based upon *The Hobbit*, and there are three more Harry Potter books yet to be made into movies.

The Microsoft product strategy strongly parallels that of the movie industry. Profits from big and successful businesses such as Microsoft Office, Windows, Visual Studio, Exchange,

SQL Server, Hotmail, and MSN Messenger are invested in incubation projects that have the potential to be the next big businesses. In the software industry, incubations are common. The term *incubation* is usually applied to a small start-up software company that has yet to release a product but whose idea seems sound and whose target market looks to be worth going after. Start-up teams at Microsoft are typically managed by a General Manager (GM) for large efforts or by a Product Unit Manager (PUM) for smaller efforts. These teams are usually self-contained units that have most of the engineering resources they need in-house. Their destiny then lies in their own hands.

I once worked for a BUM

In 1997, I was part of a group called the Internet Services Business Unit (ISBU; pronounced "is-boo") that had spun off from MSN. On the original MSN team, we had developed a lot of new technology to launch MSN: We had an e-mail service that scaled better than Microsoft Exchange Server did, we had a login server that scaled better than the Microsoft Active Directory directory service did, and we had a content management server and many other servers that just about every Internet service provider (ISP) such as CompuServe, Comcast, and AOL had or needed.

Then, someone somewhere must have said, "Hey, let's try to package this stuff up and sell it to smaller ISPs and telephone companies." Thus, ISBU was formed. Many engineers from MSN moved to join ISBU and a number of smaller companies were acquired to build up what would become Site Server, Commerce Server, and Microsoft Commercial Internet Server (MCIS). Instead of a Product Unit Manager (PUM) or a General Manager (GM) acting as the engineering manager in charge of each product team, we had a small handful of Business Unit Managers. That's how all of us engineers in ISBU ended up working for a bunch of BUMs.

Microsoft invests in internal incubation projects such as our IPTV, Auto PC, and robotics projects as well as all the work done by Microsoft Research (*http://research.microsoft.com*). We also invest in projects that can help spur change in the software industry as a whole. In April 2007, with more than 10 partners we launched the Microsoft Software as a Service (SaaS) Incubation Center Program.

In Microsoft, there are many models for incubations. Established products often incubate features in the larger organization. For example, the Office 12 ribbon, a new feature that changed the Office user interface, and the Windows Vista shuffle feature were incubations. The code coverage tools that ship in the latest versions of Visual Studio were based on concepts developed first as internal tools projects in Microsoft Research and Windows.

Another approach we've used to incubate innovations is using an internal venture capital team. Any employee can submit an idea, and the venture capital team will examine the feasibility of the idea using a process much like an industry venture capital firm would use. Just like in industry, very few ideas get funding through this mechanism.

The Bill Gates ThinkWeek is another source of ideas that can become incubations. Microsoft employees can submit white papers detailing new ideas and innovations, and during ThinkWeek, which occurs approximately twice each year, Bill reads and comments on scores of papers. At the end of the week, Bill's notes, once hand-written, are shared with the company. In 2005, the *Wall Street Journal* described ThinkWeeks in this way:

> *It's a twice-yearly ritual that can influence the future of Microsoft and the tech industry. A Think Week thought can give the green light to a new technology that millions of people will use or send Microsoft into new markets. One week in 1995 inspired Mr. Gates's paper, "The Internet Tidal Wave," that led Microsoft to develop its Internet browser and crush Netscape. Plans to create Microsoft's Tablet PC, build more-secure software and start an online videogame business were also catalyzed during Think Weeks.[1]*

For the Fall 2008 ThinkWeek, 375 papers were submitted and Bill was able to comment on 125 of them. This program was established to encourage employees to submit innovative and forward-thinking ideas. Many of the more promising ideas receive funding for initial development. Bill also publishes his recommended reading list to the company. Recently, a white paper I wrote on how to improve our software services testing made Bill's recommended reading list, and for me it was like receiving a stamp of approval on what until then was just theories.

From the minds of employees...

The concept for the Microsoft Surface (*http://www.microsoft.com/surface/*) was once a white paper written by a few folks in Microsoft Research. After Bill read that paper, a Product Unit Manager joined the team and began to drive the process of turning the idea into a viable product. The result is a computer built into a table where the computer screen is the table surface. I think they look a lot like the tabletop video games that showed up briefly in bars during the 1990s. Users can interact with Surface by using hand gestures as well as placing physical objects such as a business card or a Zune MP3 music player on the table.

Microsoft recently began using a process called *Quests* to innovate new ideas. The dictionary defines the verb *quest* as "to search and seek." At Microsoft, a Quest is about mapping our long-term aspirations and goals. The Quest process brings together senior technical thought leaders from across Microsoft to create a 5- to 10-year vision for technology innovation. Through the Quest process, Microsoft's top technologists work collaboratively across organizations and product groups and with the business leadership to architect technology advances that will offer the greatest potential to transform people's lives at work and at home, and create new business opportunities for Microsoft, our customers, and our partners.

---

[1] Robert A. Guth, "In Secret Hideaway, Bill Gates Ponders Microsoft's Future," Wall Street Journal, March 28, 2005, http://online.wsj.com/article_email/SB111196625830690477-IZjgYNklaB4o52sbHmla62Im4.html.

Quests do not raise simple problems with simple answers. Typically, a Quest takes many years to complete and likely requires new research, generates many prototypes, and discovers unique insight that often precedes the creation of a new market. A successful Quest must be customer-centered, visionary, directional, and rigorous. This last point is the part where our values of Integrity and Honesty and Open and Respectful intersect. *Rigorous* for Microsoft Quests means extensive peer review combined with oversight from the company's Senior Leadership Team, which includes all three presidents, Steve Ballmer, and a few other executives.

Quests are not about producing another version of a product but are more about managing a portfolio of long-range technology problems that by design require us to work across groups to find and use synergies. The number and areas of focus for Quests continue to change every year as some Quests end and others merge. Currently, more than 50 Quests spanning the entire range of Microsoft businesses and all customer segments, from consumer and information worker to IT pros and developers, are in progress.

Employing Many Types of Engineers

Because Microsoft is both a product and a platforms company, it has a vast array of partners who have their own software engineers working to innovate on top of what Microsoft has shipped. Vendors and partners who work with Microsoft make the engineering force of Microsoft well more than 100,000 software engineers worldwide. Compared with the full ecosystem made up of millions of software engineers around the world working on Apple, IBM, Sun, Oracle, and open source software such as Linux, the Microsoft engineering force is a small percentage. Still, it is perhaps the most powerful and influential engineering force in the market today.

 Note There are more than 35,000 software engineers working full time for Microsoft in more than 40 countries around the world. Each year Microsoft hires more than 5,000 new software engineers and more than 1,000 new software design engineers in Test.

Compared with most other companies, Microsoft is unique in both its engineering processes and its management of software engineers. Some might look at the company's success in the software industry and point to these unique differences as key competitive advantages. Others point to some of our products and their major slips and wonder if these differences are a weakness.

So, what are the software engineering factors that make Microsoft unique and different from any other company in the world?

The Engineering Disciplines

When you break down the roles of the more than 80,000 employees worldwide that work directly for Microsoft, of the total employee base, you find that more than 35,000 are in sales, marketing, and IT. Product Engineering is the part of the company that develops and supports the software products, and as of early 2008, Microsoft employs nearly 35,000 engineers worldwide. The other 10,000 employees span a number of other disciplines ranging from business administration to legal. Although Microsoft continues to grow at a rapid rate, the balance of sales, marketing, and IT with Product Engineering has been a relative constant for many years.

Product engineers are the employees who actually work to create and ship the products— hardware, software, and services—that Microsoft sells to customers. Microsoft engineering roles break down into the following 10 product-engineering disciplines:

■ **Test**   Software Development Engineers in Test (SDETs) are usually just called Test and sometimes Software Testing. SDETs are responsible for maintaining high testing and quality-assurance standards for all Microsoft products.

■ **Development**   Software Development Engineers (SDEs) are often referred to as Software Development. SDEs write the code that drives Microsoft products and upgrades.

■ **Program Management (PM)**   PM is a rather unique role in Microsoft that combines elements of project management, product planning, and design into one discipline. The PM's job is to define a new product's technical aspects and oversee its hands-on development.

■ **Operations (Ops)**   Ops is part of Microsoft Information technology (IT). The Ops discipline manages and maintains Microsoft online services as well as internal corporate IT infrastructure, from networks to servers. Ops works closely with the product teams on service architecture to lower production costs and make our services more reliable.

■ **Usability and Design**   Usability Experience and Design (UX) combines the roles we advertise as product design and usability. Design focuses on the visual and functional front-end user experience for Microsoft products. Usability also focuses on the end user experience but conducts new research to see how the user works with existing products and new prototypes, and then analyzes the results to help improve products during development.

■ **Content**   Content is still called User Assistance and Education on our external sites. This discipline plans and delivers assistance—including UI text, Web articles, training, templates, columns, books, quizzes, and Help files—to help customers get the most from Microsoft products. The shift to the title *Content* emphasizes Microsoft's need to focus on content that can be used across multiple delivery vehicles.

- **Creative**   Creative positions exist most often in the Games group. Engineers in this discipline develop and improve Microsoft's cutting-edge games software for the PC and for the Xbox game console. The Creative discipline includes game designers as well as artists.

- **Research**   Research includes subroles for developers and testers. The difference between a research developer and a product developer is the emphasis upon research, publishing papers, and incubating new technologies as opposed to shipping a product on a schedule.

- **Localization**   International Project Engineering (IPE) used to be known as Localization. The localization component of the discipline focuses on translation of Microsoft software into multiple languages and adaptation of software for different cultures. The IPE discipline is also responsible for adapting Microsoft software for specific market needs.

- **Engineering Management**   Engineering Management is made up of the managers who run teams that include multiple engineering disciplines. They often go by titles such as Product Unit Manager, General Manager, or Group Manager.

> **Note** Hardware is considered a specialty area and includes disciplines such as Hardware Developer, Hardware Tester, and even Hardware Program Manager. These disciplines are similar to their cousins in the software and services spaces but are different enough to warrant their own career path and training support.

Product engineers are aligned by disciplines. The number of engineers in each discipline varies from more than 10,000 in the largest discipline down to hundreds in the smallest discipline. The three largest disciplines are Development (SDE), Program Management (PM), and Test (SDET). The fourth largest and rapidly growing discipline with the corporation's shift to services is IT Operations (Ops).

Microsoft didn't always have this separation of disciplines. In the early years, everyone's title was "technician." Specialization into roles started in 1979, and the use of different standard titles to identify career paths for engineers started in the early 1980s.

The *triad* is the name we use for the Test, Development, and Program Management disciplines, as shown in Figure 1-5. These are the three largest engineering disciplines in Microsoft, and significant numbers of engineers in each triad discipline are involved on a product team. With the shift in focus to software and services, IT Operations is growing quickly.

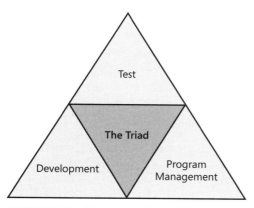

FIGURE 1-5 The Test, Dev, and PM triad.

Most of these engineering disciplines are common to any large software company. Each has its industry events such as the Software Testing Analysis and Review (STAR) conferences for Test or DEFCON (*http://www.defcon.org*) for security developers. Conferences are designed to develop skills and promote the overall profession.

Software testing is one of the larger disciplines both in Microsoft and in the whole software industry. In this book, we hope to share with you the stories of Microsoft testers to help illustrate points and to share what makes Microsoft testers both similar to and sometimes different from their industry counterparts.

Testers break the 128-KB RAM barrier

In 1985, money for equipment for testers was very tight. Excel for Mac could run on 128 KB, so that was the best test computer anyone had. As the team started working on the next version of Excel, the memory requirements grew to 512 KB. For quite a while, the testers didn't get new equipment. Finally, though, when it became clear that the testers just couldn't do our jobs, we were given memory upgrades.

—*Carole Cancler, former Microsoft Tester*

Being a Global Software Development Company

People often ask whether all of the products Microsoft creates are developed in Redmond, Washington. The short answer is, most are, but not all. Microsoft was a global company well before moving into its Redmond headquarters in February 1986. In fact, Microsoft's first international office opened in Japan in 1979. In 1998, Microsoft was still very Redmond-centric with more than 90 percent of product development engineering happening on the main campus.

Today Microsoft has sizable and rapidly growing development centers all across the United States and around the world. The largest U.S. sites are in California, North Dakota, Massachusetts, New York, South Carolina, Texas, and Colorado. Internationally, the Microsoft development centers in China and India each employ more than 1,200 engineers. For the release of the new Windows Vista operating system, major components were developed in North America, Europe, and Asia. Future releases of the Windows operating system and Office system will have even larger international contributions.

As shown in Figure 1-6, by 2004 the Redmond workforce had dropped from 90 percent of the total engineering workforce to just 81 percent of the total workforce.

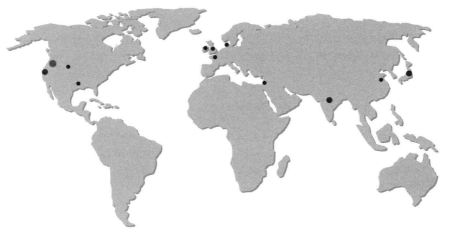

Area	% of total
United States (Redmond, WA)	81%
United States (California)	4%
Ireland	2%
Japan	2%
India	2%
United States (Texas)	1%
United States (North Dakota)	1%
United Kingdom	1%
Denmark	1%
China	1%
Israel	0.5%
France	0.3%

FIGURE 1-6 Top 12 Microsoft development centers in 2004.

This trend to spread the engineering workforce across multiple development centers continues to accelerate. In recent years, Microsoft has made large acquisitions and has chosen to keep the employees in their original locations. Rates for hiring employees in China and India have been ahead of Redmond for several years. As shown in Figure 1-7, by early 2008 Redmond-based engineers represented just 73 percent of the global product engineering workforce.

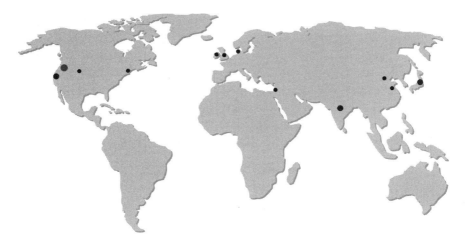

Area	% of total
United States (Redmond, WA)	73%
Hyderabad, India	7%
United States (California)	4%
Beijing, China	2.3%
Ireland	1.6%
United Kingdom	1.6%
Denmark	1.3%
North Dakota	1%
Japan	1%
Shanghai, China	1%
Israel	0.9%
United States (Massachusetts)	0.5%

FIGURE 1-7 Top 12 Microsoft development centers in 2008.

The internationalization trend is by design, but the design, unlike that of many other multinational companies, is not about cheaper labor. The globalization of the Microsoft engineering workforce is about access to talent, access to markets, and taking advantage of new technologies. As graduation rates for computer science majors continue to fall in the United States and the wait for work visas to enter the United States continues to grow, Microsoft must go to where the talent is, and some great engineers just don't want to move to Redmond, Washington, to work for Microsoft. Also, by hiring many engineers in a specific country, Microsoft can help open and stabilize the market there. For example, with so many Microsoft engineers now working in China in that country's rapidly growing technology sector, the government of China now has a vested interest in reducing software piracy because it affects its own citizens and the work they do. In addition, the technology that Microsoft develops allows for greater collaboration among our global engineering workforce. Small teams are better able to be connected to the whole than they were even just a few years ago. Judging by the current rate of change, I expect Redmond to be the home of less than 50 percent of the total engineering workforce in the next decade.

 Note At the beginning of 2008, the Microsoft India Development Center (IDC) employed more than 2,400 engineers. Microsoft employs more than 1,400 engineers in the Shanghai and Beijing facilities.

Summary

Microsoft is the world's biggest software company and the best place in the world to be a software test engineer. We build successful world class businesses that generate big revenue and big profits. The rich history of Microsoft, our broad vision to empower the people of the world and a core set of values that help guide the test engineers of Microsoft in shipping world class high quality software.

As businesses evolve, the engineering practices used by the large successful business groups have evolved from the PUM-based organization structure to the more scalable and efficient Shared Team organization structure. Microsoft invests in incubations both in established products and in brand-new product categories.

More than 35,000 product engineers work for Microsoft across 10 different engineering disciplines. Microsoft engineers develop hardware, desktop application, server, and service products. Product development at Microsoft is becoming more and more globalized. As of 2008, more than 28 percent of product development is happening outside of Redmond, Washington, and this trend of global development is expected to continue.

Chapter 2
Software Test Engineers at Microsoft

Ken Johnston

In the beginning, there were no testers at Microsoft, no localization engineers, no program managers, and no usability engineers. In the beginning, there were just engineers; oh, and sales and marketing.

Chapter 1, "Software Engineering at Microsoft," introduced the 10 different engineering disciplines Microsoft uses today to organize and develop our engineering workforce. Even before we began to break out different engineering disciplines there were a few different titles, such as product support for shipped products. Positions like these were seen as a role for an engineer rather than a different career path. During these early days, all engineers had the same title and one common career path. Of course, in these early days Microsoft had less than 50 employees, software wasn't even really an industry, and Microsoft was not yet a public company.

The move to supporting separate disciplines with distinct career paths has taken quite a while to evolve. Program Management and Usability are two of the older disciplines at Microsoft. Around 1990, the Usability discipline, engineers that work to make our software easy to use for real-world users, became a formal role and eventually a recognized discipline. Usability formed largely because of such features as the Microsoft Office Word mail merge (think snail mail and printing out form letters or stick-on labels) that just didn't seem to work for the average person. Some customers might argue that we are still working to make mail merge easy to use, but that story is better suited for a book on how we design software at Microsoft.

Shortly after the creation of the software development position, the software tester position broke off as the second distinct discipline. As the story goes, the first-ever tester at Microsoft was a young high school intern by the name of Lloyd Frink, who started in June 1979. The Microsoft Archive team places the hiring of the first full-time tester to be 1983 followed by a wave of testers hired in 1985, as illustrated in Figure 2-1. Test as a separate standard title with a fully articulated career path did not show up until the late 1980s.

FIGURE 2-1 *Seattle Times* 1985 advertisement for software testers.

Maybe we should have someone test the code before we ship it

I had met Bill a few times before—that is how I got the job. My mom knew Bill's mom, Mary. I was going to school at Lakeside, and at a school fund-raising auction they were talking and found out both of their sons were interested in computers. Both Bill and I were also at the auction, so they introduced us. I was 14 at the time, and Bill was 24. We decided to all have lunch together. So, a few weeks later, my mom and I went over to Microsoft to have lunch with Mary, Bill, and Bill's younger sister Libby, who was one year ahead of me at high school. I showed Bill some of the computer games I had written and sold, and he offered me a summer internship. That's how the whole thing got started.

The first summer I was mainly testing the BASIC Compiler for Greg Whitten. We had a bunch of BASIC programs that I would run through the compiler and see if they worked."

—*Lloyd Frink, former Microsoft employee and co-founder of zillow.com*

What's in a Name?

A rose by any other name may still smell as sweet, but a title can have a significant impact on the prism through which a person, or in this case an engineer, looks out onto his world. Developers at Microsoft have the common title of Software Development Engineer, or SDE. They develop features by writing code. The formal title for a software tester at Microsoft is Software Development Engineer in Test, or SDET. The similarity in the names of the two disciplines is by design because testers at Microsoft are developers. Among other things, testers design tests, influence product design, conduct root cause analysis, participate in code reviews, and write automation. Occasionally testers check bug fixes or work on small features. Testing is a heavy workload, so writing features is not very common for testers.

The concept of hiring a software engineer with a passion for testing is powerful and is the biggest differentiator between the Microsoft approach to software testing and the typical industry approach. The most common conclusion drawn is that we hire these "coders" for test positions because we want to automate everything and eliminate manual testing. Although we do want testers who can write effective automation, that's only a small part of the equation. Testers who understand programming concepts and computer architecture typically have the analysis skills that testing requires. They can also find bugs earlier and understand the root cause so that they can quickly find other similar bugs and implement early detection. This strong grounding in computer science—the same grounding a developer has—reinforces the tester skills and gives us a more dynamic and flexible workforce of testers.

A common question that comes up during industry events is why Microsoft doesn't hire subject matter experts (SMEs) as testers. For example, international accounting rules are very complex and a tester with just a background in engineering wouldn't know all the nuances. Another example is vertical products such as customer relationship management (CRM) solutions. The theory is that it would be better to hire an SME and Microsoft could focus on being really good at training our testers in computer science and engineering skills. The counterargument to this question is whether a company would hire a CPA, train that individual to be a world-class developer, and then have that individual write the company's accounting solution. Of course, this approach just isn't practical. Learning to be a great developer requires passion for technology and many years of formal training.

Just about every software company starts with a developer and teaches her the problem space and customer scenarios for the product she will be developing. This holds true whether the company develops operating systems or software to control the flow of power across electrical grids. With testing, we actually have two challenges. First, we must teach the engineer to be an SME for the product area she is working on, and second, we must teach her how to test.

The rule of thumb, therefore, is to hire someone who has solid engineering skills, who can code as well as an entry-level developer, and who has the other attributes we look for in a great tester. We call these attributes the *tester DNA*, and I discuss them later in this chapter.

As with any rule of thumb, there are exceptions. The vast majority of testers at Microsoft are developers in test, but in some areas, we do find that we need some of the team members to be SMEs. Global accounting rules specialists or researchers in speech recognition algorithms are two examples of areas in which we hire a lot of SMEs as testers. As we move into more consumer products, we have hired manufacturing process experts to test our designs against the needs of high-volume cost-controlled manufacturing. In these cases, the title of the SME test engineers is usually not SDET but rather something more appropriate such as Linguistics Test Engineer or Manufacturing Test Engineer.

Testers at Microsoft Have Not Always Been SDETs

Until 2005, Microsoft actually used two different titles for testers. Software Test Engineer (STE) and Software Development Engineer in Test (SDE/T). This dual-title process was very confusing. In some groups, the SDE/T title meant the employee worked on test tools, and in others it meant he had a computer science degree and wrote a lot of test automation. There wasn't even a fully articulated career path for an SDE/T at this time. Table 2-1 lists the tasks SDE/Ts and STEs were responsible for.

> **Note** Here is an excerpt from the *SDET Ladder Level Guide 2004*, "An SDE/T should use either the test or development ladder level guide, whichever is most applicable."

TABLE 2-1 SDE/T and STE Tasks

Common SDE/T tasks	Common STE tasks
Develop test harness for test execution	Write test plans
Develop specialty test tools for security or performance testing	Document test cases
Automate API or protocol tests	Run manual tests
Participate in bug bashes	Write automation for core tests
Find, debug, file, and regress bugs	Find, file, and regress bugs
Participate in design reviews	Participate in design reviews
Participate in code reviews	

Even without a clear career path, the notion of having one foot in the tester world and one in the development world was attractive. Over time, the number of employees with the SDE/T title grew to the point that we decided to merge the two disciplines.

In 2002, there was a push to drop the SDE/T title because it was causing confusion in the workforce. In 2005, the title SDE/T was changed to SDET and there was a push to merge the STE and SDET career paths, as illustrated in Figure 2-2. Test Architect first showed up as a formally recognized title in 2003 and is included in the SDET calculations.

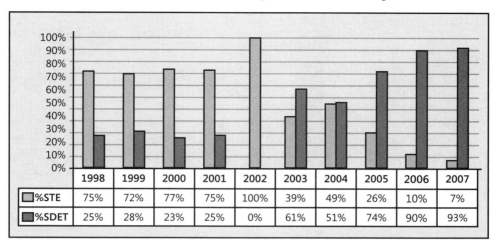

FIGURE 2-2 STE to SDET shift, 1998–2007.

	1998	1999	2000	2001	2002	2003	2004	2005	2006	2007
☐%STE	75%	72%	77%	75%	100%	39%	49%	26%	10%	7%
■%SDET	25%	28%	23%	25%	0%	61%	51%	74%	90%	93%

We can't call them SQEs (Software Quality Engineers)

"OK, let's just call them all Zebra for a moment," Grant George said to the room. We were debating what the new title for test engineers should be and had been debating for several hours now with no consensus.

"We all agree that software testing is fundamentally an engineering problem. We all agree that great test engineers need to have a strong grounding in engineering and ideally computer science skills. We also all agree that a great tester has something different in them than a developer. They have that tester DNA built into their core." Grant was on a roll now and headed to the whiteboard with marker in hand.

I looked around the room at the assembled Directors of Test. We had more than 200 years of Microsoft test management experience represented in the meeting. Some of us had grown up in Microsoft Windows, others working on Microsoft Visual Studio, and still others from Web services. Grant came at the problem from his background working on Microsoft Office. He was also the most senior of all of us in the room and at the time the only VP of test in all of Microsoft.

Grant started writing out a list on the whiteboard. "Tester DNA has to include a natural ability to do systems level thinking, skills in problem decomposition, a passion for quality, and a love of finding out how something works and then how to break it," he put the marker down and looked at the room. "Now that is what makes up a tester that makes them different from a developer. The way we combine that DNA with engineering skills is by testing software. The name we choose should reflect this but also be attractive to the engineers we want to hire. Something that shows we use development skills to drive testing."

"We've already established all this, Grant," someone from the table chimed in, but then fell silent.

"I'd like to go with SDE/T. We've used it in the past to essentially describe what you're saying, but it just has such a loaded past I don't know," Gregg said.

"Well, what if we went with SDET without the slash," offered David White. He was the Career Model project lead from HR working with the Test Leadership Team to define a unified career path for all our test engineers. "It will allow you to quickly say to campus and industry candidates that we need developers in software testing, but they are focused on testing."

"It's a better name than SQE," shouted one of the late arrivers who was sitting on the counter above the recycling and trash bins. "SQE always makes me think of those squeegee guys that wash your windows at the stoplight and want you to pay them a buck."

Darrin Muir the GM of Test for Windows chimed in, "I like it. It's simple, just get the slash out."

We debated for another hour but in the end the new title for all testers at Microsoft was SDET. The difference between an SDE and an SDET came down to core DNA that motivated that engineer to work on testing problems rather than development.

Going with a strong title reinforcing the similarity to the development discipline was critical to our strategy for ever increasing product quality and testing efficiency. The next three parts of this book delve into much more detail about the techniques we use to test software at Microsoft. The approach we take is possible only because of the skills we recruit for and develop in our test engineer workforce.

In the early stages, the use of the SDE/T title was simply to help with recruiting from colleges. Many candidates didn't want to graduate with a computer science degree and not use their coding skills on the job. The SDE/T title and the original role of tools developer in test sold much better than the STE title.

Although all STEs were expected to be able to create automation when necessary, many of our products just didn't warrant the high level of automation we expect today, so the amount of time STEs would spend writing code was a small percentage of their total time testing.

In 2001, a major change to Microsoft product support policies had a bigger impact on software testing than any other engineering discipline. The change was the length of support for our products. Most major products, including the Windows operating system, moved to a 10-year support commitment. The criticality of software in the enterprise and the long process to upgrade an enterprise from one operating system or productivity suite to another collided with our then policy of current minus one (*N* - 1) product support policies. As software shipping cycles became shorter, support windows needed to overlap. Instead of a policy based upon numbers of supported versions, we went with a model based on years, ranging from 3 years for consumer products that had an annual release cycle to 10 years for servers, operating systems, and critical productivity applications.

When we developed Windows 95, we never imagined supporting it until the year 2005. Although Windows 95 had a solid core set of test automation that validates most major functionality and key user scenarios, it also included vast numbers of documented (and undocumented) manual tests. Manual exploratory testing (covered in Chapter 4, "A Practical Approach to Test Case Design") was a common technique used on products shipped through the late 1990s. Armies of vendors and full-time employees were hired to do this button-pushing testing.

The change in support lengths meant test automation could be used for many more years and thus was more justifiable during the R&D phase of product development. That realization pushed us to emphasize the hiring of more SDE/Ts. As more computer science graduates flooded the ranks of the test organizations, we discovered an increased ability to affect design and drive improvement in testability.

Other factors such as increasing levels of integration, complexity, and challenging security testing such as threat modeling, fuzz testing, or fault injection have continued to drive our need for computer science and coding skills in test. Even the shift to services and the rapid rate of product shipping they go through is driving us to new models for automated testing. The impact of online services to our testing strategy is covered in Chapter 15, "Testing Software as a Service."

I Need More Testers and I Need Them Now!

Microsoft continues to increase its engineering workforce every year. Test alone adds approximately 500 new positions a year. We have a nearly even split in hiring testers from other companies and computer science graduates straight from colleges both in the United States and in leading universities around the world.

A great SDET candidate possesses that tester DNA covered earlier in this chapter. We also look for some very specific skills or, in HR lingo, "competencies." To prevent this section from reading too much like an HR manual, I just briefly cover what a *competency* is and how it relates to tester DNA.

Competencies describe behaviors that differentiate outstanding results from typical results. Competencies have different levels indicating relative strength. To begin with, most successful candidates have some but probably limited strength in most of our engineering competencies. Test shares the same set of competencies with all 10 engineering disciplines, but over time, some competencies such as analytical problem solving become more pronounced with testers than they might be with other disciplines.

Ten competencies are considered core to all engineers. There are additional competencies for individuals in, say, management roles, finance, or sales and marketing. Following are the 10 engineering competencies:

- **Analytical Problem Solving**   Very critical for testers because problem decomposition and root cause analysis are key to driving quality upstream.

- **Customer-Focused Innovation**   Does the candidate care about customers and see how software can help solve problems or wow them with fun experiences?

- **Technical Excellence**   We look to see if the candidate understands networks, operating systems, and not just how to code but how to optimize code.

- **Project Management**   For testers, this is more around personal time management as well as structuring a plan to get work that can have a lot of dependencies completed on time.

- **Passion for Quality**   If you don't have this, you need not apply for any engineering job let alone test.

- **Strategic Insight**   This competency usually starts weak with new hires, but when we look to hire employees who can help us find that great breakthrough that vaults us ahead of the competition and adds to shareholder value, this competency must be present from the very beginning.

- **Confidence**   Testers at Microsoft still get a lot of pushback on bugs. A tester must have confidence to push back when needed.

- **Impact and Influence**   Influence comes from confidence and experience. Impact comes from knowing how to make a change happen. Starting off, most candidates exhibit this competency when they talk about how they drove a change in their current company or rallied their project team while in college.

- **Cross-Boundary Collaboration**   Innovation often happens across organizational boundaries. An employee with a bunker mentality that just cares about her feature and her tests won't be successful.

■ **Interpersonal Awareness**   This competency is about self-awareness. Many great candidates are self-critical and able to express how they are looking to improve their skills. Call this the continuous personal improvement plan.

Campus Recruiting

A big part of Microsoft's hiring is done through campus recruiting. *Campus recruiting* is the term we use to describe when we hire someone within a year of his or her graduation from an undergraduate or graduate program. Hundreds of recruiters work year-round with university programs, developing relationships with schools and professors, and providing information about Microsoft and the different engineering careers we offer.

As candidates are identified, the Microsoft interviews are scheduled. These first interviews usually happen on campuses or at regional events, but sometimes candidates come to Microsoft for their interviews. Hiring managers such as SDET or SDE managers actually conduct the formal face-to-face interviews. To be a campus interviewer you must be an "A" interviewer. Yes, interviewing is so important to Microsoft we track and rate the interviewing skills of our employees.

It's not unusual for the candidates to try to cram for their Microsoft interview by going out on the Internet and researching the sample questions former candidates have posted. The problem is we look at those sites too and continue to evolve our questions over time.

After several rounds of interviews by different "A" interviewers, a hire or no-hire decision is made. Whether an offer of full-time employment is made or not our goal is to ensure that the interview process is a good experience for all candidates. They wouldn't have gotten this far in the process if they weren't smart and motivated.

After the offer is made, we often have to go into sell mode. For tester jobs this is when we explain how test at Microsoft is very different from test at most other companies. For a number of years, we encouraged candidates to read such books as *Testing Computer Software* (2nd ed.) by Cem Kaner, Jack Falk, and Hung Quoc Nguyen (Wiley, 1999), but those books didn't really cover the technical side of testing at Microsoft.

Fortunately, one of our Test Architects, Keith Stobie, was able to convince author Robert Binder to allow us to refer candidates to a portion of his book on testing: *Testing Object-Oriented Systems: Models, Patterns, and Tools* (Addison-Wesley, 1999), specifically, Chapter 3, "Testing: A Brief Introduction." This chapter provides a concise description of testing very much in alignment with how Microsoft approaches testing. Although the book as a whole covers a great deal more than an introduction to testing, I still refer all testers to Chapter 3 of "the Binder book."

Can I talk to someone doing the job?

One of the things that I truly enjoy doing is being a Test Manager at Microsoft. I came out of school and went to work for another company as a developer, but then came to Microsoft 12 years ago as a tester. I know the role of a tester at Microsoft is more unique than common when compared to other companies.

Our recruiting team does an amazing job trying to explain and represent all of the different roles and opportunities at Microsoft by providing materials or talking to the candidates, but the candidates always want to have the opportunity to talk to the people who actually do the job day in and day out. When I'm on a campus recruiting trip, I am often asked to be that person. In most colleges, testing is something we do after we complete one of our coding projects. I write the code the professor wants, and then I make sure it works. Testing is an afterthought and not something rigorously taught.

The SDET role at Microsoft is one of the most important roles we have and carries an enormous amount of responsibility in shipping the products we do. When I first start talking to the candidates, I really want them to understand that testing is just as much a science as writing code and understanding the algorithms. I start talking to them about the wide range of things that testers must be able to do.

One of the things that most candidates don't understand is that we must be good designers for the automation development we need to test the products. As coders we might be challenged to develop the automation that pushes our system harder and faster than the products do themselves; we must be able to simulate data coming into the system that would represent a year's worth of data but in a shorter period of time for our testing. You might need to build an automation system that allows your automated tests to work across different browsers or you need to build a system that allows you to test all the different languages our product ships in. At that point, I think most of the candidates would admit they had no idea that was the kind of work we might have to do. It doesn't stop with automation though.

As tester you must challenge yourself not only to know your features but all the features that interact with them. You will get to know how things like client and server software work together and what the end-user experience is like. We must be good at understanding the way systems are put together using firewalls, routers, backend servers, or a wide range of things. You must be able to understand and represent customers in all areas ranging from usability, accessibility, security, and so forth....Our learning never stops and it is unlimited to what we want to learn and need for our jobs.

Another one of the things that most candidates think is that we don't have impact or input into the design or can influence the design of features. One of the best things about Microsoft is that anyone can influence the design with sound reasoning, especially testers who need to understand the customer and how the system works. At Microsoft, there isn't one person who builds the software, but many people. Testers have the right and the responsibility to speak up about the features and how they are built or even recommend features we need. I always push on the design as do all of my testers.

Testing is a little bit like taking a course where the grade rests solely on the final exam. I remember taking my finals and waiting for my grade. The professor gave me the grade and I was happy or sad. Now as a tester at Microsoft, I work some number of years to build a great product and ensure that it has the quality it needs, and then I release it to millions of people. Those millions of people get to tell me the grade I get, and that is incredible!

—*Patrick Patterson, Microsoft Office Test Manager*

Industry Recruiting

Industry recruiting is the term used to describe when we hire someone who has been working full time in software or a related industry for at least a year or more. You can consider industry to be more along the lines of hiring an experienced engineer as compared to a campus hire who is all about potential. We do hire entry level from industry, so it is not all about experience.

About half of our yearly hiring for SDETs comes through the campus recruiting pipeline, the other half through industry. Although some industry candidates do come from a test role at other companies, most, including the authors of this book, did not work full time in a testing position. When hiring from the industry, we often look for developers who have done some test work or who have been in a position where quality practices are prevalent. Usually, when we see résumés from individuals with a number of years in a test job, they might not have the computer science or programming skills we are looking for. The ideal industry candidate is usually someone who is working at a company where the role of product developer and software tester are combined.

The biggest shock to most industry candidates is the sheer size of the test discipline at Microsoft and the amount of clout we wield. The developer to tester ratio at Microsoft is about 1 to 1. Typical for industry is about 5 developers to 1 tester and sometimes 10 to 1 or higher. When you are outnumbered like that, a test organization is usually focused on survival rather than evolving their engineering skills and practices.

Learning How to Be a Microsoft SDET

After new employees starts at Microsoft, they go through the on-boarding process. This consists of going through New Employee Orientation (NEO) for the first few days. NEO combines all employees into a single class regardless of discipline. After NEO, new SDETs find their team administrator to find out what office they are in. Next, it's off to find their immediate manager and find out who their mentor will be.

Among other things, the Engineering Excellence (EE) group at Microsoft is chartered to deliver technical training to employees. The first test course from Engineering Excellence a new SDET takes is *Testing at Microsoft for SDETs*. This class is usually taken within 12 months of the employee start date. Portions of this book cover much of what we teach in this 24-hour course. Although many of our technical classes and lecture series are online, milestone classes such as this one and the others in the SDET Training Roadmap, as shown in Figure 2-3, are taught in classrooms by experienced testers. This approach allows the students a rich opportunity for extensive discussions and to go deeper in many areas during exercises.

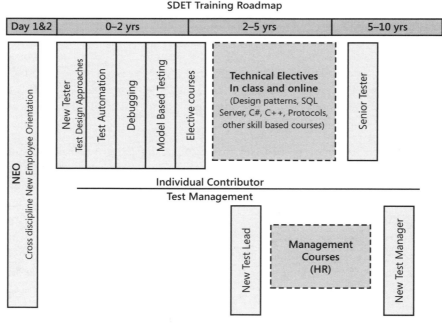

FIGURE 2-3 High-level SDET Training Roadmap as of 2008.

The Engineering Career at Microsoft

Any employee can change disciplines, and many do each and every year. In each engineering discipline, there are really only two options: to be an individual contributor (IC) or a manager. All junior engineers start as ICs. Each career path has major inflection points. For managers, it might be going from managing a team of individual contributors (a Lead position) to managing other Leads. For an IC, the scope expands from affecting a product to affecting a product line. These inflections are called *career stages*. Our use of career stages is based largely upon the work Stephen Drotter did while at General Electric.[1] Each career stage comes with a full career stage profile that helps each employee see the expected results for the next career step.

It is fairly common for an employee to "test the water" of the management career path, and then to opt back to being an IC. As senior ICs continue to develop, they require many of the same leadership skills and business acumen skills of senior engineering managers, as shown in Figure 2-4. In some cases, even very senior engineers can jump back and forth between IC and management roles.

Career Stages

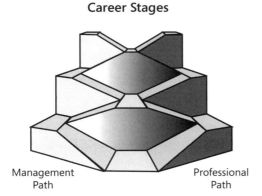

Management Path   Professional Path

FIGURE 2-4 Intermingled management and professional career paths.

For example, David Cutler joined Microsoft in 1988 to drive the creation of Microsoft Windows NT, which is still at the core of every release of the Windows operating system. Although David has managed teams during his career at Microsoft, he is generally considered an Architect and has risen to be the most senior individual contributor at Microsoft. He is recognized for his technical prowess, knowledge of systems architecture, and industry influence rather than his skills managing and developing employees.

Two other examples include Eric Rudder (Senior Vice President, Technical Strategy) and Jon DeVaan (Senior Vice President, Windows Core Operating System Division). Both men

---

[1] Ram Charan, Stephen Drotter, and James Noel, *The Leadership Pipeline: How to Build the Leadership Powered Company* (San Francisco: Jossey-Bass, 2000).

have spent multiple years in small team strategic leadership roles, and both have managed organizations made up of thousands of engineers.

The highest level a person can go on the individual contributor career path is Technical Fellow. This title is equivalent to being a Senior Vice President on the management career path. Technical Fellows and Distinguished Engineers (equivalent to a Corporate Vice President) often participate in industry efforts such as standards bodies and are viewed in the software industry as the best in their area of expertise. These senior engineers work on real shipping products but also do other company-wide influencing work such as participating in the Bill Gates ThinkWeek process by submitting their own whitepapers and commenting on others.

Career Paths in the Test Discipline

In some companies, test is seen as a junior job with development being a position that a tester could potentially grow into. At Microsoft, the test position is completely parallel to development with all the same career possibilities.

The Test Architect

In 1999, the Test Architect title was created for senior ICs with product-wide impact. The Test Architect title reflects the broad product impact role the SDET is working in, whereas the more common Senior, Principle, or Partner SDET titles are used when an individual focuses on features of a product. An important point to keep in mind in this discussion is that a Test Architect is a role and not a position. Although there is definitely a path for a senior tester to become a Test Architect, not all senior testers become Test Architects. An organization will generally choose to create a role for a Test Architect when there is sufficient business need or strategic requirement to do so. You will also see senior testers who function very much like a Test Architect, but who do not have the Test Architect title. This is a discussion of the role of a Test Architect, and not a discussion of the title.

There is no "typical" Test Architect role. Test Architects focus on a diverse set of goals and perform a wide variety of tasks. Some spend time developing testing infrastructure, testing authoring frameworks, or evaluating features to create complex tests. Some are in charge of a particular technology for their group. Others spend time consulting on how to improve test effectiveness. The common thread across all Test Architect roles and the primary responsibility of a Test Architect is to provide technical leadership and strategic direction for their testing organization. The level of the Test Architect generally dictates whether their scope is primarily focused on a family of features, a product line, or across an entire division. It is also expected that in addition to accountability to the current product senior Test Architects consistently look beyond the current release and possibly have several deliverables not tied to a particular product release.

A Test Architect is expected to be able to effect change not only across the testing community, but between development and program management as well. Test Architects must drive quality across all disciplines, providing guidance, feedback, and suggestions to improve quality practices across an entire engineering team.

It is also important to note what the Test Architect title is not. Test Architect is not a title that is awarded simply by level or experience. Creation of a Test Architect is an investment that combines an area in need of assistance with a strong individual capable of delivering invigorating change. It is also worth reiterating that Test Architect is not a career track. The skills of a Test Architect align with the career stage profile criteria for similar levels with an emphasis on cross-organizational communication and ability to drive change across an organization.

 Note As of 2008, there were just over 40 Test Architects out of more than 9,000 test engineers worldwide.

The IC Tester

The IC career path in test starts at SDET 1 (also known as IC1) and progresses through Partner SDET (IC6), as shown in Table 2-2. The major differentiators of the different levels are technical depth, technical breadth, and scope of influence. An SDET 1 is usually learning test, learning about Microsoft and how we develop software, and finding bugs in a very well defined feature. A more senior SDET might specialize in an area such as performance testing or security testing. By the time an SDET reaches Partner level, she should have spent time in many of these roles and probably a few years as a Test Architect.

TABLE 2-2 Career Stage Profile Example from the SDET IC Career Path

Career stage name	Software Development Engineer in Test	Software Development Engineer in Test 2	Senior Software Development Engineer in Test	Principal Senior Software Development Engineer in Test	Partner Software Development Engineer in Test
Customer impact	Seeks out customer feedback by means of PSS and other channels to clarify features and write test cases	Interacts directly with customers to provide critical feedback on feature areas and to develop test cases	Addresses customer expectations concerning product integration and creating specific scenarios or personas	Implements customer connection techniques that improve the interaction between customers and the organization	Leads deep customer understanding across the product line to improve designs
Test impact	Clarifies how features should work to eliminate ambiguous requirements	Provides critical feedback that improves specifications and technical designs	Identifies design patterns that are at high risk for generating future bugs	Leads innovation in test methods and technologies across the major product	Leads innovation in test methods and technologies across the product line

Scope of influence expands from a narrowly defined feature to a set of features, a full product such as Microsoft Office Word or Windows Media Player, and finally to a product line such as Office or Windows. The influence can be broad based on all aspects of testing such as the Test Architect (TA) role, or it might center around a deep technical area such as protocol security.

The IC career path for engineers does not stop at Partner SDET, but the test career path does. Partner SDET is one level below Distinguished Engineer (Corporate VP level IC). This is not because Microsoft does not see a need for a Distinguished Engineer (DE) in the test discipline. It is our belief that as engineers progress further and further along their career paths they start to look and behave more similarly to each other and the discipline distinction becomes less valuable. In a sense, every IC from every one of the 10 engineering disciplines can progress to the point that they are back to being just another engineer.

Many well-known industry luminaries exist in the Microsoft tester ranks with successful blogs, frequent conference appearances, and books. James Whittaker, author of the How to Break Software series, joined Microsoft in 2005 as a member of the TrustWorthy Computing team focused on software reliability. Keith Stobie writes the TestMuse blog on Spaces.live.com and is active in planning and supporting the Pacific Northwest Software Quality Conference (PNSQC) held annually in Portland, Oregon. The Test Verification and Metrics team headed by Tom Ball is a small team of researchers producing new and unique results around the use of data to drive product quality improvements.[2] Every member of the team is recognized widely for their research on test metrics.

These are just a few examples of how we invest in developing and supporting world-class test experts at Microsoft.

Becoming a Manager is Not a Promotion

Test management is the other major career path for an SDET. A test manager can move up the ranks, managing larger teams and areas. Of course, the management career path is one of an ever narrowing pyramid, so many test managers plateau long before reaching VP. There is one more major inflection point for the test management career path, as shown in Table 2-3, and that is to become a general manager. As described in Chapter 1, general engineering managers run organizations made up usually of Dev, Test, and Program Management (PM).

---

[2]   Microsoft Research, "Software Reliability Research," *http://research.microsoft.com/research/srr.*

TABLE 2-3 Career Stage Profile Example from the SDET Management Career Path

Career stage name	Lead Software Development Engineer in Test	Software Development Engineer in Test Manager	Director, Software Development Engineer in Test
Career stage	Manager	Manager of managers	Functional leader
Product scope	Feature Areas	Product	Product Line
	An SDET Lead works on a collection of feature areas, a highly complex feature area or component forming a small subsystem, or a simple product. Examples of feature areas include the speech recognition server, the C# compiler, the graphics engine for Microsoft Office PowerPoint, and the IP stack.	An SDET Manager works on a major product or highly complex feature areas forming a product, a large subsystem, or a simple product line. SDET Managers are major contributors to the product line. Examples of a product include Word, Microsoft Money, and the Windows shell.	An SDET Director works on a product line generally representing a Profit and Loss center (P&L) or a highly complex system or architecture underlying a product line. Examples of a product line include Windows, Office, MSN, and Microsoft Exchange.
Recruiting	Leads recruiting processes for the team	Proactively optimizes the group's recruiting processes and practices	Leads a comprehensive and effective recruiting plan for the product line

One question common at Microsoft, as well as in the whole software industry, is what it takes to get "promoted" into test management. That is a fairly loaded question because it implies that managers get paid more or perhaps get a better office than individual contributors do. The reality is that when an engineer moves into a management position, it is a *lateral* move—that is, there is no promotion involved. Future promotions are based upon the engineer's skills and individual results in leading his team. This is a different model from that used in most companies and public sector jobs where the job defines the pay scale and management jobs are almost always a higher pay scale than nonmanagement jobs are.

SDET Lead is the first rung of management in Test. An SDET Lead manages a team ranging in size from 2 to 10 employees. The team size is most often based upon the work needed to ship a specific feature or component such as printing, graphics, or a shared feature. The team might also be organized to drive a specialized test area such as performance, scale, or security. All of these employees report directly to the SDET Lead. There are no other layers of management between them and their employees.

It is important to note that technical complexity and the skills of the SDET Lead are more important in determining career advancement and rewards than is the size of the test team the SDET Lead manages. Security is an example where a small, highly skilled team can have a major impact on product quality and where you might find a more senior-level SDET Lead.

With smaller teams, the SDET Lead is expected to do a lot of his own testing, coding, analysis, and filing of bugs. All members of the product team from the highest executive down to the most junior new hire are expected to file product bugs when they find them. As a team becomes larger, more management tasks fall on the Lead and the less time he has for hands-on engineering work. Regardless of team size, SDET Leads are expected to have strong technical skills and function as technical leaders for their teams. Often, the SDET Lead is the most knowledgeable engineer on the team for a feature area and is typically one of the best testers and developers on the team.

The expectation for Leads to be very hands-on and technical is consistent with this expectation for all engineering disciplines. Development Leads often contribute to product development as much as any member on their team. Program Management Leads often design the most complex features or handle the most complex coordination issues. The expectation that all engineers, whether in a management role or not, are technical and hands-on is core to Microsoft DNA. It is easy to trace this culture back to the very early days of Microsoft, when Bill Gates would read through code at night and even rewrite portions.

Test Managers

Test Managers have many different titles and a wider variation in roles than SDET Leads do. As discussed in Chapter 1, Microsoft is a big company, and for every rule there are exceptions. Titles for management positions also have rules and variations. Table 2-4 lays out the most common titles and how they typically reflect team size and roles.

TABLE 2-4 Test Management Titles

Title	Team size	Org depth
SDET Lead or Senior SDET Lead	2-10	1
Test Manager, Senior SDET Manager, or SDET Manager	15-50	2
Group Test Manager, Principal Test Manager, or Director of Test	30-100	3-4
General Manager or VP of Test	200+	4-5

Test Managers are less hands-on with respect to writing and running tests, but every tester, regardless of level, files bugs in every product cycle. Test Managers are still expected to be technical but do tend to focus more on the processes and tools used in testing than how best to automate a particular class of tests.

A Test Manager spends a lot of time focused on how to develop and improve the skills of the test team and working with Product Management on assessing product quality and readiness to ship.

Summary

Microsoft takes a unique approach to software testing compared to industry norms. We have more test engineers than developers, and we emphasize software engineering skills with all testers. This unique approach goes all the way down to the title we give testers: Software Development Engineer in Test (SDET). By design, this title is virtually the same as the Software Development Engineer title used for developers.

With Microsoft adding more than 500 new tester positions every year, we have a very active recruiting program to hire experienced engineers from other companies as well as graduates from computer science and related programs upon graduation. Most new testers do not know much about software testing, so we have a very strong training program to teach software testing techniques.

Our emphases in very technical approaches to software testing allow us to have a fully articulated career path for testers both in management and as individual contributors (ICs). ICs can have the ability to grow to the most senior levels of engineering just as they do in the development discipline.

The 9,000 test engineers at Microsoft play a major role in developing our products and ensuring that the products ship with high quality. This vibrant community of engineers uses a wide range of engineering techniques to drive continuous improvement in our engineering practices and products.

Chapter 3
Engineering Life Cycles

Alan Page

I love to cook. Something about the entire process of creating a meal, coordinating multiple dishes, and ensuring that they all are complete at the exact same time is fun for me. My approach, learned from my highly cooking-talented mother, includes making up a lot of it as I go along. In short, I like to "wing it." I've cooked enough that I'm comfortable browsing through the cupboard to see which ingredients seem appropriate. I use recipes as a guideline—as something to give me the general idea of what kinds of ingredients to use, how long to cook things, or to give me new inspiration. There is a ton of flexibility in my approach, but there is also some amount of risk. I might make a poor choice in substitution (for example, I recommend that you never replace cow's milk with soymilk when making strata).

My approach to cooking, like testing, depends on the situation. For example, if guests are coming for dinner, I might measure a bit more than normal or substitute less than I do when cooking just for my family. I want to reduce the risk of a "defect" in the taste of my risotto, so I put a little more formality into the way I make it. I can only imagine the chef who is in charge of preparing a banquet for a hundred people. When cooking for such a large number of people, measurements and proportions become much more important. In addition, with such a wide variety of taste buds to please, the chef's challenge is to come up with a combination of flavors that is palatable to all of the guests. Finally, of course, the entire meal needs to be prepared and all elements of the meal need to be freshly hot and on the table exactly on time. In this case, the "ship date" is unchangeable!

Making software has many similarities with cooking. There are benefits to following a strict plan and other benefits that can come from a more flexible approach, and additional challenges can occur when creating anything for a massive number of users. This chapter describes a variety of methods used to create software at Microsoft.

Software Engineering at Microsoft

There is no "one model" that every product team at Microsoft uses to create software. Each team determines, given the size and scope of the product, market conditions, team size, and prior experiences, the best model for achieving their goals. A new product might be driven by time to market so as to get in the game before there is a category leader. An established product might need to be very innovative to unseat a leading competitor or to stay ahead of the pack. Each situation requires a different approach to scoping, engineering, and shipping the product. Even with the need for variation, many practices and approaches have become generally adopted, while allowing for significant experimentation and innovation in engineering processes.

For testers, understanding the differences between common engineering models, the model used by their team, and what part of the model their team is working in helps both in planning (knowing what will be happening) and in execution (knowing the goals of the current phase of the model). Understanding the process and their role in the process is essential for success.

Traditional Software Engineering Models

Many models are used to develop software. Some development models have been around for decades, whereas others seem to pop up nearly every month. Some models are extremely formal and structured, whereas others are highly flexible. Of course, there is no single model that will work for every software development team, but following some sort of proven model will usually help an engineering team create a better product. Understanding which parts of development and testing are done during which stages of the product cycle enables teams to anticipate some types of problems and to understand sooner when design or quality issues might affect their ability to release on time.

Waterfall Model

One of the most commonly known (and commonly abused) models for creating software is the waterfall model. Waterfall is an approach to software development where the end of each phase coincides with the beginning of the next phase, as shown in Figure 3-1. The work follows steps through a specified order. The implementation of the work "flows" from one phase to another (like a waterfall flows down a hill).

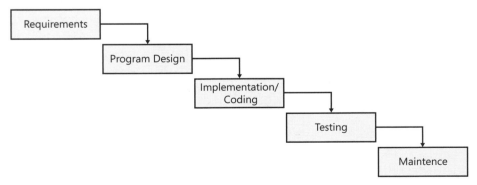

FIGURE 3-1 Waterfall model.

The advantage of this model is that when you begin a phase, everything from the previous phase is complete. Design, for example, will never begin before the requirements are complete. Another potential benefit is that the model forces you to think and design as much as possible before beginning to write code. Taken literally, waterfall is inflexible because it doesn't appear to allow phases to repeat. If testing, for example, finds a bug that leads back to a design flaw, what do you do? The Design phase is "done." This apparent inflexibility has led to many criticisms of waterfall. Each stage has the potential to delay the entire product cycle, and in a long product cycle, there is a good chance that at least some parts of the early design become irrelevant during implementation.

An interesting point about waterfall is that the inventor, Winston Royce, intended for waterfall to be an iterative process. Royce's original paper on the model[1] discusses the need to iterate at least twice and use the information learned during the early iterations to influence later iterations. Waterfall was invented to improve on the stage-based model in use for decades by recognizing feedback loops between stages and providing guidelines to minimize the impact of rework. Nevertheless, waterfall has become somewhat of a ridiculed process among many software engineers—especially among Agile proponents. In many circles of software engineering, *waterfall* is a term used to describe *any* engineering system with strict processes.

Spiral Model

In 1988, Barry Boehm proposed the spiral model of software development.[2] Spiral, as shown in Figure 3-2, is an iterative process containing four main phases: determining objectives, risk evaluation, engineering, and planning for the next iteration.

- **Determining objectives** Identify and set specific objectives for the current phase of the project.

- **Risk evaluation** Identify key risks, and identify risk reduction and contingency plans. Risks might include cost overruns or resource issues.

- **Engineering** In the engineering phase, the work (requirements, design, development, testing, and so forth) occurs.

- **Planning** The project is reviewed, and plans for the next round of the spiral begin.

---

[1] Winston Royce, "Managing the Development of Large Software Systems," *Proceedings of IEEE WESCON* 26 (August 1970).

[2] Barry Boehm, "A Spiral Model of Software Development," *IEEE* 21, no. 5 (May 1988): 61–72.

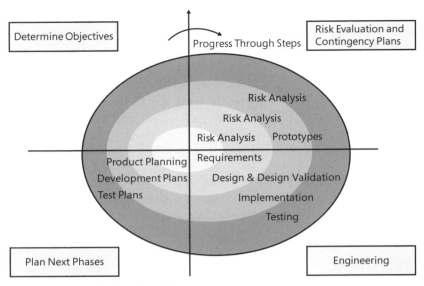

FIGURE 3-2 Simplified spiral model.

Another important concept in the spiral model is the repeated use of prototypes as a means of minimizing risk. An initial prototype is constructed based on preliminary design and approximates the characteristics of the final product. In subsequent iterations, the prototypes help evaluate strengths, weaknesses, and risks.

Software development teams can implement spiral by initially planning, designing, and creating a bare-bones or prototype version of their product. The team then gathers customer feedback on the work completed, and then analyzes the data to evaluate risk and determine what to work on in the next iteration of the spiral. This process continues until either the product is complete or the risk analysis shows that scrapping the project is the better (or less risky) choice.

Agile Methodologies

By using the spiral model, teams can build software iteratively—building on the successes (and failures) of the previous iterations. The planning and risk evaluation aspects of spiral are essential for many large software products but are too process heavy for the needs of many software projects. Somewhat in response to strict models such as waterfall, Agile approaches focus on lightweight and incremental development methods.

Agile methodologies are currently quite popular in the software engineering community. Many distinct approaches fall under the Agile umbrella, but most share the following traits:

- **Multiple, short iterations** Agile teams strive to deliver working software frequently and have a record of accomplishing this.

- **Emphasis on face-to-face communication and collaboration** Agile teams value interaction with each other and their customers.

- **Adaptability to changing requirements** Agile teams are flexible and adept in dealing with changes in customer requirements at any point in the development cycle. Short iterations allow them to prioritize and address changes frequently.

- **Quality ownership throughout the product cycle** Unit testing is prevalent among developers on Agile teams, and many use test-driven development (TDD), a method of unit testing where the developer writes a test before implementing the functionality that will make it pass.

In software development, to be Agile means that teams can quickly change direction when needed. The goal of always having working software by doing just a little work at a time can achieve great results, and engineering teams can almost always know the status of the product. Conversely, I can recall a project where we were "95 percent complete" for at least three months straight. In hindsight, we had no idea how much work we had left to do because we tried to do everything at once and went months without delivering working software. The goal of Agile is to do a little at a time rather than everything at once.

Other Models

Dozens of models of software development exist, and many more models and variations will continue to be popular. There isn't a best model, but understanding the model and creating software within the bounds of whatever model you choose can give you a better chance of creating a quality product.

Milestones

It's unclear if it was intentional, but most of the Microsoft products I have been involved in used the spiral model or variations.[3] When I joined the Windows 95 team at Microsoft, they were in the early stages of "Milestone 8" (or M8 as we called it). M8, like one of its predecessors, M6, ended up being a public beta. Each milestone had specific goals for product functionality and quality. Every product I've worked on at Microsoft, and many others I've worked with indirectly, have used a milestone model.

---

[3] Since I left product development in 2005 to join the Engineering Excellence team, many teams have begun to adopt Agile approaches.

The milestone schedule establishes the time line for the project release and includes key interim project deliverables and midcycle releases (such as beta and partner releases). The milestone schedule helps individual teams understand the overall project expectations and to check the status of the project. An example of the milestone approach is shown in Figure 3-3.

FIGURE 3-3 Milestone model example.

The powerful part of the milestone model is that it isn't just a date drawn on the calendar. For a milestone to be complete, specific, predefined criteria must be satisfied. The criteria typically include items such as the following:

- **"Code complete" on key functionality**   Although not completely tested, the functionality is implemented.

- **Interim test goals accomplished**   For example, code coverage goals or tests completed goals are accomplished.

- **Bug goals met**   For example, no severity 1 bugs or no crashing bugs are known.

- **Nonfunctional goals met**   For example, performance, stress, load testing is complete with no serious issues.

The criteria usually grow stricter with each milestone until the team reaches the goals required for final release. Table 3-1 shows the various milestones used in a sample milestone project.

TABLE 3-1 Example Milestone Exit Criteria (partial list)

Area	Milestone 1	Milestone 2	Milestone 3	Release
Test case execution		All Priority 1 test cases run	All Priority 1 and 2 test cases run	All test cases run
Code coverage	Code coverage measured and reports available	65% code coverage	75% code coverage	80% code coverage
Reliability	Priority 1 stress tests running nightly	Full stress suite running nightly on at least 200 computers	Full stress suite running nightly on at least 500 computers with no uninvestigated issues	Full stress suite running nightly on at least 500 computers with no uninvestigated issues
Reliability		Fix the top 50% of customer-reported crashes from M1	Fix the top 60% of customer-reported crashes from M2	Fix the top 70% of customer-reported crashes from M3

Area	Milestone 1	Milestone 2	Milestone 3	Release
Features		New UI shell in 20% of product	New UI in 50% of product and usability tests complete	New UI in 100% of product and usability feedback implemented
Performance	Performance plan, including scalability goals, complete	Performance baselines established for all primary customer scenarios	Full performance suite in place with progress tracking toward ship goals	All performance tests passing, and performance goals met

Another advantage of the milestone model (or any iterative approach) is that with each milestone, the team gains some experience going through the steps of release. They learn how to deal with surprises, how to ask good questions about unmet criteria points, and how to anticipate and handle the rate of incoming bugs. An additional intent is that each milestone release functions as a complete product that can be used for large-scale testing (even if the milestone release is not an external beta release). Each milestone release is a complete version of the product that the product team and any other team at Microsoft can use to "kick the tires" on (even if the tires are made of cardboard).

The quality milestone

Several years ago, I was on a product team in the midst of a ship cycle. I was part of the daily bug triage, where we reviewed, assigned, and sometimes postponed bugs to the next release. Postponements happen for a variety of reasons and are a necessary part of shipping software. A few months before shipping, we had some time left at the end of the meeting, and I asked if we could take a quick look at the bugs assigned to the next version of our product. The number was astounding. It was so large that we started calling it the "wave." The wave meant that after we shipped, we would be starting work on the next release with a huge backlog of product bugs.

Bug backlog along with incomplete documents and flaky tests we need to fix "someday" are all items that add up to *technical debt*.[4] We constantly have to make tradeoffs when developing software, and many of those tradeoffs result in technical debt. Technical debt is difficult to deal with, but it just doesn't go away if we ignore it, so we have to do something. Often, we try to deal with it while working on other things or in the rare times when we get a bit of a lull in our schedules. This is about as effective as bailing out a leaky boat with a leaky bucket.

Another way many Microsoft teams have been dealing with technical debt is with a *quality milestone*, or MQ. This milestone, which occurs after product release but before

---

4   Matthew Heusser writes about technical debt often on his blog (*xndev.blogspot.com*). Matt doesn't work for Microsoft...yet.

getting started on the next wave of product development, provides an opportunity for teams to fix bugs, retool their infrastructure, and fix anything else pushed aside during the previous drive to release. MQ is also an opportunity to implement improvements to any of the engineering systems or to begin developing early prototypes of work and generate new ideas.

Beginning a product cycle with the backlog of bugs eliminated, the test infrastructure in place, improvement policies implemented, and everything else that annoyed you during the previous release resolved is a great way to start work on a new version of a mature product.

Agile at Microsoft

Agile methodologies are popular at Microsoft. An internal e-mail distribution list dedicated to discussion of Agile methodologies has more than 1,500 members. In a survey sent to more than 3,000 testers and developers at Microsoft, approximately one-third of the respondents stated that they used some form of Agile software development.[5]

Feature Crews

Most Agile experts state that a team size of 10 or less collocated team members is optimal. This is a challenge for large-scale teams with thousands or more developers. A solution commonly used at Microsoft to scale Agile practices to large teams is the use of *feature crews*.

A feature crew is a small, cross-functional group, composed of 3 to 10 individuals from different disciplines (usually Dev, Test, and PM), who work autonomously on the end-to-end delivery of a functional piece of the overall system. The team structure is typically a program manager, three to five testers, and three to five developers. They work together in short iterations to design, implement, test, and integrate the feature into the overall product, as shown in Figure 3-4.

The key elements of the team are the following:

- It is independent enough to define its own approach and methods.
- It can drive a component from definition, development, testing, and integration to a point that shows value to the customer.

Teams in Office and Windows use this approach as a way to enable more ownership, more independence, and still manage the overall ship schedule. For the Office 2007 project, there were more than 3,000 feature crews.

---

[5] Nachiappan Nagappan and Andrew Begel, "Usage and Perceptions of Agile Software Development in an Industrial Context: An Exploratory Study," 2007, *http://csdl2.computer.org/persagen/DLAbsToc.jsp?resourcePath=/dl/ proceedings/&toc=comp/proceedings/esem/2007/2886/00/2886toc.xml&DOI=10.1109/ESEM.2007.85.*

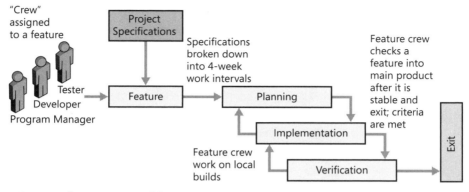

FIGURE 3-4 Feature crew model.

Getting to Done

To deliver high-quality features at the end of each iteration, feature crews concentrate on defining "done" and delivering on that definition. This is most commonly accomplished by defining *quality gates* for the team that ensure that features are complete and that there is little risk of feature integration causing negative issues. Quality gates are similar to milestone exit criteria. They are critical and often require a significant amount of work to satisfy. Table 3-2 lists sample feature crew quality gates.[6]

TABLE 3-2 Sample Feature Crew Quality Gates

Quality gate	Description
Testing	All planned automated tests and manual tests are completed and passing.
Feature Bugs Closed	All known bugs found in the feature are fixed or closed.
Performance	Performance goals for the product are met by the new feature.
Test Plan	A test plan is written that documents all planned automated and manual tests.
Code Review	Any new code is reviewed to ensure that it meets code design guidelines.
Functional Specification	A functional spec has been completed and approved by the crew.
Documentation Plan	A plan is in place for the documentation of the feature.
Security	Threat model for the feature has been written and possible security issues mitigated.
Code Coverage	Unit tests for the new code are in place and ensure 80% code coverage of the new feature.
Localization	The feature is verified to work in multiple languages.

---

6   This table is based on Ade Miller and Eric Carter, "Agile and the Inconceivably Large," *IEEE* (2007).

The feature crew writes the necessary code, publishes private releases, tests, and iterates while the issues are fresh. When the team meets the goals of the quality gates, they migrate their code to the main product source branch and move on to the next feature. I. M. Wright's *Hard Code* (Microsoft Press, 2008) contains more discussion on the feature crews at Microsoft.

Iterations and Milestones

Agile iterations don't entirely replace the milestone model prevalent at Microsoft. Agile practices work hand in hand with milestones—on large product teams, milestones are the perfect opportunity to ensure that all teams can integrate their features and come together to create a product. Although the goal on Agile teams is to have a shippable product at all times, most Microsoft teams release to beta users and other early adopters every few months. Beta and other early releases are almost always aligned to product milestones.

Putting It All Together

At the micro level, the smallest unit of output from developers is code. Code grows into functionality, and functionality grows into features. (At some point in this process, test becomes part of the picture to deliver *quality* functionality and features.)

In many cases, a large group of features becomes a *project*. A project has a distinct beginning and end as well as checkpoints (milestones) along the way, usage scenarios, personas, and many other items. Finally, at the top level, subsequent releases of related projects can become a product line. For example, Microsoft Windows is a product line, the Windows Vista operating system is a project within that product line, and hundreds of features make up that project.

Scheduling and planning occur at every level of output, but with different context, as shown in Figure 3-5. At the product level, planning is heavily based on long-term strategy and business need. At the feature level, on the other hand, planning is almost purely tactical—getting the work done in an effective and efficient manner is the goal. At the project level, plans are often both tactical and strategic—for example, integration of features into a scenario might be tactical work, whereas determining the length of the milestones and what work happens when is more strategic. Classifying the work into these two buckets isn't important, but it is critical to integrate strategy and execution into large-scale plans.

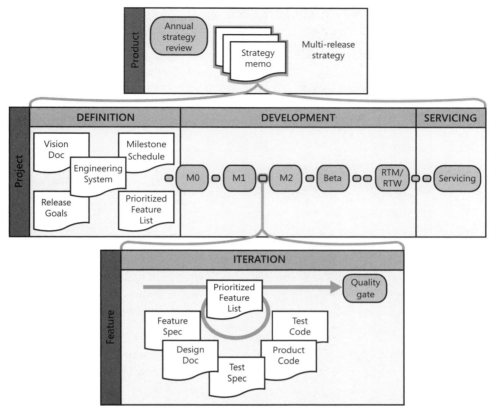

FIGURE 3-5 Software life cycle workflow.

Process Improvement

In just about anything I take seriously, I want to improve continuously. Whether I'm preparing a meal, working on my soccer skills, or practicing a clarinet sonata, I want to get better. Good software teams have the same goal—they reflect often on what they're doing and think of ways to improve.

Dr. W. Edwards Deming is widely acknowledged for his work in quality and process improvement. One of his most well known contributions to quality improvement was the simple *Plan, Do, Check, Act* cycle (sometimes referred to as the Shewhart cycle, or the PDCA cycle). The following phases of the PDCA cycle are shown in Figure 3-6:

- **Plan**   Plan ahead, analyze, establish processes, and predict the results.
- **Do**   Execute on the plan and processes.

- **Check**   Analyze the results (note that Deming later changed the name of this stage to "Study" to be more clear).

- **Act**   Review all steps and take action to improve the process.

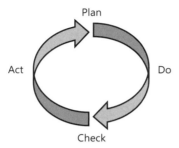

FIGURE 3-6 Deming's PDCA cycle.

For many people, the cycle seems so simple that they see it as not much more than common sense. Regardless, this is a powerful model because of its simplicity. The model is the basis of the Six Sigma DMAIC (Define, Measure, Analyze, Improve, Control) model, the ADDIE (Analyze, Design, Develop, Implement, Evaluate) instructional design model, and many other improvement models from a variety of industries.

Numerous examples of applications of this model can be found in software. For example, consider a team who noticed that many of the bugs found by testers during the last milestone could have been found during code review.

1. First, the team plans a process around code reviews—perhaps requiring peer code review for all code changes. They also might perform some deeper analysis on the bugs and come up with an accurate measure of how many of the bugs found during the previous milestone could potentially have been found through code review.

2. The group then performs code reviews during the next milestone.

3. Over the course of the next milestone, the group monitors the relevant bug metrics.

4. Finally, they review the entire process, metrics, and results and determine whether they need to make any changes to improve the overall process.

Formal Process Improvement Systems at Microsoft

Process improvement programs are prevalent in the software industry. ISO 9000, Six Sigma, Capability Maturity Model Integrated (CMMI), Lean, and many other initiatives all exist to help organizations improve and meet new goals and objectives. The different programs all focus on process improvement, but details and implementation vary slightly. Table 3-3 briefly describes some of these programs.

TABLE 3-3 Formal Process Improvement Programs

Process	Concept
ISO 9000	A system focused on achieving customer satisfaction through satisfying quality requirements, monitoring processes, and achieving continuous improvement.
Six Sigma	Developed by Motorola. Uses statistical tools and the DMAIC (Define, Measure, Analyze, Implement, Control) process to measure and improves processes.
CMMI	Five-level maturity model focused on project management, software engineering, and process management practices. CMMI focuses on the organization rather than the project.
Lean	Focuses on eliminating waste (for example, defects, delay, and unnecessary work) from the engineering process.

Although Microsoft hasn't wholeheartedly adopted any of these programs for widespread use, process improvement (either formal or ad hoc) is still commonplace. Microsoft continues to take process improvement programs seriously and often will "test" programs to get a better understanding of how the process would work on Microsoft products. For example, Microsoft has piloted several projects over the past few years using approaches based on Six Sigma and Lean. The strategy in using these approaches to greatest advantage is to understand how best to achieve a balance between the desire for quick results and the rigor of Lean and Six Sigma.

Microsoft and ISO 9000

Companies that are ISO 9000 certified have proved to an auditor that their processes and their adherence to those processes are conformant to the ISO standards. This certification can give customers a sense of protection or confidence in knowing that quality processes were integral in the development of the product.

At Microsoft, we have seen customers ask about our conformance to ISO quality standards because generally they want to know if we uphold quality standards that adhere to the ISO expectations in the development of our products.

Our response to questions such as this is that our development process, the documentation of our steps along the way, the support our management team has for quality processes, and the institutionalization of our development process in documented and repeatable processes (as well as document results) are all elements of the core ISO standards and that, in most cases, we meet or exceed these.

This doesn't mean, of course, that Microsoft doesn't value ISO 9000, and neither does it mean that Microsoft will never have ISO 9000–certified products. What it does mean at the time of this writing is that in most cases we feel our processes and standards fit the needs of our engineers and customers as well as ISO 9000 would. Of course, that could change next week, too.

Shipping Software from the War Room

Whether it's the short product cycle of a Web service or the multiyear product cycle of Windows or Office, at some point, the software needs to ship and be available for customers to use. The decisions that must be made to determine whether a product is ready to release, as well as the decisions and analysis to ensure that the product is on the right track, occur in the *war room* or *ship room*. The war team meets throughout the product cycle and acts as a ship-quality oversight committee. As a name, "war team" has stuck for many years—the term describes what goes on in the meeting: "conflict between opposing forces or principles."

As the group making the day-to-day decisions for the product, the war team needs a holistic view of all components and systems in the entire product. Determining which bugs get fixed, which features get cut, which parts of the team need more resources, or whether to move the release date are all critical decisions with potentially serious repercussions that the war team is responsible for making.

Typically, the war team is made up of one representative (usually a manager) from each area of the product. If the representative is not able to attend, that person nominates someone from his or her team to attend instead so that consistent decision making and stakeholder buy-in can occur, especially for items considered plan-of-record for the project.

The frequency of war team meetings can vary from once a week during the earliest part of the ship cycle to daily, or even two or three times a day in the days leading up to ship day.

War, What Is It Good For?

The war room is the pulse of the product team. If the war team is effective, everyone on the team remains focused on accomplishing the right work and understands why and how decisions are made. If the war team is unorganized or inefficient, the pulse of the team is also weak—causing the myriad of problems that come with lack of direction and poor leadership.

Some considerations that lead to a successful war team and war room meetings are the following:

- Ensure that the right people are in the room. Missing representation is bad, but too many people can be just as bad.

- Don't try to solve every problem in the meeting. If an issue comes up that needs more investigation, assign it to someone for follow-up and move on.

- Clearly identify action items, owners, and due dates.

- Have clear issue tracking—and address issues consistently. Over time, people will anticipate the flow and be more prepared.

- Be clear about what you want. Most ship rooms are focused and crisp. Some want to be more collaborative. Make sure everyone is on the same page. If you want it short and sweet, don't let discussions go into design questions, and if it's more informal, don't try to cut people off.

- Focus on the facts rather than speculation. Words like "I think," "It might," "It could" are red flags. Status is like pregnancy—you either are or you aren't; there's no in between.

- Everyone's voice is important. A phrase heard in many war rooms is "Don't listen to the HiPPO"—where HiPPO is an acronym for highest-paid person's opinion.

- Set up exit criteria in advance at the beginning of the milestone, and hold to them. Set the expectation that quality goals are to be adhered to.

- One person runs the meeting and keeps it moving in an orderly manner.

- It's OK to have fun.

Defining the Release—Microspeak

Much of the terminology used in the room might confuse an observer in a ship team meeting. Random phrases and three-letter acronyms (TLAs) flow throughout the conversation. Some of the most commonly used terms include the following:

- **LKG**   "Last Known Good" release that meets a specific quality bar. Typically, this is similar to self-host.

- **Self-host**   A self-host build is one that is of sufficient quality to be used for day-to-day work. The Windows team, for example, uses internal prerelease versions of Windows throughout the product cycle.

- **Self-toast**   This is a build that completely ruins, or "toasts," your ability to do day-to-day work. Also known as *self-hosed*.

- **Self-test**   A build of the product that works well enough for most testing but has one or more blocking issues keeping it from reaching self-host status.

- **Visual freeze**   Point or milestone in product development cycle when visual/UI changes are locked and will not change before release.

- **Debug/checked build**   A build with a number of features that facilitate debugging and testing enabled.

- **Release/free build**   A build optimized for release.

- **Alpha release**   A very early release of a product to get preliminary feedback about the feature set and usability.

- **Beta release**   A prerelease version of a product that is sent to customers and partners for evaluation and feedback.

Mandatory Practices

Microsoft executive management doesn't dictate how divisions, groups, or teams develop and test software. Teams are free to experiment, use tried-and-true techniques, or a combination of both. They are also free to create their own mandatory practices on the team or division level as the context dictates. Office, for example, has several criteria that every part of Office must satisfy to ship, but those same criteria might not make sense in a small team shipping a Web service. The freedom in development processes enables teams to innovate in product development and make their own choices. There are, however, a select few required practices and policies that every team at Microsoft must follow.

These mandatory requirements have little to do with the details of shipping software. The policies are about making sure that several critical steps are complete prior to shipping a product.

There are few mandatory engineering policies, but products that fail to adhere to these policies are not allowed to ship. Some examples of areas included in mandatory policies include planning for privacy issues, licenses for third-party components, geopolitical review, virus scanning, and security review.

Expected vs. Mandatory

Mandatory practices, if not done in a consistent and systematic way, create unacceptable risk to customers and Microsoft.

Expected practices are effective practices that every product group should use (unless there is a technical limitation). The biggest example of this is the use of static analysis tools. (See Chapter 11, "Non-functional Testing.") When we first developed C#, for example, we did not have static code analysis tools for that language. It wasn't long after the language shipped, however, before teams developed static analysis tools for C#.

One-Stop Shopping

Usually, one person on a product team is responsible for release management. Included in that person's duties is the task of making sure all of the mandatory obligations have been met. To ensure that everyone understands mandatory policies and applies them consistently, every policy, along with associated tools and detailed explanations, is located on a single internal Web portal so that Microsoft can keep the number of mandatory policies as low as possible and supply a consistent toolset for teams to satisfy the requirements with as little pain as possible.

Summary: Completing the Meal

Like creating a meal, there is much to consider when creating software—especially as the meal (or software) grows in size and complexity. Add to that the possibility of creating a menu for an entire week—or multiple releases of a software program—and the list of factors to consider can quickly grow enormous.

Considering *how* software is made can give great insights into what, where, and when the "ingredients" of software need to be added to the application soup that software engineering teams put together. A plan, recipe, or menu can help in many situations, but as Eisenhower said, "In preparing for battle I have always found that plans are useless, but planning is indispensable." The point to remember is that putting some effort into thinking through everything from the implementation details to the vision of the product can help achieve results. There isn't a *best* way to make software, but there are several *good* ways. The good teams I've worked with don't worry nearly as much about the actual process as they do about successfully executing whatever process they are using.

Part II
About Testing

Chapter 4
A Practical Approach to Test Case Design

Alan Page

When you design tests that will run long after the initial version of a software program has shipped, it is imperative that you make a significant effort to design long-lasting and effective test cases. Many Microsoft applications have support plans that last as long as 10 years. After they are designed and written, test cases run continuously until the moment the product is released, but that's not the end of life for the tests. After an application ships to end users, the ownership of source code, documentation, test tools, test automation, and all other relevant collateral material passes either to a separate team or a subset of the product team who are responsible for making any necessary ensuing changes. The changes made by these *sustained engineering teams* include fixes for security, quick fix engineering (QFE) changes, and service pack development. The tests created for a specific release of a product run many thousands of times through the entire support cycle of the product. Nearly every test team approaches their test case design with the knowledge that the tests they create will need to run for many years.

Because of the emphasis on long-term supportability at Microsoft, we use test automation extensively. This does not mean, however, that we do not value or perform manual testing. A good test strategy identifies areas where automation is or is not applicable and dictates an appropriate test approach. Chapter 10, "Test Automation," contains a detailed discussion of automated testing.

Design is the act of systematically thinking or planning through a solution before beginning implementation. Careful planning and design by an architect ensures that a building will be sound and fit the needs of its occupants. Careful planning and design of tests can increase the value over the lifetime of those tests. This chapter discusses the basics of test design.

 Note There were more than a million test cases written for Microsoft Office 2007.

Practicing Good Software Design and Test Design

Design might be the most important step in the process of developing software. Software design includes planning and problem solving. It includes foresight into user experience and critical analysis of solutions and alternatives. Well-designed software anticipates many

61

problems that might occur, and design is an essential step in creating software that works well for the customer. Great design doesn't necessarily require big design up front (BDUF). Projects that use Agile methodologies, where the code is considered to be the design, still require planning and foresight and can be designed well. Any product, whether it's a software program or a kitchen appliance, needs a good design to avoid frustration and confusion among its customers. If design is not given full and sufficient attention, customers are bound to have problems.

Test design has many parallels with good software design, and with good design in general. Test design requires planning and problem solving to determine which kinds of tests to run and which types of testing will be most effective at verifying functionality and confirming that failure paths are handled gracefully. One of the most important aspects of test design is anticipating customer needs and expectations, and then creating tests that address these needs appropriately. Good test design often starts with a review, or critique, of the software design. Often, design reviews are treated much like a code review, where the designer explains the design and participants ask questions and provide feedback. A good design critique involves in-depth comparisons of choices and alternatives for all major design decisions, with a goal of a shared vision of what needs to be built, how it is going to be built, and, perhaps most important, how it is going to be tested. Good design and good execution are critical pieces of a successful software development project.

Using Test Patterns

Design patterns, solutions for common software design issues, are popular in software development. They provide guidelines or strategies that can be used in many different situations. Most important, they provide a common language for communicating solutions between developers.

The concept of *test patterns* has been around for many years. In *Testing Object-Oriented Systems: Models, Patterns, and Tools*, Robert Binder[1] includes 37 test design patterns, plus another 17 for test automation. In 2001, Brian Marick, author of *The Craft of Software Testing*, conducted several Patterns of Software Testing (PoST) workshops and made further progress in defining types and uses of test patterns.

Like design patterns, test patterns solve common issues and provide guidelines and strategies for testers to design tests. Some test patterns are approaches for structured testing, others are heuristics, and other patterns are a combination of ideas or something completely different. The importance of a test pattern is that testers can use it to communicate the intent of a testing approach and can share different test design techniques in a way that is understandable and actionable.

---

[1] Robert V. Binder, *Testing Object-Oriented Systems: Models, Patterns, and Tools* (Indianapolis, IN: Addison-Wesley, 1999).

A common format for sharing test patterns is by using a template. Robert Binder's test design pattern template includes 10 different attributes. Testers at Microsoft who are interested in test design patterns usually use a simplified template based on Binder's that has the following attributes:

- **Name**   Give a memorable name—something you can refer to in conversation.

- **Problem**   Give a one-sentence description of the problem that this pattern solves.

- **Analysis**   Describe the problem area (or provide a one-paragraph description of the problem area) and answer the question of how this technique is better than simply poking around.

- **Design**   Explain how this pattern is executed (how does the pattern turn from design into test cases?).

- **Oracle**   Explain the expected results (can be included in the Design section).

- **Examples**   List examples of how this pattern finds bugs.

- **Pitfalls or Limitations**   Explain under what circumstances and in which situations this pattern should be avoided.

- **Related Patterns**   List any related patterns (if known).

This particular template provides ample flexibility in creating different types of patterns but provides enough information to facilitate communication between testers using the patterns for test design. Table 4-1 is an example of a well-known test design approach that uses this template.

TABLE 4-1 Boundary-Value Analysis Test Pattern

Name	Boundary-Value Analysis (BVA)
Problem	Many errors in software occur near the edges of physical and data boundaries. For example, using > instead of >=, or off-by-one indexing errors (zero-based vs. one-based).
Analysis	Choose test cases on or near the boundaries of the input domain of variables, with the rationale that many defects tend to concentrate near the extreme values of inputs. A classic example of boundary-value analysis in security testing is to create long input strings to probe potential buffer overflows. More generally, insecure behavior in boundary cases is often unforeseen by developers, who tend to focus on nominal situations instead.
Design	For each input value, determine the minimum and maximum allowed value (min and max). Design a set of test cases that tests min, max, min − 1, and max + 1 (note that BVA is sometimes defined to include min + 1 and max − 1). Test cases should include the following: ❐ Input(s) to the component ❐ Partition boundaries exercised ❐ Expected outcome of the test case

Name	Boundary-Value Analysis (BVA)
Oracle	Minimum and maximum values are expected to pass. Values outside of this range are expected to fail gracefully.
Examples	For an input field that expects a number between 1 and 10, test 0, 1, 10, and 11.
Pitfalls or Limitations	Boundaries are not always known. Knowledge of the domain or access to source code might be necessary to achieve useful boundary-value analysis.
	If the input range contains "special" values—values within the boundaries that are handled differently by the application—BVA might miss issues with these values.
Related Patterns	Equivalence Class Partitioning

A patterns-based approach to test design is a useful system for communicating testing ideas, and it frequently accelerates the test design process. It is also a simple way for new testers to learn about test design, for experienced testers on the team to share ideas, and for entire bodies of knowledge on test design to be transferred from one organization to another.

Estimating Test Time

"How long will it take you to test?" This can be a difficult question to answer for any test team, and a lot of thought and planning are essential to give an accurate answer. I have seen unsuccessful teams simply add a few weeks of "buffer" or "stabilization" time at the end of a product cycle. As you can expect, projects planned this way rarely meet customer expectations. Accurately estimating the testing task is at least as important as the act of writing software features, and it deserves equal attention.

How do you estimate how long it will take you to test a feature or an application? One rule of thumb I have seen used often is to copy the development time. For example, if a particular development task is scheduled to take 2 man-weeks, estimating that 2 man-weeks are necessary for writing automation and describing manual test cases can be useful. This approach is usually accurate, but in practice it is merely a starting point because so many factors can influence the testing task. The goals of the product team, customer expectations, technical ability of the test team, and complexity of the project all influence the testing process, and every tester must consider these factors when estimating test time. Table 4-2 includes examples of things to consider in test time estimation.

TABLE 4-2 **Factors in Test Time Estimation**

Attribute	How to consider this attribute
Historical data	At the very least, you can estimate test design based on previous projects.

Attribute	How to consider this attribute
Complexity	Complexity relates directly to testability. Simple applications can be tested more quickly than complex programs can be.
Business goals	Is the application a prototype or demonstration application? Or is it flight control software for a spaceship? The business goals influence the breadth and depth of the testing effort.
Conformance/Compliance	If the application must conform to a standard, these requirements must be considered when estimating the testing task.

Starting with Testing

When I began my career as a software tester more than 15 years ago, I sometimes heard project managers say things like, "Why do we need to hire more testers? We're not code complete for another month." I'm happy to say that those days are long behind me, but in some cases, we testers often debate about the right things to do if we are lucky enough to be involved from the initial stages of product development.

One place to start test design is with a review of requirements or functional specifications of the software. If good requirements are available, requirements-based testing can be a good place to start. If requirements aren't available (or if they aren't good), the best place to start test design is probably by asking questions. Ask how the software is supposed to work. Ask how it handles data. Ask how it handles errors. Asking questions about the software can help testers get a jumpstart on design before any of the code is ever written.

Ask Questions

If the code already exists, and requirements and functional specifications are either missing or incomplete, the best place to get started on test design is by running the application. Ask yourself questions about how the program should work. You might answer those questions, or they might lead to more questions. If something is confusing, ask questions. If the source code is available, refer to the code and, if necessary, ask more questions. *Exploratory testing*, the act of testing and designing tests at the same time, can significantly influence test design and is a beneficial part of the overall test design process.

If you are testing a feature or type of application you haven't tested before, or even if you are just stuck testing something that is familiar to you, it can be useful to ask someone else who has tested something similar for ideas. Many bugs in software are missed during testing because testers didn't ask enough questions or they didn't ask the right questions. Test design requires a comprehensive and careful examination of the software under test. Asking questions is one of the best ways to gain the knowledge needed to carry out this examination.

> ## Exploratory testing with a debugger
>
> Frequently, when I am testing a component or feature for the first time and I have source code available, I use the debugger to test. Before I even write test cases, I write a few basic tests. These might be automated tests, or they might be just a few ideas that I have scribbled onto a pad. I set a breakpoint somewhere in the component initialization, and then use the debugger to understand how every code path is reached and executed. I note where boundary conditions need testing and where external data is used. I typically spend hours (and sometimes days) poking and prodding (and learning and executing) until I feel I have a good understanding of the component. At that point, I usually have a good idea of how to create an efficient and effective suite of tests for the component that can be used for the lifetime of the product.

Have a Test Strategy

A test strategy guides test design and can be a method for providing a direction in test design for the test team. A good test strategy provides vision for the team, helps everyone determine which testing activities are most important, and helps them determine when and where to apply different types of testing.

The strategy includes types of testing, processes, and methods the test team will use when testing. It includes an evaluation of risk that helps the team determine where failures are more likely to occur or whether certain components might need more exhaustive testing.

The strategy often includes plans for training or education of the test team. The education strategy can include conferences, workshops, or consultant-led training, or it could include peer sharing among the test team. Regardless of how the training is conducted, a first-rate test strategy includes a plan for growing the skills and knowledge of the test team. Example attributes of a test strategy are included in Table 4-3.

TABLE 4-3 Example Test Strategy Attributes

Attribute	How to consider this attribute
Introduction	Provides an overview of the strategy and describes how the strategy will be used. The strategy is based on the features and quality goals of the project.
Specification Requirements	Lists the documentation plans for the test group, as well as expectations for documentation from other engineering disciplines.
Key Scenarios	What are the primary customer scenarios that will drive the testing effort? This section answers that question and ties testing efforts to the product plan.

Attribute	How to consider this attribute
Test Methodology	This section describes test methodologies that will be used to test the product along with the value and risk of using any specified methods. Code coverage, test automation, test case management, and other approaches or tools can be included in this section.
Test Deliverables	What are the stated expectations of the test team? Example deliverables can include status on the following: ❏ Test results ❏ Code coverage ❏ Spec signoff status ❏ Bug rates and trends ❏ Performance scenario results
Training	If success against the strategy requires training, those needs should be described, including analysis of how the training supports the strategy.

Thinking About Testability

Another thing testers can and should do both to influence the product and to help design tests is to think about testability early. *Testability* is the degree to which software can be tested completely and efficiently. Making specific design choices, choosing simple algorithms, enabling test *hooks* (additional functionality written solely to make testing easier), and making internal variables visible are all examples of how to increase testability.

The most common method a tester can use to drive testability is simply to ask, "How are we going to test this?" during requirements or design reviews. This is not only a fantastic method for clarifying ambiguous statements, but over time it pushes into the minds of the development team the idea of writing testable software. Development teams who have embraced writing unit tests as part of their daily grind have already begun to understand the importance of testability—but keep in mind that testability matters reach far beyond small units and must be considered at all levels of the product. Table 4-4 defines the acronym SOCK, a simple model for increasing the testability of software.

TABLE 4-4 A Simple Model for Testability: SOCK

Term	Definition
Simple	Simple components and applications are easier (and less expensive) to test.
Observable	Visibility of internal structures and data allows tests to determine accurately whether a test passes or fails.
Control	If an application has thresholds, the ability to set and reset those thresholds makes testing easier.
Knowledge	By referring to documentation (specifications, Help files, and so forth), the tester can ensure that results are correct.

> ## How do you test hundreds of modems?
>
> We needed to test modem dial-up server scalability in Microsoft Windows NT Remote Access Server (RAS) with limited hardware resources. We had the money and lab infrastructure only for tens of modems, but we had a testability issue in that we needed to test with hundreds of modems to simulate real customer deployments accurately. The team came up with the idea to simulate a real modem in software and have it connect over Ethernet; we called it RASETHER. This test tool turned out to be a great idea because it was the first time anyone had created a private network within a network. Today, this technology is known as a virtual private network, or a VPN. What started as a scalability test tool for the Windows NT modem server became a huge commercial success and something we use every time we "tunnel" into the corporate network.
>
> —*David Catlett, Test Architect*

Test Design Specifications

Asking questions about testability forces everyone involved to think about how a piece of software is going to be tested. It also requires the tester to consider the design of the test cases. The process of designing tests is often at least as important as the act of designing end-user software. Testers often create formal test design documents describing the strategy and approach of their tests. A test design specification (TDS) is applicable for both manual and automated tests, and it typically has the same review process as other documents such as specifications and design documents used in the software engineering process. Because the TDS describes both the approach and intent of the testing process, it becomes an integral part of the testing process throughout the entire life of the product, especially during the post-ship phases of the software's life when a sustained engineering team might own the product support.

Example Elements in a Test Design Specification

Following are items that might be found in a typical test design specification:

- Overview/goals/purpose
- Strategy
- Functionality testing
- Component testing
- Integration/system testing
- Interoperability testing
- Compliance/conformance testing

- Internationalization and globalization

- Performance testing

- Security testing

- Setup/deployment testing

- Dependencies

- Metrics

Testing the Good and the Bad

Two plus two equals four, but what happens when you divide two by zero? In the calculator program that ships with the Microsoft Windows operating system, two divided by zero results in the text "Cannot divide by zero." Attempting to divide by zero in other applications might result in a similar error, or it might result in a program crash. Test cases include both *verification* tests (tests that verify functionality using expected inputs) and *falsification* tests (tests that use unexpected data to see whether the program handles that data appropriately). Verification tests are necessary to prove that the application works as intended, but the falsification tests are perhaps even more important. Applications need to be robust and handle bad data without error.

Many years ago, a program error or crash caused by using bad data resulted in a response from a developer such as, "A user would never do that." I once accidentally renamed an application with a file name extension used by the application's document files. Opening this file in the application caused a crash that was resolved as "won't fix" because it "was not a user scenario." The bug existed for many years but was finally fixed during a large security push by Microsoft teams around 2002. In fact, one of the great things that has happened because of the enormous emphasis on security at Microsoft is that far fewer bugs found by falsification tests are resolved as "the customer would never do that."

The happy path should always pass

I arrived at work one morning to see an e-mail message from Adam, a software developer on my team, saying that he had checked in code for the new component he was working on over the weekend and that he would like me to do some ad-hoc testing as soon as the build came out. My schedule was tight, but I was excited about finally being able to test the component. In fact, I had already written down a few dozen test cases I wanted to try out based on the discussions we had had during the design review.

Later that morning, the build was released to the test team and I installed the application on my test computer. I immediately went to the portion of the application containing Adam's new functionality, entered some data, and clicked one of the buttons. It didn't work. It didn't do anything. I wasn't trying to see how the feature reacted to bad data. I was using simple inputs that should always work. I refer to simple inputs that should always work as "the happy path."

Because the happy path should always work, I immediately assumed that I must have made a mistake. (*I knew I went through setup too fast—I must have missed selecting an option.*) I had a second "clean" computer in my office, so I took some time to carefully install the application on this computer. I didn't notice anything that seemed like it would affect this feature, so I guessed that my test computer must have had some stale files on it that caused the feature not to work. Unfortunately, after starting the application again, I had the same results. *I must be doing something wrong.*

I got out of my chair and walked down the hall. I stopped at a few offices where fellow testers were working and asked if I could borrow their computer for a minute. Try as I might, I couldn't find a computer where the new feature worked at all. Finally, I went back to my office and called Adam and told him the bad news. When I described to him what I had been doing for the last hour, he said, "Hmm, I made a change just before checking the files in, but didn't think that change would make a difference. I guess I was wrong." At this point, having wasted more than an hour, I was a bit irked and replied, "Seriously, Adam, the happy path should always pass."

These days, the cases where the happy path fails are becoming quite rare. But I remember and repeat this phrase every time something that should always work doesn't.

Other Factors to Consider in Test Case Design

Schedules, resources (budget), and quality are dependent attributes that influence software testing as much as they influence software development. For example, if time and money did not matter, testing could continue indefinitely or additional testers could be added to the project as needed. However, software needs to ship for customers to be able to use it, and in most cases, additional headcount is generally not an option. To this end, adequate test case design requires that a tester think in advance about the scope of testing that is possible and that the tester be able to consolidate and prioritize that testing to fit the schedule while still testing the product sufficiently. It is never feasible to test everything, so it's important that the tester is able to choose the best set of tests to test software efficiently and thoroughly in the time constraints given.

Consider the scope of the product, the size of the customer base, the size of the test team, and the skills of the test team when considering test case design. Answers to questions on these factors can help you choose a set of tests that can verify functionality, find errors, and handle customer issues efficiently.

Black Box, White Box, and Gray Box

One way to classify approaches to test case design is to describe the level of knowledge that testers and their tests have of the application under test. A commonly understood system is that of black box and white box testing. *Black box testing* is an approach based on testing an application without any knowledge of the underlying code or functionality of the application. Given that users of an application are only concerned with whether or not the application fits their needs and do not care (nor should they) how the application was designed or written, a black box approach to testing is a useful method of simulating and anticipating how the customer will use the product. On the other hand, pure black box approaches often end up overtesting certain parts of the application while undertesting other portions. Conversely, *white box testing* is an approach that uses test design based on analysis of the underlying source code or schemas not visible to the end user. Test cases founded solely on a white box approach are typically thorough, but nearly always miss key end-user scenarios.

The answer to this dilemma is a *gray box* (sometimes called *glass box*) approach. Tests are designed from a customer-focused point of view first (that is, black box), but white box approaches are used to ensure efficiency and test case coverage of the application under test. Testers are responsible for both the customer viewpoint and for determining the correctness of an application. They cannot cover both areas effectively without considering both black box and white box approaches. Testers at Microsoft must have a holistic viewpoint on testing and consider all of these perspectives when designing tests.

Exploratory Testing at Microsoft

Microsoft's recent emphasis on test automation has caused some to think that Microsoft has devalued the importance of exploratory testing. *Exploratory testing* is a (generally) manual approach to testing where every step of testing influences the subsequent step. During exploratory testing, testers use their previous knowledge of the application under test as well as their knowledge of test methodologies to find bugs quickly. The Windows Application Compatibility test team, for example, is highly dependent on exploratory testing to verify the functionality of hundreds of applications during the development of a new version of the operating system.

On teams where there is an increased emphasis on automated tests, exploratory techniques are beneficial early in the test design phase to influence the structure and goals of the automated tests. Teams often schedule "bug bashes" throughout the product cycle, where testers take part of a day to test their product using an exploratory approach. This approach simulates the customer experience and is typically successful at finding bugs that other tactics might have missed. Many teams analyze the bugs found during the bug bash and use the findings to influence the design of future automated tests.

In teams where a higher level of automated tests is necessary, testers often use exploratory techniques in conjunction with specifications and other relevant information to influence test case design. In testing, it is essential to find the important bugs as early as possible while also striving to design tests that will find bugs and verify functionality and correctness for the entire life of the application.

One novel and successful approach to exploratory testing used at Microsoft is the practice of *pair testing*. Inspired by pair programming, this practice groups two testers together for an exploratory testing session. One tester sits at the keyboard and exercises the feature or application while the other tester stands behind or sits next to the first tester and helps to guide the testing. Both testers are performing exploratory testing, but while one concentrates on driving the functionality, one is thinking about the application from a high level. The testers switch roles at regular intervals. In a single 8-hour session, 15 pairs of testers found 166 bugs, including 40 classified as *severity 1* (bugs that must be fixed as soon as possible). In feedback collected from a survey sent to the 30 participants, only 3 thought that pair testing was less fun than an individual approach is, and 4 four thought it was less effective.

Summary

Continuously exercising a variety of techniques and methodologies and using any information gained to influence future activities is a key part of designing tests that can last a decade or longer. There isn't a right way or a wrong way to test, and there are certainly no silver bullet techniques that will guarantee great testing. It is critical to take time to understand the component, feature, or application, and design tests based on that understanding drawn from a wide variety of techniques. A strategy of using a variety of test design efforts is much more likely to succeed than is an approach that favors only a few techniques.

Most engineers beginning their careers in test do not have a lot of experience with test design. Although many great testers "pick up" good test design ideas by practicing the art of testing or by interacting with peers who are more knowledgeable or experienced, it is often better to teach and communicate good practices in approaching test design early in the career development of testers.

The following chapters cover a few test design approaches referenced in Microsoft's technical training courses for testers. These are techniques commonly considered across Microsoft when designing test cases.

Chapter 5
Functional Testing Techniques

Bj Rollison

When I was young lad, I was very curious about how things worked. One Christmas I received a demolition derby slot car set from Santa Claus. I am not sure if it was my father or I who was more excited about it because we immediately set it up on the dining room table, and he and I spent the better part of Christmas Day racing the cars around the track trying to crash into each other. It was amazingly fun especially when various parts of the car's body would fly off after some spectacular crash. Perhaps it was at this early age that I developed my penchant for breaking things. Eventually, much to our chagrin, my mother insisted the track come off the table for Christmas dinner. But after dinner Dad and I were back at it trying to out-maneuver each other until bed time. It was indeed a great day!

Thereafter, when my father was busy, I cajoled my sisters into playing, but they were no match for my cunning and superb slot car handling skills. This was all great fun, but after several weeks passed, my curiosity got the better of me. I wanted to—no, I needed to—understand how the cars worked. So, one evening in the solitude of my bedroom I completely disassembled one of the cars to discover how the electric motor caused the wheels to turn through a series of small gears. But how did the electric motor work? I discovered magnets and small coils of copper wire wrapped around plastic shafts. I watched with amazement as the electric motor spun when I touched the contacts on the track. I wondered if there was anything underneath the copper wire and proceeded to peel off the thin layer of varnish and unwind one of the coils of wire. In retrospect, that was not a very good idea because I never got that car to run again. My father was not too happy with me disassembling my new toy but nevertheless took me to the hobby shop to purchase another slot car to continue our contest.

I learned a lot about electric motors and gears that day. Throughout my life, I discovered that I can learn quite a bit about some things by dissecting them and putting them back together piece by piece to understand how each part works. That passion for finding out how things work still courses through my veins today. Incessant curiosity seems to be a trait engrained in most testers. Exploring software from a user interface is important, but if testers really want to understand how software works and what it is capable of doing, we must look below the surface of the user interface and peer into the system under test. Great testers not only use their curiosity to explore the product, but also dig deeper to investigate things at a much more granular level to perform a more in-depth analysis of the capabilities and attributes of the software under test.

One way to gather more in-depth information is to deconstruct the product's feature sets and test the discrete functional attributes and capabilities of the various components.

Functional techniques provide testers with systematic approaches that can help achieve a more comprehensive investigation of individual features and components. There are several functional testing techniques, but in this chapter I discuss a few of the key functional testing techniques commonly used throughout Microsoft.

The Need for Functional Testing

Modern software is extremely complex, and testing today's software is especially challenging because testers must be able to design and execute a set of tests that will provide project leaders with the appropriate information that highlights potential risks and qualifies important attributes and capabilities of the software. Testers must define a finite set of tests from all possible tests that provides the organization with high levels of confidence that testers have exposed critical issues and appropriately evaluated the important features of the product. And testing is expected to be completed in a limited amount of time! So, any potential approach we choose to test software should be reasonably systematic or methodic and render a relatively small subset of effective tests capable of proving or disproving any predetermined hypothesis.

One approach to software testing is *exploratory testing*.[1] Exploratory testing (ET) is a commonly used approach that primarily focuses on behavioral testing, and it is effective for gaining familiarity with new software features. ET is quite useful during the initial evaluation of software and helps the tester get a quick sense about the software. ET is also valuable in providing a quick, high-level overview of the operational capabilities and the general usability of software. Exploratory testing can be sufficient for small software projects, or software with limited distribution, or software with a limited shelf life.

However, exploratory testing generally doesn't scale well for large-scale complex projects or mission-critical software. At Microsoft, we have also learned that exploratory testing is generally not the best approach for sustained engineering necessary for the long-term maintenance of software releases. We realize that simply relying on testers and domain experts to explore and question the product's capabilities from the user interface does not provide the qualified information to the project leaders that is necessary for informed rational decision making about product quality and risk. Huge bug numbers look impressive to number ninnies, but data such as raw bug count or time testing a particular feature area does not really provide information beyond the time expended investigating something and some amount of bugs being discovered, or not. So, when the management team desires more information about the software to minimize potential risks and make rational decisions, we must perform a more complete analysis of the functional components of the software under test.

---

[1]   Exploratory testing is discussed in more detail in Chapter 12, "Other Tools."

Boris Beizer states that behavioral testing from a black box approach accounts for only somewhere between 35 percent and 65 percent of all testing.[2] Behavioral testing from the user interface is important, but when it is the only or primary approach to testing, we are very likely to waste time with ineffective tests and also miss important areas of the product, as illustrated in Figure 5-1. Internal studies at Microsoft and elsewhere in the industry provide empirical data that consistently demonstrates the limited effectiveness of behavioral testing (see the following sidebar titled "Weinberg's triangle revisited"). So, the question testers must ask is, How can we increase the effectiveness of our tests to limit redundancy and reduce our team's overall exposure to risk?

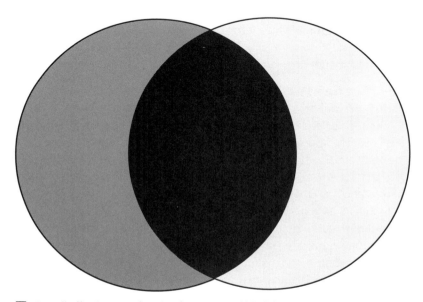

■ Overall effectiveness of testing from a typical black box perspective

☐ Testing effort that is potentially redundant or provides no new information

▣ Area of untested software – assumed risk must be 100% in untested areas

FIGURE 5-1 Venn diagram illustrating black box testing effectiveness.

---

[2] Boris Beizer, *Black-Box Testing: Techniques for Functional Testing of Software and Systems* (New York: John Wiley, 1995).

Weinberg's triangle revisited

For more than five years, our internal training for new Software Development Engineers in Test (SDETs) relied on a triangle simulation based on Gerald Weinberg's original triangle problem to establish a baseline skill assessment. Newly hired SDETs are instructed to use their existing skills and knowledge within 15 minutes to explore the application and to define the set of tests necessary to determine the ability of the software to satisfy the functional requirement. The functional requirement states that the program reads three integer values representing the lengths of the sides of a triangle. The program then displays a message that states whether the triangle is scalene, isosceles, or equilateral. Some SDETs grumble about the time limitation, but this simulates the reality of schedule pressures and our ability to identify the most important tests that will provide valuable information in a specified period.

In reviewing the more than 5,000 samples collected, we discovered that the majority of SDETs included only one test in which valid integer inputs would result in an invalid triangle type, one test for equilateral, one test for scalene, and one test for isosceles. These four tests exercise approximately only 50 percent of the paths in the most critical method in the software. Further analysis of the inputs also demonstrated an extremely low probability of tests exercising a third conditional clause in a compound predicate statement that determines whether the valid integer inputs would result in an invalid triangle type. Empirical data proves that less than 10 percent of any random sample of the total population of tests would completely exercise all three conditional subexpressions in the compound predicate statement. I also use this simulation when teaching at the University of Washington and in conference workshops and find very similar results. Fortunately, our internal studies demonstrate a 60 percent to 75 percent increase in test case effectiveness and more effective test prioritization on similar simulations after several hours of hands-on training on the proper use of testing techniques.

One way to increase the effectiveness of our tests and gather important information about certain aspects of the product is to employ functional testing techniques. *Functional techniques* are systematic procedures that can help us perform a comprehensive investigation of the software's functional attributes and capabilities. Functional techniques are generally applied from the user interface but can be used to design tests from both black box and white box test perspectives. When we use functional testing techniques correctly and in the appropriate context, they can help us achieve a more thorough analysis of the system under test and reduce the susceptibility to the pesticide paradox.[3]

---

3   Boris Beizer, *Software Testing Techniques*, 2nd ed. (New York: Van Nostrand Reinhold, 1990).

The pesticide paradox

One of the things I enjoy in my spare time is organic gardening. My daughter and I sow seeds in the early spring in a greenhouse and wait until late April or early May before transferring the seedlings to the garden. But, once in the garden, the plants are susceptible to a variety of insects and pests and I must find natural defenses against the rabbits, slugs, and other insects that would otherwise decimate our vegetable crop. Rabbits don't really eat much from the garden and my daughter gets a thrill when she sees them, so by far the most menacing critter I encounter in my backyard is the slug.

Believe it or not, slugs are attracted to beer, and a beer trap works wonders to rid any slugs that might find their way into the garden. I don't think the slugs know the difference between cheap can beer and the Pacific Northwest microbrews, so I go with the cheap stuff. A copper strip around the raised garden beds provides a barrier against slugs, and of course salt periodically sprinkled around the outside of the raised beds inhibits slug invasions. Wood ash and egg shells are other ways to help control the marauding slugs. Regardless of what I do to kill or deter slugs in my gardens, invariably some slugs still seem to make it through.

Similar to how I try to stop the onslaught of slugs I must also use an assortment of methods and approaches when testing software to expose potential bugs. Any experienced tester will tell you that no single approach to testing is effective in exposing all types of defects or completely evaluating the capabilities of software; this dilemma is known as the *pesticide paradox*. The pesticide paradox is derived from Beizer's First Law: "Every method you use to prevent or find bugs leaves a residue of subtler bugs against which those methods are ineffectual." Essentially, there is no single technique or approach that is completely effective in software testing, so by increasing the diversity of methods used in testing and considering different perspectives, we are more likely to be successful in both exposing potential issues as well as increasing the effectiveness of our testing.

Organic gardening is a lot of work and presents some unique challenges. But it is worth the effort when I watch my 6-year-old daughter pick a banana pepper or a cherry tomato off the vine and eat it while harvesting our bounty. Likewise, software testing is hard work and has inimitable challenges, but when done correctly using a variety of approaches, the rewards can be great for the entire product team.

Another benefit of functional testing techniques is the potential to instill a high level of confidence in testing coverage of specific functional areas of the product with a fewer number of redundant tests. However, as I previously stated, the value or effectiveness of using any test technique ultimately depends on the individual tester's system and domain knowledge and ability to apply the applicable technique in the correct situation. It is important to remember that functional testing techniques are merely tools used by professional testers to help gather important information about the capabilities and attributes of software and to help us expose potential issues. We must know which techniques to use in a specific situation and how to use those techniques effectively.

Are testing techniques foolish gimmicks?

Some people suggest that techniques are foolish gimmicks or they are too trivial to worry about. I suppose to an untrained observer techniques can seem like thoughtless tricks. But a technique is a systematic procedure that simply provides one approach to solve one type of complex problem, often relying on well-established heuristics. Many professionals use techniques, and when techniques are properly used by a skilled tester, they can be effective tools. Testing techniques are useful in providing a more thorough critical analysis of the capabilities and attributes of software features and aid us in increasing effective test coverage.

It is important to realize that proper application of a testing technique is not a brain-dead or rote activity. Techniques are not some magical panacea in testing, and they are certainly not the only way we should approach software testing. In fact, the application of systematic software testing techniques for functional and structural testing requires extensive domain and system level knowledge, logical deduction, analytical reasoning, critical thinking, and a tester's cognitive ability to determine the outcome of a test or the accuracy of a preconceived hypothesis in a given context. And many techniques are extremely useful in helping us prove or disprove the existence of specific types or classes of defects or validate product functionality.

Functional testing techniques such as boundary value analysis (BVA), equivalence class partitioning (ECP), combinatorial analysis, and state transition testing are similar to tools in a toolbox, and each tool serves different purposes. Used correctly in the appropriate situation, these tools can be quite effective in helping testers systematically evaluate specific functional attributes of software features. Systematic testing techniques are not the only tools in a professional tester's toolbox and are best applied when more detailed handiwork is required. But we must remember that to be effective any tool in our toolbox requires an intelligent and knowledgeable person who knows how and when to use the tool as a potential solution in the proper context.

Equivalence Class Partitioning

The first functional testing technique testers should learn to master is *equivalence class partitioning* (ECP). Understanding how to use this technique is important because it provides a foundation for many other techniques and approaches to software testing. The

ECP technique is simply a tool that enables the tester to evaluate input or output variables systematically for each parameter in a feature. But to be most effective equivalence class partitioning requires us to perform a comprehensive analysis of the variable data for each parameter in the context of the specific system. So, before designing the ECP tests, we must meticulously decompose and model the variable data for each input and/or output parameter in discrete subsets of valid and invalid classes. The ECP tests are then derived from creating unions of valid class subsets until all valid class subsets have been used in a test, and then evaluating each invalid data subset individually. This seems like a simple enough explanation; however, this technique requires both in-depth and broad knowledge to decompose input and/or output variable data precisely into discrete valid and invalid class subsets. The subsets are defined in such a way that any element of a given subset would logically produce the same result as any other element in that subset. We can then design both positive and negatives tests to systematically evaluate the functional capabilities of input and/or output parameters and the system's ability to handle any errors adequately.

The value of the ECP technique is twofold. First, it helps us systematically reduce the number of tests from all possible tests and still provides us with a high degree of confidence that other variables or variable combinations in the same subset will produce the same expected result repeatedly. For example, assume you are testing a text box control that accepts a string variable of Unicode characters between upper case *A* and *Z* with a minimum string length of 1 and a maximum string length of 25 characters. Exhaustive testing would include each letter one time (26^1) and each letter combination for every possible string length. So, to test for all possible inputs the number of tests is equal to $26^{25} + 26^{24} + 26^{23} \ldots + 26^1$. That is a really big number (RBN)! But let's make an assertion that testing the string "BCD" is similar to testing the string "WXY." So, logical deduction of the valid class subsets for this specific parameter would include the following:

- The uppercase Unicode characters between uppercase *A* and *Z*
- A string of characters with a string length between 1 and 25 characters

Based on this model of valid data for the sample input parameter, a string of "ABCDEF" should produce the same result as a string of "ZYXWVUTSRQPONM," and the same result for a string composed of "KUGVDSFHKIFSDFJKOLNBF."

The second advantage of the ECP technique is that we can effectively increase the breadth of data coverage by randomly selecting elements from a given subset to use as test data because any element from a specific valid or invalid class subset should produce the same result (if the data is correctly decomposed into discrete subsets and there is no errant behavior) as any other element in that subset. Using the previous example, tests for the given name parameter will surely include nominal real-world test data such as "Bob," "Nandu," "Elizabeth," or "Ling." But static test data provides very little value in terms of new information or evaluating the robustness of the algorithm after the first iteration (unless there are fundamental changes to the algorithm). Static data also does not exercise randomized variable permutations. Randomly selecting elements from the valid or invalid subsets provides great variability in subsequent iterations of the test case and increases the probability of exposing unusual anomalies that might not otherwise be exposed using typical or real-world valid class static data. This is the basis of using probabilistic stochastic test data to enrich our tests.

I cannot overemphasize that the overall effectiveness of ECP relies primarily on the ability of the tester to decompose the variable data for a given parameter accurately into well-defined subsets in which any element from a specific subset would logically produce the same expected result as any other element from that subset. We spend a lot of time going over these concepts in our SDET training. Of course, modeling the variable data into equivalent class subsets is based on our knowledge of the system in a given context. So, the less testers know about the system and the domain space, the greater the probability of incorrectly applying this technique and the greater the potential to miss critical defects and execute redundant tests.

Decomposing Variable Data

The most difficult and challenging aspect of equivalence class partitioning is our ability to decompose data into unique valid and invalid class subsets. We must be familiar with various types of data and understand how the program and the system process, manipulate, transfer, and store data. We must also know common or likely input variables and review failure indicators such as historically problematic variables (for example, known problematic test data, high-risk data). We must also take into consideration external factors such as user profiles, specifications, and requirements that often help us define the appropriate context.

Overgeneralizing and insufficiently decomposing the variable data results in a reduction in the number of subsets in a particular class, and the likelihood of missing errors increases. Hyperanalyzing or overly decomposing variable data into nonunique subsets increases the number of potentially redundant tests; however, redundant tests might not expose additional errors and have a low probability of providing new relevant information. I recommend you err on the side of caution because you can always cull redundant tests. However, if you miss a critical problem as a result of overgeneralizing the test data, the cost could be quite large. The data decomposition theory for equivalence class partitioning provides the basis for understanding why knowledge of the system and the domain space is critical for the greatest success and the maximum effectiveness of this technique.

> ### ECP data decomposition theory
>
> Overgeneralization of variable data reduces the base number of ECP tests but increases the probability of missing errors or generating false negatives or false positives. Hyperanalysis of variable data increases the probability of redundancy, which can reduce the overall efficiency of the test approach.

Initially, we must separate the data into two classes. Valid class data includes the set of variable elements that return a positive result under usual circumstances. In other words, the data is expected not to generate an error condition or cause an unexpected failure. Invalid class data includes the set of variable elements that are expected to result in an error condition. Most error conditions are trapped by an error handler, but occasionally invalid class data has an increased probability of exposing errant behavior or failures.

Once the data is separated into valid and invalid classes of data, the tester must carefully analyze the data in each class and further decompose the data in each class into discrete subsets in that class. Essentially, any element in any individual subset of data in either the valid or invalid class should produce the same result when used in a test. That is why we don't have to test every single uppercase Unicode character between *A* and *Z*, or every possible combination of characters in the previous example.

ECP and the case of the mysterious error message

When I was developing one of our internal training courses I stumbled upon a rather odd problem with file names on the Windows XP operating system. The exercise I designed had students decompose the set of ASCII characters into equivalence class subsets for a file name passed as an argument through the common Save dialog box using Notepad on the Windows XP operating system. This is no easy task because success requires a deep understanding of the hardware platform, the operating system environment, and the character set.

In a past life, I built custom PC systems for clients from the motherboard up through various software configurations. It was in those early days when I became all too familiar with flashing EPROMs for BIOS updates and changing jumper settings for IRQs and DMA channels to get hardware from different manufacturers to play nicely with each other. I knew a few other esoteric details such as reserved memory space for LPT and COM ports 1–9 by the PC/AT BIOS. This means that a base file name composed of a literal string of *LPT1* or *COM 6* should result in a similar error message on the Windows platform indicating that the file name is a reserved device name, or something to that effect. So, as I prepared the solution to the exercise I logically concluded that base file names that use the literal string of characters *LPT1* through *LPT9* or *COM1* through *COM9* are equivalent and should produce the same expected result.

But when I tested my assertion to validate the solution for the exercise I came across some rather unexpected behavior. When I entered *LPT2* as the base file name parameter, the system displayed the expected error message, "This file name is a reserved device name." But when I entered *COM7* as the base file name to test my equivalence hypothesis, I was greeted with a completely different message that read, "The above file name is invalid."

It didn't take me too long to figure out that LPT1 through LPT4 and COM1 through COM4 took one path through the code to present the expected reserved device name error message, and LPT5 through LPT9 and COM5 through COM9 took a different error path through the code, resulting in a more ambiguous message. One can only speculate why a logical equivalent set would somehow be arbitrarily segregated, and fortunately this little coding faux pas has been resolved in the Windows Vista operating system. But we still use this example in our training to reinforce the best practice of using multiple elements from each equivalence class data set to increase the breadth of coverage and reduce the probability of errant functionality.

To help us decompose the data into discrete subsets in each class Glenford Myers[4] proposes four heuristics in his book *The Art of Software Testing*. A *heuristic* is a guideline, principle, or rule of thumb that is often useful in performing tasks such as decision making, troubleshooting, and problem solving. The four heuristics we can use in decomposing data into discrete subsets in the valid and invalid classes include range of values, similar groups of variables, unique values, and special values:

- **Range**   A contiguous set of data in which any data point in the minima and maxima boundary values of the range is expected to produce the same result. For example, a number field in which you can enter an integer value from 1 through 999. The valid equivalence class is >=1 and <=999. Invalid equivalence class ranges include integers <1 and >999.

- **Group**   A group of items or selections is permitted as long as all items are handled identically. For example, a list of items of vehicles used to determine a taxation category includes truck, car, motorcycle, motor home, and trailer. If truck, car, and motor home reference the same taxation category, that group of items is considered equivalent.

- **Unique**   Data in a class or subset of a class that might be handled differently from other data in that class or subset of a class. For example, the date January 19, 2038, at 3:14:07 is a unique date in applications that process time and date data from the BIOS clock and it should be separated into a discrete subset.

- **Specific**   The condition *must be* or *must not be* present. For example, in Simple Mail Transfer Protocol (SMTP) the at symbol (@) is a specific character that cannot be used as part of the e-mail name or domain name.

---

4 Glenford Myers, *The Art of Software Testing* (New York: John Wiley, 1979).

Equivalence Class Partitioning in Action

A simple example can help you better understand how to decompose parameter variables into discrete subsets of valid and invalid data. The Next Date program, illustrated in Figure 5-2, takes three integer inputs that represent a specific month, day, and year in the Gregorian calendar and returns the next Gregorian calendar date in the month/day/year format. The algorithm to determine the next date is based on the Gregorian calendar, which is commonly used throughout the world today. The program is implemented in C#, and the output is always in the m/d/yyyy format regardless of the user's locale setting (meaning the output is not culture sensitive).

FIGURE 5-2 A C# implementation of the Next Date program.

On the surface, the input and output data for this program appear rather simple. In this particular case, the tester must have domain knowledge of the Gregorian calendar, the papal bull *Inter gravissimas*,[5] and must even know a bit of English history! System knowledge is also used to identify potential subsets. For example, the system includes the hardware BIOS clock that measures ticks and the programming language used to develop the program; both are important considerations in accurately identifying and logically segregating variables into discrete valid and invalid class subsets. Table 5-1 illustrates the most effective breakdown of the data sets for this particular program.

TABLE 5-1 ECP Table for the Next Date Program Input and Output Parameters

Input/output	Valid class subsets	Invalid class subsets
Month	v1—30-day months v2—31-day months v3—February	i1—>= 13 i— <= 0 i3—any noninteger i4—empty i5—>= 3 integers

---

5 A *papal bull* is a letter of patent or charter issued by a pope. The papal bull *inter gravissimas* instituted the Gregorian calendar to alleviate problems with the old Julian calendar. See *http://en.wikipedia.org/wiki/Inter_gravissimas* for more information.

Input/output	Valid class subsets	Invalid class subsets
Day	v4—1–30 v5—1–31 v6—1–28 v7—1–29	i6—>=32 i7—<= 0 i8—any noninteger i9—empty i10—>= 3 integers
Year	v8—1582–3000** v9—non–leap year v10—leap year v11—century non–leap year v12—century leap year	i11—<= 1581 i12—>= 3001 i13—any noninteger i14—empty i15—>= 5 integers
Output	v13—1/2/1582– 1/1/3001	i16—<= 1/1/1582 i17—>= 1/2/3001

Unique or special dates	v14—9/3/1752–
	    9/13/1752
	v15—1/19/2038
		i18—10/5/1582–
		    10/14/1582

Analyzing Parameter Subsets

The first parameter is the input for the month. This parameter accepts a range of integer type variables from 1 through 12 representing the months of the year. Internally, the implementation must distinguish between the 30-day months, the 31-day months, and February in non–leap years and leap years. Therefore, you can segregate the variable for the month parameter into three valid class subsets so that there is a valid class for 30-day months, 31-day months, and February, which is a unique variable state compared to the other valid class subsets. You can also create a fourth valid class subset of 1 through 12 to help identify the minima and maxima boundary conditions for this input parameter. But creating only a subset of 1 through 12 for months might be an overgeneralization and result in missing critical tests. The invalid class subsets include integer inputs above 12 and less than 1, any noninteger value, an empty string, and three or more characters entered in the control.

The variable data for the day parameter is separated into four subsets based on the number of days for 30-day months, 31-day months, February in leap years, and February in non–leap years. The primary reason to decompose the variables for the day parameter into discrete subsets for each month type is to aid in the determination of specific boundary conditions in the overall physical range between 1 and 31. An added benefit of the equivalence class subsets is that they generally indicate specific boundary conditions. For example, the day parameter clearly identifies five specific boundary conditions (depending on the exact implementation) of 1, 28, 29, 30, and 31. Also, dividing the day ranges into exclusive subsets helps ensure that you don't generate false positives. For example, if you overgeneralize the month and day parameter valid class subsets to just 1 through 12 for month and 1 through 31 for day, an automated test could randomly generate a number of 2 for month and 30 for day and expect the next day to be 2/31/xxxx, which is a false positive.

The year parameter includes one subset that specifies the range of valid years and also one subset for leap years, one subset for non–leap years, one subset for century leap years, and one subset for non–century leap years. Leap years, century leap years, and non–leap years are easily determined by using a mathematical formula implemented in an algorithm similar to the following one.

```
//Example algorithm used to calculate leap years
public static bool IsLeapYear(int year)
{
    return (year % 4 == 0 && year % 100 != 0 || year % 400 == 0);
}
```

Because determining leap years is based on a mathematical formula, testing any leap year and any century leap year between 1582 and 3000 always produces the same exact result and returns true. Also note that no specific boundary conditions are related to leap years or century leap years. For this parameter, the specific input minima and maxima boundary values are 1582 and 3000, respectively. The year 3000 was arbitrarily chosen for this particular program because I suspect we will all be bored with this simulation by then!

Finally, there are two ranges of unique dates and one unique date that are more interesting than any of the other possible dates. The first unique range of dates includes the invalid class subset of dates between 10/5/1582 and 10/14/1582. These dates were excluded from the Gregorian calendar as instituted by the papal bull *inter gravissimus,* and any date in this range should result in an error message or a message indicating the date is invalid according to the functional requirements. The range of unique dates in the valid class is between 9/3/1752 and 9/13/1752. England and her colonies didn't adopt the Gregorian calendar until 1752, so they had to exclude 10 days to synchronize the calendar with the lunar cycle. But, because the program is based on the original Gregorian calendar instituted by the papal bull, this range of dates is more unique than others are because a developer who remembers English or American history might inadvertently exclude these dates, which would actually be a defect in this particular case.

The date 1/19/2038 is one specific date that is more unique than other possible valid dates are. The BIOS clock provides a tick count the developer can use to measure time. Although it is highly unlikely that the developer would use tick counts in the implementation of this program, testers should use all available information and at least initially consider this as a unique subset until they can verify the program's implementation.

The Friday the 13th bug

The Y2K issue was highly publicized and nearly drove a panic in financial circles. But a potentially more serious problem looms on the horizon. It seems that the BIOS clocks on PC/AT computers were initialized to start on January 1, 1970, at 00:00:00. There is nothing magical about that date, but the BIOS clock uses a 32-bit integer to measure tick counts to track time. This means that on January 19, 2038, at 03:14:07 the BIOS clock tick count will be at the maximum limit or boundary of a 32-bit integer value. So, at exactly 03:14:08 on January 19, 2038, the BIOS will reset the computer time to 00:00:00 with a date of December 13, 1901. Interestingly enough, December 13th also happens to be a Friday! Fortunately, I plan to be sailing somewhere in the South Pacific by that time.

Knowledge of the programming language used in the implementation can also assist testers in decomposing data into discrete subsets. In this example, C# is used as the programming language, and in C# all input variables are passed as string types. The developer must convert the string to an integer value using an *Int32.Parse* or *Convert.ToInt32* method. These methods throw an overflow exception for any integer value outside the range of a signed 32-bit integer value, or they throw a format exception for any variable input that does not convert to an integer value. So, if the developer uses one of these methods to convert the input variable to an integer value, you can safely assert that an input of the character *A* is in the same invalid equivalence subset as the ideographic character 金 or an input of a number with a decimal point (radix) or thousands delimiter. This is because any character in the input that does not convert to an integer causes the format exception to be thrown. An empty string also throws a format exception; however, I recommend including a test for an empty string by defining it as a unique subset for input parameters.

The ECP Tests

Exhaustive testing of this particular program includes all valid dates between 1/1/1582 and 12/31/3000. The total number of positive tests is approximately 500,000. If it takes 5 seconds to manually input and verify the correct result of all valid dates in the valid range of dates, it would take one tester approximately 29 days to test the valid inputs exhaustively. You might not have time to test all possible variable input combinations—doing so is probably not the best use of your time—and many tests will have an extremely low probability of providing new information beyond what previous tests have given. The assertion you can make with ECP testing is that a valid input of 6/12/2001 would produce the next calendar date on the Gregorian calendar, as would 9/29/1899 and 4/3/2999.

As previously stated, one benefit of ECP is that it aids the tester in systematically reducing the number of tests from all possible tests. After the data is decomposed into discrete subsets, the next step in the ECP technique is to define how the data subsets will be used in a test.

The most common approach is to create combinations of valid class subsets for all parameters until all valid class subsets have been included at least once in a validation test. Then, test each invalid class subset individually for each parameter while setting the other parameters to some nominal valid value. For example, the first test for valid input data would be a combination of valid class subsets v1, v4 (or v6 or v7), and v8. The test data represented by a combination of these three subsets is any 30-day month, any day between 1 and 30, and any year between 1582 and 3000. Table 5-2 lists the test data inputs for the Next Date program.

TABLE 5-2 ECP Test Design Matrix

ECP test	Month	Day	Year	Other	Expected result
1	V1 ∪ V2 ∪ V3	V6	V8		Next date
2	V1	V4	v9 ∩ V8		Next date
3	v2	V5	V10 ∩ V8		Next date
4	v3	V6	V11 ∩ V8		Next date
5	v3	V7	V12 ∩ V8		Next date
6				V13	Next date
7				v14	Next date
8				v15	1/20/2038
9	i1	V4	v8		Error Message
10	i2	V4	v8		Error Message
11	i3	V4	v8		Error Message
12	i4	V4	v8		Error Message
13	i5	V4	v8		Error Message
14	V1 ∪ V2 ∪ V3	I6	V8		Error Message
15	V1 ∪ V2 ∪ V3	I7	V8		Error Message
16	V1 ∪ V2 ∪ V3	I8	V8		Error Message
17	V1 ∪ V2 ∪ V3	I9	V8		Error Message
18	V1 ∪ V2 ∪ V3	I10	V8		Error Message
19	V1 ∪ V2 ∪ V3	V6	I11		Error Message
20	V1 ∪ V2 ∪ V3	V6	I12		Error Message
21	V1 ∪ V2 ∪ V3	V6	I13		Error Message
22	V1 ∪ V2 ∪ V3	V6	I14		Error Message
23	V1 ∪ V2 ∪ V3	V6	I15		Error Message
24				I16	Error Message
25				I18	Error Message

In this example, the ECP technique illustrates that the number of equivalence class tests for valid inputs is reduced from more than 500,000 possible tests to 8 positive tests and 17 negative tests. There are only 17 negative tests because a test for invalid subset I17 is redundant with ECP test 19 for invalid subset I11. Likewise, you can probably also eliminate test number 6 for valid class subset V13 because it is redundant with ECP test numbers 1, 2, 3, 4, and 5. However, you should not eliminate those redundant subsets from the ECP table because they can help you later identify potential boundary conditions when you perform boundary value analysis.

Limiting the number of validation tests to only eight tests seems a bit risky, and I would never advocate executing only eight tests. You certainly want to run more positive tests with different input elements. This is where using probabilistic stochastic test data generation or randomly selecting data elements in the specified subsets for a given test provides a greater breadth of coverage of the possible variable data. Now, to design test inputs (either manual or automated) for Test 1 you can randomly select a month between 1 and 12 (or iterate through each month sequentially), randomly select any integer value between 1 and 28 for the day input, and randomly select any integer value between 1582 and 3000 for the year input. By executing the test several times and randomly selecting variable elements from the specified subsets for that test, you increase the breadth of coverage of all data points in that defined subset and also design a test that provides a great deal of flexibility for the tester or for an automated test while still proving (or disproving) the test hypothesis. By preserving the random month, day, and year selected for any iteration of ECP Test 1 either in memory or in a file or database, you can use a proto-algorithm as an oracle to verify the output of any automated ECP tests for this example.

Why don't the ECP tests include tests for boundary conditions?

Note that none of the ECP tests specifically target boundary conditions. That is because ECP tests are designed to identify a specific type of error, and boundary testing is designed to identify a different category of errors. The decomposed data subsets in the ECP table are valuable in identifying the minima and maxima boundary conditions for a linear range of physical values and can help identify a specific physical value in a range of values that might represent a special case boundary condition. However, the ECP technique looks for problems with nominal variable data and samples of probabilistic data from the population of possible data. ECP testing does not specifically target minima and maxima boundary conditions, and neither does it specifically include boundary value analysis or boundary testing.

I often see many novice testers combine the ECP technique with boundary testing in an attempt to reduce tests or save time. Although the ECP technique is often used in conjunction with boundary testing because the ECP subsets provide a basic framework that can help identify potential boundary conditions for boundary value analysis, attempting to consolidate these two techniques can be a dangerous practice because it can lead to missed tests or faulty assumptions. In general, when applying techniques to test software it is better to focus on one technique at a time for greatest effectiveness.

Summary of Equivalence Class Partitioning

ECP is a functional testing technique used to design a set of black box or white box tests to evaluate the functionality of input or output parameters. The technique is not a systematic procedure intended to evaluate boundary conditions, interdependent parameter combinations, or sequential or ordered inputs. Input and output conditions are generalized into two separate classes: valid class data, which returns a positive result or does not produce an error condition, and invalid class data, which ideally generates error messages. The data in each class is further decomposed into subsets in each class. In a test, any data element from a specific subset in a given class should produce the same exact result regardless of which data element from that subset is used. There are four useful heuristics for decomposing data into subsets: range of values, similar groups of variables, unique values, and special values. Equivalence class partitioning is a useful technique used to reduce the number tests from all possible tests logically and methodically. When combined with stochastic data generation, the execution of ECP tests increases the breadth of coverage beyond simple static variables, effectively increasing overall confidence while also testing for robustness.

Although application of the ECP technique often requires more time as compared to simply plugging in likely variables and a few variables that have proved problematic in the past, there are several significant benefits to equivalence class partitioning. When applied correctly this technique can do the following:

- Force the tester to perform a more detailed analysis of the feature set and the variable data used by input and output parameters

- Help testers identify corner cases they might have overlooked

- Provide clear evidence of which data sets were tested and how they were tested

- Increase test effectiveness systematically, which helps reduce risk

- Increase efficiency by logically reducing redundant tests

However, equivalence class partitioning is not a silver bullet, and the effectiveness of the ECP technique in detecting anomalies in the software and increasing test coverage primarily depends on testers' skills and in-depth knowledge of the domain space and the overall system. When used properly, the ECP technique is a valuable tool in a tester's toolbox and can often expose corner cases or test data that might not otherwise be used in other testing approaches.

Single fault assumption

The single fault assumption in reliability theory states that failures are rarely the result of the simultaneous occurrence of two or more faults. So, the primary purpose of ECP testing and boundary testing is to expose single faults, especially at linear boundaries of variables or at the so-called corner cases of equivalent data that might be handled differently by the application. Both ECP and BVA techniques are designed to provide a more rigorous inspection and systematically evaluate discrete input and output parameters individually while setting other parameters to valid nominal conditions. Of course, this should not be the only type of fault model to consider, but after you establish confidence in the functional capabilities of each parameter independently from other parameters, it is much easier to expand testing to include additional approaches that evaluate parameter interaction and investigate areas that might be susceptible to multiple fault models.

Boundary Value Analysis

Boundary value analysis (BVA) is perhaps the best-known functional test technique. Unfortunately, it is also typically misused because many testers assume it to be relatively easy or trivial. Historical evidence demonstrates that a surprising number of problems occur at boundaries of linear variables, so we must carefully analyze the boundary conditions of linear variable data to avoid overlooking boundary class defects. When BVA is used in conjunction with equivalence class partitioning, the BVA functional technique can be very effective in systematically analyzing the boundary values of linear variables for independent input and output parameters. BVA or boundary testing is especially useful for detecting the following types of errors:

- Incorrect artificial constraints of a data type
- Erroneously assigned relational operators
- Wrapping of data types
- Problems with looping structures
- Off-by-one errors

What is a boundary value in software?

In the context of a software program, a *boundary value* is a specific value at the extreme edges of an independent linear variable or at the edge or edges of equivalence class subsets of an independent linear variable.

Similar to how borders mark a country's physical territory, boundary values are specific data points at the extreme ranges of a linear variable. For example, in the Next Date program the minimum input date is 1/1/1582 and the maximum input year is 12/31/3000. These values represent the extreme minimum and maximum boundaries, respectively, for the combined month, day, and year variables. The minimum input of 1 and maximum input of 12 are the boundary conditions for the extreme linear range for the month parameter.

Many countries are subdivided into states or territories. Likewise, a linear variable can also have subboundary values in the minima and maxima range. These subboundaries are often identified by various equivalence class partition range subsets or unique subsets of a variable. For example, the ECP data in Table 5-1 shows a unique range of 10/5/1582 through 10/14/1582. This ECP range also denotes two additional subboundary values in the extreme linear range of allowable input dates.

Many countries occupy the physical space of a continent, but not completely. Similarly, although the input variable for the year parameter is predefined to be between 1582 and 3000, the developer must declare that variable to be some sort of data type. A plethora of tools enable testers to determine the data types of variables used by methods or functions, but assume the developer declared a 16-bit integer in C# to store the year variable. The minimum and maximum range of a 16-bit integer value is −32,768 through +32,767. Obviously, the developer artificially constrained the overall linear range of the 16-bit integer to 1582 through 3000. (Ideally, the developer would have also changed the properties of the input text box control to allow only four characters.) So, although the year parameter could accept any value within the minimum and maximum range of a signed 16-bit integer data type, the acceptable range is artificially constrained to a linear range of values (1582 through 3000) in the overall range of the data type.

BVA is especially useful at methodically analyzing two types of boundary values commonly found in software: fixed-constant values and fixed-variable values. Fixed-constant boundaries are mathematical constants, or real numbers that are significantly interesting and remain constant during run time and typically cannot be changed by a user. For example, in the Next Date program 1582 and 3000 are predefined constant values that specify an allowable range for the year input variable. Another predefined constant value in the Next Date program is the maximum number of characters a user can enter in the Year text box. The text box properties for the Year text box control are predefined to allow the user to input only four characters.

The second type of a boundary value is a fixed-variable boundary represented by a measurement that can be changed but that is constant at some point in time. For example, the height and width of a window can vary in size along the x- and y-axes; however, at any given moment in time they are constant linear values that can be measured in pixels, millimeters, or inches. Fixed-variable boundary values can be harder to identify because the linear measures might not be readily visible from the user interface. Figure 5-3 illustrates fixed-variable boundaries for the height and width attributes of the canvas size in Microsoft Paint.

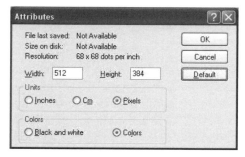

FIGURE 5-3 Width and Height variables, examples of fixed-variable boundaries that can be changed by the user at run time.

Defining Boundary Tests

Paul Jorgensen[6] suggests that the number of tests for basic boundary value analysis can be calculated by using the formula $4n + 1$ (or $6n + 1$ including the minimum –1 and maximum +1 values for robust boundary testing), where n is equal to the number of independent parameters. Jorgensen's formula includes a test for a nominal value. Although this formula is useful in analyzing the values at the extreme ranges of linear variables for simple independent parameters, it might be too simplistic in complex situations.

For example, a more thorough data analysis suggests Jorgensen's formula can potentially overlook critical boundary conditions identified by an equivalence class subset denoting a range of values in the extreme minima and maxima range of a linear variable. Also, unique values in an equivalence class subset might not be the extreme ranges of a linear variable, or a particular equivalence class range of values might be more interesting to analyze compared to other values in that range. For example, Figure 5-4 illustrates the Microsoft Windows 874 ANSI code page. The extreme linear range of character code points for this ANSI character set extends from 0x00 to 0xFF.

However, if the input parameter specifically excludes the use of unassigned character code points, several valid and invalid equivalence class subsets are required to define the ranges of assigned and unassigned character code points, as indicated in Table 5-3. Although the overall physical range extends from 0x00 through 0xFF, if you don't carefully analyze the boundaries between the assigned character code points and unassigned character code points, you could easily overlook a potential problem.

---

[6]   Paul C. Jorgensen, *Software Testing: A Craftsman's Approach* (Boca Raton, FL: CRC Press, 1995).

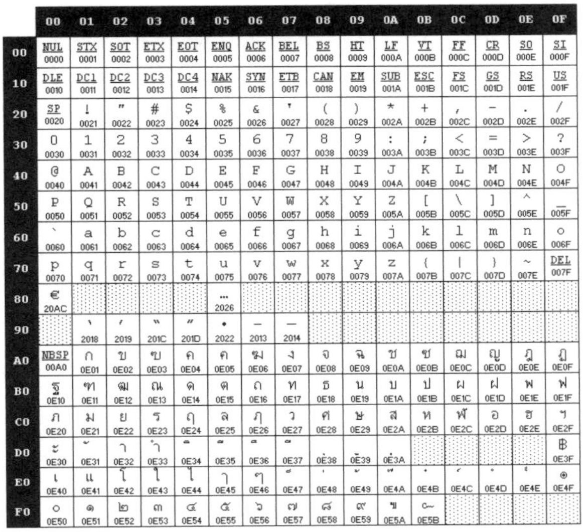

FIGURE 5-4 Windows ANSI code page 874.

TABLE 5-3 ECP Subsets of Assigned and Unassigned Character Code Points for Windows ANSI Code Page 874

Assigned character code points	Unassigned character code points
0x00–0x80	0x81–0x84
0x85	0x86–0x90
0x9 –0x97	0x98–0x9F
0xA0–0xDA	0xDB–0xDE
0xDF–0xFB	0xFC–0xFF

A New Formula for Boundary Value Analysis

Improved analysis of boundary values that might not be at the extreme ranges for an independent parameter requires an alternative approach and a different formula for calculating the minimum set of test data for basic boundary value analysis. It should be clear that effective boundary value analysis relies on our ability as testers to identify accurately all unique boundary conditions for any given independent parameter. Equivalence class subsets are also valuable in helping us identify potential boundary conditions. The ECP subsets not only reveal the extreme linear ranges of values, but if the variable data is accurately decomposed, the ECP subsets also expose several values that might indicate additional important boundary conditions.

After identifying all boundary conditions for independent input and output parameters a minimum set of test data can be calculated with a simple formula: 3(BC), where BC is equal to the number of specific boundary conditions. To illustrate the differences between Jorgensen's robust formula and the 3(BC) formula, compare the two approaches using the Next Date program.

The extreme physical input values for the month, day, and year parameters are 1 and 12, 1 and 31, and 1582 and 3000, respectively. Using Jorgensen's $6n + 1$ formula for robust boundary testing, the number of boundary tests of input variables is $(6 * 3) + 1$, or the 19 tests listed in the BVA text matrix in Table 5-4.

TABLE 5-4 **Simple BVA Test Matrix Based on Jorgensen's Robust $6n + 1$ Formula**

Test	Month	Day	Year	Expected result	Notes
1	0	1–28	1582–3000	Error	Month minimum –1, Day nominal, Year nominal
2	1	1–28	1582–3000	Next date	Month minimum, Day nominal, Year nominal
3	2	1–28	1582–3000	Next date	Month minimum +1, Day nominal, Year nominal
4	11	1–28	1582–3000	Next date	Month maximum –1, Day nominal, Year nominal
5	12	1–28	1582–3000	Next date	Month maximum, Day nominal, Year nominal
6	13	1–28	1582–3000	Error	Month maximum +1, Day nominal, Year nominal
7	1–12	0	1582–3000	Error	Day minimum–1, Month nominal, Year nominal
8	1–12	1	1582–3000	Next date	Day minimum, Month nominal, Year nominal
9	1–12	2	1582–3000	Next date	Day minimum +1, Month nominal, Year nominal
10	1–12	30	1582–3000	Next date	Day maximum –1, Month nominal, Year nominal
11	1–12	31	1582–3000	Next date	Day maximum, Month nominal, Year nominal
12	1–12	32	1582–3000	Error	Day maximum +1, Month nominal, Year nominal
13	1–12	1–28	1581	Error	Year minimum –1, Day nominal, Month nominal
14	1–12	1–28	1582	Next date	Year minimum, Day nominal, Month nominal
15	1–12	1–28	1583	Next date	Year minimum +1, Day nominal, Month nominal
16	1–12	1–28	2999	Next date	Year maximum –1, Day nominal, Month nominal
17	1–12	1–28	3000	Next date	Year maximum, Day nominal, Month nominal
18	1–12	1–28	3001	Error	Year maximum +1, Day nominal, Month nominal
19	1–12	1–28	1582–3000	Next date	All nominal conditions

However, the detailed decomposition of the data using the equivalence class technique illustrated in Table 5-1 identifies several additional boundary values that haven't been taken into account. For example, the day input parameter has three additional boundary conditions in the maximum range of 31. There are also four additional boundary conditions for the valid and invalid unique date ranges, and two boundary conditions for the output parameter. Applying the 3(BC) formula for boundary testing reveals the test set required to analyze more adequately the potential boundary conditions for each parameter increases to (3 * 18), or 54, as illustrated in the BVA matrix in Table 5-5.

TABLE 5-5 BVA Test Matrix for the Next Date Program Using the 3(BV) Formula

BVA test	Boundary condition	Month	Day	Year	Expected	Notes
1	1	0	1–28	1582–3000	Error Msg.	Month minimum –1
2		1	1–28	1582–3000	Next date	Month minimum
3		2	1–28	1582–3000	Next date	Month minimum +1
4	2	11	1–28	1582–3000	Next date	Month maximum –1
5		12	1–28	1582–3000	Next date	Month maximum
6		13	1–28	1582–3000	Error Msg.	Month maximum +1
7	3	31-day month	0	1582–3000	Error Msg.	Day minimum –1 (31-day month)
8		31-day month	1	1582–3000	Next date	Day minimum (31-day month)
9		31-day month	2	1582–3000	Next date	Day minimum +1 (31-day month)
10	4	31-day month	30	1582–3000	Next date	Day maximum –1 (31-day month)
11		31-day month	31	1582–3000	Next date	Day maximum (31-day month)
12		31-day month	32	1582–3000	Error Msg.	Day maximum +1 (31-day month)
13	5	30-day month	0	1582–3000	Error Msg.	Day minimum –1 (30-day month)
14		30-day month	1	1582–3000	Next date	Day minimum (30-day month)
15		30-day month	2	1582–3000	Next date	Day minimum +1 (30-day month)
16	6	30-day month	29	1582–3000	Next date	Day maximum –1 (30-day month)

BVA test	Boundary condition	Month	Day	Year	Expected	Notes
17		30-day month	30	1582–3000	Next date	Day maximum (30-day month)
18		30-day month	31	1582–3000	Error Msg.	Day maximum +1 (30-day month)
19	7	2	0	Leap year	Error Msg.	Day minimum −1 (leap year in range)
20		2	1	Leap year	Next date	Day minimum (leap year in range)
21		2	2	Leap year	Next date	Day minimum +1 (leap year in range)
22	8	2	28	Leap year	Next date	Day maximum −1 (leap year in range)
23		2	29	Leap year	Next date	Day maximum (leap year in range)
24		2	30	Leap year	Error Msg.	Day maximum +1 (leap year in range)
25	9	2	0	Non–leap year	Error Msg.	Day minimum −1 (non–leap year)
26		2	1	Non–leap year	Next date	Day minimum (non–leap year)
27		2	2	Non–leap year	Next date	Day minimum +1 (non–leap year)
28	10	2	27	Non–leap year	Next date	Day maximum −1 (non–leap year)
29		2	28	Non–leap year	Next date	Day maximum (non–leap year)
30		2	29	Non–leap year	Error Msg.	Day maximum +1 (non–leap year)
31	11	1–12	1–28	1581	Error Msg.	Year minimum −1
32		1–12	1–28	1582	Next date	Year minimum
33		1–12	1–28	1583	Next date	Year minimum +1
34	12	1–12	1–28	2999	Next date	Year maximum −1
35		1–12	1–28	3000	Next date	Year maximum
36		1–12	1–28	3001	Error Msg.	Year maximum +1
37	13	12	31	1581	Error Msg.	Output minimum −1

BVA test	Boundary condition	Month	Day	Year	Expected	Notes
38		1	1	1582	1/2/1582	Output minimum
39		3	2	1582	3/3/1582	Output minimum +1
40	14	12	30	3000	12/31/1582	Output maximum −1
41		12	31	3000	1/1/3001	Output maximum
42		1	1	3001	Error Msg.	Output maximum +1
43	15	9	2	1752	9/3/1752	Unique date range minimum −1
44		9	3	1752	9/4/1752	Unique date range minimum
45		9	4	1752	9/5/1752	Unique date range minimum +1
46	16	9	12	1752	9/13/1752	Unique date range maximum −1
47		9	13	1752	9/14/1751	Unique date range maximum
48		9	14	1752	9/15/1752	Unique date range maximum +1
49	17	10	4	1582	10/15/1582	Unique date range minimum −1
50		10	5	1582	Error Msg.	Unique date range minimum
51		10	6	1582	Error Msg.	Unique date range minimum +1
52	18	10	13	1582	Error Msg.	Unique date range maximum −1
53		10	14	1582	Error Msg.	Unique date range maximum
54		10	15	1582	10/16/1582	Unique date range maximum +1

In both examples, the boundary values and the values immediately above and immediately below are evaluated for each parameter while the other parameters are set to some nominal value. ECP tests on these parameters would have already confirmed that the nominal values work as expected in independent parameters. Here again, designing a BVA test to use a probabilistic stochastic value in the valid range when a nominal value is required provides greater flexibility and minimizes hard-coded or static data in tests. In some cases, a boundary test must use specific combinations of variables to drive the test to evaluate specific boundaries. In cases where probabilistic stochastic test data can be used as a variable for a nominal parameter, testers must rely on their cognition to determine the outcome of a test, and automated tests can confidently rely on a proto-algorithm as an oracle to compare the actual result against an expected result.

Hidden Boundaries

Not all boundaries are identified by numerical inputs or outputs, or are they linear measures that are represented directly to the user. The width and height of a window or a control can be measured in pixels or other linear measures. Also, there are often numerous looping algorithms in code, and looping structures are notoriously problematic at the boundary conditions. For example, the following method counts the number of characters in a string (actually, it counts the number of Unicode character code points in a string). Boundary testing this method requires that you bypass the loop once by passing an argument of an empty string (minimum –1), and then pass a string of one character (minimum) and a string of two characters (minimum +1). The tests to analyze the maximum range require a string of 2,147,483,646 characters (maximum –1), 2,147,483,647 characters (maximum), and 2,147,483,648 characters (maximum +1). The *ToCharArray* method copies a maximum number of Unicode characters from a string to a character array equal to a signed 32-bit integer data type. So, although it is extremely unlikely in practical application, passing this method a string of 1,073,741,824 Unicode surrogate pair characters the *cArray* will appear to have two Unicode code points for each surrogate pair character and the index will increment to 2,147,483,648, which will throw an out-of-range exception.

```
private static int GetCharacterCount(string myString)
{
    try
    {
        char[] cArray = myString.ToCharArray();
        int index = 0;
        while (index < cArray.Length)
        {
            index++;
        }
        return index;
    }
    catch (ArgumentOutOfRangeException)
    {
        throw;
    }
}
```

However, it is sometimes difficult to identify the boundaries of looping structures. Familiarity with programming language, data types, and algorithm structures certainly helps and provides testers with insights into hidden boundaries. In the preceding example, if you were not aware of different Unicode encoding patterns (especially surrogate pair encoding) and simply tested the extreme boundary conditions using only simple Unicode characters, the method would appear to return the correct number of characters in a string up to and including the maximum length of 2,147,483,647 characters. But passing a string of 2,147,483,647 characters in which even one character in that string is a surrogate pair will cause an out-of-range exception error to be thrown.

Boundary testing loops and the déjà vu heuristic

Loops are common structures in software and (depending on the programming language) are susceptible to boundary defects. Boundary value analysis of a loop structure involves (at a minimum) bypassing the loop, iterating through the loop one time, iterating through the loop two times, iterating through the loop the maximum number of times and one minus the maximum number of times, and finally trying to exceed the maximum number of iterations through a loop structure by one time. It is often difficult to identify looping structures when designing tests from only a black box test design approach.

In Windows XP, if the user attempts to save a file name using a reserved device name (LPT1, COM) as the base file name that includes the extension (.txt) as an argument in the File Name edit control, the system displays an error message indicating the file already exists and asking, "Do you want to replace it?" Of course, you cannot save a file name that is a reserved device name in the Windows operating system, so when I was testing this condition, I clicked Yes in that dialog box. The document window title actually changed to display LPT1 – Notepad; however, the file was not saved, and after I closed the file the contents of the file were lost. An update to Windows XP attempted to correct this defect; however, boundary testing revealed the problem was only partially fixed.

After the fix, I repeated the same set of steps, but this time after I clicked the Yes button a new error message appeared that said, "Cannot create the [lpt1] file. Make sure that the path and filename are correct." After clicking OK, control flow returned me to Notepad. Any time I encountered an error message, I repeated exactly the same set of steps to make sure I got the same exact error message. Guess what? The second time in traversing the same path to the error message revealed the same problem encountered prior to the fix.

How did I know to test for a loop in the Save dialog box? Quite simply, any time I encounter an error message I use a rule of thumb I refer to as the *déjà vu heuristic*. (A *heuristic* is a commonsense rule (or set of rules) intended to increase the probability of solving some problem. Heuristics are valuable because they generally add value, but they might also be fallible.) The déjà vu heuristic specifically analyzes the minimum boundary value and the values immediately above and immediately below that boundary value. In this case, the minimum –1 value is not executing the error path; the minimum boundary condition is executing the path that instantiates the error message, and the minimum +1 value is repeating the same steps to ideally traverse the same path through the code.

Summary of Boundary Value Analysis

Boundary value analysis is a functional technique that targets data values at, immediately above, and immediately below a specific boundary condition. Historical experience and root cause analysis of recurring problems demonstrate that anomalies are common occurrences at or near the boundary conditions of independent input or output parameters. A systematic analysis of the variables at and near boundary conditions increases test effectiveness, provides better-qualified information, and increases the likelihood of detecting specific classes of defects that can occur with linear variables in input or output parameters earlier in the testing cycle.

With the 3(BC) formula, you can better approximate the number of boundary tests needed and provide a more comprehensive set of tests as compared to using other formulas because tests are based on the number of identified boundary values, not on the number of parameters. A detailed examination of the data is the only way to identify additional boundary conditions that are otherwise not exposed if the focus is on only the extreme ranges of the physical parameter or through random input of nominal values. Boundary testing provides a more precise systematic technique for qualified evaluation of variables for independent parameters. However, you must remember that no single approach in testing is faultless, and the effectiveness of boundary value analysis relies on our ability to decompose variables into discrete equivalence subsets and to identify important boundary conditions. Also, basic boundary testing is based on the single-fault assumption. With this underlying assumption, BVA testing is generally not effective in evaluating complex combinations of dependent or semicoupled parameters.

Combinatorial Analysis

So far, I have focused on testing the discrete functional capabilities of each input or output parameter while holding other parameter variable states to valid nominal conditions. However, the variable states for some parameters are dependent, or at least semicoupled, to the variable states of other parameters. This simply means that the output state of a parameter is dependent on various combinations of input parameter variable states. To test the interactions between the variable states of several dependent parameters systematically, combinatorial analysis is a best practice as compared to alternative approaches.

To put things in perspective, consider the Security Settings dialog box in Microsoft Internet Explorer. This dialog box has several parameters that have between two and five variable states for each of the 24 parameters. If you assume that all these parameters are at least semicoupled, the total number of tests for exhaustive testing is equal to the Cartesian product of all variable states. In this example, the total number of combinations is about a half trillion, and at one test per millisecond it would take approximately 3,300 years to complete testing. Obviously, exhaustive combination testing is only possible in trivial programs. But, to test the functional interactivity of complex variable states more efficiently, empirical evidence throughout the industry conclusively demonstrates that combinatorial analysis is the most effective solution.

Combinatorial analysis is a functional testing technique widely used by SDETs at Microsoft to analyze methodically dependent and semicoupled parameter interactions in a complex feature set to select an effective subset of tests systematically from all possible combinations. There are many benefits of the combinatorial analysis technique when it is used correctly and in the appropriate context. Some of these benefits include the following:

- Identifies most defects caused by variable interaction
- Provides greater structural coverage
- Has great potential to reduce overall testing costs (when used appropriately)

It is important to note that the advantages of this technique apply when you are testing a feature in which the parameters are directly interdependent or semicoupled, and the parameter input is unordered. Occasionally, novice testers try to apply this technique to a set of parameters or inputs without performing a comprehensive analysis of the feature. However, you must understand that this technique does not apply to any program or feature with multiple inputs. Combinatorial analysis is not an effective technique for testing independent parameters with no direct or indirect interaction, mathematical calculations, ordered parameter input, or inputs that require sequential operations.

Combinatorial Testing Approaches

There are two common approaches to testing parameter interaction. The first approach typically involves random or ad hoc methods, and the second approach includes more systematic procedures. The random evaluation approaches include best guess or ad hoc testing, and random selection. The systematic evaluation approaches include testing each variable or each choice once (EC), base choice (BC), orthogonal array (OA), combination tests (pair-wise through n-wise or $t = n$), and exhaustive testing (AC).

Best guess or ad hoc methods rely primarily on intuition and luck of the tester. They are useful in testing commonly used combinations or the happy path and can expose subtle defects resulting from unusual combination scenarios. However, experiments in controlled environments demonstrate that testers quickly reach a threshold of coverage and additional tests tend to execute the same code paths, providing little value to the overall testing effort. Random selection methods rely on selecting a set of tests from the complete set of all possible combinations. A recent study by Schroeder and colleagues[7] found no significant difference in the failure detection effectiveness of n-wise testing and a set of random

---

[7] Patrick J. Schroeder, Pankaj Bolaki, and Vijayram Gopu, *Comparing the Fault Detection Effectiveness of N-Way and Random Test Suites*, 2004 International Symposium on Empirical Software Engineering.

combinatorial tests selected from all possible combinations. Random selection from all possible combinations could include tests that involve variable states that are mutually exclusive or invariant conditions where certain parameters must be different. This method is interesting from an academic perspective but is not especially practical for testing commercial software when more efficient and effective tools are readily available.

Each choice (EC) is simply testing each variable at least once. EC provides the minimum amount of tests as compared to virtually any other combinatorial analysis approach; however, it is generally ineffective in any complex system. Base choice (BC) identifies a combination of variables as the base test. This is usually the happy path or the most commonly used combinations of variable states. Additional tests change the variable state for one parameter at a time while keeping the other parameter variable states constant with the base test state. BC testing satisfies $t = 1$ or 1-wise coverage and is effective in detecting single combination errors. But some studies suggest that BC testing is useful when coupled with n-wise combinatorial testing.

Orthogonal arrays (OA) involve processes adopted from industrial manufacturing. The use of orthogonal arrays in software testing is a nontrivial process. A simple OA approach expects an equal number of variable states for each interdependent parameter, and those states are mapped into an array. In more complex features where the number of variable states is different between the interdependent parameters, the selection of orthogonal arrays becomes quite complex. The output of an OA is comparable only to pair-wise test coverage. Also, the OA output is less than optimal because it includes each tuple the same number of times, leading to redundant pair-wise test combinations. Orthogonal arrays are beneficial in experimentation and performance analysis and optimization. However, OAs are a difficult solution to a difficult problem and they are not practical in functional testing of interdependent parameters given the availability of more efficient alternative solutions for combinatorial testing.

One of the most efficient and effective solutions for testing variable combinations of interdependent parameters is combinatorial analysis or n-wise testing using coverage arrays. Several combinatorial analysis tools are available, and multiple algorithms are used to produce a combinatorial test matrix. For a basic understanding of a common coverage array algorithm for pair-wise analysis, consider a simple font style feature for a single font whose style can be set to any combination of bold, italic, strikethrough, or underline. In this example, there are four parameters (bold, italic, strikethrough, and underline), and each parameter has two variable states (checked and unchecked).

For a simple pair-wise or 2-wise analysis, first identify the unique variable state combinations for the bold and italic parameter pair from all possible combinations. In the following graphics, c stands for checked and u stands for unchecked.

	1	2	3	4	5	6	7	8	9	10	11	12	13	14	15	16
Bold	c	c	c	c	u	u	u	c	u	u	c	c	u	c	u	u
Italic	u	c	c	c	c	c	c	c	u	u	u	u	u	u	c	u
Underline	u	u	c	c	u	c	c	u	c	c	c	c	u	u	u	u
Strikethrough	u	u	u	c	u	u	c	c	u	c	u	c	c	c	c	u

Next , identify the variable state combinations for each subsequent pair of parameters from all possible combinations, and combine those sets of variable state combinations with test combinations from the previous set of combinations for other parameter pairs, as illustrated in the following sequence of tables.

	1	2	3	4	5	6	7	8	9	10	11	12	13	14	15	16
Bold	c	c	c	c	u	u	u	c	u	u	c	c	u	c	u	u
Italic	u	c	c	c	c	c	c	c	u	u	u	u	u	u	c	u
Underline	u	u	c	c	u	c	c	u	c	c	c	c	u	u	u	u
Strikethrough	u	u	u	c	u	u	c	c	u	c	u	c	c	c	c	u

	1	2	3	4	5	6	7	8	9	10	11	12	13	14	15	16
Bold	c	c	c	c	u	u	u	c	u	u	c	c	u	c	u	u
Italic	u	c	c	c	c	c	c	c	u	u	u	u	u	u	c	u
Underline	u	u	c	c	u	c	c	u	c	c	c	c	u	u	u	u
Strikethrough	u	u	u	c	u	u	c	c	u	c	u	c	c	c	c	u

	1	2	3	4	5	6	7	8	9	10	11	12	13	14	15	16
Bold	c	c	c	c	u	u	u	c	u	u	c	c	u	c	u	u
Italic	u	c	c	c	c	c	c	c	u	u	u	u	u	u	c	u
Underline	u	u	c	c	u	c	c	u	c	c	c	c	u	u	u	u
Strikethrough	u	u	u	c	u	u	c	c	u	c	u	c	c	c	c	u

	1	2	3	4	5	6	7	8	9	10	11	12	13	14	15	16
Bold	c	c	c	c	u	u	u	c	u	u	c	c	u	c	u	u
Italic	u	c	c	c	c	c	c	c	u	u	u	u	u	u	c	u
Underline	u	u	c	c	u	c	c	u	c	c	c	c	u	u	u	u
Strikethrough	u	u	u	c	u	u	c	c	u	c	u	c	c	c	c	u

	1	2	3	4	5	6	7	8	9	10	11	12	13	14	15	16
Bold	c	c	c	c	u	u	u	c	u	u	c	c	u	c	u	u
Italic	u	c	c	c	c	c	c	c	u	u	u	u	u	u	c	u
Underline	u	u	c	c	u	c	c	u	c	c	c	c	u	u	u	u
Strikethrough	u	u	u	c	u	u	c	c	u	c	u	c	c	c	c	u

Combining each table reveals a test matrix of five tests (numbers 2, 7, 11, 14, and 16) from the total number of 16 possible combination tests. These five tests effectively test every parameter pair combination at least once. Notice that this set of tests does not include a test in which all styles are checked, and if the tester determines that to be an important test, he should certainly add that to the output matrix.

Combinatorial Analysis in Practice

Tools used to analyze *n*-wise combinations of parameter interaction are only tools and rely on the tester's comprehensive knowledge of the complete system to be most effective. The output of any tool is limited to that tool's capabilities and the skill and knowledge of the person using that tool. A tool in the hands of an untrained or unskilled person appears to be ineffective and can be said to be a foolish tool; likewise, an untrained or unskilled person who attempts to use a tool she does not understand is simply a toolish fool. Microsoft SDETs primarily use the Pair-wise Independent Combinatorial Testing (PICT) tool for combinatorial testing of interdependent parameters. PICT is a highly customizable tool that overcomes many of the limitations of other available tools and in less time can help testers design tests that are more effective than manually generated test combinations are.

However, using PICT (or any testing tool) and application of a combinatorial analysis technique are not a matter of simply identifying input parameters and variable states and feeding that data into a tool. The process requires the tester to perform an in-depth analysis of the feature being tested to identify directly dependent and semicoupled parameters, and decomposition of the parameters to define the appropriate variable states for each interdependent parameter. After the tester completes a comprehensive analysis of the feature and defines the variable states for each parameter, he is ready to apply a systematic procedure to determine a set of combinatorial tests:

1. Create an input matrix of BC tests.

2. Create an input matrix of common or probable scenarios and historical failure indicators.

3. Create an input model file of the variable states for each parameter.

4. Customize the model file to exclude mutually exclusive variable states or invariant parameters.

5. Apply all input files to the PICT tool.

6. Review the tool output.

7. Refine and customize the model file if necessary.

8. Reapply all input files to the PICT tool.

9. Revalidate output.

10. Execute tests.

You can examine each step in sequence to understand how to apply this technique correctly on a relatively simple simulation. Say you are testing a simple font dialog box such as the one shown in Figure 5-5. This dialog box lets the user choose one of four possible fonts, a font style of bold and italic, font effects of strikethrough and underline, font color (black, white, red, green, blue, or yellow), and font size (1–1,638 including half sizes). The total number of combinations for exhaustive testing is 1,257,600 (assuming all font size values are tested). Testing all combinations might not be possible or feasible, so you must select a reasonable set of tests that are effective in reducing overall risk.

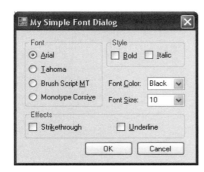

FIGURE 5-5 Simple font dialog box illustrating directly dependent and semicoupled parameters.

First, identify the interdependent parameters. In this example, the directly dependent parameters are font type and font styles because some font types cannot be bold only or italic only but might be bold and italic or bold or italic, or use no style at all. The font size, color, and effects are semicoupled parameters because they apply to all font types and affect the output accordingly. After you identify the interdependent parameters, you must define the variable states for each parameter. The variable states for font type are Arial, Tahoma, Brush Script MT, and Monotype Corsive. The font style and font effects each have two parameters (bold and italic, and strikethrough and underline) and each parameter has two variable states (select and clear). The font color uses six colors (black, white, red, green, blue, and yellow). There are 3,275 possible values for font size. It might not be reasonable to test all values, so you can construct equivalence ranges of values and randomly select one value from each ECP subset when that subset range is selected.

So, for the font size parameter define five variable states using equivalence class subsets of Small (font sizes 1–9.5), Nominal (font sizes 10–12), Large (font sizes 12.5–72), Extra large (font sizes 72.5–1638), and Half sizes (font sizes 1.5–1637.5) to ensure that you force at least one test combination with a font size that is not an integer value. By creating equivalent class subsets of font size ranges, the test designer gives greater flexibility to the tester (or well-designed test automation) to select a test value in the specified range for a given combination. In this example, partitioning the range of font sizes into equivalence class subsets also eliminates hard-coded test values, which unnecessarily restrict the test data to a very small set of data values, which might or might not be interesting values to include in tests.

After you have thoroughly analyzed the features to determine which parameters are interdependent and have decomposed the variable states for each parameter to select the appropriate variables to test with, you can create a BC matrix, as shown in Figure 5-6. The BC matrix is important because studies have demonstrated that the inclusion of a base choice matrix in conjunction with higher levels of *n*-wise tests increases the likelihood of exposing a greater number of potential defects resulting from parameter interaction, and pair-wise or *n*-wise combination tests might not necessarily include BC combinations. The BC matrix generally defines the most common variable state combination, and then changes the variable state for each parameter one at a time while holding the other parameter variable states to the original value until all variables are tested at least once.

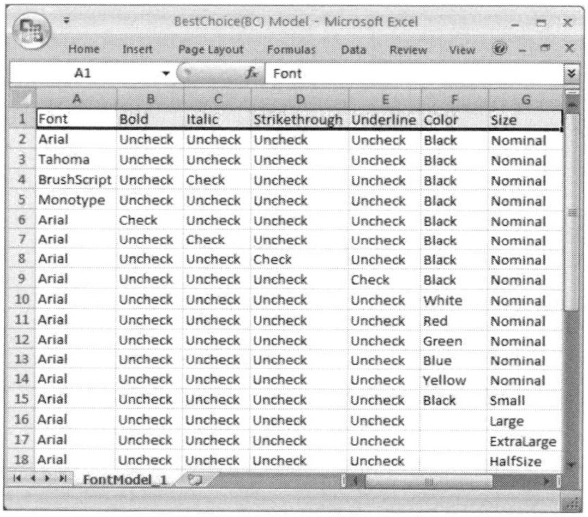

	A	B	C	D	E	F	G
1	Font	Bold	Italic	Strikethrough	Underline	Color	Size
2	Arial	Uncheck	Uncheck	Uncheck	Uncheck	Black	Nominal
3	Tahoma	Uncheck	Uncheck	Uncheck	Uncheck	Black	Nominal
4	BrushScript	Uncheck	Check	Uncheck	Uncheck	Black	Nominal
5	Monotype	Uncheck	Uncheck	Uncheck	Uncheck	Black	Nominal
6	Arial	Check	Uncheck	Uncheck	Uncheck	Black	Nominal
7	Arial	Uncheck	Check	Uncheck	Uncheck	Black	Nominal
8	Arial	Uncheck	Uncheck	Check	Uncheck	Black	Nominal
9	Arial	Uncheck	Uncheck	Uncheck	Check	Black	Nominal
10	Arial	Uncheck	Uncheck	Uncheck	Uncheck	White	Nominal
11	Arial	Uncheck	Uncheck	Uncheck	Uncheck	Red	Nominal
12	Arial	Uncheck	Uncheck	Uncheck	Uncheck	Green	Nominal
13	Arial	Uncheck	Uncheck	Uncheck	Uncheck	Blue	Nominal
14	Arial	Uncheck	Uncheck	Uncheck	Uncheck	Yellow	Nominal
15	Arial	Uncheck	Uncheck	Uncheck	Uncheck	Black	Small
16	Arial	Uncheck	Uncheck	Uncheck	Uncheck		Large
17	Arial	Uncheck	Uncheck	Uncheck	Uncheck		ExtraLarge
18	Arial	Uncheck	Uncheck	Uncheck	Uncheck		HalfSize

FIGURE 5-6 BC combinatorial test matrix for MyFontDialog example.

A common problem with many combinatorial testing tools is the inability of the tester to define highly probable combinations in the output. PICT overcomes this limitation with an important feature that allows the tester to define and pass in a tab-delimited file with seeded combinations as input into the tool. A tab-delimited input file with seeded combinations gives the tester greater control over specific combinations to test while still allowing the tool to determine the complete set of test variables for complete *n*-wise coverage.

So, after completing the BC test matrix the next step is to identify any common customer combinations or combinations that might be especially problematic based on failure indicators that aren't defined in the BC matrix. You can list these combinations in a tab-delimited seed file that will be passed to the PICT tool and used as part of the output of test combinations, as shown in Figure 5-7. For example, if you know that a combination of the Arial font with a style of Bold and an effect of Underline and a large font size is commonly used by a large segment of customers, you can include that in a seed file. You might also assert that a combination of Tahoma font with Bold, Italic, Strikethrough, and Underline selected and a font color of Yellow and a small font size has historically resulted in erroneous outputs, so you will also specify this combination in the seed file. The seed file forces the PICT tool to include these combinations in the output and guarantees that highly probable and highly problematic combinations always get tested.

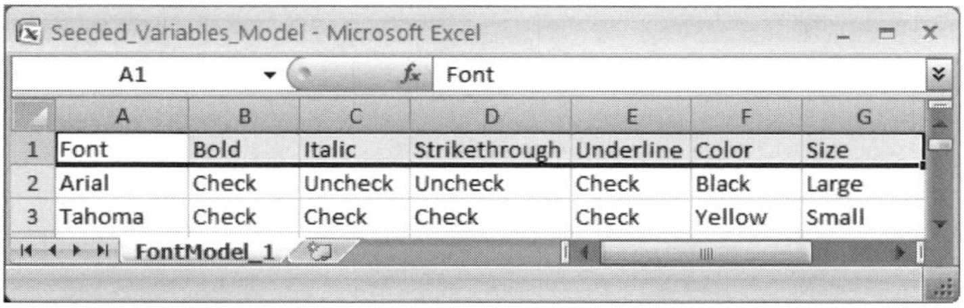

	A	B	C	D	E	F	G
1	Font	Bold	Italic	Strikethrough	Underline	Color	Size
2	Arial	Check	Uncheck	Uncheck	Check	Black	Large
3	Tahoma	Check	Check	Check	Check	Yellow	Small

FIGURE 5-7 A tab-delimited seed file defining likely combinations based on customer information or other failure indicators that can be input into the PICT tool.

Next, you must create an input file that models the appropriate variable states for each parameter. Using a simple text editor such as Notepad, you can create a simple text file that lists the parameter followed by the variable states for that parameter.

```
Font: Arial, Tahoma, BrushScript, Monotype
Bold: Check, Uncheck
Italic: Check, Uncheck
Strikethrough: Check, Uncheck
Underline: Check, Uncheck
Color: Black, White, Red, Green, Blue, Yellow
Size: Small, Nominal, Large, ExtraLarge, HalfSize
```

Now you are ready to generate the initial default output of a pair-wise test combination using the PICT tool. PICT is a command-line tool that generates a tab-delimited output file of test combinations for *n*-wise coverage. The command-line syntax to generate an output of test combinations based on a seeded file and the model file is the following:

```
pict.exe myModelFile.txt /e:mySeededInput.txt > output.xls
```

In a fraction of a second, you have a pair-wise output of the modeled parameters and the seeded inputs provided by the tester in a tab-delimited output that is easily reviewed for correctness using Microsoft Office Excel. By using the seeded input file and the model file defined earlier, you see that there are now only 218 total combinations of the variable states, and a pair-wise analysis of variable states using the PICT tool further reduces the number of tests to 30. However, you must carefully analyze the results to validate the output combinations of the tool by checking for conditional or invariant constraints of specific parameters or variable states. Figure 5-8 demonstrates why verifying the output of the tool and revising the input model are critical to avoid false negatives.

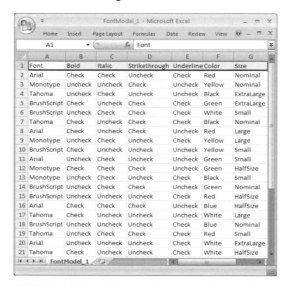

	A	B	C	D	E	F	G
1	Font	Bold	Italic	Strikethrough	Underline	Color	Size
2	Arial	Check	Check	Uncheck	Check	Red	Nominal
3	Monotype	Uncheck	Uncheck	Check	Uncheck	Yellow	Nominal
4	Tahoma	Uncheck	Check	Uncheck	Uncheck	Black	ExtraLarge
5	BrushScript	Check	Uncheck	Check	Check	Green	ExtraLarge
6	BrushScript	Uncheck	Check	Check	Check	White	Small
7	Tahoma	Check	Uncheck	Check	Check	Black	Nominal
8	Arial	Check	Uncheck	Check	Uncheck	Red	Large
9	Monotype	Uncheck	Check	Uncheck	Check	Yellow	Large
10	BrushScript	Check	Uncheck	Uncheck	Uncheck	Yellow	Small
11	Arial	Uncheck	Check	Uncheck	Uncheck	Green	Small
12	Monotype	Check	Check	Uncheck	Uncheck	Green	HalfSize
13	Monotype	Check	Check	Uncheck	Check	Black	Small
14	BrushScript	Uncheck	Check	Check	Uncheck	Green	Nominal
15	BrushScript	Uncheck	Uncheck	Check	Check	Red	HalfSize
16	Arial	Check	Check	Check	Uncheck	Blue	HalfSize
17	Tahoma	Check	Uncheck	Uncheck	Uncheck	White	Large
18	BrushScript	Uncheck	Uncheck	Uncheck	Check	Blue	Nominal
19	Tahoma	Uncheck	Check	Check	Check	Red	Small
20	Arial	Uncheck	Uncheck	Uncheck	Check	White	ExtraLarge
21	Tahoma	Check	Uncheck	Uncheck	Check	White	HalfSize

FIGURE 5-8   The initial pair-wise test matrix reveals tests with mutually exclusive variable combinations.

What about negative testing

In this example, you create a model file for positive tests, meaning the expected output of each combination should not result in an error state. When the OK button is clicked in the dialog box, the imaginary text editor changes the font, style, effect, color, and size of the selected glyphs accordingly, and you can verify the correct results either visually if you are manually testing or programmatically through the *GetFont* application programming interface (API) as an oracle for automated tests.

But what about negative testing, where you expect an error state or condition? The PICT tool also includes the ability to define invalid variable states in a model file. When testing with invalid variable states, each test should have only one invalid parameter value to avoid *input masking*. Input masking occurs when a program throws an error condition on the first invalid variable and subsequent values are not tested.

When designing tests (especially automated tests), I prefer to separate the model used for positive testing and the model used for negative testing to simplify the test code and to reduce the possibility of false negatives by keeping the appropriate oracle focused on the specific purpose of the test.

You know that font styles are directly dependent on certain font types. For example, the Brush Script font can have a font style of only italic or bold and italic. So, as you can see in Figure 5-8, rows 5, 12, and 16 would result in a false negative. Also, the Monotype Corsive font can be regular, or bold and italic only. The rows 4 and 15 in Figure 5-8 violate these dependency rules and would also result in a false negative for these tests. It is not uncommon to encounter features that rely on mutually exclusive variable states between parameters to restrict or constrain certain events or actions that are mutually exclusive. It would be foolish to try to manually change these values in the output because you might not be aware of which other parameter variable states were used in determining the *n*-wise combinations. To overcome this problem PICT includes the ability to define conditional and invariant constraints of specific variable states using a basic *if-then* syntax in the model file.

In the model file, add conditional constraints to ensure that any time the Font variable is Brush Script the Bold parameter variable state is Uncheck and the Italic parameter variable state is Check, or both the Bold and Italic parameter variable states are Check. Also, you can add a conditional constraint to ensure that any time the Font variable is Monotype Corsive the variable states for both style parameters are either set to Check or Uncheck. Following is the modified model file:

```
Font: Arial, Tahoma, BrushScript, Monotype
Bold: Check, Uncheck
Italic: Check, Uncheck
Strikethrough: Check, Uncheck
Underline: Check, Uncheck
Color: Black, White, Red, Green, Blue, Yellow
Size: Small, Nominal, Large, ExtraLarge, HalfSize
#
# Conditional constraints for Brush Script and Monotype
#
IF [Font] = "BrushScript" AND [Italic] = "Uncheck" THEN [Bold] <> "Check";
IF [Bold] = "Uncheck" AND [Italic] = "Uncheck" THEN NOT [Font] = "BrushScript";
IF [Font] = "Monotype" THEN [Bold] = [Italic];
```

After modifying the model file by specifying the appropriate constraints, you can regenerate the output for the tests. It is important to review the output each time the model or seeded input files are modified to validate the *n*-wise output combinations from the tool. Now that you have updated the model file notice that in Figure 5-9 there are no occurrences of Brush Script with a style of Bold only or with no style applied.

	Font	Bold	Italic	Strikethrough	Underline	Color	Size
2	Arial	Check	Check	Uncheck	Check	Red	Nominal
3	Monotype	Uncheck	Uncheck	Check	Uncheck	Yellow	Nominal
4	Tahoma	Uncheck	Check	Uncheck	Uncheck	Black	ExtraLarge
5	Tahoma	Check	Uncheck	Check	Check	Green	ExtraLarge
6	BrushScript	Uncheck	Check	Check	Check	White	Small
7	Arial	Check	Uncheck	Check	Check	Black	Nominal
8	Arial	Check	Uncheck	Uncheck	Uncheck	Black	Small
9	Monotype	Check	Check	Uncheck	Check	Yellow	Large
10	Arial	Check	Uncheck	Uncheck	Uncheck	Yellow	HalfSize
11	Arial	Check	Uncheck	Uncheck	Uncheck	Blue	ExtraLarge
12	BrushScript	Uncheck	Check	Uncheck	Uncheck	Green	HalfSize
13	Tahoma	Check	Uncheck	Check	Uncheck	Yellow	ExtraLarge
14	BrushScript	Uncheck	Uncheck	Check	Uncheck	Red	Small
15	Tahoma	Check	Uncheck	Uncheck	Uncheck	White	Nominal
16	Arial	Uncheck	Uncheck	Check	Uncheck	Red	Large
17	BrushScript	Uncheck	Check	Check	Check	Blue	Nominal
18	Tahoma	Check	Uncheck	Uncheck	Check	Red	ExtraLarge
19	Tahoma	Check	Uncheck	Uncheck	Uncheck	White	Large
20	Arial	Check	Uncheck	Check	Check	Black	Large
21	BrushScript	Check	Check	Check	Check	Black	HalfSize

FIGURE 5-9 Updated pair-wise test matrix using a revised model file to eliminate mutually exclusive variables.

You can further customize the PICT model file by aliasing or making some variable states equivalent. For example, the Arial font and the Tahoma font are very similar font types, so you could assert that Arial is equivalent to Tahoma when tested in combination with variable states from other parameters. You can alias the Arial and Tahoma font by removing the comma and inserting a pipe character (|) between the Arial and Tahoma variable states in the PICT model file, as illustrated in the following code example. Using another feature of the PICT tool, you can potentially increase the occurrences of highly probable combinations or variable states in the output of test combinations. For example, you can assert that the most common font color is black and the most common font size is a nominal font size. Again, you can modify the PICT input model file by providing weights to those variable states as illustrated in the following code. A weighted variable state is useful to give preference to a value once all *n*-wise conditions are satisfied for that variable state.

```
Font: Arial | Tahoma, BrushScript, Monotype
Bold: Check, Uncheck
Italic: Check, Uncheck
Strikethrough: Check, Uncheck
Underline: Check, Uncheck
Color: Black (10), White, Red, Green, Blue, Yellow
Size: Small, Nominal (10), Large, ExtraLarge, HalfSize
#
# Conditional constraints for Brush Script and Monotype
#
IF [Font] = "BrushScript" AND [Italic] = "Uncheck" THEN [Bold] <> "Check";
IF [Bold] = "Uncheck" AND [Italic] = "Uncheck" THEN NOT [Font] = "BrushScript";
IF [Font] = "Monotype" THEN [Bold] = [Italic];
```

After you are satisfied that the output includes highly probable combinations to ensure that likely customer settings are thoroughly tested, and that the output excludes mutually exclusive combinations to avoid a test inadvertently resulting in a false negative, you are ready to execute the tests. The tests can be executed manually or the output of the PICT tool can be input into a data-driven automated test. But, because you know that simply reusing the same set of variables every time the test is run provides very little value and virtually no new information you need a way to change the output of variable combinations. Again, attempting to manually alter the output might not be wise because it can disrupt *n*-wise combinations you are unaware of, especially in highly complex outputs. So, PICT includes another great feature that randomizes the output while still maintaining *n*-wise coverage of all variable states. Passing the */r:[seed]* argument to the PICT tool randomizes the output, which effectively increases breadth of coverage and can even identify defects that were missed using previous combinations.

Is BC and pair-wise coverage enough?

Historical evidence suggests that a majority (greater than 50 percent) of defects resulting from parameter interaction occur between simple pair combinations. But, in addition to executing the tests in the BC matrix as well as several randomized pair-wise outputs from the PICT tool, recent studies have shown that sequentially increasing the *n*-wise combinations tested can expose subtle defects that weren't previously discovered. Current studies suggest that 6-wise coverage is comparable to exhaustive coverage with regard to defect removal effectiveness and structural code coverage measures. However, the number of tests increases approximately quadratically with each sequential increase in *n*-wise coverage, which ultimately increases the overall cost of testing.

I recommend using the output matrix randomization feature of the PICT tool of pairwise combinations to expand breadth of coverage. Microsoft's expert in this area, Jacek Czerwonka, recommends that you start with BC and pair-wise combinatorial tests, and that 3-wise and 4-wise combinations should also be tested. This provides reasonable depth of coverage. Jacek also suggests that 5-wise and 6-wise might expose only a few subtle problems and should be run if the cost of executing those tests is relatively low; 7-wise or greater is extremely unlikely to increase defect detection or expand coverage based on current studies. Jacek maintains the Pairwise Testing Web site (*http://www.pairwise.org*) that provides a wealth of information on this topic.

Effectiveness of Combinatorial Analysis

There are many ways to evaluate the effectiveness of a testing technique or approach. Defect detection effectiveness (DDE) is one of the most common measures of test effectiveness (although it is completely arbitrary except in controlled academic environments where the total number of defects is known or in environments where the number of defects can be predicted using defect density ratios and other measures). Because exposing defects is the most readily apparent result of testing, you can analyze the DDE of *n*-wise testing. Many studies suggest that a large number of defects result from the combinations of variable states of interdependent parameters, and that more than 50 percent of all interdependent fault defects result from simple pair interactions or pair-wise combinations. One academic study[8] "found no significant difference" in the DDE of *n*-wise versus randomly selected combinatorial test suites in which each test was programmatically chosen from a matrix of all possible combinations. Another industry study[9] found 98 percent of all detectable combinatorial faults using a combination of BC and pair-wise testing. And more recent industry studies conclude that subtle combinatorial defects might still be exposed by sequentially increasing the number of combinations up to 6-wise coverage. So, I recommend that testers start with BC and pair-wise testing, and then both randomize the pair-wise output and sequentially increase the number of *n*-wise combinations to a maximum of 6-wise coverage.

Another way to measure effectiveness of testing is to look at the information the tests are providing. A lot of empirical data proves most black box–designed and executed tests provide less than 65 percent structural coverage of a complex program. So, by increasing the structural testing of a complex algorithm, the tests provide additional information and help reduce overall risk. One study found that pair-wise testing increased structural testing of blocks and decisions by more than 25 percent with a fewer number of tests as compared to random input testing. Microsoft has collected empirical data to show increases in both block and arc coverage of product code using pair-wise coverage as compared to a set of black box–designed tests, as illustrated in Table 5-6. The data also reveals additional increases in both block and arc coverage with sequential increases in *n*-wise coverage. Although increases in structural testing help reduce overall risk, this result comes with additional cost.

TABLE 5-6 Testing Effectiveness of Combinatorial Testing by Increased Code Coverage

Total block = 1,317	Manual tests	Pair-wise tests	n-3 coverage	n-4 coverage
Number of tests	236	136	800	3,533
Block covered	960	979	994	1,006
Code coverage	73%	74%	75%	76%
Functions not covered	11	11	10	10

Another measure of effectiveness is reduced operational costs. At Microsoft, several teams have significantly reduced operational costs in various ways. For example, because the output of the PICT tool is a tab-delimited file it is relatively easy to incorporate into data-driven test

[8] Patrick J. Schroeder, Pankaj Bolaki, and Vijayram Gopu, *Comparing the Fault Detection Effectiveness of N-Way and Random Test Suites*, 2004 International Symposium on Empirical Software Engineering.

[9] Mats Grindal, Birgitta Lindstrom, Jeff Offutt, and Sten F. Andler, "An Evaluation of Combination Testing Strategies," *Empirical Software Engineering* 11, no. 4 (December 2006): 583–611.

automation. Many teams have realized a large increase in the number of automated tests as well as an increase in the breadth of coverage provided by those tests through randomizing the test variables used. Other teams have significantly reduced the number of environment configurations, resulting in fewer tests with no degradation in overall effectiveness. And the adoption of PICT has revealed several defects that were previously undetected in other test passes prior to release of software.

Summary of Combinatorial Analysis

Combinatorial analysis is not a panacea for all testing woes. It is possible for novices to abuse the tool or misapply the technique to test feature areas that do not involve interdependent parameters. Testers must be able to analyze the feature parameters accurately to identify dependent and semicoupled parameters and decompose the variable states and identify conditional and invariant constraints. Compared to other approaches of combinatorial testing, when the procedures outlined in this book are properly employed by highly skilled testers with in-depth system knowledge this technique is highly effective in detecting defects earlier, increasing structural coverage, and reducing operational costs. In fact, it is a well-established best practice at Microsoft.

Summary

This chapter discusses a sampling of the functional testing techniques employed at Microsoft that we use to evaluate the functional attributes and capabilities of a software program more effectively. These techniques systematically analyze a program's functional components to increase test coverage, reduce costly redundancy, better assess overall risk, and provide qualified information to the decision makers so that they can make more informed business decisions. We also find that application of these techniques often forces us to scrutinize the software under test in different ways. Additional functional techniques used include cause and effect graphing and decision tables, and state transition testing. These additional techniques build upon equivalence class partitioning, boundary value analysis, and combinatorial analysis by requiring us to methodically examine input and output interactions and sequential operations or transaction flow through a program.

When techniques are used correctly they are very good at exposing the specific categories of defects they are intended to identify. But they won't find all problems and that is why you need to learn to use various methods and techniques, and understand when to use them in the appropriate context. Functional testing techniques used in conjunction with other approaches such as exploratory testing are quite useful, especially when the decision makers require a more systematic analysis of the software project. Techniques are methodical procedures that rely on heuristics, fault models, and historical evidence to help solve the difficult problems in testing complex systems. For greatest effectiveness, functional techniques require comprehensive domain and system knowledge. These techniques do not replace other approaches to software testing but can significantly increase testing effectiveness, help identify and reduce redundancy, and also reduce the susceptibility of the testing effort to the pesticide paradox.

Chapter 6
Structural Testing Techniques

Bj Rollison

A kindergarten teacher asked her students, "Who knows the color of apples?" A student dutifully raised his hand and the teacher said, "Ethan, what is the color of apples?" Young Ethan proudly stood up and stated, "Apples are red." Then, several other hands raised and the teacher picked another child. "Yes, Emma?" queried the teacher. Emma replied, "But some apples are green." "Correct!" exclaimed the teacher. Then, several more hands went up, and the teacher again selected an anxious student who was vigorously waving his hand. But young Caroline couldn't control herself and before the selected student could answer she shouted out, "And some apples are yellow." "Yes, that's right! Apples are red, green, and yellow," stated the teacher. But before she continued with the lesson, the teacher noticed a quiet little girl in the corner of the room with her hand still raised. The teacher called upon the child and the little girl said, "Apples are also white." The somewhat puzzled teacher politely replied, "Elizabeth, there are red apples, and green apples, and yellow apples, but I have never seen a white apple." The other children in the room began to laugh. Elizabeth stood up, peered over her glasses at the teacher and bluntly declared, "All apples are white on the inside!"

Too often we tend to assess software quality simply from the behavior aspects and neglect to consider the computational characteristics that remain hidden below the user interface. When treating some illnesses doctors know they must not only consider the physical manifestation of symptoms in a patient, but in some situations they must also consider various tests of internal systems. In-depth diagnostic evaluations such as blood tests or CT scans can sometimes help detect potential issues earlier before they cause serious illness. Similarly, for highly critical systems, or when it is imperative to perform a more detailed analysis of extremely complex software, we must look beyond the exterior and perform a more complete inspection of what lies underneath the outer layer. Structural testing techniques help reduce overall risk through a more rigorous analysis of control flow through a function. Structural testing is especially effective in investigating the parts of a program's code that have been previously unexercised by extensive behavioral or more methodical functional testing using tests designed only from a black box perspective.

Unlike functional testing techniques that can be applied to design tests from both a black box and a white box perspective, structural testing techniques are one of several white box test design approaches. Designing tests from a white box perspective is based on the internal structure and implementation of the program. So, it goes without saying that for a tester to design white box tests to provide more information and further reduce overall risk, testers must be familiar with the programming language used in the implementation. However, it should be noted that tests designed from the white box test approach can be executed from either the user interface (UI) or below the user interface at the component level using stubs or mock objects, assuming program functionality is separated from the UI layer.

A common misconception concerning white box testing approaches is the assumption that testers are biased by the code and will design tests that only prove the function does what it is supposed to do. I don't necessarily agree with this viewpoint because a good tester simply doesn't prove that the code does what it is supposed to do. A good tester with direct insight into data types, function calls, and program structure can identify different types of problems more effectively as compared to other testing approaches. This doesn't imply white box testing is superior to other approaches. Tests designed from a white box perspective such as those designed using structured testing techniques only supplement behavioral and functional testing techniques and approaches; they do not supersede other approaches to testing. We would never advocate simply designing tests from a white box approach or designing tests that only test the structural integrity of a program. Structural testing and application of these techniques are typically used in conjunction with code coverage analysis and are very effective in designing additional tests to increase code coverage. Structural testing also provides additional valuable information when a more in-depth analysis and rigorous inspection of a program is required to reduce overall risk.

Do we need structural testing?

There is no doubt that behavioral and exploratory testing (a test execution approach where the tester uses information gained while performing tests to intuitively derive additional tests) provides value to the testing effort. Behavioral and exploratory testing is generally good at evaluating the "look and feel" of a project, but several recent studies raise important questions about the overall effectiveness and efficiency of behavioral testing and popular exploratory testing approaches to software testing. One study at Helsinki University[1] "found no significant difference in the defect detection efficiency" or in the types or severity of defects detected when comparing test case–based testing and exploratory testing. An earlier study[2] also provided empirical data refuting claims that exploratory testing increased productivity. Another case study[3] by Marnie Hutcheson revealed exploratory testing is less effective in finding certain problems as compared to comprehensive requirements-based testing after formal training. And a

---

[1] Juha Itkonen, Mika V. Mantyla, and Casper Lassenius, "Defect Detection Efficiency: Test Case Based vs. Exploratory Testing," *ESEM*, 2007, 61–70, First International Symposium on Empirical Software Engineering and Measurement.

[2] Juha Itkonen and Kristian Rautiainen, "Exploratory Testing: A Multiple Case Study," *International Symposium on Empirical Software Engineering*, November 2005.

[3] Marnie L. Hutcheson, "Exploratory Testing versus Requirements-Based Testing: A Comparative Study," paper presented at Practical Software Quality and Testing Conference, 2007.

yet unpublished internal study at Microsoft found no significant difference in the level of code coverage between scripted tests and exploratory testing.

In the five-year study at Microsoft, we found no significant difference in the code coverage effectiveness of exploratory or behavioral testing as compared to scripted tests. More than 3,000 testers participated in this experiment and the findings have remained consistent with each group of 25 participants. In this study, scripted tests designed from a specification achieved a nominal 83 percent code coverage of the application under test. The participants were then allowed to perform exploratory testing of the application for an additional 15 minutes for total of five cumulative hours. Surprisingly, the code coverage metric increased only an average of 3 percent. But when the participants were able to analyze the results of the instrumented code and design tests using white box structural test design techniques, the code coverage measure rose to 91 percent (the maximum practical achievable code coverage metric without code mutation or fault injection) in less than 20 minutes. Also testers could better explain why the remaining 9 percent of uncovered code is not testable from a value add or cost versus benefit perspective. Figure 6-1 shows the code coverage effectiveness of the different testing techniques.

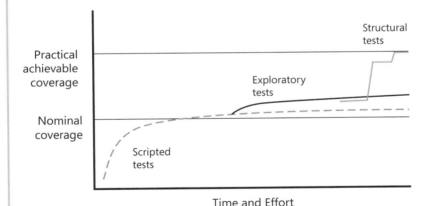

FIGURE 6-1 Code coverage effectiveness of different testing approaches.

These studies do not suggest that exploratory testing or other behavioral testing approaches are ineffective. In fact, exploratory testing can be valuable in specific situations and reveal certain categories of defects more readily than other approaches can. But the overall effectiveness of behavioral testing approaches is heavily influenced by the tester's in-depth system and domain knowledge and experience. Empirical evidence also now suggests that simply increasing the sheer number of testers or including testers with diverse perspectives to perform behavioral or exploratory testing does not significantly reduce risk and can leave critical areas of the product untested or undertested. Additionally, the effectiveness of any test method eventually plateaus or becomes less valuable and testers must employ different approaches to further investigate and evaluate the software under test. What these studies do tell us is that when decision makers need more qualified information to reduce or analyze potential overall risk of highly complex or mission-critical systems, systematic testing techniques that evaluate the program's structural integrity might be required.

Block Testing

There are a few simple techniques for basic structural testing approaches of a function including statement testing and block testing. The purpose of statement testing is to exercise all statements in a function. By comparison, block testing exercises groups of sequential statements or blocks of statements that are free from branches or function calls. Because block testing provides greater sensitivity for evaluating control flow through a function, and many coverage tools currently in use measure block coverage, we typically use block testing for designing our minimum set of structural tests.

Block coverage vs. statement coverage

Statement coverage measures the number of statements in a program that have been executed during testing. Block coverage measures the number of contiguous groups of statements unbound by branches. Conditional clauses that cause control flow to branch can include multiple blocks. This might seem like a minor difference; however, the distinction between statement testing and block testing is important because block testing provides better sensitivity to control flow as compared to statement testing.

Example1 function

```
public static void BlockExample1 (bool condition)
{
    int x = 0, y = 0, z = 0;        } 1 Block
    if (condition)
    {
        x = 1;
        y = 2;                      } 1 Block       } 1 Block
        z = 3;
    }
    return x + y + z;               } 1 Block
}
```

Example1 function illustrates the basic difference between how block and statement coverage are measured. In this example, there are 5 statements, but there are only 4 basic blocks as indicated. A test in which the *condition* parameter is false results in statement coverage measurement of 40 percent because only two statements are executed. But the block coverage measurement would be 75 percent because the test executed 3 of the 4 blocks of code. Of course, if the *condition* parameter is true, both the statement and block coverage measurements would be 100 percent.

The advantage of block testing over statement testing is revealed in more complex structures. For example, in the *Example2* function, passing true arguments to both the *condition1* and *condition2* parameters would result in 100 percent statement coverage, but only 85.71 percent block coverage. The *Example2* function requires a second test where *condition1* is false, and *condition2* is true to achieve 100 percent block coverage.

Example2 **function**

```
public static void BlockExample1 (bool condition1, bool condition2)
{
    int x = 0, y = 0, z = 0;              } 4 Blocks
    if (condition1 && condition2)
    {
        x = 1;                            } 1 Block      } 1 Block
        y = 2;
        z = 3;
    }
    return x + y + z;                     } 1 Block
}
```

Of course, both of these examples also illustrate the weaknesses of statement or block coverage measures. In simple functions, it is somewhat easy to get high levels of code coverage measures with a relatively few number of tests. That is why it is important to remember there is no direct correlation between code coverage and quality, and only an indirect association between code coverage and test effectiveness. The value of structural testing lies in the ability of the tester to critically analyze control flow through a function and design tests that ensure various control flow paths are executed at least once.

In the following *SimpleSearch* function example, we can exercise all statements in this function with one test by passing a string argument of AB and a character argument of B to the function's input parameters. With one simple test, control flow would enter the *while* loop because the *index* variable is less than the length of the array, and the character variable passed to the function through the *myCharacter* parameter is not equal to the element in the array indicated by the current index value. In the *while* loop, we execute a statement to increment the *index* variable by 1 and loop back around to evaluate both conditional clauses in the *while* loop again. The value of the *index* variable is still less than the length of the array, but the second element in the array is the character B, which is equal to the *myCharacter* variable. The second conditional clause is true because the value of the *index* variable is less than the length of the array, so we enter this block and increment the value of *index* by 1 and assign it to the *retVal* variable. Finally, control flow exits the decision block and returns the value of the *retVal* variable to the calling function. So, with one simple test we are able to execute all statements in this function. However, no professional tester would be satisfied with one simple test of this function!

SimpleSearch function

```
// Simple search function that searches for the first instance of a character in a
// string and returns the position of that character in the string, or a -1.
public static int SimpleSearch (string myString, char myCharacter)
{
    int index = 0, retVal = -1;
    char[] strArray = s.ToCharArray();
    while ( index < strArray.Length && strArray[index] != c)
    {
        index++;
    }
    if (index < strArray.Length)
    {
        retVal = index++;
    }
    return retVal;
}
```

By comparison we would need a minimum of two tests for block testing of this function. For the first block test, we would pass this function a string A and a character A to the first and second parameters, respectively. This test would execute 9 of the 11 blocks, as illustrated in Figure 6-2.

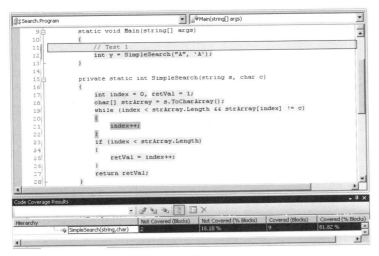

FIGURE 6-2 Block coverage results of first test.

In the second test, we pass a string argument of A and a character argument of B to the function and execute 10 of the 11 blocks, as illustrated in Figure 6-3. Notice that this second test now executes the previously untested blocks, but also skips over one block that was exercised in the previous test. With these two simple block tests we can achieve 100 percent block coverage of this function.

FIGURE 6-3 Block coverage results of second test.

Modeling control flow

Control flow diagrams (CFDs) are simply models of a function or a class. A CFD must have one entry point and an exit point. Between the entry and exit points of a function the CFD provides an abstract representation or model of the program's code to help a tester trace the control flow as it could traverse the various paths through a complex function. There are two basic types of CFDs, as illustrated in Figure 6-4.

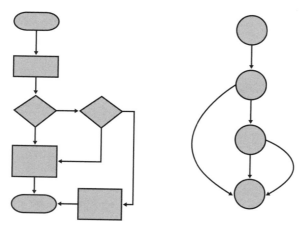

FIGURE 6-4 Control flow diagram examples.

A basic CFD uses typical flowchart symbols to model the function. The basic CFD uses a rectangle to represent statements or blocks of statements, and a diamond to represent decisions or conditional clauses. Basic CFDs are easier to read and understand by people unfamiliar with the function and essentially model the control flow step by step through process blocks and conditional clauses. The simplified CFD uses circles to represent decision points in the function where control flow can change depending on the outcome of a relational condition. The simplified CFD is a more abstract representation of the function because it does not explicitly model blocks of statements. This level of abstraction is sometimes confusing at first, but it increases the efficiency of the modeling process.

It is important to remember that block testing is generally sufficient for unit testing purposes, but it is a relatively weak form of structural testing. However, there are a few programmatic structures for which testers might need to design block tests to ensure adequate structural coverage of a function. One type of structure where block testing is appropriate is the switch/case statement. A switch statement is an effective method to handle control flow through a function that involves multiple choices or selections for a parameter. When we step through a switch/case statement in the debugger, we can see control flow transfer immediately to the case statement that matches the parameter passed to the switch statement.

For example, programmatic platform profiling is quite common in automated tests when the procedures or outcome might be different depending on the specific Microsoft Windows operating system version. A function similar to the *SimpleGetNT5ClientVersion* function can help us determine whether the program or automated test is running on a Windows 2000–based or a Windows XP–based client. The sequential control flow diagrams (CFDs) in Figure 6-5 illustrate control flow through the *SimpleGetNT5ClientVersion* function for a non-NT5 kernel operating system, a Windows Server 2003 operating system, and the Windows 2000 Server and Windows XP operating systems, respectively.

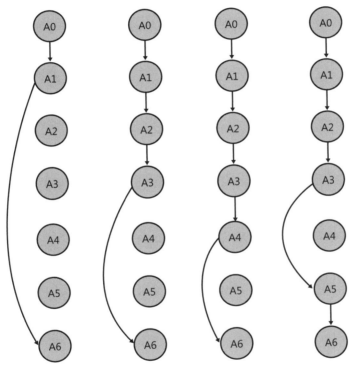

FIGURE 6-5 Sequential control flow diagrams for *GetOSVersion* function.

SimpleGetNT5ClientVersion function

```
//**********************************************************************************
// SimpleGetNT5ClientVersion.cs © 2008 by Bj Rollison
// Returns the Windows NT operating system environment
//**********************************************************************************
private const int WINDOWS_NT5_KERNEL = 5;
private const int WINDOWS_2000 = 0;
private const int WINDOWS_XP = 1;

A0   private static string SimpleGetNT5ClientVersion()
     {
         OperatingSystem osVersionInfo = Environment.OSVersion;
         string osVersion = string.Empty;

A1       switch(osVersionInfo.Version.Major)
         {
A2          case WINDOWS_NT5_KERNEL:
A3              switch(osVersionInfo.Version.Minor)
                {
A4                  case WINDOWS_2000:
                        osVersion = "Win2K";
                        break;
A5                  case WINDOWS_XP:
                        osVersion = "WinXp";
                        break;
                }
                break;
         }
         return osVersion;
A6   }
```

The first CFD demonstrates how control flow would simply bypass the case statements and return an empty string if the operating system's major version number is not equal to an integer value of 5. If the operating system environment is Windows Server 2003, control flow jumps from the switch statement at A3 to A6 and also returns an empty string as illustrated in the second CFD. The third CFD shows the control flow from A3 to the case statement at A4 when the operating system environment is Windows 2000 Server and returns the string *Win2K*. And, if the operating system environment is Windows XP, the fourth CFD demonstrates how the control flow jumps around A6 to the A7 case statement and returns the string *WinXp*.

Another place where block testing is important is in exception handling. Interestingly enough, behavioral testing typically does not exercise many of the exception handlers in a program, so designing structural tests to reduce risk and ensure exceptions are handled correctly is important. If the application handles exceptions and an exception occurs during the execution of the application's code, the system will search for the appropriate exception handler and control flow will transfer to that exception handler.

ConvertToPositiveInteger function

```
A0   private static int ConvertToPositiveInteger(string s)
     {
         try
         {
A1           return (int)Convert.ToUInt32(s);
         }
A2       catch(FormatException)
         {
             return -1;
         }
A3       catch(OverflowException)
         {
             return -1;
         }
A4   }
```

The preceding *ConvertToPositiveIntValue* function is a simple example of control flow for exception handlers. The sequential CFDs in Figure 6-6 for the *ConvertToPositiveIntValue* function illustrate how control flow jumps around or to the appropriate exception handler. A block test that passes a string argument of whole numbers between 0 and 2147483647 will convert the string passed to the *number* parameter to an integer and exit the function, as illustrated by the first CFD in Figure 6-6. To test the exception handlers we require a minimum of two additional tests. For the second test, we pass a noninteger value (string, empty string, characters, and so forth) to the number parameter. Any noninteger value will cause a format exception error to be thrown and control jumps from A1 to A2 where the return value is set to –1 before control flow exits and returns to the calling function. The third test must exercise the overflow exception handler. A string argument representing a whole number larger than 2147483647 or any negative whole number results in an overflow exception within the *try* block A1 and control jumps to the overflow exception handler.

In the CFD, the statements *int.Parse()* and *(int)Convert.ToUInt32()* are represented by the single node A1 because it is not important to differentiate between the two statements for the purpose of block testing. However, testers must also realize that these two process statements set up specific input minimum and maximum boundary conditions for the *number* parameter. The *int.Parse()* function converts a string representation of a whole number to a signed integer value within the range of –2,147,483,648 to 2,147,483,647. The *Convert. ToUInt32* function converts a *System.String* representation of a whole number to an integer value between 0 and 4,294,967,296. Although we require only one block test to evaluate control flow through the overflow exception handler, the professional tester also realizes that additional boundary testing is required for adequate evaluation of this function.

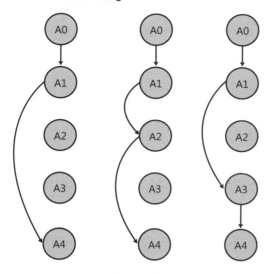

FIGURE 6-6 Sequential control flow diagrams for *ConvertToPositiveIntValue* function.

Summary of Block Testing

Block testing is a common testing approach used for unit testing, and it is quite valuable to quickly evaluate the basic functionality of a function. It is also a valuable technique to design tests to exercise control flow of switch/case statements and exception handlers. However, block testing is a weak criterion for robust structural testing and can miss important branches of control flow. It is also very easy to overlook potential problems, especially if the only purpose of the testing is to achieve increased code coverage and not to carefully analyze the code under test.

Decision Testing

Decision testing evaluates conditional clauses where simple Boolean expressions cause control flow to branch depending on whether the condition evaluates true or false. The primary goal of decision testing is to design tests that evaluate both the true and false outcome of a Boolean expression. This approach to structural test design is similar to block testing, but instead of designing tests to execute contiguous blocks of code, decision testing focuses on evaluating each conditional clause in a function. The advantage of decision testing over block testing is that it provides even better sensitivity to control flow as compared to block testing. The *CreateNewFile* function helps illustrate the effectiveness of decision testing as compared to block testing.

CreateNewFile function

```
// Simplified function to check for an existing file and delete that file if it exists
// and create a new file
A0   private static void CreateNewFile (string myFilename)
     {
A1     if (File.Exists (myFilename))
       {
         File.Delete (myFilename);
       }
       File.Create (myFilename);
A2   }
```

In this example, we can achieve 100 percent block coverage of the *CreateNewFile* function with one test. By passing the function a valid file name to the *myFilename* parameter (a file that already exists on the system at the specified location), we can execute all blocks in this function. However, as the control flow diagram in Figure 6-7 reveals, only the true outcome of the simple conditional clause in the function was evaluated. The false outcome of the conditional clause at A1, indicated by the dotted line in the CFD in Figure 6-7, is not traversed. Again, this is one weakness of block coverage measures.

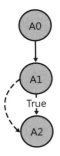

FIGURE 6-7 Control flow diagram for *CreateNewFile* function.

Decision testing of the *CreateNewFile* function requires a minimum of two tests of this function. For the first test, we pass a file name as an argument to this function that exists on the system to force the conditional clause to evaluate to its true outcome. A second decision or branch test requires us to pass a valid file name that does not exist as an argument to this function to evaluate the false outcome of the conditional clause. Although this is a simple example, it demonstrates how decision testing provides better sensitivity to control flow for simple conditional clauses as compared to block coverage.

Also note that we are not passing invalid file name strings to the *myFilename* parameter to check for various error conditions. The purpose of structural testing is not to test all possible inputs or outputs, but simply to help us test control flow through a function. In this example, we assume that the *myFilename* string is validated somewhere else and a valid string is passed as an argument to the *myFilename* parameter.

However, testers should be cautious with looping structures because it is easy to design ineffective tests that evaluate both the true and false outcomes of the conditional clause without effectively testing the loop structure. For example, we could design one test for the *GetCharacterCount* function and pass an argument of A to the *myString* parameter and an argument of A to the *myCharacter* parameter, which would evaluate the conditional clause in the *for* loop as true. The next iteration through the loop evaluates the conditional clause as false because the index value is equal to the length of the *myStringArray* variable.

GetCharacterCount.cs

```
// This function counts the number of specified characters in a string
private static int GetCharaacterCount (string myString, char myCharacter)
{
  char[] myStringArray = myString.ToCharArray();
  int result = 0;

  for (int i = 0; i < myStringArray.Length; i++)
  {
    if (myStringArray[i] == myCharacter)
    {
      result++;
    }
  }
  return result;
}
```

A more effective test strategy for decision testing is to execute a minimum of three tests for more comprehensive structural testing of this function. The basis path testing technique described later in this chapter provides a technique that ensures that a more thorough set of structural tests for functions with simple conditional clauses is used. Also note that there are additional tests that we would want to design to completely test the capabilities of this function, but for decision testing of the function, we require only two tests.

Summary of Decision Testing

In general, decision testing provides greater sensitivity to control flow as compared to block testing. Decision testing is effective for simple conditional clauses in which one Boolean conditional clause is being evaluated such as if statements or looping structures. But, similar to block testing, decision tests do not adequately evaluate relational operators in a conditional clause. The decision tests for the conditional clause

```
if ( x <= 5)
```

would include a test where *x* is equal to 5, forcing the condition to evaluate as true. A second test where *x* is greater than 5 would force the conditional expression to evaluate as false. With two tests we are able to evaluate both the true and false outcomes of the conditional clause, but these two tests do not adequately test the relational operator. Testing the relational operator requires an additional test where *x* is less than 5. Although this third test seems self-evident, incorrect usage of relational operators is one of the leading causes of boundary class defects.

Decision tests also do not effectively evaluate control flow of a compound conditional clause. For example, the looping structure in the *SimpleSearch* function contains two conditional clauses or subexpressions. Decision tests are designed to evaluate compound conditional clauses to their true and false outcomes regardless of the number of conditional expressions. So, if we pass a string of ABC as the *myString* parameter, and a character of B as the *myCharacter* parameter to the *SimpleSearch* function, we can evaluate both the true and false outcomes of the looping structure. However, we didn't adequately evaluate the false outcome of the conditional subexpression that evaluates the index against the length of the string array. For adequate testing of compound conditional clauses with multiple conditional subexpressions, we use a slightly different structural technique called condition testing.

Condition Testing

Sometimes control flow through a function depends on the outcome of multiple conditional clauses. But rather than writing cascading conditional clauses, developers can often simplify the function by writing a single conditional clause composed of multiple Boolean subexpressions that are separated by logical AND or logical OR operators. For example, the *IsNumberBetweenMinAndMax* function checks for a number between minimum and maximum values. This implementation uses two simple conditional clauses to return either a true or false output.

IsNumberBetweenMinAndMax() function

```
private static bool IsNumberBetweenMinAndMax (int number)
{
   int minValue = 1;
   int maxvalue = 10;

   if !(number < minValue)
   {
      if !(number > maxValue)
      {
         return true;
      }
   }
   return false;
}
```

But we can rewrite the two simple conditional clauses using a logical AND operator to separate the two Boolean expressions in this function. The advantages to refactoring the code as illustrated in the following example include the reduction of lines of code, increased maintainability index, and reduced number of blocks. In the preceding function, the number of decision tests is three, and in the following refactored code, the number of condition tests is also three if we assume short-circuiting.

RefactoredIsNumberBetweenMinAndMax function

```
private static bool IsNumberBetweenMinAndMax (int number)
{
  int minValue = 1;
  int maxvalue = 10;

  if (!(number < minValue) && !(number > maxValue))
  {
    return true;
  }
  return false;
}
```

When a conditional clause contains two or more Boolean subexpressions, we can use the structural testing technique condition testing. Condition testing is similar to decision testing, but tests for condition testing are designed to evaluate the true and false outcomes for each subexpression in a compound conditional clause. Condition testing provides better sensitivity to control flow as compared to decision testing when testing compound conditional clauses.

For example, the Next Date program that we tested in Chapter 5 contains the *IsInvalidGregorianCalendarDate* function that checks to verify the input variables are not within the date ranges identified by the i18 Invalid equivalence class subset in Table 5-1. The *IsInvalidGregorianCalendarDate* function uses a compound conditional clause to determine whether the three input variables that are passed to the month, day, and year parameters are valid (meaning the variables are not within the specified date ranges) or invalid (meaning the variables are within the specified date ranges). Decision testing of the *IsInvalidGregorianCalendarDate* function requires only two tests to evaluate the conditional clause to both the true and false outcomes. But it should be obvious that simple decision testing is inadequate to test the structure and control flow of this function effectively.

IsInvalidGregorianCalendarDate() function

```
// The following function checks for dates between 10/5/1582 and 10/15/1582
// which are dates excluded on the original Gregorian Calendar
private static bool IsInvalidGregorianCalendarDate (int year, int month, int day)
{
  if (year == 1582 && month == 10 && !(day < 5) && !(day > 14))
  {
    return true;
  }
  return false;
}
```

Condition testing of the *IsInvalidGregorianCalendarDate* function requires five tests to effectively evaluate the true and false outcome of each Boolean subexpression in this single compound conditional clause. The control flow diagram in Figure 6-8 represents a model of the control flow at each conditional clause in the function. The tests and the outcome for each conditional clause are outlined in the truth table in Table 6-1.

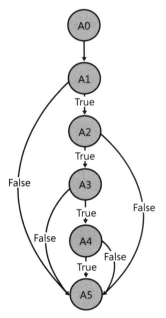

FIGURE 6-8 Control flow diagram for *IsInvalidGregorianCalendarDate* function.

TABLE 6-1 Truth Table for *IsInvalidGregorianCalendarDate* Function

Tests	Parameters			Conditional clauses				Expected result
	Month	Day	Year	Year	Month	!(day < 5)	!(day > 14)	
1	10	11	1582	True	True	True	True	True
2	10	21	1582	True	True	True	False	False
3	10	3	1582	True	True	False		False
4	5	7	1582	True	False			False
5	10	5	1994	False				False

The variables passed as arguments to the *month*, *day*, and *year* parameters are a representative sample of the elements from the valid equivalence class subsets for each parameter, as illustrated in Table 5-1. The Boolean outcomes for tests 3, 4, and 5 that are highlighted in gray in Table 6-1 are for illustration purposes only and would not be evaluated during program execution if we assume short-circuiting. When the first conditional clause resolves as false, control flow will jump to the return false process statement. Also, Table 6-1 does not include all combinations of possible outcomes for each conditional clause. Again, this is because we are assuming short-circuiting of the control flow. If, short-circuiting is not a common practice or cannot be assumed, the *IsInvalidGregorianCalendarDate* function would require 16 tests to exercise all combinations of each outcome for each conditional clause.

Summary of Condition Testing

Condition testing provides better sensitivity to control flow through compound conditional clauses with multiple Boolean subexpressions separated by logical operators as compared to other types of structural testing. So, condition testing subsumes both block and decision testing when dealing with functions that include compound conditional clauses. Condition tests are designed to evaluate the true and false outcome of each subexpression in a compound conditional clause. But condition testing does not exercise all combinations of true and false outcomes of compound conditional clauses because short-circuiting is typically enforced at Microsoft. In general, there is never a good excuse for not short-circuiting. However, testers should check with their developers to determine whether short-circuiting is a standard practice.

Basis Path Testing

Path testing attempts to traverse every possible path through a program. Looping structures in a function pose an especially challenging problem to path testing because every time control flow iterates through a loop it is considered a different path. So, testing every possible path in any nontrivial function is simply impractical. Consider a function, as shown in

Figure 6-9, with four conditional clauses inside a looping structure, and control flows through the loop up to a maximum of 20 times. If we regard each subsequent path through the loop as a different path, there are 5^{20} or approximately 100 trillion possible tests. Exhaustive testing of every possible path would take more than 3,000 years at one test per millisecond!

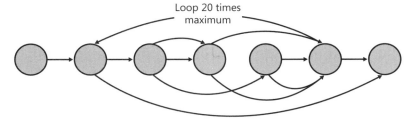

FIGURE 6-9 Control flow diagram of a function where control can loop up to 20 times.

Testing every possible path through a function is mathematically infeasible—and rarely practical for that matter. Thomas McCabe suggested a possible solution to this testing dilemma. McCabe hypothesized a direct correlation between the cyclomatic complexity metric and the number of tests required to perform adequate path testing of that function. The exception to this heuristic occurs in functions where the same conditional clause is evaluated twice. When identical conditional clauses are evaluated, the number of possible basis paths and corresponding basis path tests is less than the cyclomatic complexity metric. An example of this is illustrated in the *IsValidMod10Number* function described later in this chapter.

What is cyclomatic complexity?

Cyclomatic complexity is one measure to help developers gauge the complexity of their functions. It is a commonly used metric in the software development life cycle to evaluate potential reliability, testability, and maintainability of a module. But it can also be used by testers to determine a minimum number of tests for more rigorous testing of control flow through a function as compared to block or decision testing. Cyclomatic complexity measures the decision logic used to control flow through a module or a function. The formula to calculate cyclomatic complexity is $v(G) = \text{Edges} - \text{Nodes} + 2$, but if you must calculate cyclomatic complexity by hand an easier formula is to simply count the number of conditional clauses and add 1 ($v(G) = p + 1$).

A *basis path* is defined as a linearly independent path through a function. A complete explanation of linear independence is nontrivial and beyond the scope of this book. However, for the sake of simplicity linearly independent basis paths are a finite set of unique paths through a function. For example, in a function with one conditional clause there are two linearly independent basis paths, as illustrated in the control flow graphs in Figure 6-10. Linear combinations of the set of linearly independent basis paths represent all possible paths through a function such that any other path through the function is a superset of the basis path set. The structural testing technique of basis path testing provides an effective approach to the virtually insurmountable problem of exhaustive path testing.

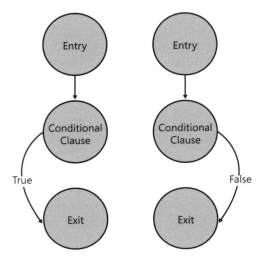

FIGURE 6-10 Linearly independent control flow graphs.

McCabe and Watson also proposed the baseline path technique that testers can use to systematically identify the set of linearly independent basis paths through a function. There are actually two different approaches the tester can use to identify the set of basis paths. The *simplified baseline path technique* is perhaps the most commonly known and the most systematic approach used to identify the set of basis paths in a function. The simplified baseline path technique employs a methodical process in which the tester completes the following steps:

1. Identifies the shortest baseline path (the path with the fewest number of conditional clauses) through a function from the entry point to the exit point of the function being tested.

2. Return to the entry point of the function.

3. Trace control flow from the entry point to the first conditional clause that has not been evaluated to both its true and false outcomes.

4. Change the conditional clause to its alternate outcome.

5. Follow the shortest path from that conditional clause to the exit point.

6. Repeat steps 2 through 6 until all basis paths (equal to the cyclomatic complexity metric) are defined.

Although the simplified baseline path technique is effective in quickly identifying a set of basis paths, it can result in a set of basis paths that are too restrictive, or the set might include unlikely paths through the function. So, to provide the tester with an alternative and more creative method of identifying basis paths McCabe and Watson also proposed the *practical baseline path technique* to identify the set of basis paths in a function. The practical baseline path technique is also a systematic process, but instead of following the shortest paths through a function, the tester uses the following procedure:

1. Identify a likely functional baseline path through the function that is representative of highly probable control flow through the function that is most commonly encountered at run time, or the most important or critical path through the function.

2. Return to the entry point of the function.

3. Trace control flow from the entry point to the first conditional clause that has not been evaluated to both its true and false outcomes.

4. Change the conditional clause to its alternate outcome.

5. Follow a path to the exit point that includes the maximum number of conditional clauses traversed by the baseline path.

6. Repeat steps 2 through 6 until every conditional clause has been evaluated to both its true and false outcomes and all basis paths are defined.

The effectiveness of basis path testing is clearly revealed in the prototypical example first published in the National Institute of Standards and Technology Special Publication 500-235.[4]

CountC function

```
// This function counts the instances of the letter C
// in strings that begin with the letter A
A0   private static int CountC (string myString)
     {
         int index = 0, i = 0, j = 0, k = 0;
         char A = 'A', B = 'B', C = 'C';
         char[] strArray = myString.ToCharArray();

A1       if (strArray[index] == A)
         {
A2           while (++index < strArray.Length)
             {
A3               if (strArray[index] == B)
                 {
                     j = j + 1;
                 }
A4               else if (strArray[index] == C)
                 {
                     i = i + j;
                     k = k + 1;
```

---

[4] Arthur H. Watson and Thomas J. McCabe, *Structured Testing: A Testing Methodology Using the Cyclomatic Complexity Metric*, NIST Special Publication 500-235 (Gaithersburg, MD: National Institute of Standards and Technology, 1996).

```
                    j = 0;
                }
            }
            i = i + j;
        }
        return i;
A5  }
```

The *CountC* function contains four conditional clauses. If we only wanted to evaluate each conditional clause to both its true and false outcomes at least once, we would need only two tests. Table 6-2 is the truth table that would result from two tests in which the first test passes an argument of D and the second test passes an argument of ABCD to the *CountC* function.

TABLE 6-2 Truth Table for Decision Testing of *CountC* Function

Test	Param	Conditional clauses				Result	
		A1	A2	A3	A4	Expected	Actual
1	D	False				0	0
2	ABCD	True	True/False	True/False	True/False	1	1

The control flow diagram illustrated in Figure 6-11 reveals the true and false outcomes for each conditional clause in the *CountC* function for decision test 2 in Table 6-2. Decision test 2 traverses a path of A0 → A1(T) → A2(T) → A3(T) → A2(T) → A3(F) → A4(T) → A2(T) → A3(F) → A4(F) → A2(F) → A5.

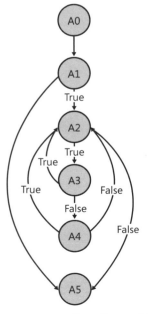

FIGURE 6-11 *CountC* control flow diagram.

However, application of the simple baseline path method to identify the set of basis paths and the expected result predicted for each basis path test quickly reveals two errors of commission. The *CountC* function has four conditional clauses and a cyclomatic complexity of five. Therefore, there are five basis paths for this function. Table 6-3 lists the set of basis paths and the inputs required to test those paths and the expected result, and Figure 6-12 illustrates each linear independent basis path.

TABLE 6-3 Basis Path Table for *CountC* Function

Basis path	Path	Input	Expected
1	A0 → A1(F) → A5	D	0
2	A0 → A1(T) → A2(F) → A5	A	0
3	A0 → A1(T) → A2(T) → A3(T) → A2(F) → A5	AB	0
4	A0 → A1(T) → A2(T) → A3(F) → A4(T) → A2(F) → A5	AC	1
5	A0 → A1(T) → A2(T) → A3(F) → A4(F) → A2(F) → A5	AD	0

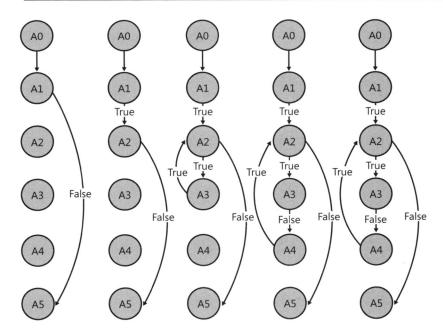

FIGURE 6-12 Linear independent paths in *CountC* function.

Table 6-4 for the *CountC* function reveals that each independent true and false outcome for each conditional clause is executed at least one time. But as we execute the basis path tests and systematically traverse each linear independent path we soon realize there are two separate errors in this simple function. The first error is detected with basis path test 3. The expected output is 0, but in fact it will be 1. The second error is found with basis path test 4, for which the expected output is 1, but the return value is actually 0.

TABLE 6-4 **Truth Table for *CountC* Function**

Test	Param	Conditional clauses				Expected	Actual
		A1	A2	A3	A4		
1	D	False				0	0
2	A	True	False			0	0
3	AB	True	True/False	True		0	1
4	AC	True	True/False	False	True	1	0
5	AD	True	True/False	False	False	0	0

This is just a simple example to explain the principles of basis path testing and how to methodically analyze a function. Some people will look at the *CountC* function and focus on the poor quality of the code. For example, they ask why we are even checking for the character B or realize the variable *k* does absolutely nothing. Interestingly enough, we sometimes see things such as this in production code. The conditional clause could be for future use or a feature that was removed. The *k* variable is an example of dead code. Sometimes people focus on the poorly written code, but a professional tester can take even the most convoluted function and design structural tests for it.

Of course, both of these errors might have been found during behavioral testing. But the dead code could not be detected by behavioral or exploratory testing from the user interface (and that is an error of commission) and if the error of counting the letter *B* is found, the tester has no way of determining which of the more than 100,000 other Unicode characters might also be incrementing the return value. So, which of the more than 100,000 Unicode characters do you choose? Would you try them all? Or perhaps would structural testing reduce the number of tests, increase efficiency, improve test coverage, provide more qualified information, identify different types of errors and help us understand why they occur, and potentially help reduce overall risk?

The *IsValidMod10Number* function is another great example of how basis path testing provides greater sensitivity to control flow as compared to block and decision testing in a real-world example.

IsValidMod10Number.cs

```
// This function takes a string input, converts it to a number array, and applies a
// mathematical formula to check the number's ability to meet the criteria for a valid
// Mod 10 number and returns a Boolean result.
A0  public static bool IsValidMod10Number (string number)
    {
       int[] numberArray = new int[number.Length];
       bool checkBit = false;
    int sumTotal = 0;

A1      for (int i = 0; i < number.Length; i++)
        {
    numberArray[i] = int.Parse(number.Substring(i, 1));
        }

A2      for (int index = numberArray.Length - 1; index >= 0; index--)
        {
A3          if (checkBit)
          {
         numberArray[index] *= 2;
A4        if (numberArray[index] > 9)
          {
              numberArray[index] = 9;  // correct statement is number -= 9;
          }
          }
          sumTotal += numberArray[index];
          checkBit = !checkBit;
        }
        return sumTotal % 10 == 0;
A5  }
```

What is a mod 10 number?

Hans P. Luhn patented a simple checksum algorithm known as the "modulus 10" or "Luhn formula" commonly used to validate certain identification numbers. Basically, the algorithm multiplies every digit in the number by a 1 or a 2 starting from the ones column and progressing leftward. If the result of a digit's computation is greater than 10, the two digits in the result are simply added together (or the result is simply subtracted by 9). The sum of all computed digits is then divided by 10. If the quotient has no remainder (sum % 10 == 0), the number passes the mod 10 algorithm. This algorithm is commonly used to verify numbers such as credit card numbers and Canadian Social Insurance Numbers.

With a single input we could achieve 100 percent block and decision code coverage of the *IsValidMod10Number* function. A test input of 4291 would evaluate the true and false outcomes for each conditional clause and return a Boolean value of true to the calling function, which is the expected result. A second test of 1 would return false to the calling function. Both tests passed and the code coverage results reveal 100 percent decision and block coverage, as illustrated in Table 6-5, but both tests missed the critical errors in the *IsValidMod10Number* function.

TABLE 6-5 Truth Table for Decision Testing of *IsValidMod10Number* Function

Test Number	Parameter number	Conditional Clauses				Result	
		A1	A2	A3	A4	Expected	Actual
1	4291	True/False	True/False	False/True	True/False	True	True
2	1	True/False	True/False	False		False	False

The *IsValidMod10Number* function has four conditional clauses. Using a simplified formula of counting the number of conditional clauses and adding 1, we calculate a cyclomatic complexity of 5. There are logically five basis paths; however, in this example we are able to traverse only four basis paths. This is because it is impossible for duplicate decisions within a function to have conflicting outcomes. If two conditional clauses evaluate the same Boolean expression, the outcome for the same conditional clauses must be identical. The conditional clauses in A1 and A2 in the *IsValidMod10Number* function are identical because they are evaluating the number of characters in the string against an incrementing index value and the number of elements in the array after converting the string to an array against an incrementing index value. In this case, the number of characters in the string is equal to the number of elements in the array, so the conditional clauses are essentially identical and we have only four basis paths, as illustrated in Figure 6-13.

The four basis path tests indicated in Table 6-6 reveal three of the five critical errors. (The two errors not identified by basis path testing in this example include an unhandled format exception when the argument value is a negative number or contains noninteger characters, and when the argument value is an integer larger than 2,147,483,647 and an unhandled overflow exception error will occur.)

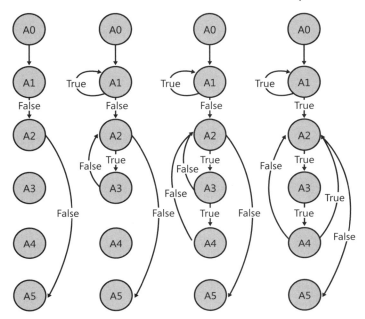

FIGURE 6-13 Basis path set for *IsValidMod10Number* function.

TABLE 6-6   Truth Table for Basis Path Testing of *IsValidMod10Number* Function

Test number	Parameter number	Conditional clauses				Result	
		A1	A2	A3	A4	Expected	Actual
1	empty	False	False			False	True
2	0	True/False	True/False	False		False	True
3	10	True/False	True/False	False/True	False	False	False
4	59	True/False	True/False	False/True	True	True	False

The first two critical errors identified by basis path testing also occur as a result of faulty input validation. If the input parameter is an empty string or the string 0, the return Boolean value in these cases is true instead of false. The third critical error found by basis path testing is test 4 using the minimum valid number that will cause A4 to evaluate as true and satisfy the mathematical formula for the mod 10 algorithm.

Of course, we could miss the critical error in the function by passing a string of 50 to the *number* parameter. This is the minimum input value that would traverse the same structural path as test 4 and cause the conditional clause A4 to be true. In this case, the expected output would be false and the actual output is false. This example serves to reinforce problems associated with the pesticide paradox and the importance of testers not relying on a single approach or technique for effective testing.

This example also illustrates how visibility into the code can reveal hidden boundary conditions or other corner cases. For example, by applying the principles of boundary value analysis to this function, we discover several subboundary conditions. For example, assume that the developer validates the argument value as an integer greater than 0 before passing it to the *IsValidMod10Number* function. The minimum boundary condition of the extreme range is 1, which is an invalid number. But the minimum valid number is 18, so that is a boundary condition identified by our equivalence class partition of minimum valid numbers according to the mod 10 algorithm. An input of 18 in the faulty function would return an actual value of true, as expected. However, the minimum valid number that will traverse the true path of the conditional clause A4 is 59. So, 59 is a subboundary condition and a unique value within the valid class range of valid numbers because it is handled differently from how other valid numbers preceding it are handled. In this example, identifying boundary conditions and using them as test inputs for structural tests can help identify certain types of errors more efficiently.

Summary of Basis Path Testing

Basis path testing is different from block and decision testing in that each outcome for each conditional clause must be tested independently. For example, it is possible to evaluate the conditional clause in a while or for loop to both its true and false outcomes with one (poorly designed) test to satisfy decision or block testing. However, basis path testing requires one test that forces control flow to bypass the loop and another test in which program control flows through the looping structure. So, similar to condition coverage, basis path testing subsumes both block and decision testing.

Basis path testing provides better sensitivity to control flow as compared to block or decision testing when analyzing a function composed of simple conditional clauses, especially those employing looping structures. But basis path testing appears to produce similar results to condition testing when evaluating a compound conditional clause.

Summary

Structural testing techniques are systematic procedures that help testers design effective tests more efficiently when analyzing the program's source code to improve code coverage. But we would never advocate structural testing as the initial or the only approach to testing software. Structural testing techniques are designed to support and enhance other testing approaches and methods. Structural testing can also provide more in-depth information and reduce risk exposure by designing and executing tests to evaluate paths through the code that were not traversed by other testing approaches. This is important because logic errors are inversely relational to a path's probability of execution. If we don't execute a path through code, we must assume 100 percent risk. If we execute that path, our risk is reduced by some percentage, and the more we successfully traverse a path through code, especially with different data, the more we reduce our overall exposure to risk.

Behavioral testing approaches, systematic functional testing methods, and structural testing methods are each intended to provide different types of information and evaluate the software from different perspectives. Complex problems require a plethora of perspectives to provide the qualified information the decision makers require to better assess risk and make informed business decisions. Structural testing simply provides a different perspective to a complex problem. But structural testing is an organizational investment. This level of testing costs more in terms of time and skills needed by testers to design white box structural tests. However, structural testing can prove invaluable in reducing long-term costs and minimizing risk for highly critical or complex systems that require a high degree of reliability.

Chapter 7
Analyzing Risk with Code Complexity

Alan Page

My uncle Frank has fished the rivers of Montana his entire life. To this day, he is a great fisherman. He always knows which combinations of pole, line, and bait have the best chance of catching a fish, and his friends consider him an expert in the field. As good as he is at fishing, he can't catch fish if there aren't any in the area of the river where he is fishing. He knows that great equipment and bait aren't enough, so he also knows how to read depth and flow of the rivers and uses this information to predict accurately where fish will be. The combination of knowing what to do and developing a strategy based on analysis of the fishing area is what makes him so successful.

Techniques such as *boundary-value analysis* and *pairwise testing* are effective for reducing the number of needed test cases while minimally affecting risk. The problem is that there is not an even distribution of bugs throughout the source code. In fact, in a typical software project, some components tend to have many bugs while others have few or none. My uncle uses a variety of techniques to predict where the fish will be. Similarly, one of the necessities of software testing is to anticipate where pockets of bugs will be, and then target test cases toward those areas of the project.

Risky Business

Testing is often a process of managing risk. *Risk-based testing* is an approach to testing based on mitigating potential risks in a product. This approach intends to focus available testing resources on the most appropriate areas. In a sense, all testing is risk based; it is not possible to test everything, so as testers, we make choices based on a variety of criteria on where to concentrate our testing efforts.

Italian economist Vilfredo Pareto created a formula to describe the irregular distribution of wealth in his country, observing that 80 percent of the wealth belonged to 20 percent of the people. Many people believe that the *Pareto principle*[1] (the 80:20 rule) applies as well to software projects. Applied generally, the Pareto principle states that in many measurements, 80 percent of the results come from 20 percent of the causes. When applied to software, the Pareto principle can mean that 80 percent of the users will use 20 percent of the

---

[1] Wikipedia, "Pareto Principle," *http://en.wikipedia.org/wiki/Pareto_principle*.

functionality, that 80 percent of the bugs will be in 20 percent of the product, or that 80 percent of the execution time occurs in 20 percent of the code. One aspect of a risk-based approach attempts to classify which portion of the product contains these popular user scenarios and drives the creation of more tests directed at that portion of the product. The other side of the risk in this approach is that this approach relies on accurately determining where the majority of the testing effort should be and misses the fact that there will be customers who will use the features and code paths that fall outside of the 20 percent range.

Another manner in which to apply risk-based testing is to write more tests for the parts of the product that have a higher potential of containing bugs. Just as my uncle knows where to cast his line to have the best chance of catching a fish, a risk-based testing approach knows which tests to run to have the best chance of finding critical bugs.

A Complex Problem

Complexity is everywhere. I remember making chocolate chip cookies ever since I was old enough to reach the knobs on the oven. I used my grandmother's recipe, and it only included a few ingredients. I rarely referred to the recipe, but the cookies were perfect every time. The measurements of the various ingredients were consistent (that is, two sticks of butter, two cups of flour, one cup each of white and brown sugar, and one bag of chocolate chips), and the cooking time was a round number (10 minutes). The key to my success was that the recipe was simple. Barring a catastrophe (such as rancid butter or a broken oven), I could not find a way to make bad chocolate chip cookies.

As an adult, I still love to cook, but I have run into various problems many times in the kitchen while attempting to reproduce a favorite dish or re-create a recipe inspired by the pictures included in some of my cookbooks. Recipes with dozens of ingredients and multiple cooking steps are primed for mistakes to happen. Usually, I make it through unscathed, but often enough, I end up with three pans cooking on the stove before I realize that I missed an entire step or misread the recipe and put a *tablespoon* of cayenne pepper into the soup instead of a *teaspoon*. The complexity of the recipe and the interaction of dealing with multiple recipes at once make it more likely that I will make a mistake. Similarly, complex code and interactions of complex portions of code are generally more prone to mistakes.

One method sometimes used to predict where bugs might be is to seek out the areas where the code is more complicated. Complex code has a tendency to have more bugs, and simple code tends to have fewer bugs. Complicated code also has the enormous drawback of being much more difficult to maintain. Code complexity is an important measure of the "difficulty" of the code. The greater the complexity of the code, the more difficult the code is to test.

Gut feel or subjective measurement from cursory code review is at times sufficient for gauging code complexity. *Code smell* is a term used often in Agile programming circles that describes code that might be too complex because of large functions or a large number of dependencies. Smells are typically a subjective measurement that can depend on the programming language or environment, and they are useful for identifying code that potentially should be refactored or rewritten.

Don't touch that

When I worked on the Microsoft Windows 95 team, I tested networking components. In one particular component I tested, we would occasionally find a minor bug, and on rare occasions, a beta user would report an issue with this component. Luckily, all of the bugs were minor because all of the bugs in this component were resolved as "won't fix," meaning that a fix was not planned for this release or for any future release. The reason for these resolutions was simple: The code was "too scary to touch" and the original developer had left the company years earlier. The code was so complex and difficult to comprehend that not a single developer was comfortable fixing bugs for fear that he or she would cause a dozen other failures.

Fortunately, that component was completely rewritten for the following release of the Windows operating system, but every once in a while, I still hear stories about bugs that can't be fixed because everyone is too scared to touch the code.

Any time simplicity isn't part of the initial design and implementation of the software, there is potential for the code to grow into a nonmaintainable mess. Subjective methods such as intuition or gut feel can be effective means to identify complex code, but there are objective measures of code complexity that can assist in determining where bugs can be hiding.

The simplest measure of code complexity might be lines of code (LOC). An application with 1,000 lines of code typically is less complex than an application with 10,000 lines of code is. Mathematics alone can lead you to believe that the 10,000-line project would have 10 times as many bugs as the 1,000-line project, but in practice, the 10,000-line project often has many, many more bugs. However, because of discrepancies in how lines of code are counted (see the following section), as well as numerous other external factors, lines of source code is generally discarded as an accurate complexity metric. Many other complexity measurements can be used to predict where bugs can occur, and some of those measurements are described in subsequent sections.

Counting Lines of Code

How many lines of code are in a program? How can such a simple question be so difficult to answer? Let's start with something simple:

```
if (x < 0)
    i = 1;
else
    i = 2;
```

The preceding excerpt contains four lines. How many does it contain if formatted like this?

```
if (x < 0) i = 1;
else i = 2;
```

You would have a hard time counting the second example as four lines—it is two lines, or at least it is *formatted* as two lines. Personally, I don't like the formatting of either example. Given the same code, I'd prefer to write it like this:

```
if (x < 0)
{
    i = 1;
}
else
{
    i = 2;
}
```

So, is this example two, four, or eight lines long? The answer depends on whom you ask. Some LOC measurements count only statements (in C, for example, this includes only lines ending in a semicolon). Other measurements count all lines except blank lines and comments. Others still count the number of assembly instructions generated (each of the preceding examples generates the exact same assembly language or intermediate language when compiled as managed code).

Although there are many methods for counting LOC, all you have to do if you want to measure LOC is pick a method that you like, and use it consistently. Measuring program length through lines of code is rarely an actionable metric but is simple to calculate and has potential for such tasks as comparing the deltas between two versions of a product or two components in a project.

Measuring Cyclomatic Complexity

Computer programs contain thousands of decisions: *If this happens, do that...unless the other thing happened, then do this first.* Programs that contain numerous choices or decisions have more potential to contain failures and are often more difficult to test. One of the most common methods of determining the number of decisions in a program is by using a measurement called *cyclomatic complexity.* Cyclomatic complexity is a measurement developed by Thomas McCabe[2] that identifies the number of linearly independent paths (or decisions) in a function. A function that contains no conditional operators (such as conditional statements, loops, or ternary operators) has only one linearly independent path through the program. Conditional statements add branches to the program flow and create additional paths through the function.

Program maintenance becomes an issue when cyclomatic complexity numbers rise. Psychologists have demonstrated that the average person can hold only five to nine pieces of information in short-term memory at one time; thus, when the number of interrelated choices grows beyond five to nine there is a much higher potential for the programmer to make a mistake when modifying the code. Exceptionally high numbers of decisions can lead to code that is difficult to maintain and even more difficult to test.

The most common method of computing McCabe's complexity measurement is by first creating a control flow graph based on the source code, and then calculating a result based on the graph. For example, consider the code in Listing 7-1.

LISTING 7-1 Simple cyclomatic complexity

```
int CycloSampleOne(int input)
{
    int result;
    if (a < 10)
        result = 1;
    else
        result = 2;

    return result;
}
```

This code is represented by the control flow graph shown in Figure 7-1.

---

2   Thomas McCabe, "A Complexity Measure," *IEEE Transactions on Software Engineering* SE-2, no. 4 (December 1996): 308–320.

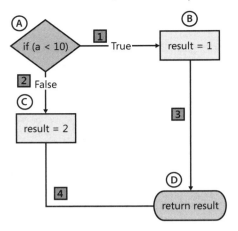

FIGURE 7-1 Control flow diagram for the example of simple cyclomatic complexity in Listing 7-1.

Based on the control flow graph, McCabe identifies the formula to calculate cyclomatic complexity for a function as *edges – nodes + 2*. In the graph in Figure 7-1, nodes appear as shapes, and the edges are the lines connecting the nodes that show potential paths through the program. The nodes in Figure 7-1 labeled A through D show the statements in the function. Using the formula described earlier, there are four nodes, and four edges, or paths between nodes. Analysis shows that the complexity of this function is 2 (edges (4) – nodes (4) + 2 = 2). An accurate shortcut to calculate cyclomatic complexity is simply to count the number of conditional (predicate) statements and add 1. In the preceding example, there is one condition (*if (a < 10)*), and thus the cyclomatic complexity is 2.

The code sample in Listing 7-2 shows a slightly more complex (yet still relatively simple) example. The control flow graph in Figure 7-2 represents this code.

LISTING 7-2 More complex cyclomatic complexity

```
void CycloSampleTwo(int value)
{
    if (value !=0)
    {
        if (value < 0)
            value += 1;
        else
        {
            if (value == 999) //special value
                value = 0;
            else //process all other positive numbers
                value -= 1;
        }
    }
}
```

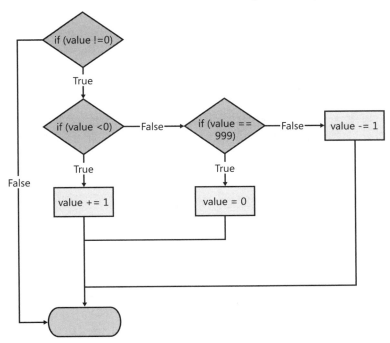

FIGURE 7-2 Control flow graph for the example of slightly more complex cyclomatic complexity in Listing 7-2.

The previous two examples are in all probability much simpler than most code you will find in production, and creating a complete set of test cases for these code examples would be relatively quick work. For simple functions, calculation of cyclomatic complexity is straight-forward and easily performed manually. For large functions with many decision points, or for automatically calculating cyclomatic complexity across a large code base, many tools are available (including tools from McCabe such as McCabe IQ,[3] or free tools such as CCCC, NDepend, and Code Analyzer). For managed code development, several free tools are on the market that calculate the cyclomatic complexity of a given piece of code, including Sourcemonitor, Reflector, and FxCop.

A primary use of cyclomatic complexity is as a measurement of the testability of a function. Table 7-1 contains McCabe's guidelines on using cyclomatic complexity.

TABLE 7-1 Cyclomatic Complexity Risk Analysis

Cyclomatic complexity	Associated risk
1–10	Simple program with little risk
11–20	Moderate complexity and risk
21–50	High complexity and risk
50+	Very high risk/untestable

---

[3] McCabe IQ, home page, *http://www.mccabe.com/iq.htm.*

Consider these values as guidelines. I have seen code with low cyclomatic complexity filled with bugs and code with cyclomatic complexity well over 50 that were well tested and contained few defects.

Halstead Metrics

Halstead metrics are an entirely different complexity metric based on the following four measurements of syntax elements in a program:

- Number of unique operators (n1)

- Number of unique operands (n2)

- Total occurrences of operators (N1)

- Total occurrences of operands (N2)

These measurements are used to derive a set of complexity metrics. For example, a measure of code length is determined by adding N1 and N2. Halstead metrics also can calculate a Difficulty metric with the following formula: (n1 / 2) * (N2 / n2). In the following code sample, there are six unique operators and four unique operands, used a total of 6 and 12 times each, respectively. Table 7-2 shows how I calculated these counts.

```
void HalsteadSample(int value)
{
    if (value !=0)
    {
        if (value < 0)
            value += 1;
        else
        {
            if (value == 999) //special value
                value = 0;

            else //process all other positive numbers
                value -= 1;
        }
    }
}
```

TABLE 7-2 Halstead Metrics Example

| | Operators | | Operands | |
	Operator	Count	Operand	Count
1	!=	1	value	6
2	<	1	999	1
3	+=	1	0	3
4	==	1	1	2
5	=	1		
6	-=	1		
Total	**6 (n1)**	**6 (N1)**	**4 (n2)**	**12 (N2)**

- n1 = 6
- n2 = 4
- N1 = 8
- N2 = 12

Using Halstead metrics, the *Length* of this function is 18 (N1 + N2), and the *Difficulty* ((n1 / 2) * (N2 / n2)) is 9 ((6 / 2) * (12 / 4)).

Like cyclomatic complexity, Halstead metrics are valuable for determining the maintainability of a program, but there are varying views on this value ranging from "unreliable"[4] to "among the strongest measures of maintainability."[5] As with cyclomatic complexity (and nearly every other metric I can think of), use this measurement primarily as an indicator of which code *might* need additional rework or analysis.

Object-Oriented Metrics

Object-oriented metrics are metrics related to classes and class structure in languages such as C++, Java, and C#. The most popular of these are the object-oriented metrics created by Chidamber and Kemerer[6] known as CK metrics. CK metrics include the following:

- **Weighted methods per class (WMC)**   Number of methods in a class

---

4 Capers Jones, "Software Metrics: Good, Bad, and Missing," *Computer* 27, no. 9 (September 1994): 98–100.

5 P. Oman, *HP-MAS: A Tool for Software Maintainability, Software Engineering* (#91-08-TR) (Moscow, ID: Test Laboratory, University of Idaho, 1991).

6 S. R. Chidamber and C. F. Kemerer, "A Metrics Suite for Object Oriented Design," *IEEE Transactions in Software Engineering* 20, no. 6 (1994): 476–493.

- **Depth of inheritance tree (DIT)**   Number of classes a class inherits from
- **Coupling between object classes (CBO)**   Number of times a class uses methods or instance variables from another class

Advocates of object-oriented metrics suggest that classes with a large number of methods, deep inheritance trees, or excessive coupling are more difficult to test and maintain, and are more prone to contain defects.

In object-oriented programming, *fan-in* and *fan-out* metrics are a measurement of how many classes call *into* a specific class and how many classes are called *from* a specific class. For example, if a class contains methods called by 5 other classes and in turn calls methods in 10 other classes, its fan-in measurement is 5, and its fan-out measurement is 10. These measurements are frequently quite effective as maintainability metrics, but they also indicate where additional testing might be needed. For example, if a class is called by dozens of other classes (high fan-in measurement), there is a high potential for any code changes in that class to cause a new failure to occur in one of the calling classes.

Fan-in and fan-out measurements are also quite valuable in non-object-oriented programming when used at either the function or module level. Functions called by a high number of other functions can be some of the most difficult functions to maintain and test, and often simply cannot be changed. The biggest example of this I have seen in my career has been with Windows application programming interface (API) functions. Many of the core Windows functions are called by thousands of applications. Even the most trivial change to any of these functions has the potential to cause one of the calling functions to suddenly fail. Great care must be taken during maintenance of any function or module with a high fan-in measurement. From the testing perspective, this is a great place to be proactive. Determine as early as possible which functions, modules, or classes of your application will have the highest fan-in measurement, and concentrate testing efforts in that area.

Conversely, fan-out measurements tell you how many dependencies you have. If you have a function or class that calls 10 or 20 methods, this means there are 10 or 20 different methods where changes might affect you. This problem is often magnified when other developers or other teams entirely are responsible for the maintenance of these called functions.

Complexity usage on the Windows Sustained Engineering Team

The Windows Sustained Engineering (SE) Team is responsible for all of the ongoing maintenance of the released versions of Windows. This includes hotfixes, security patches, updates (critical and noncritical), security rollups, feature packs, and service packs.

Whenever a hotfix is released, the SE team must decide how many of the 4,000+ binaries that make up Windows they should test. With a hotfix, they have a very short amount of time to ensure that a change in one binary doesn't affect some other binary, but they don't have time to test each and every binary in Windows for every hotfix. They use a combination of complexity metrics to do a risk ranking of each binary based on the changes being made for a particular hotfix as well as the overall historical failure likelihood of a binary.

Once ranked, they take a very conservative approach and eliminate the bottom 30 percent of the least risky binaries from the regression test pass. This means they don't have to spend time running tests for more than 1,000 binaries and can concentrate their testing on the remaining higher-risk binaries. As they hone their process, they will be able to eliminate even more binaries, increasing the test efficiency while remaining confident that the changes being made don't cause an undetected regression.

—Koushik Rajaram

High Cyclomatic Complexity Doesn't Necessarily Mean "Buggy"

Being able to quantify how complex a given piece of software is doesn't necessarily dictate an action item for the test team. It is possible for each of the preceding metrics to indicate a high level of complexity in code that contains very few bugs. I often refer to metrics such as this as *smoke alarm metrics*. When a smoke alarm starts screeching, it doesn't guarantee that there is a fire, but it does indicate that you should look for a fire and respond appropriately. Similarly, when complexity metrics are high, it doesn't necessarily mean that the code is "buggy" or unmaintainable; but it does mean that you should take a closer look.

For example, consider cyclomatic complexity and code using a long switch statement, such as the message loop used often in Windows programming. Each case statement in the loop creates a separate path and increases the cyclomatic complexity (and number of test cases needed) by one but doesn't necessarily make the application difficult to test. Consider Microsoft Paint. Paint is quite simple compared to other graphic manipulation applications, but it has nearly 40 menu choices, another 16 choices for drawing tools, and another 28 choices for color selection. I didn't look at the source code for Paint, but I wouldn't be surprised if the code to handle all of these choices is contained in a single case statement! Add to this the drawing- and size-related messages that applications have to handle, and you have a function that some complexity metrics will tell you is so untestable that you should run screaming (but you probably shouldn't).

The following code represents part of a typical Windows message loop. Message loops, by design, have dozens or more case statements resulting in a high measurement of cyclomatic complexity. Bugs in message loops definitely do occur, but not nearly in the amount that complexity metrics could lead you to believe.

```
int HandleMessage(message)
{
    switch (message)
    {
        case Move :
            // code omitted...
            break;

        case Size :
            // code omitted...
            break;

        ...
        // dozens more deleted
    }
}
```

In many other situations, however, you will likely find that areas of the source code with high complexity are also the areas that contain more bugs. Numerous studies have shown a high correlation between complexity metrics and bugs. Often, complexity is also associated with the *maintainability* of source code. Overly complex code is extremely difficult for maintenance programmers to work with. Getting familiar with the code requires extra time, and bug fixes or additional features can be challenging to implement without adding even more complexity to the code.

What to Do with Complexity Metrics

There are several other methods of measuring code complexity. Just about any reasonably well known complexity measurement likely has some merit and has demonstrated some success in identifying areas of code that might contain more bugs or be more difficult to maintain. Complexity measurements are all also quite capable of reporting *false positives*—that is, code that shows high complexity through analysis, but that contains few or no bugs and is simple to maintain. One method for moderating the false positives is to look at several different complexity metrics and combine, merge, or weigh the data to weed out some of the false positives. If several different complexity metrics all classify a function, module, or file as being highly complex, chances are that it actually might be more prone to containing bugs and could be difficult to maintain. On the other hand, if one measurement shows high complexity for a section of code, but other complexity measurements disagree, there is a realistic chance that the code is not too complex, too difficult to maintain, or prone to containing bugs.

What do you do with complex code? If it's new code, high complexity indicates code that can need refactoring. Some teams at Microsoft have experimented with setting limits on the level of cyclomatic complexity for new functionality. (Most teams that have tried this have discovered that, by itself, cyclomatic complexity isn't always an accurate indicator of code that is in need of refactoring.) Other teams, including the Windows team, look at a combination of several different complexity metrics and use the combined data to help determine the risk of changing a component late in the product cycle.

Consider, for example, the functions listed in Table 7-3. The *OpenAccount* function has high cyclomatic complexity but has few calling functions (fan in) and a low number of lines of code. This function might need additional rework to reduce the cyclomatic complexity, or review might show that the code is maintainable and that tests for all branches are easy to create. *CloseAccount* has a high number of calling functions but few branches. Additional inspection of this function might be warranted to reduce the number of calling functions, but this function probably does not have a significant amount of risk. Of the three functions, *UpdatePassword* might have the most risk. Cyclomatic complexity is moderate, there are nearly 20 calling functions, and the length of the function is nearly three times the length of the other functions. Of course, you want to test when changes are made to any of the functions, but the metrics for *UpdatePassword* should make you wary of any changes made at all to that function.

TABLE 7-3 Complexity Examples

Function name	Cyclomatic complexity	Number of calling functions	Lines of code
OpenAccount	21	3	42
CloseAccount	9	24	35
UpdatePassword	17	18	113

The latest version of the Microsoft Visual Studio toolset contains measurements for complexity metrics, including cyclomatic complexity; Halstead metrics, shown in Figure 7-3 as *maintainability index*; and lines of code.

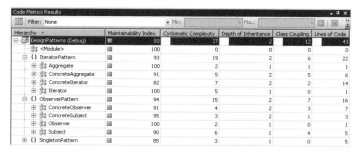

FIGURE 7-3 Complexity metrics in Visual Studio 2008.

Summary

Code complexity is an essential metric for identifying where bugs might exist in your application and is equally valuable in identifying code that can cause maintenance issues. If you are not measuring complexity in any part of your code, start by measuring it in your most critical functionality or features. Over time, you can expand the scope of your complexity measurements and begin to compare complexity between components or feature areas.

Complexity is also an easy metric to misuse, so it is critical that you use the metrics wisely and monitor the value to ensure that these metrics are discovering what you expect them to discover. Remember that high complexity tells you only that the code *might* be prone to having more bugs. You might need additional investigation to know for sure.

Chapter 8
Model-Based Testing

Alan Page

When Boeing designs a new jet such as the 787 Dreamliner, they model the airplane in software, where they run millions of simulations to understand how the shape of the fuse-lage, weight of the components, position of the cockpit, and numerous other variables affect lift and fuel efficiency.

When I first learned how to drive a car with a stick shift, I was horrible. For some reason, I just couldn't get the timing right between releasing the clutch and pressing the gas. Finally, someone drew a diagram for me, showing me what happened when I pressed the clutch in, and how giving the car gas interacted with the process. Amazingly, once I visualized the system, I didn't have a problem with the manual transmission anymore. I never even had a problem with "riding the clutch"—the entire system made sense to me.

Models help us understand how complex things work. In school, I learned basic math through models. Rather than starting directly with "9 – 4 = 5," a teacher uses a model to explain the concept, as shown in Figure 8-1.

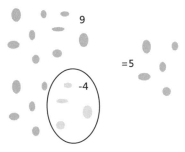

FIGURE 8-1 Math model.

If you start with 9 objects, and then remove 4, your are left with 5 objects. The model explains this simply and efficiently. It is a perfect way to express a complex (to a 6-year-old) problem. Throughout our lives, models help explain what we do not fully understand. They give meaning to the abstract and answer what-if questions and help drive design. The act of modeling forces the modeler to break down complex issues into understandable and well-defined units, and in the end allows for better understanding of the entire problem space.

Model-based testing (MBT) is one (very natural) way to approach this perennial problem. This chapter outlines the basic workflow testers at Microsoft often take to render a model in their mind to some actionable form. The form might be a drawing on a whiteboard or a sketch on the back of an envelope. Modelers that are more ambitious use a visualization tool such as Microsoft Visio or custom modeling tools to create their models. Of course, a model alone is not sufficient for testers; they need test cases. Testers' favorite modeling technology is one that can generate test cases from their models.

Modeling Basics

Figure 8-2 is a model of how testers at Microsoft approach modeling. It is a model of a model! Testers often write models on napkins during lunch conversations, write them on a whiteboard, or sketch them on the backside of a specification. They might even create them directly in Visio or use internal tools that assist testers in creating model-based tests.

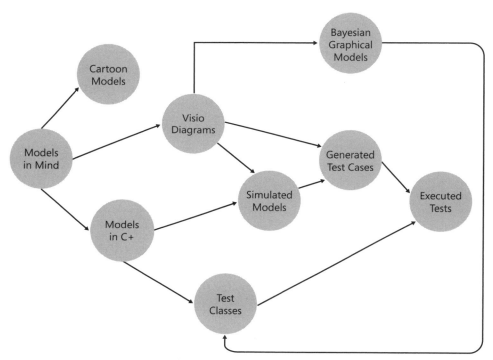

FIGURE 8-2 A model of modeling.

A model can be any description of a system. A typical behavioral model contains a *starting state*, one or more *transitions*, and an *ending* state. In the math model in Figure 8-1, the starting state is 9, the action is "remove 4," and the ending state is 5.

A *finite state machine* (FSM) is the term used to describe a collection of states and associated transitions. FSMs are a natural way to express any functionality that is represented by states and transitions. Figure 8-3 represents the FSM for the mathematical expression "nine minus four."

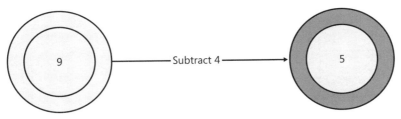

FIGURE 8-3 Finite state machine representing 9– 4.

Testing with Models

Testing can be (and often is) done through models. Many testers have used models without even knowing it. I've seen many testers sketch the functionality of the feature they were testing in a diagram on their whiteboard, and then trace the program flow to understand how the feature works. My hunch is that these testers could be even more effective after they learn how to take explicit advantage of model-based testing.

Designing a Model

Creating models isn't terribly difficult. It is often more difficult to know *when to stop* creating models. My first car was a 1962 AMC Rambler. It was fun to drive, yet quite simple. It had push button gears—one each for Drive, Low 1, Low 2, and Reverse. The Neutral button doubled as the starter. When I got in the car to go somewhere, it was always in the same state—parked and off. After I got in the car, I would take an action (pressing the green start button) to take the car to a new state—running! From here, I usually put the car into drive (yet another state) and went to school. Sometimes I forgot something and had to return the car to the previous state (off) while I ran inside to grab my homework, books, or whatever else I missed the first time I ran out the door. I could also go from gear to gear whenever necessary. Technically, the car could be put into reverse at any time (I never tested that), but for simplicity, let's pretend that I had to put the car into neutral first, as shown in Figure 8-4.

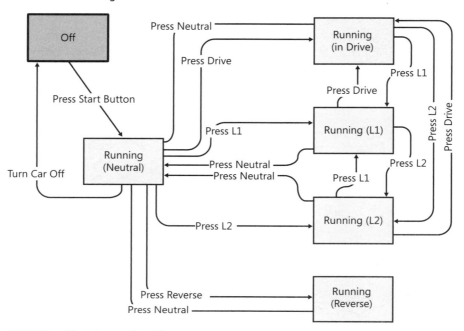

FIGURE 8-4 Modeling my Rambler.

This model (like my Rambler) is rather simple. The "problem" is that there are many more actions I could take with my car. The model in Figure 8-4 doesn't take the actions of the brake or gas pedal into account and those could be modeled as well. The windows could be in varying states of openness, and the headlights could be in any of three different states (off, on, bright). The heating system, the windshield wipers, and the radio all had entirely different models, some, unbelievably, that interacted with each other. Models can grow quite quickly. As mine grow, I always recall a bit of advice I heard years ago: " 'Too small' is just about the right size for a good model." By starting with small models, you can fully comprehend a sub-area of a system before figuring out how different systems interact. When I first learned to drive, I learned the basics of each part of the car (how to make it go, how to turn, and how to stop). As I gained experience and learned more about each subsystem of the car, I got better at driving. I never *drew* models of my Rambler, but I'm certain that in some sense, I *thought* of the different pieces of the system as models.

Modeling Software

A great deal of software is state based and can benefit from a state-based testing approach. Figure 8-5 shows a simple application with three buttons. The first button prints "Hello" to a text box, the second prints "World" to a text box, and the third button clears the fields. When the application starts, both text boxes are clear regardless of their state when the application terminated.

FIGURE 8-5 Simple application for modeling.

As far as applications go, this one is as uncomplicated and minimal as you will ever find. The first thing a tester on this application might do is generate simple, serial test cases, as shown in Figure 8-6.

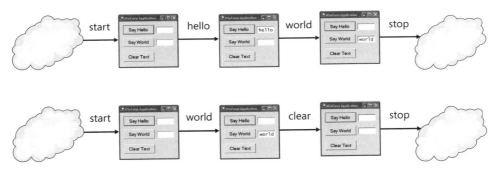

FIGURE 8-6 Simple application model.

At first glance, you might think that there are only three actions that need to be tested, one for each button. Experienced testers might wonder, "What happens if I click 'Say Hello' twice in a row—or 50 times in a row?" (Good testers seem to understand that no matter how absurd clicking a button 50 times in a row might sound, somewhere, a customer will do exactly that.) Scripted tests for this application could look like the four tests listed in Table 8-1.

TABLE 8-1 Sample Tests

Test 1	Test 2	Test 3	Test 4
1. Start	1. Start	1. Start	1. Start
2. Hello	2. Hello	2. Clear	2. World
3. Clear	3. World	3. World	3. Stop
4. Hello	4. Hello	4. Clear	
5. Hello	5. World	5. World	
6. Stop	6. Clear	6. World	
	7. Stop	7. Hello	
		8. Stop	

For this application, these test cases may be enough for adequate testing. There are, however, drawbacks to tests like this. First, these test cases require manual maintenance. If a tester forgets to add a new test case (for example, the tester later realizes that he needs to create a test where he closed the application without clicking any button), the tester would need to make updates to the scripts. More important, because these tests are static, they will always test the same thing. Although this is often a good (and expected) attribute (any regressions in functionality will be found quickly), many scripted test cases never find bugs after they are created and executed once. In a sense, the tests train the software to succeed against the test cases. Figure 8-7 shows a state model for this application, along with bold lines to show which transitions and states in the model the tests in Table 8-1 "visit."

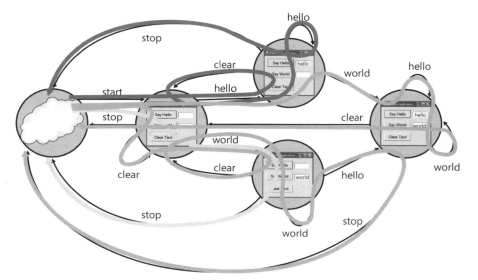

FIGURE 8-7 Exercising a model with static tests.

A state model can clarify understanding of how the application works and what the differ-ent test permutations might be. Figure 8-8 contains a state model for this application. The four boxes represent the four possible states of the application, and the lines represent the actions that can be taken from each state. The states are as follows:

1. Both text boxes are clear (S1).

2. The first text box contains "Hello" and the second text box is clear (S2).

3. The first text box is clear and the second text box contains "World" (S3).

4. The first text box contains "Hello", and the second contains "World" (S4).

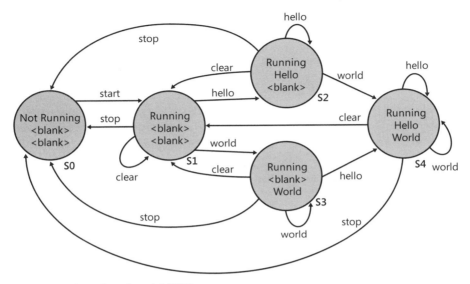

FIGURE 8-8 State-based model (FSM).

The connecting lines represent actions that cause transitions from state to state. For example, from the start state (both text boxes clear), there are three possible actions. Clicking the clear button returns the application to the same state (or does nothing depending on your point of view). Clicking either "Say Hello" or "Say World" changes the application to a new state.

A random walk through the transitions and expected states might look like what is shown in Table 8-2.

TABLE 8-2 RANDOM WALK OF STATE-BASED MODEL

Test step	Action	Text box 1	Text box 2
0	Start Application	Empty	Empty
1	Say World	Empty	World
2	Clear	Empty	Empty
3	Say Hello	Hello	Empty
4	Say Hello	Hello	Empty
5	Clear	Empty	Empty
6	Say World	Empty	World
7	Say Hello	Hello	World
8	Say World	Hello	World
9	Clear	Empty	Empty
10	Stop Application	Empty	Empty

Building a Finite State Model

Building a model can be a little challenging at first but with practice becomes an almost unconscious act for most testers. As I explore applications or specifications and draw models, I find myself thinking of the following same three questions repeatedly as I generate the model:

- **Where am I?** I need to know what state the application is in now, and I need to be able to describe (or know how to verify) the current state.

- **What actions can I do?** From my current state, what are the different things I can do?

- **What happens when I do them?** If I take an action, what state does it bring me to?

As my model grows, I find it useful to continue to think of scenarios and expectations as I work. Because the model lets me see early how all of the states interact, I frequently find bugs before I ever actually run any of the tests.

Automating Models

The automation approach for state-based models is slightly different from traditional approaches. Rather than automate an end-to-end scenario, test automation for models focuses on automating the transitions and verifying the states.

The application modeled in Figure 8-8 contains four possible states and three possible actions: "Say Hello," "Say World," and "Clear Text." Each of the actions is valid in all four states.

To create model-based automation for this application, I would implement just a few functions, one each for the three buttons (the actions), and four others to verify each of the states.

At this point, I can execute any of the available actions and have oracles in place to ensure that the application is in the expected state. Tools and frameworks for MBT (discussed later in this chapter) take this testing to a new level by running through transitions and states using a myriad of different paths.

Graph Theory and MBT

In 1737, Leonhard Euler solved the problem of the Seven Bridges of Königsberg. The city of Königsberg is set on a river and connected across the mainland and two islands by seven bridges. Apparently, the popular pastime of the day was to determine whether it was possible to walk a path that crossed each bridge once (and only once).

Euler determined that the task was impossible. In doing so, he defined relationships between nodes (dry land in this case) and edges (the bridges), and created theorems that demonstrated conditions (using a different number of bridges or connections) where the task could be completed. Euler's solution is considered to be the first theorem of graph theory.

In mathematics, a graph is a collection of edges (or links) and nodes. In MBT, edges and nodes represent transitions and states, respectively. It turns out that the math behind graph traversal is very interesting for testing state models. Much of the power in MBT is in the traversal algorithms. Tests that run randomly through every state are interesting and often find bugs, but applying graph theory concepts to the traversal is powerful and effective.

A *random walk* traversal chooses an available transition at random. It has no guidance or plan; it just strolls through the states for as long as you let it. Random walks often find bugs (some consider these to be a "smart monkey test"), but can take an extremely long time to traverse through large models.

A *weighted traversal* is a slightly better solution. A weighted traversal is somewhat of a guided random walk. The choices of which transition to choose are still random, but the most likely choices are weighted so that they occur more often.

The *shortest path* traversal walks the path between two nodes using the least number of transitions.

There are many other ways to traverse a state model using graph theory algorithms. An *all transitions* path, as its name implies, ensures that all transitions have been exercised. Note that an all transitions path includes all nodes as well. The *all states* traversal, on the other hand, does not guarantee that all transitions have been exercised. Revisiting the model from Figure 8-8, Figure 8-9 shows an example of a traversal that exercises all states, and Figure 8-10 shows an example traversal that reaches all transitions.

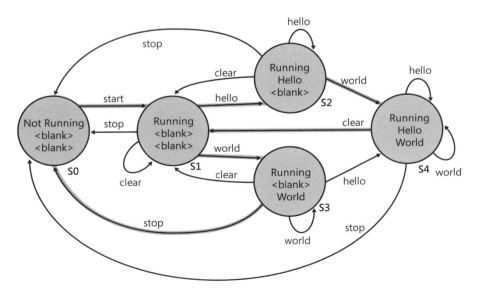

FIGURE 8-9 All states traversal.

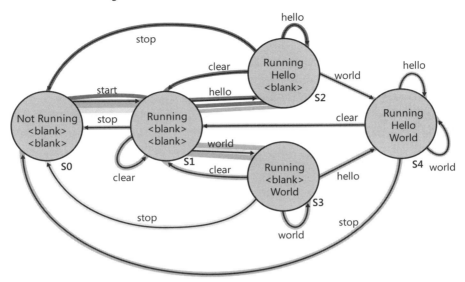

FIGURE 8-10 All transitions traversal.

Models for API Testing

At a lower level, testing of many operating system or platform functions is also amenable to a state-based approach. Common file reading and writing functionality is one such example. Common file APIs can change the state of the file system by creating files, opening files, modifying files, and closing files.

The model shown in Figure 8-11 is simple and provides a starting point for a suite of file function tests. As the model grows, I might differentiate between opening a file, creating a new file, or attempting to open a file that is already open. Over time, I will add the actions of reading from a file, writing multiple times to the same file, and closing a file previously closed. Other related file functionality, such as functions that set the location of the reader within the file, could also be included in this model. Models can grow quickly, so it is important to start small and grow as you understand more about the functionality you are modeling.

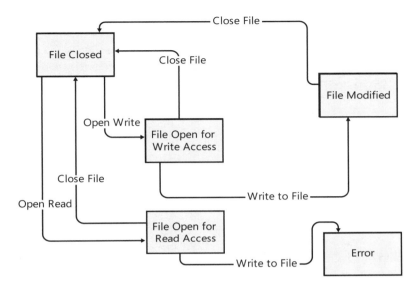

FIGURE 8-11 Partial model of file API.

Random Models

Another simple form of model-based testing is *monkey testing.* A monkey test[1] gener-ates random (or pseudo-random) input with the hope of finding a bug. Monkey tests are common in stress testing and are typically not difficult to create. I wrote an extremely simple one several years ago that looked something like the pseudo-code in Listing 8-1.

Listing 8-1 Sample Monkey Test

```
Launch Text Editor

// "simulate" typing
Repeat 1000 times //slightly less than infinite, but suitable for this example!
{
  Repeat 500
  {
    Press Random Key
  }
  Select some portion of text
  Select Random Font, Font Size, and Font Color
  Press one of ToolBar Buttons [Cut | Copy | Paste | ]
}
Close Text Editor
```

---

[1] The term *monkey test* comes from the infinite monkey theorem, which states that a thousand monkeys at a thousand typewriters will eventually type the complete works of William Shakespeare.

This test was fun to watch, but the only bug it ever found was a slight memory leak (which is a critical bug on embedded systems). The drawback of monkey tests is that they are generally difficult to debug. Finding the exact combination of commands that led to the memory leak required that I write some additional tests. In this case, it was a leak in the Clipboard functionality, so a targeted test on cut, copy, and paste would have found the bug sooner.

Grammar Models

Another common form of MBT is testing with a *grammar model*. A grammar model describes the characteristics and structure of data such as an e-mail address, name, or text.

Regular expressions are an example of an implementation of a grammar model. A common use of regular expressions is to search text. If I wanted to find all occurrences of my name (Alan) across a large set of documents, I could use a search tool to find instances of *Alan* in the text. However, if I want to search for alternate spellings such as Allen and Allan at the same time, I could build a model using regular expressions to search for all three at the same time. For example, a search for *Alan|Allan|Allen* (the model) would find all instances of all three spellings of my first name. The model language of regular expressions also allows me to simplify (although some would argue) the model to *(A|Al)l(a|e)n.*[2] A model for the former pattern is in Listing 8-2

Listing 8-2 Regular Expression Model

```
<Name>        ::= Alan | Allan | Allen
```

Grammar models are great for creating test data. Let's say that you are testing Microsoft Windows Live Hotmail and want to send 10,000 e-mail messages covering a variety of different inputs (assume that you have ample test accounts and sufficient automation to accomplish this). The first thing you might do is create a model of the data you care about for the message. The model can look like Listing 8-3 and generate the data in Table 8-3:

Listing 8-3 Grammar Model for E-Mail Fields

```
<To>       ::= <Valid Address | Invalid Address>
<Cc>       ::= <Valid Address | Invalid Address>
<Bcc>      ::= <Valid Address | Invalid Address>
<Subject> ::= <Empty | Not Empty>
<Body>     ::= <Empty | Not Empty>
```

---

[2] Note that this regular expression also would find instances of *Alen*. This is simple to fix, but outside the scope of this book.

TABLE 8-3 **Partial Data for Grammar Model**

Valid address	Invalid address	Empty	Not empty
testacc1@hotmail.com	<blank>	Length == 0	Length > 0
testacc2@hotmail.com	nobodythere1@hotmail.com		
testacc3@hotmail.com	nobodythere2@hotmail.com		
...	...		

A test generator could use the model along with a database containing valid and invalid e-mail addresses, random subject lines, and message bodies to generate 10,000 unique e-mail messages. Note that yet another tester could easily create another grammar model to create random strings for the subject and message body.

A modeling success

Our test team used model-based testing on several new features from the Windows Vista operating system time frame and found that very extensive coverage could be achieved with a small amount of work. One of the hardest problems was creating a model that accurately depicts the system in question. Once this was achieved by properly defining all possible inputs, transitions, and outputs, we found it very easy to accurately define an expected result from any possible set of parameters. The model in essence becomes the ideal representation of the system you are testing and any deviation should be readily apparently.

We found model-based testing very robust because we could apply it to test areas ranging from APIs to UIs. This allowed us to do away with manual testing completely when the models were implemented. In particular with our UI, this saved us countless hours of manually verifying its functionality for all possible actions (button clicks, text inputs, and so forth). When properly scaled, our model-based tests could provide coverage ranging from quick verification tests to full-scale functional tests. This was done by paring down our list of inputs, transitions, and outputs to the subset that we were interested in. It would have been very difficult to achieve such a wide range of coverage if we relied on developing specific test cases one by one.

One of our successful implementations of modeling involved testing a new API that shipped out to developers in Windows Vista. Rather than write test applications that used the API or script a series of possible scenarios, we used modeling to generate a state machine for all possible function calls that a developer could make. This means for a given function call with given parameters, we could determine how all other subsequent function calls would react. We realized the true value of our framework in testing

> whether the API reacted correctly to different options/parameters/completion schemes without writing one-off applications for each interesting scenario. Our test footprint was much smaller with the model while achieving more coverage compared with our older approaches.
>
> *—Jim Liu, SDET, Windows Networking*

Modeling Without Testing

As exciting as modeling sounds, model-based testing is not the same thing as modeling. Many testers, however, fail to make this distinction. A model can be a very powerful tool for the design/development team, even if it never generates a test case. In this section, we examine two examples of modeling power that do not directly affect test cases. One example demonstrates how to model uncertainty or risk, and the other provides a method for testers to use to ensure that their models behave as they should.

Bayesian Graphical Modeling

Bayesian Graphical Modeling (BGM)[3] is notably different from the other modeling approaches used at Microsoft.[4] The goal of BGM analysis is to *measure and reduce the uncertainty of testing*. It is a method of modeling for risk analysis. Every tester comes to an application to test with some measure of confidence in the code she tests. Many factors inform this confidence (reputation of the developer, complexity of the code, number of dependencies on other binaries taken, time and cost of testing, and other factors). If every tester and every application starts out with the same presumption, we have a good starting point for measuring and reducing uncertainty.

If a tester presumes the quality of the code tested is good (especially if there are strong internal development controls in place), a proper starting point for all testers is to answer this question: How confident am I that there are no defects in this code? In a BGM, the tester specifies his confidence for all the components he will test and fully describes his reasoning in a model. The BGM takes into account that uncertainty and risk affect dependent components as well. Testers then run tests, and as they find bugs, they update the BGM. The model and tests form a feedback loop of updates throughout the product cycle. An example of a BGM is shown in Figure 8-12.

We testers will never enjoy complete certainty in our job, but we can measure and take steps to reduce the uncertainty of our task. At some point, we have to ship, and it's nice to know when the odds of success are in our favor.

---

[3] Also known as a Bayesian Belief Network (BBN).

[4] Heckerman, David, *A Tutorial on Learning with Bayesian Networks*, Technical Report MSR-TR-95-06 (Redmond, WA: Microsoft Corporation, March 1995).

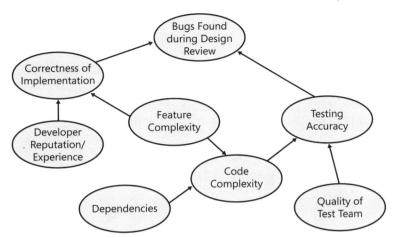

FIGURE 8-12 Product quality assessment using a Bayesian Graphical Model.

Petri Nets

A Petri net is a modeling tool that consists of *places*, *transitions*, and *arcs* that connect places to transitions. Places can contain tokens; the number of tokens in each place gives the current state of the modeled system. Transitions model activities that can occur (that is, the transition fires), thus changing the state of the system. Transitions are allowed to fire only if they are enabled, which means that all the preconditions must be fulfilled. When a transition fires, it removes tokens from its input places and adds some at all of its output places. Using Petri nets is kind of like playing a board game with the computer. The player/tester moves the tokens and observes the state of the system to get a better understanding of the system.

Petri nets provide a visual (and with Petri net tools, interactive) method of interacting with software behaviors. Petri nets are useful for a variety of purposes but are particularly useful for modeling systems with concurrency and resource sharing.

> ### Modeling victories
>
> In many cases, the simple act of creating the model has impact. Once, when I was teaching a testing class at Microsoft, we were discussing models, and the students were drawing models of the systems they were working on. About 15 minutes into the exercise, one of the students stood up and said aloud to everyone, "I just sketched a model for the product we're about to ship and realized that there was a scenario that we probably haven't thought of before. I just tested it and found a bug!" I've used models in the past as a way to ensure that I understood a specification. A picture really is worth a thousand words sometimes.

Model-Based Testing Tools at Microsoft

Perhaps the biggest mistake I've seen testers at Microsoft make in regards to model-based testing is to dive into model-based testing tools before they understand the basics of modeling. Modeling tools often behave much the same as programming languages with which testers are familiar, but for many testers thinking of tests as models is still somewhat of a mind shift that can be difficult to take on simultaneously with learning any new toolset. In many cases, and numerous times in my own career, I have had great successes merely creating the model in the first place. Drawing a picture of how the software under test works is a powerful tool and the value of this tool cannot be underrated.

For many modelers, at some point the complexity of the models, the variations in the traversals, and the scope of what they are modeling require some help. This help typically comes in the form of tools to assist in model-based testing.

The first model-based tools at Microsoft appeared sometime around 2001. Product teams and Microsoft Research both have been involved in creating tools for model-based testing, with a few tools gaining widespread use. The variety of tools provides solutions to different types of testers and testing problems. By approaching the modeling challenge from different ends of the technology spectrum, more teams can use modeling successfully.

Spec Explorer

One powerful tool used for model-based testing at Microsoft is Spec Explorer, created by Microsoft Research in 2002, and used in Microsoft product groups since 2003. The Hypervisor team created a full model of their product using Spec Explorer and developed around 10,000 lines of model code, which they successfully used to test their core technology. (See Chapter 15, "Solving Tomorrow's Problems Today," for more on Hypervisor.) More than 20 different product groups at Microsoft used Spec Explorer over the years.

The third-generation of the tool family, Spec Explorer for Visual Studio 2008, has been transferred from Microsoft Research to the Server Tools and Business division in Microsoft. Here it is used among other areas for the testing of a large number of protocols for Microsoft's interoperability initiative. Some of the characteristics of Spec Explorer for Visual Studio are that it runs as an add-in to the Microsoft development environment and allows creating models in C#, using a rich model state. The tool supports both scenario-oriented and state-oriented modeling, and it supports event-based testing and nondeterminism (the implementation has multiple choices to react).

Perhaps the best thing about Spec Explorer is that it will soon be available to everyone as a power tool for Visual Studio and should be available before this book hits the streets. Before we look inside a Spec Explorer model, let's look at its overall design. What is the intent of Spec Explorer? What problems does it solve, and how?

Modeling with Spec Explorer

Spec Explorer can do impressive analysis and transformation of the model program that generates the FSMs. The problem with a finite state machine is that it can quickly explode in complexity. Spec Explorer manages this complexity by emitting only those states that make a difference.

The model program is the most crucial part of an advanced model-based testing application. This is the place where special modeling attributes inform the runtime of which methods drive the model logic. It's in the model program that the tester specifies the contract, and the rules of engagement that make a model program a model, such as preconditions, postconditions, and invariants.

When the model program is finished, we might have a very complex state space on our hands. To step down the amperage of this model we need a separate file that can extract only specific scenarios, specific actions, or even sequences of actions that will actually drive our tests. Indeed, one test of the model's effectiveness is to check for the presence of some known scenario. If we are generating conformance tests for some implementation, we also need to bind our model and its test cases to some binary we want to test.

Spec Explorer for Visual Studio

Figure 8-13 shows Spec Explorer in action running under Microsoft Visual Studio 2008.

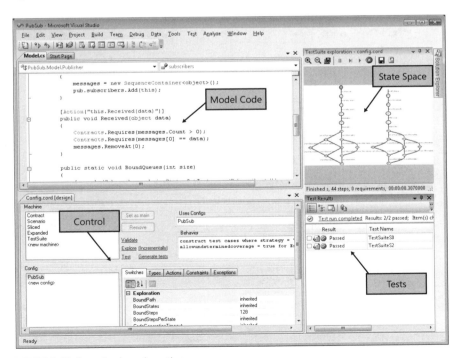

FIGURE 8-13 Spec Explorer in action.

The upper left pane contains the model program code, given in regular C# with custom attributes. The lower left part is the control center of Spec Explorer, where you can configure various parameters and select exploration goals. The upper right pane is an automatic visualization of an exploration result. The lower right part represents test cases generated from the model and then managed and executed under Visual Studio Test Tools.

To get a better idea of how to use Spec Explorer for model-based testing, consider a simple stopwatch application with the following attributes:

- The stopwatch has two display modes:
    - Current time
    - Stopper

- The watch has three buttons:
    - Switch Mode (always available)
    - Reset stopper (only available in stopper mode and when stopper is running)
    - Start/Stop stopper (only available in stopper mode)

Each button on the stopwatch represents an action, and we can query the application to know whether the stopper is running. A tester modeling the stopwatch application could create the actions and code in Listing 8-5 to describe the stopwatch model.

Listing 8-5 Stopwatch Model

```
using System; using Microsoft.Modeling;

namespace Model
{
    static class Stopwatch
    {
        static bool modeTime = true;
        static bool stopperRunning = false;

        [Action]
        static void ModeButton()
        {
            modeTime = !modeTime;
        }

        [Action]
        static void StartStopButton()
        {
            Contracts.Requires(!modeTime);
            stopperRunning = !stopperRunning;
        }
```

```
        [Action]
        static void ResetButton()
        {
            Contracts.Requires(!modeTime);
            Contracts.Requires(stopperRunning);
            stopperRunning = false;
        }

        [Action]
        static bool IsStopping()
        {
            return stopperRunning;
        }
    }
}
```

Two items in Listing 8-5 will probably be unfamiliar to most readers. The *[Action]* attribute comes from the Spec Explorer library and differentiates methods between model actions and regular C# methods, and the *Contracts* class (specifically the *Contracts.Requires* method) is used to enforce preconditions. Put differently, when you generate a finite state machine from this model, Spec Explorer will scan the model's state and execute any *Action* method if it is enabled in that state.

The configuration file is the core of modeling with Spec Explorer. The configuration represents a set of switches and parameters to control exploration, state graph display, and testing. Figure 8-14 shows the configuration file in design view.

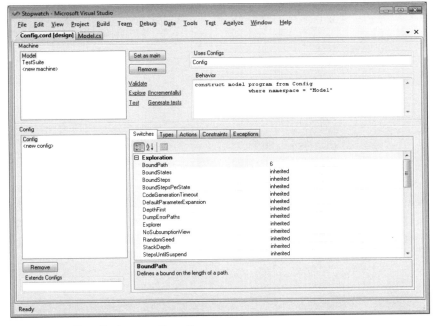

FIGURE 8-14 Spec Explorer configuration.

From here, a tester can create a model visualization, as shown in Figure 8-15, or generate test code to traverse the model.

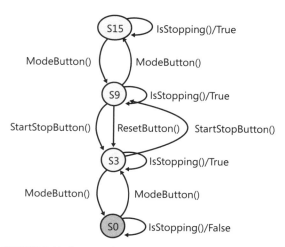

FIGURE 8-15 Stopwatch model generated by Spec Explorer.

Testers can also explore and test the model directly, create scenarios to extract "slices" from the full model, or continue to change dozens of other permutations of the model. By using the model, testers can develop testing strategies and model key scenarios (especially when they become more apparent upon viewing the graphical representation of the model).

In the model configuration file, testers can specify a strategy for the test suite. One example of a Spec Explorer strategy is in Listing 8-6.

Listing 8-6 Short Tests Strategy for Stopwatch

```
machine TestSuite() : Config
{
    construct test cases where strategy = "shorttests"
    for Model
}
```

A tester can then generate (and run!) tests from the model, or can continue to add constraints and other configuration details to the model. Model-based testing and Spec Explorer are certainly a different way to approach testing than many testers are used to, but the results so far at Microsoft have been remarkable. Figure 8-16 contains examples of tests generated from the stopwatch model using Spec Explorer.

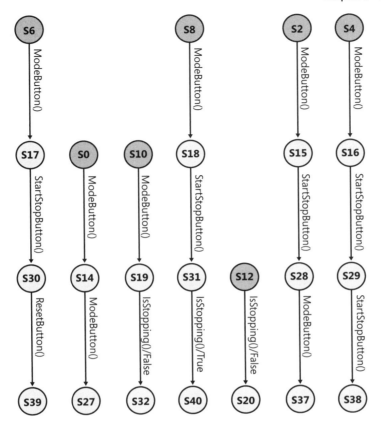

FIGURE 8-16 Generated tests for the stopwatch model.

A Language and Engine

Another successful MBT implementation in use at Microsoft also simply uses the Common Language Runtime (CLR) for language and an *engine* to exercise the entire model graph at run time. The difference with Spec Explorer is that the engine, in this case, uses the CLR for execution, too.

With this simple, yet powerful solution, testers can create models quickly. As in Spec Explorer, creating the models is similar to object-oriented programming with which most testers are familiar with using. Testers can work with multiple models, models can inherit from other models, models can nest, and models can call other models. Writing models feels like working with a programming language and feels natural for those who use it. There are no separate compilers or tools needed. Testers just write code using custom C# attributes to define the model behavior and run an execution engine to interpret those annotations. Because the models are based on annotations only, it is seamless to integrate modeled and nonmodeled tests.

The teams using this particular modeling tool are able to model quickly on a small scale, and then grow the scope of their modeling while integrating with other, sequenced tests as needed.

Listing 8-7 shows a model written in C# using attributes to describe the model, and Listing 8-8 shows code for a test that runs this model.

Listing 8-7 Modeling with C# Attributes

```
[Model]
public class AppModel : Model
{
    [ModelVariable]
    public bool _running = false;
    public bool _hello = false;
    public bool _world = false;

    [ModelAction]
    [ModelRequirement(Variable = "_running", value = false)]
    public void StartApp()
    {
        //start application
        _running = true;
    }

    [ModelAction]
    [ModelRequirement(_running = true)]
    public void SayHello()
    {
        buttonHello.Press();
        _hello = true;
    }

    [ModelAction]
    [ModelRequirement(_running = true)]
    public void SayWorld()
    {
        buttonWorld.Press();
        _world = true;
    }

    [ModelAction]
    [ModelRequirement(_running = true)]
    public void Clear()
    {
        buttonClear.Press();
        _hello = false;
        _world = false;
    }
}
```

Listing 8-8 Running the Model

```
class ApplicationTest
{
    class ApplicationTest
    {
        static void Main()
        {
            ApplicationTest test = new ApplicationTest();
            test.MainTest();
        }

        public void MainTest()
        {
            ApplicationModel app = new ApplicationModel();
            ModelEngine engine = new ModelEngine(app);
            engine.Run();
        }
    }
}
```

Spec Explorer and Windows 7

In the upcoming release of the Windows operating system, known as Windows 7, the problem of providing a new managed service account class in the Active Directory directory service for automatic password management and simplified Service Principal Name (SPN) management was addressed by a new feature: service accounts.

The feature implements a rich set of APIs for management of this new type of account. Additionally, it supports security-related system functions such as account logons. The resulting test matrix of APIs, order of calls, and parameter permutations is very complex, so it is easy to miss test cases in traditional automation. Model-based testing was a good solution because account state and API calls could be easily represented by a finite state machine.

There is a large selection of tools available for MBT. We chose Spec Explorer because of features such as C#-driven model development, integration with Visual Studio, and support for model slicing (using scenarios). A first model was created by using the example model shipped with Spec Explorer. Later the model was expanded by adding new states and transitions as well as additional parameter permutations. With Spec Explorer, you can add executable code as implementation of state transitions. Our model generated an XML file of test cases that could later be consumed by a traditional test execution engine.

Applying MBT for service accounts was very successful. Tests generated using MBT gave us greater coverage with less testing effort. Also, the models were easily expandable. It also helped us find interesting design issues very early in the development cycle.

One important lesson we learned is that, as a good modeling practice, we should start by modeling the most basic functionality and incrementally expand on it; this makes correction of modeling errors much easier. Following are some of the perspectives we gained by applying MBT versus traditional test design:

- MBT gives a different point of view on design of a feature.

- Tests are generated automatically with assurance of full coverage of the model in least steps.

- Extending the model is easy and takes advantage of previously generated tests.

To me, using MBT was fun and a great learning experience. It was easy to understand the model and gave me confidence about the extent of my test coverage. Interesting bugs were also found including design bugs, input validation bugs, and scenario bugs. I'll definitely use MBT for my next feature.

—*Sasha Hanganu, SDET, Windows Security*

Modeling Tips

I have observed many test teams add model-based testing to their arsenal of test techniques. I have seen teams succeed, and I have seen teams fail to adopt model-based testing successfully. Some of the most common errors I have observed when teams adopt model-based testing are the following:

- **Too much modeling**   Teams that try to model everything end up testing nothing. The most important item to keep in mind when beginning to model is to start with small models of simple features. Remember that not everything is a candidate for modeling, and large models are difficult to maintain.

- **Modeling doesn't replace other testing**   MBT is one tool of many that you will use to test. Teams that look to MBT as a silver bullet soon find that it isn't. Develop a test strategy that uses all of the tools in the test toolbox effectively.

- **Only model what you can verify**   Random monkey tests can be interesting, but the bugs they find are extremely difficult to debug and diagnose. Good models include verification at every step that confirms that the current state conforms to the expected state.

- **Design carefully**   When a tester makes a mistake or two writing a typical automated test, it just causes a test or two to report false results. When a tester makes a mistake creating a model, an entire suite of tests can break. The design of the model is critical and is worthy of extra caution and review—especially as the team is learning modeling.

Summary

Any sort of modeling is good, but accompanying models with tests generated from models is powerful. Models help testers understand (and explain) complex systems, they help manage risk, and they help find bugs.

Generated test cases from models can do some interesting things, things human testers might not think of or have the patience to do. This unexpected behavior in the model generates unexpected behavior in the application (and this is good for testers). For example, a test of 100 randomly generated steps might or might not (but usually does) find a bug that's deeply buried in the tested application. If you were as thorough as the random walk that generated these 100 steps, you, too, might find the bug, but why trouble yourself when, with the proper instructions, the computer can randomly walk the tested app day and night until it finds a crash?

Model-based tests, of course, do much more than random walks through an application. Microsoft teams have used model-based tests in conjunction with traditional test automation to test many features and applications effectively. Teams that are successful using modeling also understand that modeling is just one tool of many test tools in a tester's toolbox.

Recommended Reading and Tools

- *Model-Based Software Testing and Analysis with C#* by Jonathan Jacky, Margus Veanes, Colin Campbell, and Wolfram Schulte

- *Practical Model-Based Testing: A Tools Approach* by Mark Utting and Bruno Legeard

- *Testing Object Oriented Systems* by Robert Binder

- Spec Explorer, *http://research.microsoft.com/projects/specexplorer/*

- NModel Modeling tool, *http://www.codeplex.com/NModel*

Part III
Test Tools and Systems

Chapter 9
Managing Bugs and Test Cases

Alan Page

Before I came to Microsoft, I was employee number 17 at a small software company just down the road from the Microsoft corporate campus. It was there that I first learned about the challenges of software testing, and it was there where I first realized how much those challenges fit my passions and strengths. It was also my first exposure to a bug tracking system. Our system solved some problems for our team but had a few issues of its own. I was the author of this system, and as I've discovered over the years, there was a lot I didn't know about managing bugs in 1994.

Up until this point, as far as I can remember, we had tracked our bugs by using a combination of notes on whiteboards, color-coded sticky notes, and various e-mail messages. Of course, in this situation, organizing the data in one place would have obvious benefits, but we needed our system to do a few more things. We needed to assign bugs to specific people. We needed a way to provide additional information about the bug—things like the steps needed to reproduce the bug, or the version of the software where the bug occurred. We needed to know when and how bugs were fixed so that the test team (me) could verify that the fix worked. In addition, we needed reporting so that we could monitor the number and types of bugs reported and fixed. My bug tracking system supported all of this—but, unfortunately, not much more. In the end, it provided good information and helped the engineering team, but it was inflexible and slow. I hear it was replaced less than a year after I left to join Microsoft.

Microsoft, of course, had a *real* bug tracking system. The system was built by an internal team and was named after a popular brand of insect spray. It used a Microsoft SQL Server database for storing bug information, and the front-end user interface contained fields I had never thought of when designing my system. I entered my first bug at Microsoft in this system (as well, I'm sure, as my tenth and my hundredth). This system, too, had its deficiencies, and by the time I had hit my five-year anniversary of working at Microsoft, most of the company had moved to yet another bug tracking system. This system, also developed internally, was named *Product Studio*. Product Studio has far fewer limitations than its predecessor had and is highly customizable. As of this writing, it is still widely used across Microsoft, although many teams have begun moving their bug tracking systems to the tools in Microsoft Visual Studio Team System (which, incidentally, is based largely on Product Studio).

This chapter contains information, discussions, and examples of bug tracking and test case management tools generally in use at Microsoft, along with some lessons learned and practical tips based on years of use by thousands of test teams and testers.

The Bug Workflow

Bugs and test cases comprise two of the largest repositories of artifacts created by almost any test team. In the simplest terms, test cases describe the intent of the test process, and bugs describe much of the result of those test cases. Of course, many other factors make up the full definition of these two terms, and in this chapter, I hope to expand on these thoughts.

The *bug workflow* describes the process, participants, and path of a bug report as it proceeds from creation to closure. Figure 9-1 shows the many paths and decisions included in the lifetime of a bug.

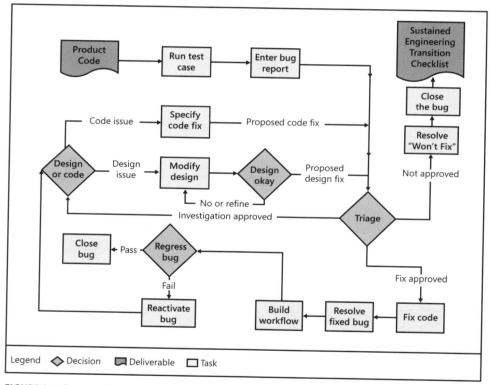

FIGURE 9-1 Bug workflow.

Bug Tracking

One of the biggest artifacts created by testers is bugs. More accurately put, programmers create the bugs, but it is the testers who examine the code and application to discover the exact sequence or combination of steps that turns up an error. Over the course of testing a product, test teams can discover thousands of bugs. Some of these bugs relate to each other, and some might even be the same issue reported by different people. The steps to determine a resolution to a bug can go through many changes and have a number of owners. A vital practice that any test team must use is a bug tracking system, along with a pragmatic and common set of guidelines for using the system.

A Bug's Life

A software bug begins its "life" as code or design or some other artifact of the development process. Similar to the riddle "If a tree falls in the forest with no one around, does it make a sound?" no one might know the bug exists until the code or design is exercised by someone, usually a customer, developer, or tester.

A bug can be found or recorded in a variety of ways, but if a tester runs a test case that finds a bug, the tester usually enters a bug report directly into the tracking system. The *triage team* regularly reviews all bugs, prioritizes them, and assigns them to the appropriate person to investigate or fix the issue. After the bug is fixed or the design is modified, the triage team might review the change before it is accepted and either allow the change or reject it for additional rework. On occasion, some changes might be determined to be too risky and are postponed to a later release. It is not uncommon for a fix that seems like it "should be trivial" to end up as a huge work item that can destabilize the entire feature area.

Having a central group of people who review both bugs and the fixes for those bugs ensures that bug fixes are implemented with the appropriate priority. Some bugs can be resolved as "won't fix"—meaning that the bug is acknowledged but will not be fixed—or postponed—meaning that the bug will be fixed in a future release. Sustained engineering and product support teams review bugs resolved in this manner. Many "won't fix" and postponed bugs end up as subjects in Microsoft Knowledge Base articles. Product support teams also have access to bug data for the products they support and often refer to this information.

After a bug fix is approved, the developer makes the appropriate changes and integrates them into the application. At this point, the original bug is resolved in the bug database, and it is the tester's job to verify that the change fixes the original problem. If the bug still occurs (that is, the fix didn't work), the bug is reactivated and assigned back to the developer. Otherwise, the tester closes the bug—but the bug's life does not end at this point. Fixed bugs are regularly analyzed for root cause or other relationships. Bug data remains relevant and useful for years beyond the day the bug is found.

Although from one angle bugs can be viewed as "something that went wrong," the bug life cycle regularly functions as the pulse of the engineering process. Bug reports provide information on the remaining work, risk, and the overall status of the project. In fact, many companies (and groups in Microsoft, for that matter) use the bug tracking system as a project management system, including work items right alongside the defects. The advantage of using a bug tracking system in this way is that it is simple to see all work (both feature development and bug fixing) needed in a specific area or to see all work assigned to a specific developer or group of developers. Table 9-1 and Table 9-2 show examples of the different ways a team can view bugs. As with any system containing large amounts of data, the ability to view the data in different ways is advantageous to good product and workflow planning. Seeing, for example, the number of bugs assigned to each developer on the team along with the bugs in each feature area can aid managing bugs in the development team.

 Note More than 15 million bug and project management entries were created in Microsoft systems in 2007.

TABLE 9-1 Bugs by Assignment

Assigned to	Number of active	Number of resolved
Adam Carter	7	2
Michael Pfeiffer	5	0
Kim Akers	11	0
Chris Preston	4	3
Nader Issa	0	7
Hao Chen	0	4
Minesh Lad	0	2
Ben Smith	0	9

TABLE 9-2 Bugs by Area

Area	Number of active	Number of resolved
Core engine	10	7
User interface	6	3
Web controls	16	16

Attributes of a Bug Tracking System

A bug tracking system is most often the first tool adopted or implemented on a new test team. Odds are that if you are reading this book, you are actively using a bug tracking system. Successful systems tend to include a few important attributes. These attributes are what separates sticky notes and worksheets from mature systems that are effectively and efficiently used by all members of the engineering team.

Ease of use is one of the most important elements in a bug tracking system. Individual testers use the system to enter bugs. Test management performs various queries against the bug data, and engineering management often runs another set of completely different queries against the bug data. Entering and viewing data in the system must be simple and efficient.

Configurability is also an important attribute of any bug tracking system. Different teams often have different needs and expectations when tracking bugs. The ability to add fields to contain additional information as well as the ability to choose which fields are required or optional in the system are essential. Some product teams at Microsoft, for example, require only that the Title, Description, Severity, and Revision Number fields are completed to save the bug report. Other teams choose to require a little (or a lot) of additional information when bugs are entered in the system.

Reliability is another crucial attribute of a bug tracking system. As one of the most used pieces of software on an engineering team, these systems must be available without inter-ruption, 24 hours a day, 7 days a week. At Microsoft, the internal IT department maintains the hardware and SQL systems that support all of the bug databases for Microsoft software. Dedicated hardware with backup power, data backups, and quick support turnaround has led to little downtime in the ability to report and act in the bug workflow.

Other attributes to consider include the following:

- **Bug notification**   The system should have the ability to notify engineers when bugs are assigned to them or if the bug changes. At Microsoft, automated e-mail systems that pull data directly from the database are the most used type of notification system, but stand-alone applications that talk directly to the SQL back end and communicate changes in real time are used as well.

- **Interoperability**   The ability to easily pull bug data from the system and display it in a worksheet, Web application, or custom control is highly beneficial.

- **External user access**   Customers or partner companies sometimes need access to view or edit bugs and the ability to share bugs through a proxy.

Why Write a Bug Report?

Bug reports are accurate, long-living records of software failures and their resolutions. On many teams, it might seem much easier to take care of bugs in e-mail or hallway conversa-tions, but there are significant advantages to recording all bugs in a bug tracking system. At Microsoft, root cause analysis of bugs is common. Other groups of bugs might be analyzed by looking at the engineering process where the bugs were introduced and the engineer-ing process where they were detected to determine how effectively bugs are found during different engineering processes. This type of analysis is usually referred to as *defect removal efficiency* (DRE). Both root cause analysis and DRE are much more effective when all bugs are recorded.

Bug reports often become historical references used by the teams who develop future versions of the product, sustained engineering teams, and product support. These teams rely on the information contained in the bug reports to understand the product, to influence their decisions, or to help customers.

On rare occasion, bug reports can become a legal defense. I know of one case in which a noncritical, yet serious bug was found late in the product cycle. Meetings involving several executives and legal counsel were held, but in the end the bug was postponed and was scheduled to be fixed shortly after release. As feared, a customer found the bug and filed a lawsuit. Fortunately for Microsoft, the documentation contained in the bug report was sufficient to prove there was no malicious intent and to have the case dismissed.

Anatomy of a Bug Report

No matter how much data you track, or how many fields your bug tracking system requires, a few key items differentiate a highly actionable bug report from data that might lead you in the wrong direction or data that might be erroneously ignored. Table 9-3 lists key features of a good bug report.

TABLE 9-3 Features of a Good Bug Report

Feature	Description
Title	At Microsoft, the bug title is perhaps the most important (or most used) bit of information in the bug report. Casual users of the system scan titles to get an idea of the types of bugs in the product or in a particular area. The title is also the most searched field in the bug database and is a quick way to find similar bugs or bugs in a particular area that cannot be tracked by using any other fields. Possibly the most important use of the title is review by the feature or product triage team. A title, in the space of 80 or so characters, needs to provide an accurate summary of the overall bug report. It needs to be descriptive, yet not overly descriptive—something that when viewed quickly gives just the right amount of information to the audience. At Microsoft, many testers quickly fill out all fields of the bug report but take extra time to carefully word a title for their bug. Some example bug titles and evaluations are as follows: ❑ Program crash—*too short* ❑ When running many instances of the program at the same time, a crash occurs in one of the dialogs—*both wordy and vague* ❑ Program crash in Settings dialog box under low-memory conditions—*specific, accurate, and tells enough of the story to understand the bug from the report*
Description	The description answers all of the questions not obvious from the title. It includes a summary of the bug, customer impact information, and expected results versus actual results. Noting actual and expected results clarifies understanding of the proper behavior of the system among all interested parties.

Feature	Description
Status	Bug status is either "Active," "Resolved," or "Closed" and reflects the work that needs to be done with the bug. The status for new bugs is Active. Bugs remain Active until a resolution is found—at which time the resolution becomes Resolved. After a bug is resolved, testers verify the fix and either reset the status to Active (if the fix didn't work) or set the status to Closed (if the original issue is, in fact, fixed).
Version number	All bugs should include the version of the software where the bug was found. At Microsoft, most products are rebuilt every day—in some cases even more often. Knowing the exact version where a bug was found is a huge help in reproducing bugs or verifying fixes.
Feature area	Most teams at Microsoft require that bugs include the area or subarea of the product where the bug is. For example, the Microsoft Windows bug database might have an area for file system bugs and subareas that include NTFS, FAT, or other areas relevant to the file system. Accurate information on the feature areas and subareas is beneficial when examining bugs across the product to determine which areas might have risk or might need additional time to understand and fix larger numbers of bugs.
Reproduction steps	Reproduction steps are often included in the description, but some systems separate this vital component of the bug report. *Repro steps*, as they are often referred to at Microsoft, are the steps that can be repeated by anyone who is involved in the bug workflow. One of the most frustrating and time-wasting experiences for a tester is a bug where the developer says, "It doesn't reproduce on my computer." A good set of repro steps doesn't guarantee that this situation will never happen, but it does make the possibility much less likely. Repro steps also must be as concise as possible. Although a bug may have been found in 10 steps, it is important to take the time to see if any of the steps are irrelevant, and if the bug will reproduce in fewer steps. Reducing the number of steps improves the chance of quickly isolating the root cause of the bug and increases the chance of making the proper fix the first time.
Assignment	The Assigned To field is required in all bug systems at Microsoft, but the usage varies from team to team. Many teams assign the bug to the developer who owns the area where the bug was found (if known). Other teams prefer that the bug is assigned to "Active" (*Active* is the default Assigned To name in Product Studio) and rely on the triage team to assign the bug to the appropriate person. Each bug is assigned to exactly one person at a time. It is the responsibility of the bug owner to address any issues (that is, fix the bug) or to reassign the bug.

Feature	Description
Severity	Severity describes the impact of the bug on the customer, the development process, and on the entire bug workflow. Severity factors in impact, frequency, and reproducibility of the bug and is usually a value from 1 to 4, where 1 is the highest severity. Most bug databases at Microsoft use the following severity definition: 1. Bug causes system crash or data loss. 2. Bug causes major functionality or other severe problems; product crashes in obscure cases. 3. Bug causes minor functionality problems, may affect fit and finish. 4. Bug contains typos, unclear wording, or error messages in low-visibility fields.
Customer impact	It is valuable to include a customer impact description in the bug report. Customer impact descriptions include how the bug affects the user and how the problem will affect customer scenarios and requirements. Items to consider when writing a customer impact description include the following: ❑ Determine the customer scenarios and requirements that the bug affects. ❑ Determine the frequency or likelihood of the customer encountering the issue. ❑ Adjust the Severity field to match the customer impact.
Environment	It is important to clearly describe the conditions of the test environment and the steps necessary to reproduce that environment as part of the bug report. You might even need to describe what conditions did not exist or were not attempted. This makes it easier for the others to find and reproduce the bug. Environment details can include the following: ❑ Hardware specifications and configuration ❑ System, component, and application versions ❑ Tools and processes employed ❑ Related connectivity and data configurations ❑ Roles, permissions, and other applicable settings ❑ Description of environmental factors that have been eliminated

Feature	Description
Resolution	This field is filled in when the bug is resolved. Nearly all Microsoft products use the following choices for the Resolution field. ❏ **Fixed** The underlying error was fixed. ❏ **Not repro** The error could not be reproduced. This typically happens when the reproduction steps were incomplete or the environment is different between the tester's and developer's computers. ❏ **Duplicate** When two separate bugs describe the same issue, one of the bugs (usually the one opened later) is resolved as duplicate. See the sidebar titled "A Note on Duplicate Bugs" later in this chapter for more information on duplicate bugs. ❏ **By Design** Sometimes, what appears to be a bug actually isn't a bug. Instead, the behavior is the intent of the design. For example, when I run Windows Calculator and press 2 / 0, the output window of Calculator reads "Cannot divide by zero" (this is expected). Then, none of the number keys work until I press the C button to clear the data. Some people might consider this to be a bug, but it's "By Design." This resolution has lead to the famous tester catch phrase "It's not a bug, it's a feature." ❏ **Postponed** This resolution is given to bugs that will be fixed in a future release of the product.

Additional fields in common use in a bug database include the following:

- **How Found**   What testing activity found the bug?

- **Issue Type**   Is the bug a coding bug, a design issue, a documentation issue, and so forth?

- **Bug Type**   Bug types might be security, performance, functionality, stress, and so forth.

- **Source**   Who found the bug? That is, did test, development, an internal user, a beta user, or someone else find the bug?

Figure 9-2 shows an example of a bug tracking system in Visual Studio Team System.

FIGURE 9-2 Bug tracking in Visual Studio Team System.

Avoid adding too many fields to your bug database. It is tempting to add extra fields every month or so to track the "cool new metric of the month." Keeping the system simple makes it much easier for everyone on the team, as well as other teams, to use the system consistently. Specialized fields in the system can be useful, but too many fields can cause confusion or cause mistakes to occur when working with bugs. If there are too many required fields, engineers might be tempted to fix bugs outside of the system, in which case none of the bug data will be captured for future analysis.

Bug Triage

Triage is a term taken from the medical industry and is used by every single product team at Microsoft. In emergency rooms, the triage process is used to determine where to focus medical resources first. In other words, it's the method used to determine that the head injury needs to be handled before the broken finger, and the broken finger needs to be dealt with before the person with the rash from poison ivy.

It's not a bug, it's a feature!

At some point, just about everyone who has worked on a software project has heard the expression "It's not a bug, it's a feature." This is said mostly when something that appears to be a bug is actually the intended behavior of the software. Sometimes the bug is reported because the tester doesn't understand the design. Other times, the tester argues that the design is in fact wrong. In most cases, however, the phrase is used with sarcasm to describe something that seems like a bug to everyone except, perhaps, the person who created the design in the first place.

One particular day, I spent several hours arguing with a developer about a "by design" bug. I thought his resolution was more a result of laziness and apathy than a sincere design decision. Eventually, I think we both gave up and decided to go home for the night. I was walking through the parking lot trying to remember where I parked (a frequent occurrence after long days at work) and couldn't help but laugh when I saw an old Volkswagen Beetle (or "Bug") parked in one of the stalls. The car was mostly navy blue but had a yellow cover on the engine with a vanity plate centered on it. The vanity plate read "FEATURE."

At Microsoft, the triage concept is applied to incoming bugs instead of incoming patients. Triage happens at all levels of the product. The primary responsibility of the triage team is to be decision makers and to ensure that the bug workflow is proceeding as expected. The triage team consists of a cross-discipline representation (usually development, test, and program management) of decision makers from the team that owns a given product or feature area. As the decision makers for the initial path of the bug workflow for any given bug, they can assign the bug to a developer for a fix, assign the bug for more investigation, or resolve the bug back to the originator as duplicate, postponed, external, by design, or some other resolution. The triage team might also review incoming bugs for duplicate bugs or group together bugs that seem related. The main thing they accomplish is the prioritization of bugs. Some bugs need to be fixed right away, while other bugs can be fixed later in the product cycle or even in a later release. Another class of bugs won't be fixed at all. These are all decisions that the triage team makes.

It is essential that the quality of the bug report be such that the triage team can make the correct decisions and ensure proper routing and prioritization of the bug reports. On some teams, the person entering the bug into the system records bug priority, and then the triage team later adjusts the priority. Some teams choose to leave the priority field blank on entry and rely on the triage team to assign initial priorities for all bugs. Bug priority is typically set using the following values:

1. **Must fix**   Fix this bug as soon as possible. Bug is blocking further progress in this area.

2. **Should fix**   This bug should be fixed soon, before product release, before the end of the milestone, or before the next iteration begins, as appropriate.

3. **Fix if time**   This is a somewhat trivial bug and can be postponed depending on the stage of product development.

It can be difficult to prioritize all bugs on a three-point scale. Some teams use additional levels of priority or use additional fields in the bug database to represent a more granular viewpoint of priority. Any priority system can be effective as long as the bugs are consistently evaluated for priority and acted upon appropriately.

As products get closer to shipping, most of the triage happens at higher levels of project management. Group or division level managers review the incoming bugs and make decisions on whether to fix each active bug. The closer to release date the team gets, the higher the criteria or *bar* is for approving bugs to be fixed. There is always some amount of risk associated with making a code change, so triage teams become hesitant to make all but the most critical fixes as the release date approaches.

The goal of the triage team late in the product cycle is to help the team successfully reach zero bugs. Of course, anyone who has ever worked on a software product knows that all software ships with a few bugs. Microsoft products aren't any different. Every product we have worked on has shipped with known bugs. The zero bugs concept really means that there are *zero bugs that we know about that will stop us from shipping this product*. Incoming bugs are triaged, and then are assigned to a developer to fix, are postponed, or are resolved as won't (ever) fix. Eventually, as the bar for fixing gets higher and higher, the active bug count hits zero. Sometimes, this is called *zero bug bounce*. If there is still a bit of work to do, or if recent changes cause other bugs, or if new bugs are discovered, the bug count *bounces* from zero to a positive number. Eventually, the count reaches zero, and the product ships. At this stage, the product still has bugs, but there are zero bugs that the triage team has recognized that should keep the product from shipping.

Common Mistakes in Bug Reports

A bug tracking system can lose much of its value when used incorrectly or inappropriately. Although the benefits of having a system far outweigh the pitfalls, it is important to keep those hazards in mind when preparing guidelines for the team or educating them on the proper use of the system. Many mistakes are simply failures to follow the features of a good bug report listed in Table 9-3. Some other interesting mistakes that happen often in bug reports are e-mail discussions, *bug morphing*, and multiple bugs in the same report. Table 9-4 lists examples of these types of mistakes.

TABLE 9-4 **Common Mistakes in Bug Reports**

Mistake	Examples
E-mail discussions	10/28/2007 5:38 PM Opened by Jim Hance Application crashes when opening multiple instances. Doesn't block testing, but should be fixed. 8/28/2007 5:53 PM Assigned by David Pelton to Jim Hance I'll fix this soon. Does the error happen on the second instance, or after more? Do you think this is related to the new manager? 8/28/2007 6:15 PM Assigned by Jim Hance to David Pelton Ha ha. The bug happens on the second instance (you could have tried it first). Nothing to do with the manager, but it could be related to the office move. 8/28/2007 6:34 PM Assigned by David Pelton to Jim Hance Now *that's* funny. By the way—if you're heading home soon, can I get a lift? 8/28/2007 6:41 PM Assigned by Jim Hance to David Pelton Sure thing—I'll be by in about 15 minutes. Don't forget to assign this back to me.

E-mail and the bug system are the two most used tools by most engineers at Microsoft, and it is not surprising that the two tools sometimes converge.

A much larger audience than just the tester and developer working on the bug use the bug reports. Any information not directly related to the bug report should not be included in the report.

Bug morphing	9/17/2007 9:34 AM Opened by Don Hall I am unable to print from our Application. Environment conditions and repro are listed below. ... 9/17/2007 9:49 AM Assigned by Ann Beebe to Don Hall I looked at the environment information, and you missed configuring the %PRINT_INFO% variable. This should clear it up. However, while looking at your notes, I found a different issue that I want to track. There are some layout problems with the Print dialog box that need to be addressed. 9/17/2007 10:37 AM Assigned by Don Hall to Ann Beebe I have updated the setup scripts we use to set that variable, and I have changed the title of this bug report to reflect the layout issues. Thanks.

Bug morphing is the phenomenon that occurs when a bug changes from one issue to a completely separate issue within the same bug report. Sometimes it happens quickly, and sometimes the morphing is drawn out over days or months. Regardless of the situation, bug morphing is never a good idea.

Bugs that have morphed are difficult to analyze for root cause. They also can cause confusion with product support or sustained engineering when they are reviewing product issues or searching to see if an issue a customer is seeing is caused by a known defect. If a bug begins to change in a bug report, it is crucial to stop and open a new bug for the new issue.

Mistake	Examples
Multiple bugs	8/28/2007 6:13 PM Opened by Jeff Ressler

While running build verification tests on the layout engine, I discovered the following errors:

1. Manually resizing the application window to a size less than 200×180 results in overlapped controls.
2. Maximizing the window draws two of the controls off of the screen boundaries.
3. The Configuration dialog box text is misspelled—it reads "configruation."

If testers are in a hurry or busy, they might group somewhat-related bugs in one bug report. Despite the extra effort involved in avoiding this problem, multiple bugs in one report is never a good idea. As with the problems listed previously, using one bug report for multiple bugs causes problems with other customers of the bug report.

A few of the problems with this practice are as follows:

❑ The priority of the individual bugs cannot be set separately.

❑ The resolution of the individual bugs cannot be set. If the triage determines that one of the bugs should be deferred to a different release, there is no way to notate this.

❑ Although the bugs seem to be in similar areas, they might need to be assigned to different developers.

❑ At some point, someone might analyze product bugs for root cause. There is likely a separate root cause for each of the bugs in a multiple-bug report.

A Note on Duplicate Bugs

When I talk about bug data—or potential uses for bug data—one thing I typically mention is my opinion on duplicate bugs. With nearly every test team I have worked on, entering a duplicate bug is considered a "bad thing" for a tester to do. Some teams even use fancy algorithms that calculate ratios between found bugs, fixed bugs, and resolution type to come up with a magic tester efficiency number.

I suppose duplicate bugs seem bad because they are potentially a waste of someone's time.

The nerve of Bobby Tester entering a bug that Jane entered so clearly just a few days before—now someone has to take the time to resolve that bug as duplicate. So what if they test different areas of the product and didn't realize that the bug was actually in a shared component. Bad Bobby, Bad Bobby!

I don't think entering duplicate bugs is bad at all—in fact, I think worrying about them is bad. Let me tell you why.

If there is any notion of a negative consequence for a tester entering a duplicate bug, that tester will err on the side of not entering a bug at all if he is worried about entering a duplicate bug. Think about this: Say I find a high-impact bug. I take some time to look and see whether the bug is known, and I find one that *might be* similar. If there is a negative consequence for entering the bug, I am more inclined to not enter the bug. Ideally, I'll make a note of the bug and verify that it fixes the problem I just found, or I'll e-mail the owner and get her opinion, but in many cases, a tester simply thinks, "This is probably a duplicate," and moves on to something else even if it means missing a potentially important issue.

The idea that entering duplicate bugs wastes somebody's time is a myth. Most testers know their own areas pretty well but might not know as much about the rest of the system. After I find a bug, it might take me 20 minutes to dig around and see whether any of the other bugs in the area are similar or possibly the same as the one I just found. If I were to just enter the bug and let the triage team (or whoever examines the incoming bugs) look at it, chances are that they would know if it was a duplicate in far less than 20 minutes. The only time wasted was my own.

Who cares if a tester enters a duplicate bug? The information in one bug report often doesn't provide enough information to diagnose the problem. Another report on the same issue might lead the developer to the root cause or to a more efficient fix. Most bug database systems have a way to mark bugs as "related" (or "duplicate") and retain a link between the bugs. In my opinion, more bug data is always better, and duplicate bugs are a necessary by-product of supplying that data.

Using the Data

One of the things that management seems to love the most about a database full of bugs is the reports they can generate to represent the variety of information available in the system. No magic formula or query tells whether your project is ready to ship or if it is in trouble, but there are countless methods of examining the data. Teams at Microsoft examine bug data in hundreds of different permutations. Some examples of potential bug metrics to examine along with potential uses are listed in Table 9-5.

TABLE 9-5 Metrics and Purpose

Metric	Metric use
Total fixed found / total bugs fixed	The ratio of bugs that are fixed versus other resolutions. Early in the product cycle, expect to find more bugs than the number that are resolved; later in the ship cycle, expect bugs to be resolved faster than they are found. This metric can also tell you how to build a prediction model of when you will hit zero bugs.
Total bugs per language	View of cost involved in testing a localized version. This metric can provide clues to a more effective localization effort.
Bug find rate over time	Too high or too low can be concerning; spikes should be explained.
Bug fix rate over time	Percentage of bugs found that are being fixed. Percentage should go down toward ship as the triage bar rises.
Bugs by code area	Sorted list of functions with the most reported bugs can influence where additional testing might be needed.
Bugs found by functional area	Percentage of bugs found by test team, by internal users, by development, by product support, and by external beta testers can help influence test strategy.
Bugs by severity	Expect to see severity 1 and severity 2 bug find rates drop as the project progresses, while percentage of severity 3 and lower bugs increases. That is, expect to find the serious bugs earlier in the product cycle.
Where found	This measure can vary depending on the type of product being tested. Understanding where in the product the bugs have been found can reveal risky areas of the product.
How found	Knowing how the bug was found can aid in root cause analysis and implementation of defect prevention techniques.
When introduced	Knowing at what stage of product development the problem was introduced (for example, specification, design, coding, bug fixing) can influence where defect prevention techniques need to be implemented.
Bug reactivation rate	Can be a good indicator of the quality of fixes that Dev provides; this often increases toward the end of the project when the bug fix rate is at its highest.
Bugs opened by testing activity	Understand which types of testing are finding bugs. Activities might include exploratory testing, structured testing, prerelease testing, test case development, configuration testing, printer testing, automated testing, general product use, beta tests, each test pass, acceptance testing, and so forth.

Metric	Metric use
Average time to resolve	Track development team's level of responsiveness to posted bugs.
Average time to close	Track general responsiveness to bugs, or the time it takes a bug to progress through the bug workflow. Ideally, bugs are quickly fixed by development, and the bug fix is verified by test promptly.

Certainly, as with most metrics, representing bug data as a graph can be advantageous. Figure 9-3 and Figure 9-4 are examples of bug trend information represented in a simple graph format. At Microsoft, these sorts of charts are sent within product teams on a regular basis as a method of quickly communicating relevant information related to bugs.

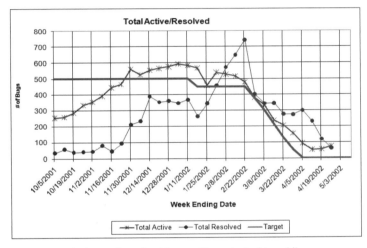

FIGURE 9-3 Active and resolved bugs with projected trend line.

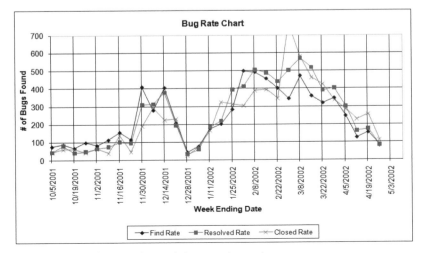

FIGURE 9-4 Bug find, resolve, and close rate by week.

How Not to Use the Data: Bugs as Performance Metrics

It is tempting to use bug data to measure tester performance. Testers are expected to find bugs, so you might expect good testers to find higher volumes of bugs. Many managers collect and track bug data for performance management. However, alone the gross number of bugs reported metric provides very little valuable information with regard to individual performance. There are simply too many variables in bug counts, especially when comparing between peers, such as the following:

- Feature complexity
- Developer ability
- Specification completeness
- Bug prevention versus bug finding
- Timeliness of reporting

Additionally, if anyone intends to use specific bug counts as a performance metric, that person must qualify the parameters of the measurement and be prepared to address questions, such as follows:

- Does the number of bugs reported have to be of a particular severity/priority? If yes, what is the breakdown?
- Do functional bugs count equally as superficial user interface type bugs do?
- Will spending time (one or more days) tracking down a critical issue (such as data loss, memory leak) that gets resolved result in not meeting expectations or indicate poor performance? If yes, what is the team policy for collaborating with developers to assist in troubleshooting these issues?
- Is bug quality a factor? If yes, how are the specific factors for bug quality determined in the group, and what are the team averages? Are the averages the target goal? What specific quality factors would exceed expectations for the goal?
- What is the minimum number of bugs per measured iteration? What is the number of bugs a tester needs to produce to exceed expectations?

Finding a high number of bugs can indicate that the tester is doing a good job, or it might mean that the developer is doing a poor job of writing code. Conversely, if a tester is finding a low number of bugs, it could be a sign that he is not performing well, or it might mean that he is testing high-quality code that has a lower bug density. It is crucial to use the metrics at the individual level only to show where additional investigation might be needed. For example, if a tester is not reporting very many bugs, it would make sense to look at the feature area and determine the cause of the low bug count. If other users (customers, developers, beta users) find bugs in the area, the tester's low bug count might be a concern. If there were a low number of tests run (measured by test cases or code coverage information), the low number of bugs might also be something worth investigating. However, if upon further investigation you determine that the area is well tested and just doesn't have very many bugs, it certainly isn't a situation where you would want to penalize the tester.

A story of bug metrics

When I first started at Microsoft, I had a bug quota. My manager told me that every tester on the team was expected to find 10 bugs per week. That seemed like a reasonable request, so I diligently went to work and started finding bugs. Like most Microsoft employees, I always wanted to do a little more than was expected of me, so I regularly reported at least 12 or 13 bugs per week.

Fortunately, the area I was testing was undergoing a lot of change, and I never had a problem reaching the quota. In fact, some weeks I would find 20 or more bugs! When this happened, however, I worried that I had somehow found too many bugs and that I wouldn't be able to reach my quota the next week. So, I reported 13 or so, and "saved" the remaining bugs for the following week just in case my well of bugs dried up.

This demonstrates another classic case of getting what you measure. My manager wanted 10 bugs per week, so that's what I gave him—regardless of whether I found more bugs. I repeatedly see attempts at using bug metrics to measure individual performance, but these metrics are rarely, if ever, effective.

Bug Bars

One process gaining popularity at Microsoft is the concept of *bug bars*. In simplest terms, a bug bar is a limit on the number of bugs that a developer can have assigned to her at any particular time. If the number of bugs assigned to the developer goes over the magic number, the developer is expected to stop feature work and fix bugs. Depending on the specific rules, developers might need to get their bug count to zero or get the number of bugs assigned to them to a specific number somewhere below the limit.

Used correctly, bug bars can be an effective engineering tool, but as with any metric targeted at the individual level, they can be misused. Unscrupulous developers might ask testers to "keep this bug in e-mail for now" or might bribe fellow developers to "take a few bugs off of my plate" to keep their bug counts low. When measuring people, you will often get what you measure regardless of whether the change supports your goals or not.

A tale of two developers

Rob and Kirk are two developers on the same product team. Their team uses a bug bar—a rule that states that if developers on their team have more than 10 product bugs assigned to them, they need to stop their feature work and fix all of the bugs before continuing to develop features.

Rob was worried that the bug bar would slow down his development work. He preferred to finish all of his feature work, and then work on all of his bugs at once, but he agreed that the bug bar would help keep the overall bug count low. As development progressed, Rob quickly started writing his features. A few bugs were reported against his code, but he was on a good pace with his development work and had only 6 bugs assigned to him, so he continued to work on feature development. A week later, just as Rob was nearing completion on his latest feature, his boss stopped by his office to tell him that he now had 12 bugs assigned to him, and that he needed to stop and fix them. Rob was frustrated that he had to stop his development work, but he was even more aggravated when he realized that the code containing most of the bugs was written nearly a month previously, and he now had to take time to relearn how the code worked before making the fixes.

Kirk was also worried that the bug bar would slow down his development work, but he was willing to give it a chance. Kirk started writing code, and soon after his first code check-in, two bugs were found in his code. Rather than wait for his bug count to reach or surpass the 10-bug limit, Kirk decided to stop and see if he could fix them immediately. Kirk had written the code with the bugs just a few days earlier and was surprised how easy it was to fix the bugs while the code was still fresh in his mind. He continued to write code and continued to address bugs assigned to him as soon as possible. He discovered that fixing bugs close to the point when they were created was always much easier than waiting until later was. He also discovered that fixing bugs early helped him write better code later—although he made mistakes in his code, he rarely made the same mistakes twice. Because of his new approach to development and addressing bugs, Kirk became one of the most productive and respected developers on the team.

Some teams see the intent of the bug bar as a process that can limit the total number of bugs open at any particular time. For example, if there are 20 developers on the team and the bug bar is 10 bugs per developer, math says (theoretically) there will never be more than 200 bugs open at any time. In practice, this theory might or might not be true, but reducing the overall bug count is not the intent of a bug bar. The intent of capping bugs per developer is to force developers to fix bugs as close to the time of bug creation as possible. In the earlier example, Kirk figured out this concept, and Rob did not. One (ill-conceived) solution is to lower the bug cap number. If, for example, the bug count was set at 5, Rob would have been forced to fix his bugs sooner! Although that solution might work (or might not), the real solution is to communicate to the entire team what the goals and intent of implementing a bug cap are.

Of course, if the goal of implementing a bug cap is to fix bugs as close as possible to the point when they were created, the bugs need to be *found* as close to the point of creation as possible. In other words, a system such as this requires that the test team be involved from the very start of feature development. If no one is finding the bugs early, no one will be able to fix them early.

Classic bugs at Microsoft

Millions of individual issues are created in the bug tracking systems at Microsoft every year. Many of the issues are product bugs, but work items, bugs duplicated in different databases, and bugs in test tools and code also contribute to the overall number of issues. However, a few issues every year fall into a completely different category. A few of these examples are as follows.

Bug #65889: The new 2% milk cartons are clearly dysfunctional. They don't open properly.
Opened by ...
The new 2% milk cartons are clearly dysfunctional. They don't open properly. This seems to be a regression from the older design. Building 35 is having the same issue.

Clearly, this is a Pri1, Sev1 bug because I'm encountering it 2 to 3 times a day.

Response from Microsoft Dining
Thank you for contacting us about the new milk. We found out the reason that the milk is hard to open is because our milk provider has just bought a brand-new machine for the pint-size milk cartons and they are adjusting the machine now so as not to have such a tight seal. Thank you for your question, and should you require additional information, please feel free to contact me.

Suggested workarounds:

1. Drink water instead.

2. Bring your own cow.

3. Use elevator doors to clip off the seal.

4. Freeze the milk carton, let the frozen milk crack the carton, and then thaw.

5. Tell your manager that you can't work without milk and let him solve the problem.

This bug is causing a lot of churn—it might sour our attempts at the RI this week. I hope we can moo-ve on this issue quickly.

The exact same problem has been reported out in the Sammamish campus. We've discovered a local workaround that might be helpful. There is an alternate dairy located approximate 1.35 miles south of our location that bottles 2% in quart-sized containers that are sufficiently easy to open. The downside is that it is typically substantially more milk than a single person can comfortably consume in one sitting. An additional step to the workaround is finding 2–3 other people who also want to consume the milk at the same time. I'm not sure that this warrants downgrading of the bug's severity because of the caveats associated with this workaround: (1) the geographic location of the alternate source being much less convenient than the kitchen fridge, and (2) that efficient consumption requires pooling of resources.

The latest information I have from our dairy provider is that they will not be able to release the fix ASAP because the new fix will be required to go through extensive testing. The testers have refused to sign off on the fix. They said that they have merely tested the private for the bug fix but haven't run their full regression pass. Currently, only three testers are handling this component and they can drink only 8 cartons a day. The team could conduct more carton-opening tests, but carton-tasting, milk flow testing, and carton pressure tests are still remaining. In addition, since the seal has been made less tight they have been observing breaks in their stress tests.

Test needs 3–4 more weeks.

Bug 68648: The Love Bug
Anne,

Over a year ago, you identified a problem with Windows 95 and worked with my manager and the product group to get me up here to see if I could help get those problems addressed with Windows 98. You provided me with suggestions and call data to get the appropriate visibility. Little did I know at that time that you would provide me with much more. You've given my life meaning, made me laugh, made me cry, and made me pick weeds. You know I have fallen madly in love with you. I love everything about you. I can't live my life without you.

I know this is not the most romantic way to do this, but I would be forever happy if you would be my wife and share your life with me forever.

Will you marry me?

Steps to reproduce:

1. Get married.
2. Reproduce.

> Sorry, I couldn't resist.
>
> Yes!
>
> I can't believe you did this!
>
>
> Bugs are typically a painful reminder of something that went wrong. The levity used on occasion when writing bugs is often an entertaining reminder that there is more to life, and more to software development, than noting work items and failures.

Test Case Management

Bugs are discovered by a wide variety of activities during product development, but targeted testing based on documented test cases finds the majority of bugs in a software product. At Microsoft, even the smallest projects have thousands of test cases. It is common for larger products to have hundreds of thousands or more test cases. A test case management system is necessary to store and organize this vast number of test cases.

A *test case manager* (TCM) is a system in which test cases can be defined, versioned, stored, and executed. The TCM shares many of the same attributes as a bug management system. These shared attributes, along with the relationship between test cases and bugs, are one of the reasons I have included both of these topics in this chapter. Another reason of interest is that the most widely used bug tracking systems at Microsoft, Product Studio and Visual Studio Team System, manage both bugs and test cases in the same system. This has the advantage of providing the ability to link test cases, bugs, and feature areas. TCM usage across the entire team is continuous and extensive, so attributes such as ease of use, configurability, and reliability are equally as essential in a TCM as they are in a bug tracking system.

What Is a Test Case?

A *test case* describes specific actions to take against a particular software component and the expected outcomes. The component can be as small as an application programming interface (API), a control in a user interface (UI), or a port handler of a device driver. It can be as large as a software system with multiple computers and applications working together.

Test cases can be a set of written steps and expected results, such as a manual test case, or a set of software instructions, such as automated test cases. Automated test cases should be self-verifying (that is, able to determine whether they passed or failed). Figure 9-5 shows a simple example of a test case management form.

Test Case Number: *0000*			
Area: *Concise Title of Test Case*			
Area		**Subarea**	
Priority	**Type**	**Frequency**	**Test Time (Min)**
1	Functionality	Every build	2
Description			
Purpose of test: Initial conditions and background: Steps: 1. 2. 3. 4. Expected results: Notes:			

FIGURE 9-5 Example test case form template

Most TCM systems are Web based, stand-alone applications, or both. Visual Studio Team System Test Edition includes a TCM that you can use to create test cases and reporting. Figure 9-6 shows an open test case.

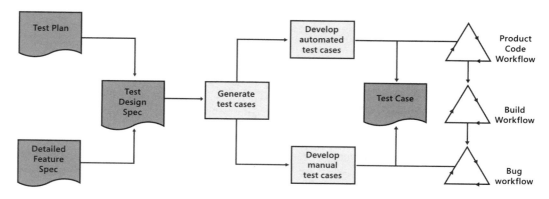

FIGURE 9-6 Test case management in Visual Studio Team System.

The Value of a Test Case

A test case is a formal document or record that describes how a specific testing activity is performed. Some test references state that the purpose of a test case is to expose bugs, but test cases are useful far beyond revealing bugs. Test cases can verify that the program functions correctly or validate that errors are handled correctly. Other test cases can attempt to increase code coverage or specifically cover seldom-used paths.

The value of a documented test case is often debated both in Microsoft and among industry software testers. Several factors contribute to the context of choosing whether to document test cases. Some of the benefits of documenting test cases include the following:

- **Historical reference**   Test cases last far beyond product release. Sustained engineering, as well as owners of future product versions often need to refer to test cases to understand what was tested and how it was tested. Documented test cases, as well as an organized system for storing them, is essential if long-term support or revisions are part of the product strategy.

- **Tracking test progress**   By documenting test cases, you can track several additional attributes, such as the number of test cases run, the number of tests that have passed or failed, and total number of test cases per feature area.

- **Repeatability**   A well-documented test case can be run by anyone at any time. This is equally applicable to both automated and manual-based test cases. The ability to repeat the same test accurately is essential to generate reproduction steps or to detect regression.

There are drawbacks to creating test cases as well. Some of these include the following:

- **Documentation time**   If the time to document the test case takes longer than running the test does, it might not make sense to document the test case. This is frequently true in situations where the test case needs to execute only a few times in a single environment.

- **Test cases get out of date as features change**   The time needed to document a test case can quickly grow out of control if the underlying feature changes often. It does not always make sense to document test cases for feature areas that change often. This scenario is frequently true when attempting to write test cases to verify user interface components.

- **Difficult to assume knowledge of reader**   People who are extremely familiar with the feature under test often are those who are writing the test cases. A mistake commonly made by these people is the use of jargon or acronyms in the test case that might not be understandable to those who run the test case in the future. When this occurs, the test case is no longer accurately repeatable, and the test case loses one of the key attributes of a good test case.

Test cases are typically documented using a test case management tool (TCM), and most teams at Microsoft record the majority of their test cases in a TCM. It is important to keep in mind that test cases do not define *all* testing activities. Activities such as *bug bashes*, when a team dedicates hours or days when the entire team can focus on using the feature or application with the intent of finding bugs that might be missed by test cases, are common on every team at Microsoft. Many teams also have time in the product cycle dedicated to customer usage scenarios. For example, some parts of the Visual Studio team dedicate regular time when the entire team does nothing but create and build various applications using the tools in the Visual Studio development environment.

Anatomy of a Test Case

Several factors contribute to the difference between a great test case and a poor test case. Some of these factors include the following:

- **Purpose**   Identify why this test case is important and what it does. The purpose could be to verify specific functionality, verify error handling, verify a specific situation, or some other specific purpose.

- **Conditions**   Identify which aspects of the environment are important or unimportant. State whether the test needs to run on specific hardware or a specific operating system, if other software is required, or if additional preconditions are necessary.

- **Specific inputs and steps**   List all steps required to accurately and repeatedly run the test case.

- **Predicted results**   Provide information that allows whoever runs the test to determine correctly whether the test has passed or failed.

Other attributes of a test case specify where and when a test case is run. These attributes include the following:

- **Test frequency**   This is often referred to as a test type, such as a build verification test (BVT), a nightly (a test that is run every night during the overnight test pass), or a milestone test that is intended to run at least once during every internal iteration. Some test case management systems list these types of tests by name, while others might assign a priority to indicate how often the test should run.

- **Configurations**   This indicates the configurations of the target software where the test case will run. For example, the attributes of one test case might state that the test run only on the PC version of an application, while another test case might run across additional supported operating systems.

- **Automation**   The automation attribute refers to the degree of automation a test has. In other words, whether the test is fully automated, partially automated, or an entirely manual test case. Automation settings are generally as follows:

    - **Manual**   Manual tests require a tester to execute all steps of the test case and record the result in the TCM.

    - **Semiautomated**   Semiautomated tests are carried out manually but require some amount of action from a tester. For example, a network test might require that a certain network topology is set up manually, but the actual test cases can be fully automated.

    - **Automated**   Automated tests (sometimes called fully automated tests) require no user intervention. Test setup, execution, and the reporting of results back to the TCM are entirely automated.

Test Case Mistakes

Creating good test cases is a difficult process. Making a single mistake can destroy the intent of the test case. Some of the areas that cause the most problems are the following:

- **Missing steps**   Hastily created test cases or test cases that assume some steps will be performed whether they are included or not are some of the most common types of test cases that are not accurately repeatable.

- **Too verbose**   Although it is important to be specific and to provide enough information, unnecessary words or lengthy explanations can make the test case hard to follow. Include just enough information to precisely run the test case.

- **Too much jargon**   Don't assume that everyone who ever runs the test case (including product support and sustained engineering) knows all of the acronyms, code names, and abbreviations that you do. Spell out everything necessary for your test case to be valuable for the entire lifetime of the product.

- **Unclear pass/fail criteria**   The test case is useless if, after running the test, it is unclear whether the test passed or failed.

Test Case Examples

Poor Test Case Example

Title: Check encrypted message

Steps:

1. Get a v3 certificate
2. Send an encrypted message
3. Create a message with 0 RSA/DH lockboxes, send it
4. Create a message with 1 RSA/DH lockbox, send it
5. Create a message with an RSA/DSA signature, send it

Verify:

- ❏ Everything works for all messages
- ❏ Certificate server produced a good certificate
- ❏ Clear text and blobs come through properly

Good Test Case Example

Title: Clear text with v3 certificate

Purpose:

Verify that an encrypted clear text message using a v3 certificate can be opened and read by a recipient

Conditions/Prerequisites:

Crypto Overview and v3 certificate (Diffie-Hellman) setup

User1 and User2 are Microsoft Exchange Server mailbox accounts

Steps:

1. User1 starts Microsoft Office Outlook.
2. On the Tools menu, click Options, and then click the Security tab.
3. Ensure that the Send clear text signed message when sending signed messages option is selected.
4. Ensure that v3 certificates are properly set up.
5. Click OK.
6. Open a new message, give it a subject "foo" and body of "bar."
7. Address and send message to User2.
8. On another computer, start Outlook with User2 account.

Verify:

- ❏ The encrypted message has been received in the Inbox and can be opened by User2
- ❏ The subject and body text of the message are "foo" and "bar", respectively

Note Each step is numbered. This is a best practice.

Managing Test Cases

The number of test cases needed for a software program grows rapidly as the product grows in size and complexity. Over time, as additional features are developed or support for additional software or hardware platforms is added, the number of test cases that need to be run and tracked grows exponentially. At some point, the only way to track this vast number of test cases is through a full-scale test case management system.

TCM systems look and feel much like bug tracking systems. The primary bug tracking systems at Microsoft (Product Studio and Visual Studio Team System) include both bug tracking and test case management tools, and they share much of the user interface and program structure between the two functionalities. An integrated system enables a few appealing features. For example, test cases can link directly to the bugs they find, and reproduction steps can link directly from the test cases or can be imported easily. To go even further, with Visual Studio Team System you can link test cases directly to functional requirements as well. This three-way linking between functional requirements, test cases, and bugs allows for several unique views, such as knowing how many test cases exist for each requirement, knowing which requirements do not have test cases, and viewing the mapping between bugs and requirements.

Cases and Points: Counting Test Cases

A test case is a list of specific actions that verifies functionality or that an error is handled correctly or some other quality attribute (performance, reliability, and so forth). A simple test case for playing an audio file might be *Open tada.wav, click Play, and verify that it plays correctly.* This is one test case, but it might need to run on 32-bit and 64-bit systems. It might also be a requirement to run the test on assorted families of audio chipsets. Depending on the implementation, the test case might also run on various localized versions of the system.

At this point, many testers might be confused as to whether to count all of these variations as one test case or as multiple test cases. Testers inside and outside of Microsoft often struggle with this situation. At Microsoft, some terminology that is gaining use is the concept of a *test point*. A test case is the single instance of a set of steps to carry out a testing activity, whereas the test point is an instantiation of that test case in a particular environment. Test point results can be compared meaningfully to one another across the testing matrix or over historic test passes, while the test case might not have changed at all. For example, when I was on the Windows CE team, we ran many of our tests on different hardware platforms and on different configurations of the operating system. We had a few hundred thousand test cases, but more than a million test points. By differentiating the tests in this way, we were able to determine quickly whether a test case was failing in all environments or only on a particular configuration or platform. Here is a list of testing terms that are handy to know:

- **Test case**   A plan for exercising a test.

- **Test point**   A combination of a test case and an execution environment.

- **Test suite**   A collection of related test cases or test points. Often, a test suite is a unit of tested functionality, limited to a component or feature.

- **Test run**   A collection of test suites invoked as a unit. Often, a test run is a collection of all the tests invoked on a single hardware or software context.

- **Test pass**   A collection of test runs. Often, a test pass spans several hardware and software configurations and is confined by a specific checkpoint or release plans.

Test case management solutions at Microsoft

My first test case manager at Microsoft was Microsoft Office Excel. In fact, on my first day as an employee, my manager handed me a fresh printout of my test cases. Over time, we expanded and modified our spreadsheet-based system, and for our needs, it worked fine. In hindsight, I realize that our solution was inefficient and inadequate. I doubt anyone has ever been able to run our test cases (or find them for that matter). When we added configuration changes to our test matrix, we typically copied the relevant test cases to a new worksheet.

Thankfully, the TCM landscape at Microsoft today is much better. Or, more accurately, Microsoft has a different problem to face with TCM systems. The problem Microsoft faces today is an explosion in the number of TCM systems. A search for "TCM" on the Web site for a company-wide tool repository shows 22 results. I remember at one point there were at least a half dozen TCM systems in Windows. Most test teams have begun to migrate toward the TCM tools in Visual Studio Team System, but major divisions such as Windows, Office, and Developer each currently have their own TCM system. Tool proliferation is inevitable in a company of 8,000 testers, but having multiple test management systems causes other problems, for example, if the Windows team wants to run application compatibility tests on Office applications on a new version of the operating system. Having nonstandard TCM systems makes the process of copying or executing tests from one TCM on another TCM difficult at best.

The situation is improving rapidly. (Almost) the entire Windows team uses a single TCM. Rather than create new TCM systems, most new teams are choosing to use either one of the major existing internal systems or Visual Studio Team System for tracking test cases and results.

Tracking and Interpreting the Test Results

One of the primary features of a TCM system is the ability to track relevant metrics such as number of test cases run and the percentage of the tests that pass or fail. A TCM can organize tests into a *test pass*, a suite of tests that execute daily, weekly, or against a specific version or build of the application. If the TCM is integrated with the bug tracking system, the TCM can report the number of bugs found in a test pass or whether bugs marked as "fixed" in the bug database are indeed fixed.

Many testers and test managers have gone down the wrong path of examining metrics first, and then trying to determine what the metrics mean. As when examining bug metrics, it is critical to determine which questions you are trying to answer before examining test case metrics. Common metrics, along with common usage, are listed in Table 9-6.

TABLE 9-6 Common Test Case Metrics

Metric	Usage
Pass rate	This is probably the most often used test case metric. This metric shows the ratio of number of passing tests to the number of failing tests. This ratio is typically calculated using test points rather than test cases.
Number of passes / failures	On systems with a large number of test cases, this metric can be more revealing. For example, a 99 percent pass rate is usually an exceptional pass rate. Systems with a million or more test points (test cases * the number of configurations they run on) are common for Microsoft products. On a system with a million test points, a 99 percent pass rate includes *10,000 failures*.
Total number of test cases / total number of planned test cases	If test cases are planned up front and implemented throughout the product cycle, this metric provides a progress metric for management.
Automation ratio	It can be interesting to know the percentage of automated tests versus tests that are manual. Some teams might have goals to increase the number of automated tests for a particular area or across the entire product team. This metric is easily abused. Not all manual tests can or should be automated. More discussion on the types of tests that benefit from automation is in Chapter 11, "Other Testing: Nonfunctional Testing."
Number of tests by type	A test manager might want to know which tests or how many tests run for a particular type of test pass. For example, build verification tests (BVTs) need to run quickly and cover the product in breadth. Viewing the number of BVTs along with the area they are testing provides quick information in this area.
Number or percentage of tests finding bugs	This metric is occasionally useful in measuring test effectiveness. It can show whether a variety of test cases is finding bugs or whether only selected test cases or types of test cases are finding the most bugs.

Summary

In simplest terms, bugs and test cases are the center of a tester's world. Whether you are testing large, complex systems or a Web site to sell travel accessories for pets, a system that allows you to track the artifacts of test creation and test execution is extremely beneficial. Good systems are highly configurable, yet exceptionally simple; they are highly usable by the most technical engineer as well as the most bumbling marketer or executive; and, most significant, they are the cornerstone of the testing effort.

Chapter 10
Test Automation

Alan Page

I have been writing automation for nearly 20 years. Of course, I haven't been writing automated tests nearly that long; rather, I have used repeatable scripts or code either to make a redundant task more efficient or to reduce the chance of error when doing some computer operation. In my early days of using a computer, I used batch files (a script containing sequences of commands for the command interpreter) to back up my files to floppy disks or to reconfigure my environment for a particular application. I have continued to use batch files for configuring command-line environments for different build systems, but I automate in other ways as well. I write and use automated scripts to install applications, set reminders, sync files between computers, and to tune my computer. I don't consider any of these activities to be an automated test, but they are automation. The automation I'm referring to removes the need for me to perform a repetitive task and allows me to execute tasks identically every time.

There is certainly a lot more to a good automated test than accurately executing a repetitive task. This chapter discusses the elements, attributes, and structure of high-quality automated tests and automated testing architecture and infrastructure.

An important point to keep in mind as you read this chapter (as well as any chapter in this book) is that test automation strategies, tools, and techniques vary widely across Microsoft. The goal of this chapter is to discuss many of the popular approaches to test automation across the company. Although many of the automation methods discussed are common practices, there is constant innovation in this area and continuous growth and expansion of automation tools and approaches.

The Value of Automation

Nothing seems both to unite and divide software testers across the industry more than a discussion on test automation. To some, automated tests are mindless and emotionless substitutes for the type of testing that the human brain is capable of achieving. For others, anything less than complete testing using automation is a disappointment. In practice, however, context determines the value of automation. Sometimes it makes sense to automate every single test. On other occasions, it might make sense to automate nothing. Some types of bugs can be found only while someone is carefully watching the screen and running the application. Bugs that have an explanation starting with "Weird—when I dismiss this dialog box, the entire screen flashes" or "The mouse pointer flickers when I move it across the controls" are types of bugs that humans are vastly better at detecting than computers are. For many other types of bugs, however, automated tests are more efficient and effective.

To Automate or Not to Automate, That Is the Question

Why should you write automated tests? Why or when should you choose manual testing over automated testing? Choosing whether to write automation and determining the extent of test automation are issues that nearly every tester must contend with at some point. If you are going to run a test only once, it doesn't make sense to automate it. However, just because you are going to run it twice doesn't mean you should automate it either. Many tests might need to run hundreds, thousands, or millions of times before product release or during the maintenance cycle of the program. Several factors contribute to accurately assessing the benefits of automation for any particular context. Some factors to consider include the following:

- **Effort**   Determining the effort or cost is the first step in determining the return on investment (ROI) of creating automated tests. Some types of products or features are simple to automate, whereas other areas are inherently problematic. For example, application programming interface (API) testing, as well as any other functionality exposed to the user in the form of a programming object, is more often than not straightforward to automate. User interface (UI) testing, on the other hand, can be problematic and frequently requires more effort.

- **Test lifetime**   How many times will an automated test run before it becomes useless? Part of the process of determining whether to automate a specific scenario or test case includes estimating the long-term value of the test. Consider the life span of the product under test and the length of the product cycle. Different automation choices must be made for a product with no planned future versions on a short ship cycle than for a product on a two-year ship cycle with multiple follow-up releases planned.

- **Value**   Consider the value of an automated test over its lifetime. Some testers say that the value of a test case is in finding bugs, but many bugs found by automated tests are only found the first time the test is run. Once the bug is fixed, these tests become regression tests—tests that show that recent changes do not cause previously working functionality to stop working. Many automation techniques can vary data used by the test or change the paths tested on each run of the test to continue to find bugs throughout the lifetime of the test. For products with a long lifetime, a growing suite of regression tests is an advantage—with so much complexity in the underlying software, a large number of tests that focus primarily on making sure functionality that worked before keeps on working is exceptionally advantageous.

- **Point of involvement**   Most successful automation projects I have witnessed have occurred on teams where the test team was involved from the beginning of the project.

Attempts at adding automated tests to a project in situations where the test team begins involvement close to or after code complete usually fail.

■ **Accuracy**   Good automation reports accurate results every time it runs. One of the biggest complaints from management regarding automated tests is the number of false positives automation often generates. (See the following sidebar titled "Positively False?") False positives are tests that report a failure, but the failure is caused by a bug somewhere in the test rather than a product bug. Some areas of a project (such as user interface components that are in flux) can be difficult to analyze by automated testing and can be more prone to reporting false positives.

Positively false?

When a test fails, even though the targeted functionality is working correctly, it is commonly referred to as a false positive report. The test reports an error (the positive), but no error actually exists (thus false). Conversely, a situation where a test passes even though the underlying functionality is broken is often called a false negative (or false pass). An example of a false positive outside of the software-testing world is a judicial court finding someone guilty for a crime the person did not actually commit, whereas a false negative would be a court finding someone innocent when that person actually is guilty. These terms come from the world of statistics, where false positives and false negatives are most often known as Type I and Type II errors, respectively.

■ **Supported platforms**   Automation is one approach for addressing the test matrix explosion that occurs in many large projects. Writing a test once that will run on multiple platforms or systems provides a huge time-saving advantage. On a small scale, this can mean that a single automated test can run on both Microsoft Windows Server and the Windows Vista operating system, but the big successes happen when a single automated test is able to run on 8 different embedded platforms or in 10 different Web browsers.

■ **Complexity**   How complex is a test to automate versus manual execution or verification? Some tests are simply too difficult to automate using existing frameworks or available technologies. For example, graphics programs can use pixel comparison algorithms to compare two images. Image comparison is notorious for causing false positives. Fuzzy matching sometimes provides better results, but the implementation is often complex and can require constant changes in the automation to produce the desired result.

■ **Other factors**   You also must consider the amount of time you have to automate as well as the skills of the testers who will be writing the automation. Automation is an investment. It is never something that can be fit in last minute, and neither is it something that an unskilled tester is able to do simply because he had programming experience in school. Remember that your goal is to do the best job testing possible, given the time and resources you have to complete the job. Keep in mind that testability factors and automation support not considered early in the design of the product can make writing automation for the product difficult. A final factor to consider is the automation philosophy of management. Automation is not a silver bullet, but it cannot be completely ignored either. Some teams might have a philosophy where they want to automate everything, whereas other teams might choose to automate very little. There is no right amount of automation, and it is imperative that all of the preceding factors are considered when determining how much and what to automate rather than making that choice purely from a management perspective.

We don't have time to automate this

I learned to write UI automation using a program called Microsoft Test. MS Test, as it was often called (which was later named MS Visual Test, and then subsequently sold to Rational Software), was a tool for writing UI automation. I started using a beta version a year or so before joining Microsoft, and by the time I started at Microsoft, I knew the program fairly well and was quite comfortable writing UI automation.

My first job at Microsoft was on the team that tested networking functionality on Japanese, Chinese, and Korean Windows 95. A big part of my job was verifying that the characters of these languages worked correctly in the UI elements of networking properties, as well as network interoperability of file names containing these characters in a variety of network topologies and operating systems. At that time, I had only a bit of experience testing non-English versions of the Windows operating system, and even less experience with Windows 95. I knew that writing automation for this area would be an interesting challenge for me, but I was excited to give it a shot.

I spent my first day or so getting used to my office, finding the test lab, meeting new teammates, setting up computers, and finding necessary tools on the internal network. My manager had asked me to stop by to talk about my testing responsibilities and I was excited to get started. We talked briefly about the areas I was responsible for to make sure I understood the scope of my testing area, and then he handed me a list of test cases printed out from a Microsoft Office Excel worksheet. I spent a few minutes scanning the list to make sure I understood everything. Everything made sense, and I was confident I could automate the test cases in short order.

Just to be sure, I asked if there was a deadline when I should complete automation. I remember the exact words of the reply.

"Oh, no, we don't have time to automate these tests, you just need to run them on every build."

"Wow," I thought, "These tests must be much more difficult to automate than I thought they were." I went back to my office and started running through test cases. I did this for a few days, found some bugs, and learned a lot more about the area. Some of the test cases were for command-line network options. I was starting to get a little bored running these tests, and as a result, I found I was sometimes forgetting steps. I thought, "Surely, a little batch file would help me run these tests more consistently." Fifteen minutes later, I had proved myself correct. I had also found a way to test additional configuration operations automatically.

A few days later, I was making some of the same mistakes in the UI testing, so I thought I would take a few minutes to see just how difficult it really was to automate. I was prepared to spend some of my own time on the weekend to experiment with writing UI automation on Windows 95, but I quickly found that for the tests I needed to run, Visual Test worked pretty well. A few hours later, most of the scenarios from the worksheet my boss gave me were now automated tests.

I ran those tests every day for months, and they saved me days or weeks of time—time that I used to expand what I was testing and to look at areas I never would have looked at otherwise. I probably found at least a hundred bugs that I might not have found if I had focused on that same script of tests every day. In hindsight, I was still a novice tester, and those tests probably weren't very good, but no matter how I look at it, automation was still the right answer in that context.

User Interface Automation

Public-facing functions such as the Windows API or any other public-facing functionality exposed through a programming interface are good candidates for test automation. You can test the programming interface without writing automation. For example, I could test a large part of the core Windows API purely by running the Microsoft Office suite, but with automation targeted at the individual API functions I could use test applications to test multiple parameter combinations efficiently.

Many facets of non-functional testing such as performance tests, load tests, stress tests, and leak tests are highly suitable for automation. (See Chapter 11, "Non-Functional Testing.") In fact, automated testing is the only way to execute many of the scenarios related to these types of testing situations. Simulating thousands of simultaneous connections to a service and timing an operation are tasks where automation is the only practical solution.

When software testers think about test automation, many of them first think of user interface (UI) testing. The software test marketplace offers many tools that assist test writers in manipulating the user interface in their automated tests. A number of these tools also offer record and playback functionality so that the test author can simply record the manual test, and then play it back as an automated test. Record and playback tools often receive criticism because the tests they generate are not resistant to subtle changes in the user interface. User interface testing, in general, has this same problem, and it can be difficult to automate many UI elements.

In practice at Microsoft, the primary methods used for automating UI bypass the presentation layer and use the underlying object model directly, or use similar methods to manipulate the core logic of the user interface. In a few cases, UI automation directly interacts with the UI by simulating mouse clicks and keystrokes.

```csharp
// C# code to start Microsoft Office Word, type text, select the text, and make the
font bold
// error checking removed for brevity

Process wordApp = Process.Start("Winword.exe");
if (wordApp.WaitForInputIdle(1000))
{
    SendKeys.SendWait("This is input to WinWord");
    SendKeys.SendWait("^a"); // send ctrl+a (select all text)
    SendKeys.SendWait("^b"); // send ctrl + b (make text bold)
}
```

Code using keystrokes or mouse clicks is the closest form of automation to reproducing the way users interact with the software but is also one of the most fragile forms of UI automation. Controls move, underlying identifications change, and text is updated and localized. It is possible to write robust automation using only methods that simulate keyboard presses or mouse clicks, but it is difficult and far from failure proof.

Another form of automation is to automate the actions that occur when the user interacts with the UI. For example, instead of simulating a button click, the automation directly calls the underlying code that the button triggers.

Figure 10-1 is a simple variation on what the object-oriented community calls an object model. An object model is a collection of objects (functionality) that allow manipulation of specific parts of the application. For example, the HTML Document Object Model (DOM) provides access to HTML controls (buttons, check boxes, and so forth), embedded links, and browsing history. Languages such as JavaScript can access those controls directly through the DOM.

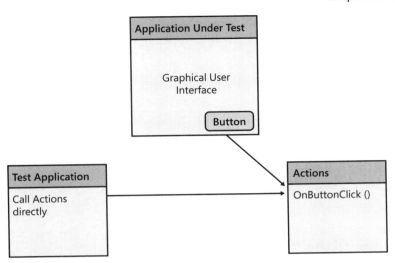

FIGURE 10-1 Calling UI functions without the UI.

Many Windows-based applications enable access to the features in the application through an object model. By using object models, combined with user interface code that separates program logic from the user interface logic, testers can automate tests to manipulate any portion of the UI without directly interacting with any of the UI controls.

This code uses the Word object model to perform the same automation as the previous example.

```
Object template = Type.Missing;
Object newTemplate = Type.Missing;
Object docType = Type.Missing;
Object visible = Type.Missing;

Word.Application wordApp = new Word.Application();
Word.Document wordDoc = new Word.Document();
wordApp.Visible = true;
// the following line is equivalent to selecting File, and then New
// to create a new document based on Normal.dot.
wordDoc = wordApp.Documents.Add(ref template, ref newTemplate, ref docType, ref
visible);

wordDoc.Selection.TypeText("This is input to WinWord");
wordDoc.Selection.WholeStory();
wordDoc.Selection.Font.Bold = 1
```

Instead of mouse clicks, this code manipulates Word using its object model. This code is slightly more verbose than the C# example using SendKeys() but is more likely to be extensible, and maintainable.

Another similar method of automating the UI is by using Microsoft Active Accessibility (MSAA). MSAA improves the way accessibility tools such as screen readers work with Windows, but it also provides a simple method for writing automation. The heart of MSAA is the IAccessible interface. The IAccessible interface supports properties that allow you to get information about the corresponding UI element. Windows common controls such as buttons, text boxes, list boxes, and scroll bars all implement an IAccessible interface. Many Windows-based applications that contain custom controls also support this interface.

Applications (or tests) use accessibility functions by obtaining a pointer to the IAccessible interface using functions such as AccessibleObjectFromWindow, AccessibleObjectFromPoint, or AccessibleObjectFromEvent. By using the interface pointer, test applications can use methods to get information about the controls, such as text or button state, or to manipulate the control (such as simulating clicking a button).

With the release of version 3.0 of the Microsoft .NET Framework, Microsoft UI Automation is the new accessibility framework for Windows and is available on all operating systems that support Windows Presentation Foundation (WPF). Like MSAA, UI Automation is an accessibility feature but is written in managed code and is most easily used from C# or VB.Net applications. UI Automation exposes every component of the UI as an AutomationElement. These elements expose common properties of the UI elements they represent, such as appearance and state. A control, such as a button click, can be performed with code such as the following.

```
// obtain an InvokePattern object, and use it to click a button
// NOTE: error checking removed for brevity
private void InvokeControl(AutomationElement targetControl)
{
    InvokePattern invokePattern =
      targetControl.GetCurrentPattern(InvokePattern.Pattern) as InvokePattern
}
invokePattern.Invoke();
```

Most groups at Microsoft that write automated UI tests use the preceding methods or hybrids of these methods. Many frameworks for UI automation wrap one or more of the solutions mentioned. An application, for example, can have an incomplete object model, and tests might use the object model for most testing but use MSAA for the remainder of UI testing.

Brute force UI automation

In most cases, UI automation that accesses controls through a model or similar methods tests just as well as automation that accesses the UI through button clicks and key presses. Occasionally, however, automating purely through the model can miss critical bugs.

Several years ago, a spinoff of the Windows CE team was working on a project called the Windows Powered Smart Display. This device was a flat screen monitor that also functioned as a thin client for terminal services. When the monitor was undocked from the workstation, it would connect back to the workstation using a terminal server client.

The software on the device was primarily composed of core Windows CE components but also contained a simple user interface that showed a history of connected servers, battery life, connection speed, and any local applications, as shown in the following graphic. The CE components were all well tested, and the small test team assigned to the device tested several user scenarios in addition to some manual functionality testing. Toward the end of the product cycle, I spent some time working with the team, helping them develop some additional tests.

One of the first things I wanted to do was create a few simple tests that I could run overnight to find any issues with the software that might not show up for days or weeks for a typical user. There was no object model for the application, and no other testability features, but given the simplicity of the application and the amount of time I had, I dove in to what I call brute force UI automation. I quickly wrote some code that could find each of the individual windows on the single screen that made up the application. I remember that I was going to look up the specific Windows message that this program used, but I'd hit a roadblock waiting for access to the source code. I've never been a fan of waiting around, so I decided to write code that would center the mouse over a specific window on the screen and send a mouse click to that point on the screen. After a few more minutes of debugging and testing, I had a simple application that would randomly connect to any available server, verify that the connection was successfully established, and then terminate the terminal server session.

I set up the application to run infinitely, started it, and then let it run while I took care of a final few projects before heading home for the day. I glanced over my shoulder once in a while, happy to see the application connecting and disconnecting every few seconds. However, just as I stood up to leave, I turned around to take one final look at my test application and I saw that it had crashed. I happened to be running under the debugger and noticed that the crash was caused by a memory leak, and the application was out of a particular Windows resource. At first, I thought it was a problem in my application, so I spent some time scanning the source code looking for any place where items had been using that type of resource or perhaps misusing a Windows API. I couldn't find anything wrong but still thought the problem must be mine, and that I might have caused the problem during one of my earlier debugging sessions. I rebooted the device, set up the tests to run again, and walked out the door.

When I got to work the next morning, the first thing I noticed was that the application had crashed again in the same place. By this time, I had access to the source code for the application, and after spending about an hour debugging the problem. The problem turned out not to be in the connection code. Every time one of the computer names was selected, the application initiated code that did custom drawing. It was just a small blue flash so that the user would know that the application had recognized the mouse click, much like the way that a button in a Windows-based application appears to sink when pressed. The problem in this application was that every time the test and drawing code ran, there was a resource leak. After a few hundred connections, the resource leak was big enough that the application would crash when the custom drawing code ran.

I don't think I ever would have found this bug if I had been writing UI automation that executed functionality without going through the UI directly. I think that in most cases, the best solution for robust UI automation is a method that accesses controls without interacting with the UI, but now, I always keep my eye on any code in the user interface that does more than the functionality that the UI represents.

What's in a Test?

When considering test cases for automation, there is much more to think about than the execution steps of the test. Before running any steps, the application must be in a state where test execution is possible. After the test is run, it is critical to know whether the test passed or failed, and test results must be saved somewhere for review or further analysis. It can also be necessary to clean up any artifacts created by the test (files, registry settings, and so forth). Finally, the test must be maintainable and comprehensible so that anyone can run or modify the test at any time when it becomes necessary.

An automated test is much more than the automatic execution of steps from a manual test case. Good automation takes advantage of the power of the computer to perform testing that a human cannot perform as effectively. Test automation is not a replacement for human testers. Several manual tests and testing activities are far more powerful when performed by a thinking human being rather than by a machine, but when used effectively, automated tests save enormous amounts of time and money.

Keith Stobie and Mark Bergman describe components of test automation in their 1992 paper "How to Automate Testing: The Big Picture" in terms of the acronym SEARCH.[1] SEARCH stands for setup, execution, analysis, reporting, cleanup, and help.

- **Setup**   Setup is the effort it takes to bring the software to a point where the actual test operation is ready for execution.

- **Execution**   This is the core of the test—the specific steps necessary to verify functionality, sufficient error handling, or some other relevant task.

- **Analysis**   Analysis is the process of determining whether the test passes or fails. This is the most important step—and often the most complicated step of a test.

- **Reporting**   Reporting includes display and dissemination of the analysis, for example, log files, database, or other generated files.

- **Cleanup**   The cleanup phase returns the software to a known state so that the next test can proceed.

- **Help**   A help system enables maintenance and robustness of the test case throughout its life.

Consider a simple test case:

Title:

Verify values larger than 32-bit integer can display in calculator program

Steps:

1. In decimal mode, enter maximum 32-bit unsigned integer value (4294967295) using the keyboard or calc controls.

2. Add any positive whole number value to the original value.

Verify:

Verify proper addition. For example, 4294967295 + 10 == 4294967305

This test case describes simple actions to determine whether a calculator program can handle values larger than 2^{32} (maximum value of a 32-bit integer).[2]

---

[1]   Keith Stobie and Mark Bergman, "How to Automate Testing: The Big Picture," March 1992, *http://keithstobie.net/ Documents/TestAuto_The_BigPict.PDF*.

[2]   Programs that do not expect values larger than 2^{32} will "roll over" (or overflow) to the minimum value of the data type. In this case, it means that the number after 4294967295 is zero. The value of 2^{32} is 4294967296. Because counting on computers starts at zero, the range of an unsigned 32-bit integer is from 0 to 4294967295.

On the surface, this test appears to be quite simple, but many more steps are required to automate this test than the preceding two steps dictate. Before the test steps can be carried out, the calculator program needs to be started and in a state where it can accept input. Even on the fastest computers, some applications take several seconds to start, so the test might need to account for this. Alternatively, perhaps the test assumes that the program is already running. No matter what the assumption is, certain conditions need to be satisfied before executing the first step of this test case.

After the preceding steps execute, it is necessary to validate the output to determine whether the test passes or not. In this case, the automated test might read the value from the output field in the calculator application, or it might evaluate the value by probing internal variables in the application (or both). After determining whether the test passes or fails, the test must log the results so that they are reviewable by anyone who needs to evaluate test status. If subsequent test cases assume that the output field is clear, or set to zero, or that the calculator program is not running, it is essential to clear the data or close the application before ending the automated test.

Finally, additional information about the test included in the test case or embedded as comments in the code is necessary to enable long-term maintenance of the test and enable other (or future) team members to easily modify or add to the existing tests.

It is important to consider the entire scope of the test from setup to maintenance when developing test automation. Extensive automation can automate every step of SEARCH, but it is occasionally useful to automate only a few parts of the approach. In some situations, for example, it can be beneficial to automate installing and configuring an application to the point where critical manual or exploratory steps can be performed—or, you might have a system where you record test results in a test case manager and results are analyzed automatically for reporting. In most cases, however, a successful approach automates most steps of the testing effort.

Many automation efforts fail because they attempt to automate only the test execution phase. A holistic automation approach requires automating much more than execution alone. Automation strategies that do not include a plan for getting the application to a stage where execution can take place and where reporting and analysis are automatic are rarely beneficial. When considering test automation, many people think primarily of automating test execution, but automation is also helpful in other testing phases. Computer-assisted testing might be a better term to describe the concept of automating each stage of testing. Thorough automation includes much more than executing a test. Computer-based tools and software are a good solution for automating the various tasks that support test execution.

Test tools and utilities

In several situations, automated tests are not a valid testing solution. One of the areas I tested on Windows 98 was font rendering. Some aspects of font testing benefited immensely from automation. Performance testing is a good example. We significantly changed the way the core graphics engine displayed non-Western characters, and I needed to test the length of time it took different fonts to draw random strings of varying lengths. There were far too many combinations for me to test manually, but I was able to write a suite of tests that could accurately track the impact of the performance gains.

Other areas of font testing were just not conducive to automation, but I needed quick and accurate methods for determining the effect of the multitude of font settings. For a lot of this testing, I used a tool that displayed the fonts in a large grid that allowed me to view each pixel of the font and rapidly adjust each of the different parameters affecting the display of the font. If, for example, a customer reported that certain characters in a specific font "looked funny," I could quickly examine the rendered font and determine the cause of the issue.

I also needed to verify that all characters in a font could draw without causing a problem. In those days, in a few obscure cases an application would crash if it attempted to draw a particular character, or ranges of characters would have printing problems. Testing printing of every character in every font certainly isn't good for saving time (or trees), but it was important to be able to spot-check new fonts and to investigate bugs reported by customers. To help myself out in this scenario, I wrote a tool capable of displaying or printing all characters in a font with any selection of sizes and attributes (bold, italic, and so forth), as shown in Figure 10-2.

The tool took only a few hours to write, but the first time I used it, I found a crash when "scrolling" through the characters in a third-party font. The other team members and I used this tool often throughout the development cycle for quick verification, smoke testing, and other investigations. We found only a few other bugs using the tool, but it was extremely beneficial in helping us verify a variety of font rendering issues. It wasn't an automated test, but it saved dozens of hours of time among several engineers.

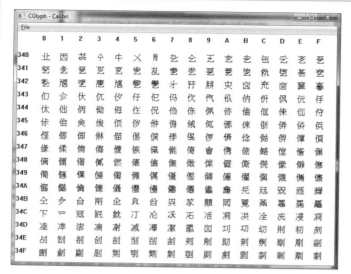

FIGURE 10-2 Font display tool.

SEARCH at Microsoft

A wide variety of approaches and solutions for test automation is used at Microsoft. Not all teams approach automation or test case generation in terms of SEARCH, but an approach that considers automating each stage of the testing effort is prevalent on most teams.

Setup

The scope of testing and the size of the test matrix on teams at Microsoft emphasize the need for automating the setup portion of testing. The simplest form of automating this phase is by using a script or command-line option that enables an unattended installation of an application. Test computers often install the latest version of an application automatically in the middle of the night so that testers can start working with a clean installation of the application when they arrive in the morning. This approach saves time but can be dangerous if product installation is rarely tested in the way that customers will install the application. If all installations run automatically, the test team will undoubtedly miss important bugs in the setup application. A common practice at Microsoft is to use automated application setup for the majority of the test team, but have a dedicated setup tester (or test team) to verify the entire setup test matrix.

The scope of preparing a system for test execution, including operating system installation (if necessary) and configuring the application under test, can grow quickly when you consider operating system version and application version constraints. Consider the test matrix shown in Table 10-1.

TABLE 10-1 Installation Test Matrix

Base operating system	Test needed
Windows XP	Full install
Windows XP	Upgrade from version 1 to version 2
Windows Vista	Full install
Windows Vista	Upgrade from version 1 to version 2
Windows XP	Install application, and then upgrade to Windows Vista

Installation and upgrade scenarios are extremely complex. When the base test configuration includes installing an operating system, or a previous version of the application, setup testing quickly becomes a huge time burden. In these situations, it is imperative to be able to get to the base setup quickly. It can take hours to install an operating system and necessary applications manually, so many teams at Microsoft use a system that quickly configures a baseline setup using imaging technology. Imaging technology takes a snapshot of a baseline system and writes it to a computer hard drive directly. If a tester needs a copy of Windows XP with Office Professional Edition 2003 installed, she simply selects that image, runs a script or application from the computer she wants to configure, and several minutes later, a computer with the required applications is ready to test. Imaging is typically a two-stage process that creates both the necessary software baseline, as well as installs drivers specific to the imaged computer and sets up necessary user accounts.

Teams that use this approach keep hundreds of images on hand and use these images for configuring a variety of manual and automated tests. Another advantage of an image library such as this is that application or operating system patches are applied to images in a central location, removing another time-consuming portion of the process of setting up an application.

Windows CE uses a similar approach. Windows CE is not designed to be installed like an application or operating system. Instead, operating system images are flashed onto a device such as a mobile phone, network router, or a development board that supports Windows CE. The Windows CE automation system selects the appropriate operating system image for a given test and hardware configuration, flashes the operating system onto the device, and then uses special hardware to automatically reset (restart) the device before executing the tests.

I didn't know you could automate that

Sometimes, parts of your testing effort can seem difficult or nearly impossible to automate. Whenever something seems impossible to automate, I think it's important to brainstorm a bit more and see if there's a way to make even the smallest portion of the testing more efficient.

The Windows and Windows CE teams use a variety of custom-built hardware to assist in their automation efforts. Testing with PCMCIA cards, for example, can be a time-consuming task. The operating systems need to support inserting and removing cards at any time. Some classes of tests such as network tests might need to be run with several different PCMCIA network cards. On the Windows CE team, we used a "PCMCIA Jukebox" to assist in this testing. The device contained six PCMCIA slots and a serial connection we could use to simulate physically inserting and removing cards from any of the six positions. We didn't have jukeboxes for every piece of peripheral hardware, but where we didn't we did have several "switcher" devices that allowed us to simulate plugging and unplugging other removable devices such as USB and 1394/Firewire devices using a serial connection.

The Windows team makes heavy use of a device simulation framework to emulate hardware. The framework enables tests that otherwise might be unpractical, such as plugging in hundreds of devices or plugging and unplugging a device thousands of times.

Execution

Running the steps of the test case is the heart of automated testing, and a variety of execution methods is possible. One simple form of execution is to write and run a script or application. A simple test case written in Microsoft Visual Basic Scripting Edition (VBScript) to open and print a specified document in Microsoft Word can be implemented as follows:

```
Set objWord = CreateObject("Word.Application")
Set objDoc = objWord.Documents.Open("c:\tests\printtest.doc")

objDoc.PrintOut()
objWord.Quit
```

Test execution is also common in stand-alone applications. I once wrote an application containing a large suite of network tests for Windows 98. After starting the application and configuring a few options, a button click kicked off an extensive set of network file sharing and copy functions. This wasn't an optimal solution. Although the tests themselves ran automati-cally, user intervention was still required to select and execute the tests.

 A much better solution, and one used by nearly every team at Microsoft today, is to use a test harness to run automated tests. A test harness is the framework needed to run tests. Good harnesses are configurable, extendable, and make automated testing easier. An ex-ample of a simple test harness architecture is shown in Figure 10-3.

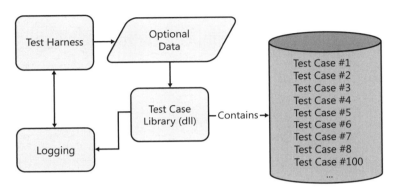

FIGURE 10-3 Test harness design.

In this example, the test harness is an application that runs tests contained in another binary—for example, Windows dynamic-link library (DLL). The harness workflow runs some-thing like this:

1. **The test harness starts and examines any additional data passed to it.**   This can in-clude environment variables, specific tests to run, locations of files, network addresses, or anything else needed by the test. This information always includes the name of the file containing the test cases. An example command line that would run test cases 1 to 100 in TestCase.dll, repeat those 100 tests 10 times, and log information to a file named test.log might look like this:

    harness.exe TestCase.dll -Tests 1-100 –Repeat 10 –output test.log

2. **The harness executes the test cases**.   Depending on the harness or optional data, one or all of the automated test cases might run sequentially, randomly, or in a specific order. For native C and C++ code, a common implementation of a test harness is to create a dynamic-link library (DLL) containing functions for each test. Typically, the DLL uses a table to track detailed test information as well as unique identification for each test. A simple example is as follows:

```
struct functionTable[] =
{
    { "API 1 "Positive Functional Test", 1, FunctionalTest },
    { "API 1 "Boundary Test", 2, BoundaryTest },
    // ...
};
```

The table in this example contains three entries used by the harness; a plain text description of the test (for example, "Positive Functional Test"), a unique identifier, and the address of the function that executes the test. This makes it possible, for example, to tell the harness to run test 2 without the need to know (or remember) that test 2 is a boundary test for a specific API.

A harness with this architecture works by calling LoadLibrary on the DLL, and then passing the address of the function from the function table to GetProcAddress to call the routine contained in the DLL directly.

The test code used in this harness architecture looks like a typical function in an application.

```
int FunctionalTest(int parameters)
{
        int testResult = 0;
        //test code here

        if(testWasSuccessful)
                testResult = 1;
        return testPass;
}
```

This variety of test harness is common in automated testing efforts at Microsoft and is effective and extensible.

More and more automation at Microsoft is being written using C# (pronounced "cee sharp"). Development in C# is generally faster than writing the equivalent native C or C++ code. Tests (or applications) written in managed code typically use less code than the native equivalent does, enabling easier reading, review, and maintenance of the code. Managed code also removes the causes of many of the bugs that are easy to create in native code; variable initialization and memory management, for example, are automatic.

When authoring test cases in C#, the test details can exist as attributes to a function. Attributes are more flexible than creating a table of functions in a header file is, and by grouping the test information next to the test in the source code rather than in a separate file, the test information is more likely to be up-to-date.

```
[TestCaseAttribute( "Build Verification Test: Math Tests", Type = TestType.BVT,
ID=42)]
public TestResult BuildVerificationTest_Math1()
{
    TestResult.AddComment("executing BuildVerificationTest_Math1");
    //code removed ...
    return TestResult.Pass;
}
```

This example uses a custom attribute to describe the test and the test type and assigns a unique ID to the test. The harness uses reflection to examine the details of the attributes and execute the test methods contained in the managed code. Command-line usage of a managed test harness can look like this:

managed-harness.exe managed-test.dll TestType=BVT

The harness using this command line might examine managed-test.dll using reflection and run all test methods with the TestType.BVT attribute.

The unit-testing framework included in Microsoft Visual Studio Team System contains built-in attributes that are as applicable to functional testing as they are to unit testing. Managed code test harnesses often implement additional attributes to enable more complete descriptions and classifications of test cases. Table 10-2 contains a list of common managed code test attributes.

TABLE 10-2 Common Managed Code Test Attributes

Attribute	Description
ClassSetup	Methods with this attribute contain actions that occur before any tests execute. Methods with this attribute can start the application, set values in a database, or configure settings needed by all tests.
ClassTeardown	Teardown actions occur after all tests have run, and they return the environment to its original state. A method with this attribute typically removes all artifacts of the test, such as files, database entries, or registry entries.
TestInitialize	Methods with this attribute run before the execution of each test and include anything needed to prepare the environment for a test, such as copying or creating files needed for the test. This reduces the amount of potentially duplicated code at the beginning of each test method, but assumes that every test in the suite needs to start from the same point.
TestCleanup	Methods with this attribute run after the execution of each test. Methods with this attribute might delete files created by the test, restore a database to known settings, or restore other system configurations.
TestMethod	Methods with this attribute represent the tests contained in the file.
Step	This attribute is used to denote methods that must occur in a specific sequence. A typical managed test harness can execute tests in an arbitrary order. If specific tests need to be run sequentially, the *Step* attribute is used to denote this.
SupportFile	This attribute indicates that a specific file is necessary for a test to run.

```
// These test methods always run in the following order

[TestCaseAttribute("Example Ordered Tests", Step=1, SupportFile="one.txt")]
public TestResult TestOne()
{
    // do something with "one.txt"
    ...
}

[TestCaseAttribute("Example Ordered Tests", Step=2, SupportFile="two.txt")]
public TestResult TestTwo()
{
    // do something with "two.txt"
    ...
}
```

In this example, the Step attribute indicates to the harness that TestOne always executes before executing TestTwo. Additionally, TestOne and TestTwo require the presence of additional support files ("one.txt" and "two.txt," respectively).

3. **Test cases can log data (including test status) to a file, to the debug stream, or to some other persistent location.**   The test harness examines logs or other information to determine whether the tests have passed or failed. Logs can be simple text files, XML-based files, HTML files, combinations of the three, or completely different outputs such as Windows system events or entries in a database. Log files are essential for tracking test results as well as for debugging test failures. Table 10-3 lists several elements that should be in every log file generated by test automation.

TABLE 10-3 Suggested Required Elements for Test Logs

Element	Notes
Test ID	Every test for a system needs a unique ID so that results can be aggregated at the highest level of reporting without conflicting IDs. Globally unique identifiers (GUIDs) are often used for test IDs.
Test Name	This is an easily understood name of the test.
Environment Information	Include operating system version, SKU (for example, Windows Vista Ultimate), operating system language, architecture (x86, 32 bit, 64 bit, and so forth), total RAM, free disk space, and computer name. Environment information is often beneficial in tracking down bugs that occur only on a subset of all test computers.

Element	Notes
Application Under Test (AUT) Information	Include the application or component version or build revision. If applicable, include the localized language of the application and version information for all application dependencies.
Test Result	Test results are typically pass or fail. Other options are possible and are discussed later in this chapter.

Regardless of the logging format and medium, consider the following several excellent practices when logging data from an automated test:

- Passing tests should generate as few log records as possible.

- Failing tests should provide enough information to debug the failure without the need to rerun the test or connect a debugger. The log file should include the binary and function under test, as well as the functionality under test and expected and actual results.

- Error codes should be clear and written in understandable text.

- Logging should be configurable without the need for recompilation. Tests should be able to run with multiple logging levels, including "no logging," "normal logging," and "verbose logging."

The following is an example of a simple log file containing information about the test, the test result, and additional status on the execution of the test.

```
<TESTCASE ID=1024>
*** TEST STARTING
*** Test Name:     Attempt to delete read-only file
*** vvvvvvvvvvvvvvvvvvvvvvvvvvvvvvvvvvvvvvvvvvvvvvvvvvvvvvvvvvvvvvvvv
   BEGIN TEST: "Attempt to delete read-only file"
     Creating read-only file c:\temp\test.tmp
     Verifying read-only attributes...
     File is read-only
     Calling DeleteFile
     DeleteFile returned ERROR_SUCCESS. Expected: ERROR_ACCESS_DENIED
   END TEST: "Attempt to delete read-only file", FAILED, Time=0.644
*** ^^^^^^^^^^^^^^^^^^^^^^^^^^^^^^^^^^^^^^^^^^^^^^^^^^^^^^^^^^^^^^^^^
*** TEST COMPLETED
***
*** Test Name:     Attempt to delete read-only file
** Test ID:       1024*
** Library Path:  \fsystst.dll
*** Command Line:  -p -Flash
*** Result:        Failed
*** Random Seed:   30221
*** Execution Time: 0:00:00.644
</TESTCASE RESULT="FAILED">
```

Another simple log file, this one in XML format, follows.

```xml
<harness harness_client="testclient1">
<harness_client_machine>testclient1</harness_client_machine>
<harness_client_ip>157.59.28.234</harness_client_ip>
  <result_information>
    <parameter name="computer_name" value="LAB-09563"/>
    <parameter name="result_filename" value="1234.LOG"/>
    <parameter name="result_testid" value="1234"/>
    <parameter name="result_comments" value="Passed"/>
  </result_information>
</message>
</harness>
```

Analysis

Execution of the steps in the test are only the beginning of an automated test. After execution, some level of investigation must occur to determine the result of the test. Occasionally, analysis is simple, but the criteria for determining whether a test has passed or not can be complex. A test oracle is a source of expected test results for a test case. The CreateFile function in the Windows API creates a new file or opens an existing file. If it succeeds, the function returns a handle (a unique integer value) to the file, and if the function fails, it returns an error code. You could test this function in a trivial manner by checking the return value to determine the test status.

```c
TEST_RESULT TestCreateFile(void)
{
    HANDLE hFile = CreateFile(...)
    if (hFile == INVALID_HANDLE_VALUE)
    {
        return TEST_FAIL;
    }
    else
    {
        return TEST_PASS;
    }
}
```

This "test" really only determines whether the CreateFile function returns a value. A significant amount of additional testing is necessary to determine whether the function actually worked to determine an accurate test result. A tester can create an oracle (or verification function) to aid in determining the test status.

```
TEST_RESULT TestCreateFile(void)
{
    TEST_RESULT tr = TEST_FAIL;
    HANDLE hFile = CreateFile(...)
    if (IsValidFile(hFile, ...) == TRUE)
    {
        tr = TEST_PASS;
    }
    return tr;
}
BOOL IsValidFile(hFile, ...)
{
    /* ORACLE:
       check handle value for INVALID_HANDLE_VALUE,
       determine if the file exists on disk,
       confirm that the attributes assigned to the file are correct,
       if file is writable, confirm that it can be written to,
       and do any other applicable verification.
       return true if the file appears valid
       otherwise, return false
    */
}
```

The difficulty with oracles is accurately predicting the result of the operations they are verifying. Accurate oracles require extensive knowledge of the functionality under test and clear documentation of the intent of the functionality. At a minimum, they must verify success, but they also must verify a variety of environment and program changes that occur in parallel or as side effects of testing functionality.

The challenge of oracles

One of my responsibilities on the Windows 98 team was testing the graphic functions of the Windows operating system, such as the drawing of text and shapes on the screen. On Windows, the SetPixel function changes the pixel at given coordinates to a specified color. The related GetPixel function retrieves the color of a pixel at a given coordinate.

I remember an interesting late-night conversation I had related to oracles and the functions that manipulated pixels on the screen. The discussion revolved around whether we could safely use GetPixel as the oracle to test SetPixel. In other words, if I set the color of a specific pixel using SetPixel, could I trust GetPixel to retrieve the data, rather than just directly return the value I used in the SetPixel call?

I started to design and prototype some code to query the display driver data structures and attempt to determine the color of the pixel without calling GetPixel, but someone obviously smarter than me pointed out that was exactly what GetPixel did anyway.

The answer was yes, I could safely use GetPixel to test SetPixel, but it's still something I hear questioned from time to time, and something that always reminds me of the philosophy of oracles.

When running manual tests, it is usually straightforward to determine whether the test passes or fails, or whether certain tests should not be run because of various circumstances in the testing environment. Automated tests, however, must try to determine this without human intervention. As discussed previously, determining pass and fail can have challenges. The gray area between pass and fail often causes confusion, but it is essential to understand results beyond pass and fail to accurately report the complete status of automated tests. Several types of potential test results are listed in Table 10-4.

TABLE 10-4 Test Result Types

Result	Description
Pass	The test passed.
Fail	The test failed.
Skip	Skipped tests typically occur when tests are available for optional functionality. For example, a test suite for video cards might include tests that run only if certain features are enabled in hardware.
Abort	The most common example of an aborted result occurs when expected support files are not available. For example, if test collateral (additional files needed to run the test) are located on a network share and that share is unavailable, the test is aborted.
Block	The test was blocked from running by a known application or system issue. Marking tests as blocked (rather than failed) when they cannot run as a result of a known bug keeps failure rates from being artificially high, but high numbers of blocked test cases indicate areas where quality and functionality are untested and unknown.
Warn	The test passed but indicated warnings that might need to be examined in greater detail.

It is possible to have more result types than listed in Table 10-4, and acceptable analysis might include only pass, fail, and unknown as result types. In test automation, the oracle is responsible for accurately determining test status and must indicate status as well as action to take on any test that has not passed.

Reporting

On small projects, log files often are the reports. Log files report pass or fail results for tests and suites of tests, and as long as there aren't too many log files to look at, this can be sufficient reporting. Many test projects at Microsoft, for example, include thousands of test suites and hundreds of thousands of tests. For projects of this size, manually examining log files is out of the question. One possible option is for tests to log results directly to a database, but the overhead of connecting to a database isn't feasible for all test scenarios. Network connectivity might not be available for all scenarios, and network connectivity to a database is much slower than is logging on directly to a local storage device or debug stream.

A common and effective solution is to automate the parsing of log files. A log file parser can execute outside the scope of running the test case and works equally well for single log files as for batches of log files. The parser can simply record the test case name and the test result, or it can record other potentially essential metadata such as the type of test, component under test, and information needed to debug a failure. A database typically stores the parsed data, and applications or Web pages display the results. Table 10-5 shows a partial list of test case results.

TABLE 10-5 Test Case Results

Component	Passed	Failed	Skipped	Blocked	Not run	Total results	%Passed	%Complete
component 1	1,262	148	194	415	0	2,019	69.15	100.00
component 2	1,145	78	18	28	0	1,269	91.53	100.00
component 3	872	18	32	4	0	926	97.53	100.00

Note that skipped tests do not affect the pass rate, but blocked test cases are part of the calculation. Pass rates in this example are calculated as Passed / (Total Results – Skipped). Using the definitions in Table 10-4, tests marked as skipped are done so purposely and reflect tests that are intentionally not run. Blocked test cases represent unknown areas. Even though the test has not run, because it is unknown whether it will pass or fail, it is included in the fail rate. There are various alternate calculations for determining pass rates, but the preceding method is the one used most prevalently at Microsoft.

Cleanup

Whenever possible, tests should return the environment to the state it was in before the test ran. This ensures that failures in subsequent tests are the result of product bugs rather than artifacts left over from the previous tests. This is especially important if the setup portion of the test is time extensive.

Although good test cleanup is preferable, it is sometimes impractical in practice. A test can intend to clean up after itself, but if the test causes memory leaks or memory corruption, cleaning up can mask the result of the corruption before it can occur. On the other hand, if no cleanup ever occurs, it can be difficult to track down the root cause of errors that occur in subsequent tests. A reasonable compromise is to perform a cleanup step with all automated tests, but also to run repeatedly in parallel another set of tests that do not clean up. For example, while running automated functional tests with a cleanup stage, also run a repeated set of scenario tests on a few other computers.

Help

As a tester's career grows, he might take on ownership of more critical components in his group, or he might change groups in the company. When this happens, another tester must take over the ownership of maintaining, configuring, and running the tests and must understand how to interpret the results. The final phase of SEARCH is the portion that enables execution and maintenance of the tests throughout the lifetime of the product.

Test code, like product code, must be maintainable. In addition to well-structured and commented code, the help phase often includes creating related documentation. Information on the purpose of the tests, known limitations, configuration notes, and instructions on interpreting results are all included in this documentation.

This step isn't as exciting to many testers as the first five steps of SEARCH are, but over the lifetime of the test, this stage can be the most important.

Note The automated tests written for many Microsoft products have more lines of code than the products they test.

Too much of a good thing?

Microsoft's internal repository for shared tools includes more than 40 entries under "test harness." Although entire divisions consolidate on some harnesses, the variety of products and unique needs of test teams at Microsoft dictate that some duplication is inevitable. The biggest problem with so many solutions is that sharing test cases or test results between teams is problematic. It also increases the time it takes for testers to ramp up when they change teams in the company. In a company the size of Microsoft, it might not be feasible or practical to have every group use the exact same toolset, but too many solutions presents problems that can be difficult to solve.

Fortunately, there is a considerable effort under way to move to a smaller set of testing tools. Several of the long-used test tools will remain in use for the near future, and many teams are moving toward the solutions available in Visual Studio Team System.

Run, Automation, Run!

Simple automation executes by running an application or script. Typically, large-scale automation must run under a complex framework, ensuring compatibility and consistent reporting between every test pass. Figure 10-4 shows an automated test infrastructure that includes all aspects of SEARCH. A well-constructed test automation system enables execution of the entire suite of automated tests with one figurative push of a button.

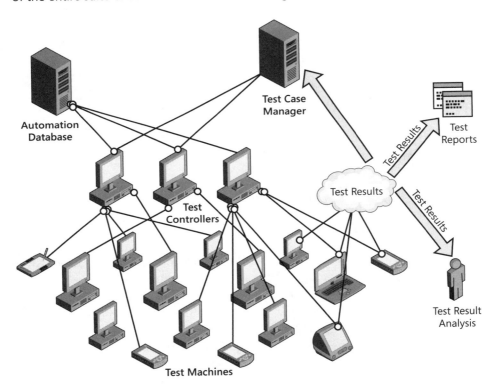

FIGURE 10-4 Automation infrastructure.

Putting It All Together

An automation system contains a variety of components. In addition to the test harness (refer to Figure 10-3), mechanisms are necessary to obtain tests from the test case management system and map those tests to the test binaries or scripts that execute the automation. Computers and devices are needed to run those tests. The results then need to be reported and recorded in the test case manager.

Note There are more than 100,000 computers at Microsoft dedicated to automated testing.

Large-Scale Test Automation

In most automation systems in use at Microsoft, the entire test pass starts with a single command executed from the command line, a Web page, or an application. In some teams, automated file monitors ensure that tests start automatically as soon as the build is available for test. The automation flow begins at the test case manager (TCM). Based on the configuration of the test pass, the TCM constructs a list of tests to run.

The test cases are then cross-referenced with the binaries or scripts that execute the test. A unique ID or globally unique identifier (GUID) shared between the TCM and an automation database is the most common method for this correlation. An advantage of maintaining a separate database for automation is that information about the automated test (such as command-line options, location of the test and any related files) is completely separate from information about the test case.

A shared directory on one of the database servers or on another computer in the system can contain test collateral—extra files needed for the tests to run, such as .doc files for Microsoft Word tests or media files for Windows Media Player.

Next, the automation database and test case manager contact test controllers, which in turn configure the test computers to run the specified tests. Usually, each controller is responsible for deploying tests to between 8 and 50 or more computers (the number depends on a variety of factors including hardware and network limitations). Once preparation of the test computer is complete, the test controller deploys the test. The test controller waits for the test to complete (or crash), and then obtains the log file from the test computer. The controller can parse the log file for results directly, but more often, it sends the log file back to the TCM or to another computer for parsing.

After the log files are examined and a test result is known, the file is saved (to ease failure analysis) and the results are recorded in the TCM. Many of the systems used at Microsoft also log all test failures directly to the bug tracking system. Finally, the results are presented in a variety of reports, and the test team examines the failures.

Common Automation Mistakes

There are numerous advantages to writing automated tests, but it is easy to make mistakes. Microsoft test developers have coding skills equal to their development peers, but there is one big difference between test code and product code: Product code is tested. To be fair, you could say that repeated test runs and constant feedback in the form of test results imply that the product tests the tests. Nevertheless, the goal of nearly every Microsoft team is for test code to have the same quality goals as production code does.

Watch out for these common errors when writing test code:

- **Hard-coded paths**   Tests often need external files during test execution. The quickest and simplest method to point the test to a network share or other location is to embed the path in the source file. Unfortunately, paths can change and servers can be reconfigured or retired. It is a much better practice to store information about support files in the TCM or automation database.

- **Complexity**   The complexity issues discussed in Chapter 7, "Code Complexity," are just as prevalent in test code as they are in production code. The goal for test code must be to write the simplest code possible to test the feature sufficiently.

- **Difficult debugging**   When a failure occurs, debugging should be a quick and painless procedure—not a multihour time investment for the tester. Insufficient logging is a key contributor to making debugging difficult. When a test fails, it is a good practice to log why the test failed. "Streaming test failed: buffer size expected 2048, actual size 1024" is a much better result than "Streaming test failed: bad buffer size" or simply "Streaming test failed." With good logging information, failures can be reported and fixed without ever needing to touch a debugger.

- **False positives**   A tester investigates a failure and discovers that the product code is fine, but a bug in her test caused the test to report a failure result. The opposite of this, a false negative, is much worse—a test incorrectly reports a passing result. When analyzing test results, testers examine failures, not passing tests. Unless a test with a false negative repeats in another test or is caught by an internal user during normal usage, the consequences of false negatives are bugs in the hands of the consumer.

Writing automation is a difficult enough task, but writing quality automation is an arduous undertaking. Despite the goals of the test teams, not all test code written at Microsoft is production quality—at least not yet. For some of the reasons mentioned earlier, as well as other related issues, false positives are more common than most teams would prefer. In Chapter 12, "Other Tools," among other things, we discuss some of the tools testers use to avoid some of the pitfalls mentioned and to write high-quality tests.

Summary

Automated testing is obviously something deeply valued at Microsoft. Sufficient testing of large, complex products such as Windows, Office, and Visual Studio cannot be done without some investment in automation. Add to that numerous localized versions and 10-year support plans, and a significant investment in automation is required.

A big goal of automated testing is to scale the testing effort. Writing even one automated test takes significant effort, but when that test can run on different application configurations and languages and can be used by the sustained engineering team for a decade, its value grows considerably. Plugging that test into an automation infrastructure that automatically configures the test bed, runs the test, reports results, and files bugs is the basis of excellent, long-lived test automation.

Chapter 11
Non-Functional Testing

Alan Page

Almost everyone has experienced or heard this story: Product development was going exceptionally well. The test team and development team worked together and made quick progress. Like clockwork, the development team released a new build of the software every day, and the test team updated their build, and then created and ran new tests every day. They found bugs in the functionality, but the development team fixed issues quickly. The release date approached, and there was little pressure. The software just worked. The tests just passed. The beta testers said the software did everything it was supposed to do. The software shipped, and the initial reaction was positive.

Two weeks later the first call came in, quickly followed by many more. The program that the team had just developed was designed to run constantly in the background. After a few weeks of continuous use, the software still "worked," but performance had degraded so much that the application was nearly unusable. The team was so proud of the features and functionality of their application that they did not think to (or forgot to) run the application as a user would—for days, weeks, and months at a time. Daily builds meant that they reinstalled the application daily. The longest the application ever ran was over the weekend, from Friday to Monday, but that wasn't enough time to expose the small resource leaks in the application that would show up in an obvious way only after nearly two weeks of constant use.

Over the next week, the development team fixed nearly a dozen memory leaks and performance issues, and the test team did their best to verify that the fixes didn't break any functionality. Twenty-five days after releasing the software the team was so proud of, they released their first high-priority update, with several others following over the subsequent weeks and months.

Beyond Functionality

Non-functional testing is a somewhat confusing phrase, but one that is common throughout the testing industry. In a way, it makes sense. Functional testing involves positive and negative testing of the functionality in the application under test. Non-functional testing is merely everything else. Areas defined as non-functional include performance, load, security, reliability, and many others. Non-functional tests are sometimes referred to as behavioral tests or quality tests. A characteristic of non-functional attributes is that direct measurement is generally not possible. Instead, these attributes are gauged by indirect measures such as failure rates to measure reliability or cyclomatic complexity and design review metrics to assess testability.

The International Organization for Standardization (ISO) defines several non-functional attributes in ISO 9216 and in ISO 25000:2005. These attributes include the following:

- **Reliability** Software users expect their software to run without fault. Reliability is a measure of how well software maintains its functionality in mainstream or unexpected situations. It also sometimes includes the ability of the application to recover from a fault. The feature that enables an application to automatically save the active document periodically could be considered a reliability feature. Reliability is a serious topic at Microsoft and is one of the pillars of the Trustworthy Computing Initiative (http://www.microsoft.com/mscorp/twc).

- **Usability** Even a program with zero defects will be worthless if the user cannot figure out how to use it. Usability measures how easy it is for users of the software to learn and control the application to accomplish whatever they need to do. Usability studies, customer feedback, and examination of error messages and other dialogues all support usability.

- **Maintainability** Maintainability describes the effort needed to make changes in software without causing errors. Product code and test code alike must be highly maintainable. Knowledge of the code base by the team members, testability, and complexity all contribute to this attribute. (Testability is discussed in Chapter 4, "A Practical Approach to Test Case Design," and complexity is discussed in Chapter 7, "Analyzing Risk with Code Complexity.")

- **Portability** Microsoft Windows NT 3.1 ran on four different processor families. At that time, portability of code was a major requirement in the Windows division. Even today, Windows code must run on both 32-bit and 64-bit processors. A number of Microsoft products also run on both Windows and Macintosh platforms. Portable code for both products and tests is crucial for many Microsoft organizations.

Testing the "ilities"

A list of attributes commonly called the ilities contains the preceding list plus dozens of other quality attributes such as dependability, reusability, testability, extensibility, and adaptability. All of these can be used to help evaluate and understand the quality of a product beyond its functional capabilities. Scalability (ability of the program to handle excessive usage) and security (ability of the system to handle unauthorized modification attempts) are two highly measured "ilities" among teams at Microsoft.

Microsoft test teams often have specialized teams to focus on many of these "ilities." In the case of usability, we even have a whole separate engineering discipline dedicated to running the tests and innovating the tools and methods we use.

In regard to organizational structure, there are two primary approaches to testing non-functional areas. Larger teams can structure themselves as shown in Figure 11-1, with test leads or test managers managing feature team testers alongside non-functional test teams.

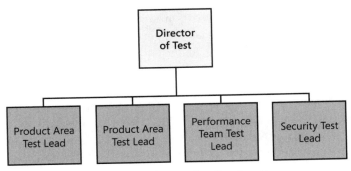

FIGURE 11-1 Dedicated teams for non-functional areas.

A more prevalent approach, shown in Figure 11-2, is the use of a virtual team to test a non-functional area. Virtual teams do not report through the same managers, but work together to address a specific aspect of testing in addition to their own feature work. Every virtual team has a designated virtual team lead who is responsible for strategy, goals, and success metrics of the team.

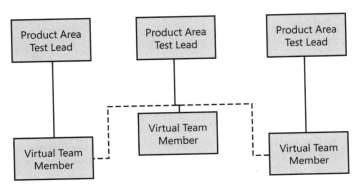

FIGURE 11-2 Virtual teams for non-functional testing.

A combination of these two approaches is also common. There might be a dedicated team for an area such as security or performance, while virtual teams take on areas like usability and accessibility.

Numerous resources describe various types of non-functional testing. In this chapter, I do not attempt to discuss every single type of non-functional testing used at Microsoft. Instead, I highlight a few of the areas of non-functional testing where Microsoft has solutions that represent something interesting in innovation, approach, or scale.

Performance Testing

Because of the scope and overlap between various non-functional attributes, the names of many attributes are used interchangeably. For example, performance testing is often associated with the concepts of stress, load, and scalability testing mentioned later in this chapter. In many test organizations at Microsoft, the same testers or test teams are in charge of all of these areas. The approaches and goals for these areas have many differences, but there are several similarities. For example, testing a server system to see how well it performs with thousands of connected users is a type of a performance test (many others would call this a load test or scalability test). Similarly, the ability of an application to perform after running for weeks or months without restarting is considered by many to be part of performance testing (most would call this test a reliability test or long-haul test).

The most common flavor of performance testing could be called stopwatch testing. Many years ago, some testers actually sat in front of the screen and used a stopwatch to measure the performance of various functional tests. This approach, although a reasonable first step in performance testing, is error prone and rarely is the best approach for timing application performance.

The concept behind this genre of performance testing is simply to measure the duration of various important actions. This type of performance test is a single test or a suite of tests designed to measure the application's response times to various user actions or to measure product functionality in controlled environments. Because the stopwatch approach just doesn't scale and isn't really reproducible, most performance testing is accomplished with automated tests that execute the tests and record timing information.

The goal of performance testing is to identify the important and significant bottlenecks in the system. You can think of the system as a series of bottlenecks; identifying and improving one bottleneck most often reveals a new bottleneck somewhere else. For example, I worked on a device running Microsoft Windows CE once where the first big performance problem we found was with the way memory management worked on a specific hardware implementation. We isolated the problem and improved the speed of the memory allocations. We ran our tests again and found a new bottleneck, this time in network throughput. After we fixed that issue, we worked on improving the next bottleneck, and then the next bottleneck until the entire system met our performance goals. One thing to keep in mind is that establishing performance goals early is critical—otherwise, you might not know when to stop performance testing.

How Do You Measure Performance?

Perhaps the most difficult part of performance testing is determining what to measure. Performance testers use several different approaches to help target their testing. One thing every experienced performance tester will tell you is that a proactive approach that involves reviewing and analyzing performance objectives early in the design process is imperative. In fact, the best way to address most non-functional testing needs is to consider those needs during program design. Some tips to help identify potential performance issues during the design phase include the following:

- **Ask questions**   Identify areas that have potential performance problems. Ask about network traffic, memory management, database design, or any other areas that are relevant. Even if you don't have the performance design solution, testers can make a big impact by making other team members think about performance.

- **Think about the big picture**   Think about full scenarios rather than individual optimizations. You will have time to dig into granular performance scenarios throughout development, but time during the design is better spent thinking about end-to-end scenarios.

- **Set clear, unambiguous goals**   Goals such as "Response time should be quick" are impossible to measure. Apply SMART (specific, measurable, achievable, relevant, time-bound) criteria to the design goals. For example, "Execution of every user action must return application control to the user within 100 milliseconds, or within 10 percent of the previous version, whichever is longer."

An additional tactic to consider is to anticipate where performance issues might occur or which actions are most important to the users and need measurement. Definition of these scenarios is most effective when addressed during the design phase. A scenario-based approach is effective as an alternative and is well suited for performance testing legacy code. Regardless of the situation, here are some helpful tips for performance testing.

- **Establish a baseline**   An important aspect of defining and measuring early is establishing baselines. If performance testing starts late in the project, it is difficult to determine when any discovered performance bottlenecks were introduced.

- **Run tests often**   Once you have a baseline, measure as often as possible. Measuring often is a tremendous aid in helping to diagnose exactly which code changes are contributing to performance degradation.

- **Measure responsiveness**   Users don't care how long an underlying function takes to execute. What they care about is how responsive the application is. Performance tests should focus on measuring responsiveness to the user, regardless of how long the operation takes.

- **Measure performance**   It is tempting to mix functionality (or other types of testing) in a performance test suite. Concentrate performance tests on measuring performance.

- **Take advantage of performance tests**   The alternate side of the previous bullet is that performance tests are often useful in other testing situations. Use automated performance tests in other automated test suites whenever possible (for instance, in the stress test suite).

- **Anticipate bottlenecks**   Target performance tests on areas where latency can occur, such as file and print I/O, memory functions, network operations, or any other areas where unresponsive behavior can occur.

- **Use tools**   In conjunction with the preceding bullet, use tools that simulate network or I/O latency to determine the performance characteristics of the application under test in adverse situations.

- **Remember that resource utilization is important**   Response time and latency are both key indicators of performance, but don't forget to monitor the load on CPU, disk or network I/O, and memory during your performance tests. For example, if you are testing a media player, in addition to responsiveness, you might want to monitor network I/O and CPU usage to ensure that the resource usage of the application does not cause adverse behaviors in other applications.

- **Use "clean machines" and don't...**   Partition your performance testing between clean machines (new installations of the operating systems and application under test) and computer configurations based on customer profiles. Clean machines are useful to generate consistent numbers, but those numbers can be misleading if performance is adversely affected by other applications, add-ins, or other extensions. Running performance tests on the clean machine will generate your best numbers, but running tests on a machine full of software will generate numbers closer to what your customers will see.

- **Avoid change**   Resist the urge to tweak (or overhaul) your performance tests. The less the tests change, the more accurate the data will be over the long term.

Performance counters are often useful in identifying performance bottlenecks in the system. Performance counters are granular measurements that reveal some performance aspect of the application or system, and they enable monitoring and analysis of these aspects. All versions of the Windows operating system include a tool (Perfmon.exe) for monitoring these performance counters, and Windows includes performance counters for many areas where bottlenecks exist, such as CPU, disk I/O, network I/O, memory statistics, and resource usage. A sample view of a Perfmon.exe counter is shown in Figure 11-3.

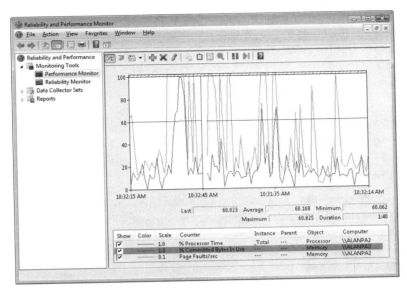

FIGURE 11-3 Windows Reliability and Performance Monitor.

Applications can implement custom performance counters to track private object usage, execution timings, or most anything else interesting in regard to performance. A comprehensive set of performance counters planned in the design phase and implemented early will always benefit performance testing and analysis during the entire life of the product.

Many books and Web references contain extensive additional information in the area of performance testing. Both the patterns & practices Performance Testing Guidance Project at http://www.codeplex.com/PerfTesting/ and http://msdn.microsoft.com/en-us/library/bb924375.aspx are great places to find further information about this topic.

Stress Testing

The ability of an application to perform under expected and heavy load conditions, as well as the ability to handle increased capacity, is an area that often falls under the umbrella of performance testing. Stress testing is a generic term that often includes load testing, mean time between failure (MTBF) testing, low-resource testing, capacity testing, or repetition testing. The main differences between the approaches and goals of these different types of testing are described here:

- **Stress testing**   Generally, the goal of stress testing is to simulate larger-than-expected workloads to expose bugs that occur only under peak load conditions. Stress testing attempts to find the weak points in an application. Memory leaks, race conditions, lock collision between threads or rows in a database, and other synchronization issues are some of the common bugs unearthed by stress testing.

- **Load testing**   Load testing intends to find out what happens to the system or application under test when peak or even higher than normal levels of activity occur. For example, a load test for a Web service might attempt to simulate thousands of users connecting and using the service at one time. Performance testing typically includes measuring response time under peak expected loads.

- **Mean time between failure (MTBF) testing**   MTBF testing measures the average amount of time a system or application runs before an error or crash occurs. There are several flavors of this type of test, including mean time to failure (MTTF) and mean time to crash (MTTC). There are technical differences between the terms, but in practice, these are often used interchangeably.

- **Low-resource testing**   Low-resource testing determines what happens when the system is low or depleted of a critical resource such as physical memory, hard disk space, or other system-defined resources. It is important, for example, to understand what will happen when an application attempts to save a file to a location that does not have enough storage space available to store the file, or what happens when an attempt to allocate additional memory for an application fails.

- **Capacity testing**   Closely related to load testing, capacity testing is typically used for server or services testing. The goal of capacity testing is to determine the maximum users a computer or set of computers can support. Capacity models are often built out of capacity testing data so that Operations can plan when to increase system capacity by either adding more resources such as RAM, CPU, and disk or just adding another computer.

- **Repetition testing**   Repetition testing is a simple, brute force technique of determining the effect of repeating a function or scenario. The essence of this technique is to run a test in a loop until reaching a specified limit or threshold, or until an undesirable action occurs. For example, a particular action might leak 20 bytes of memory. This isn't enough to cause any problems elsewhere in the application, but if the test runs 2,000 times in a row, the leak grows to 40,000 bytes. If the function provides core functionality that is called often, this test could catch a memory leak that might become noticeable only after the application has run for an extended period of time. There are usually better ways to find memory leaks, but on occasion, this brute force method can be effective.

Stapler stress

In the early days of Microsoft Office, testers were very creative with their office supplies.

The goal was to simulate real user input from a keyboard that would overload the program's input buffer. The challenge was finding the proper office accessory that was the right size with the proper dimensions that could easily be applied to the keyboard while I went to lunch. As it turns out, the stapler fit the task. When I came back from lunch, there was always an ASSERT or Hard Crash on my screen. Craig Fleischman, Test Manager

The USB cart of death

During the Windows 2000 project, we had an interesting way to test Plug and Play. We created the "USB Cart of Death." We started with a two-level cart similar to what you'd see in a library.

About 10 eight-port hubs were wired together, and then every port was filled with some different type of USB device. A USB steering wheel adorned the back of the cart, and a USB radio provided the antenna. Two cameras were on the front. All power went to a USB uninterruptible power supply (UPS). The entire cart, completely mobile, came down to two cables (power, USB). The final USB cable was plugged into a USB PCMCIA card.

We'd plug the card into a laptop, watch the operating system start up the 50 or so devices on it, and then (either before or after it finished) we'd unceremoniously yank the PCMCIA card. If a blue screen occurred, or if another error occurred, the appropriate developer would be asked to look at the computer. In the meantime, we would wheel the cart on to the next laptop, in hopes of finding a different bug. Adrian Oney, Senior Development Lead

Distributed Stress Testing

Stress testing is important at Microsoft. Most product lines run stress tests across hundreds of computers or more. Some portion of stress testing occurs over extended periods—often running 3 to 5 consecutive days or longer. On most teams, however, a more significant quantity of stress testing occurs over a 12- to 14-hour period between the time employees leave for the evening and return the next day. Everyone takes part in volunteering their computers to run the overnight stress tests. Test, Development, Program Management, and even Product Support run stress on their computers every night.

When running stress tests, failures and crashes are inevitable. On small teams, reporting stress failures and finding the owner of the code at fault can transpire by phone, e-mail, or a knock on a door. Unfortunately, if a crash occurs on a computer that nobody is paying attention to, or on Frank's computer while he's on vacation, investigation and debugging of the failure might never occur.

Large teams need a more efficient method for determining which computers have had stress failures and for determining who should investigate the failure. The most common solution is an ordinary client/server solution. Because stress tests usually run overnight, ideally, the client portion of stress runs in an idle state until reaching a specified time. Nightly stress testing is a valued part of the development life cycle, and this ensures that no one forgets to start stress before they leave for the evening. On Windows 95, for example, the client was a screen saver. The first time the screen saver ran after a specified time (19:00 by default), the stress tests would start. The Windows Vista team uses a background application that is configurable through an icon in the notification area.

Distributed Stress Architecture

The architecture for a distributed stress system is somewhat less complex than is the automation infrastructure discussed in Chapter 10, "Test Automation," but it does have some implementation challenges. Figure 11-4 shows the basic work flow for such a system.

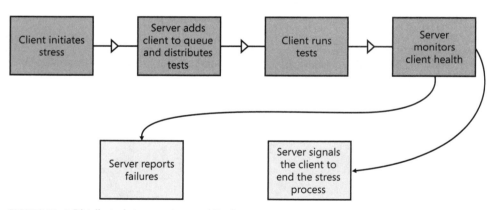

FIGURE 11-4 Distributed stress system architecture.

The Stress Client

As mentioned earlier, an application on the computer targeted for stress (the stress client) initiates the stress test run. Manual initiation of the stress tests is possible, but in many cases, stress tests start automatically at a preconfigured time. The initiation phase is a simple announcement to the server that the host computer is ready to run stress tests. At this point, the server distributes a variety of stress tests to the host computer for execution. A mix of tests runs for various lengths of time until either reaching a specified time or the stress tests are manually terminated. (Manual termination is convenient if an employee arrives in the morning before the configured end time or needs to reclaim the computer for another reason.) Figure 11-5 shows stress clients connected to a stress server.

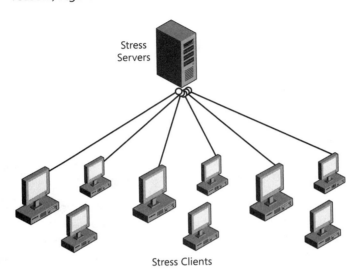

FIGURE 11-5 Distributed stress.

In the case of operating system stress, such as Windows or Windows CE, stress client computers are usually attached to a debugger to aid in investigating failures. Application-based stress suites can run with a debugger such as WinDbg or Microsoft Visual Studio attached during the entire stress run, or they might rely on starting the debugger as a just in time (JIT) debugger. The JIT approach is the most common on application and server teams, whereas an "always attached" debugger is used prevalently on teams developing operating systems.

The Stress Server

The role of the stress server is to distribute a set of stress tests (commonly called the stress mix) to all stress clients and track status on the state of the clients. After a client contacts the server, the server adds the client name to the list of known stress clients and begins distributing the tests. The clients periodically send a heartbeat pulse to the server. The heartbeat is critical for determining whether a computer is in a crashed or hung state. If a client heartbeat is not received in a reasonable amount of time, the computer name is added to the list of computers that will need additional investigation or debugging.

At the end of the stress run, the server signals all clients to end the stress testing session. The failures are examined, and then are distributed to the appropriate owners for additional debugging.

The Windows Stress team

The Windows Stress team does not have a lab filled with hundreds of computers. Instead, they rely on the internal Windows community to volunteer their computers to the stress testing effort. Every day, dozens or more stress failures are reported from the thousands of computers that run stress. Because the Windows Stress team doesn't "own" the computers running stress, their goal is to ensure that the computers are debugged quickly so that the owners can use the computers for their daily work.

Every morning around 06:30, one or more members of the Stress team arrive at Microsoft and begin to examine all failures found over the previous evening (or weekend). They spend the next two to three hours debugging and assigning issues to appropriate owners. The preliminary debugging, although time intensive, helps them accurately find the correct owner for every issue. On a team with hundreds of developers, assigning issues to the right person in the first place can save a lot of time.

When they find the most probable owner for an issue, they send an e-mail message to the computer owner and the engineer assigned to investigate the issue with a description of the problem. It is possible to connect remotely to the kernel debugger (kd.exe) used by the Windows team, so those assigned to investigate don't even have to leave their office to look at the failure. Because of this, despite the vast size and disparate locations of members on the Windows Stress team, many issues are resolved before the computer owner arrives at work.

Attributes of Multiclient Stress Tests

Stress tests written for a large distributed stress system have many of the same quality goals as typical automated tests do, but also have some unique attributes:

- **Run infinitely**   Stress tests ordinarily run forever, or until signaled to end. The standard implementation procedure for this is for the test to respond efficiently to a WM_CLOSE message so that the server can run tests for varying lengths of time.

- **Memory usage**   Memory leaks by a test during stress typically manifest as failures in other tests resulting from a lack of resources. Ideally, stress tests do not leak memory. Because tests will run concurrently with several other tests, excessive use of processes, threads, or other system resources is also a practice to avoid.

- **No known failures**   On many teams, it is a requirement that all tests are run anywhere from 24 hours to a week on a private computer with no failures before being added to the stress mix. The goal of the nightly stress run is to determine what the application or operating system will do when a variety of actions run in parallel and in varying sequences. If one test causes the same failure to occur on every single stress client computer, no new issues will be found, and an entire night of stress will have been wasted.

Compatibility Testing

Application compatibility testing typically focuses on interactions between the application or system under test and other applications. Other applications can include both internal and external applications. At Microsoft, the biggest efforts in application compatibility are undoubtedly the labors of the Windows team. Every new release of Windows adds new functionality, but must continue to support applications designed for previous versions of Windows. Application compatibility (aka app compat) affects most other Microsoft products as well. Microsoft Internet Explorer must continue to support relevant plug-ins or other add-on functionality; applications with a rich developer community such as Visual Studio or Office must also support a variety of third-party-generated functionality. Even support for previous file formats in new versions of an application is critical.

The copy of Microsoft Office Word 2007 I am using to write this chapter supports previous Word document types, as well as templates and other add-ins created for previous versions of Word. Nearly every application I use supports opening files from previous versions of the application, opening files created by other applications, or a variety of add-in components that enhance program functionality. Application compatibility testing ensures that the interoperability between the application under test and all of these file formats and components continues to work correctly.

Application Libraries

Many teams at Microsoft maintain libraries of applications or components used entirely for application compatibility testing. The Windows Application Compatibility team has a library containing many hundreds of applications. There are similarly large libraries for teams such as Office, Windows CE, and the .NET Framework.

Adopt an App

Windows 95 was Microsoft's first 32-bit operating system targeted at the general consumer audience. At the time, Windows NT was the "business" version of Windows and supported a relatively minute number of applications. Windows 95, on the other hand, was expected to run new 32-bit applications, as well as a legacy code base of thousands of 16-bit Windows 3.1 applications. The big push into multimedia titles was under way, and we were finding a ton of bugs in Windows 95 running this class of applications. The schedule was already slipping and we needed action. Out of that pressure comes one of the great Microsoft stories about just getting things done that was first presented by David Cole in the book Inside Out: Microsoft—In Our Own Words (Warner Business Books, 2000):

"A boatload of multimedia titles came out for Windows 3.1 during the holiday season of 1994, and we found that many of them were not compatible with the upcoming Win 95 release. This was one of the reasons we had to delay the release. So rather than taking a pile of time ordering from the vendors, I had the wacky idea of driving my truck to the local Egghead and buying one of every multimedia title they had.

"Since we needed quick testing, the idea was to literally give these titles to our employees to test at home or at work and they could then keep the title for their own use.

"A couple of us drove on down to the Egghead and started grabbing one of everything and piling them up by the register. The three clerks there were kind of freaked out and wanted to know what the hell we were doing. We explained; their eyes opened wide and they were thrilled. One guy started ringing us up, but the cash register kept crashing. After three crashes and ringing up all these boxes three times he figured out that it crashed at about $10,000. So he rung things up to around $7K, then he would stop, get our credit card, and ring up the next batch. It took forever. I think the total was close to $20K.

"We loaded everything up on the back of the truck, and the boxes filled the entire bed. I backed it up to the front door of building 5. " David Cole

Back on campus, a few volunteers were recruited to unload this mountain of software into the cafeteria. Mail was sent to the entire product engineering team announcing the new "Adopt an App" program. Employees quickly flooded the cafeteria roaming around the tables trying to select from the hundreds of titles laid across the tables, and then sign a "contract" requiring them to report bugs—or the success with the application running on the internal dogfood builds of the new operating system. All of the applications were "adopted" within hours.

Dozens of bugs were filed and many more success stories were reported. Employees updated their computers with daily or weekly builds and continued to use their "adopted" applications. By the time Windows 95 shipped, most Windows 3.1 applications ran without a single problem—all because of the success of beta testers and the Adopt an App program.

Application Verifier

One of the key tools used by engineers testing application compatibility is the Microsoft Application Verifier. Application Verifier is used to proactively examine native user-mode applications at run time to determine whether they have potential compatibility errors caused by common programming mistakes. Applications that incorrectly check for the Windows version, assume administrative rights, or have any of dozens of other subtle programming errors can all be detected with Application Verifier. Application Verifier also detects several other classes of programming errors such as memory leaks, memory corruption, or invalid handle usage. Application Verifier is extendable and is commonly used for numerous additional fault injection scenarios.

Plug-ins for Application Verifier, such as the Print Verifier, are used to test and verify subsystems, printer drivers and print applications, in this case. The Print Verifier detects errors such as invalid printer handle usage, incorrect usage of printing functions, and incorrect implementation of functions within a printer driver. Similar plug-ins for other driver subsystems are commonly available.

Application Verifier works by "hooking" several core Windows functions and adding additional checks before calling the "real" function. For example, when the application under test is loaded, the address of the Microsoft Win32 application programming interface (API) CreateFile method is replaced with an internal Application Verifier method that will trigger a series of tests, as shown in Figure 11-6. If any of the tests fail, the failure is logged, or if a debugger is installed, a debug breakpoint might be triggered. More information about Application Verifier is available on MSDN at http://msdn2.microsoft.com/en-us/library/ms807121.aspx.

Typical application usage of a Win32 API. Application calls
a function exported from a windows library

Application Verifier creates a "shim" that intercepts the call from the application. After conducting any number of tests or modifications, the shim calls the originally called function, then has one more chance to examine the return value before returning to the calling application.

FIGURE 11-6 Application Verifier architecture.

Eating Our Dogfood

> *I mean, we talk at Microsoft about this notion we call "eating our own dog food."*
> *You're supposed to eat your own dog food before you serve it to anybody else.*
>
> —*Steve Ballmer, October 21, 2003, Office System Launch*

Sometimes, the best way to determine how a user will use an application is to be a user. At Microsoft, "eating our own dogfood" (using the product we make every day during development) is a key part of every product team's usability and compatibility strategy. Everyone on the Windows team uses daily or weekly builds of the in-development version of the operating system to develop the operating system. The Visual Studio team develops their product using Visual Studio. The Office team uses the latest builds of their own products to write specifications, deliver customer presentations, and even send and receive e-mail. When I worked on the Windows CE team, my office phone, my cell phone, and my home wireless router all ran dogfood versions of the operating system.

One disadvantage with dogfooding is that the intended audience of an application might use the product differently from how an employee working on the project uses it. For example, if engineers were the only users of early versions of Word, and they only wrote specifications and design documents, it is likely that other types of users would run into problems. Beta testers (external employees who test prerelease versions of products) are a partial solution for this problem and are enormously valuable in aiding product development at Microsoft. For Microsoft Office applications, the wide variety of nonengineering roles is also an immense advantage. Numerous Microsoft lawyers, accountants, and many other nonengineering employees use dogfood versions of the Office suite for many months preceding the product release.

A lot of dogfood

Microsoft Visual Studio Team Foundation Server (TFS) is an integrated collaboration server for Visual Studio Team System that includes such features as bug tracking, project tracking, source control, and build management. For years, Microsoft employees have used a variety of tools to accomplish these same tasks, and adoption of TFS outside of the developer division was initially slow. The team that creates TFS has a lot of interest in understanding internal usage of their product, and they publish a monthly report with updates on the internal adoption of TFS across the company.

As of March 2008, more than 11,000 distinct users were actively participating in TFS projects. These users were working on nearly 300,000 work items and had checked in nearly 240 million files. Adoption of any common toolset is advantageous to Microsoft, but the dogfood process—both of the client and server portions of TFS—has led to a much better experience for the end users of this product.

Dogfood is so important to Microsoft that we are seeing this concept extend into our services. The Windows Live Mail team has a dogfood instance with a set of customers that understand that they will be getting a version of the service that is less stable than that of other users, but they are excited to go through that pain for the opportunity to provide us feedback on how to make the service better.

Accessibility Testing

Accessibility is about removing barriers and providing the benefits of technology for everyone.

— *Steve Ballmer*

Accessibility is the availability of equal access to the information and tools that anyone can use to accomplish everyday tasks. This includes everything from copying files to browsing the Web to creating new documents. A user's capacity to create and maintain a mental model of the application, Web site, or document content, as well as the user's ability to interact with it, is the root of software accessibility.

One of Microsoft's largest customers, the United States federal government, requires that their information technologies take into account the needs of all users. In 1998, Section 508 (http://www.section508.gov) of the Rehabilitation Act was enacted to eliminate obstacles and create opportunities for people with disabilities. Microsoft is committed to supporting Section 508. An internal Accessibility Business Unit works with engineering teams, assistive-technology companies, and disability advocates to ensure that people with disabilities can use software developed by all software companies.

Several layers of specialty features—all of which play an important part in how accessible a program is—define accessibility. Some of the features that must be tested for any application include the following:

- **Operating system settings**   Operating system settings include settings such as large fonts, high dots per inch (DPI), high-contrast themes, cursor blink rate, StickyKeys, FilterKeys, MouseKeys, SerialKeys, ToggleKeys, screen resolution, custom mouse settings, and input from on-screen keyboards, as shown in Figure 11-7.

- **"Built-in" accessibility features**   Built-in features include features and functionality such as tab order, hotkeys, and shortcut keys.

- **Programmatic access**   Programmatic access includes implementation of Microsoft Active Accessibility (MSAA) or any related object model that enables accessibility features.

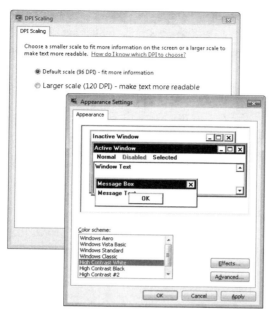

FIGURE 11-7 Selected accessibility features on Windows Vista.

- **Accessible technology tools**   Testing of applications using accessibility tools such as screen readers, magnifiers, speech recognition, or other input programs is an important aspect of accessibility testing. Microsoft maintains an accessibility lab, open to all employees, filled with computers installed with accessibility software such as screen readers and Braille readers.

Accessibility Personas

Personas are descriptions of fictional people used to represent customer segments and the way these customers use our products. By using personas, teams can focus on designing and developing the right set of features to support these users. At Microsoft, most product teams identify and create user personas early in the product cycle and refer to these personas throughout the entire life of the product.

Product teams might create three to five (or more) personas for their product, but many personas span all Microsoft products. More than 10 personas were created for helping teams gain a better understanding of how customers with specific types of disabilities use computers and how they might interact with software. For example, the persona for a blind user includes information on the person's usage of screen readers (screen readers cannot read text in bitmaps and in some custom controls) and expected navigation features. Similarly, the persona for users who are deaf or hard of hearing helps the engineering team remember that sounds should be customizable, volume should be adjustable, and that alternative options might need to be supplied for caller ID or voice mail features.

Mousetrap?

I'm one of those computer users who favors the keyboard over the mouse for nearly every task. For me, shortcut keys aren't an accessibility feature; they are a productivity feature. I'm just faster if I can keep my hands on the keyboard.

Early in my career, I was testing one of our applications and ran into an area of the product that was nearly impossible to use without a mouse. A carefully planned series of tabs and arrow keys were the only way I could discover to get to several of the controls. I knew this issue was important, so I filed a bug and went home for the night.

I was surprised the next morning when I found out that the project lead in charge of the feature had resolved the bug. I explained the need for accessible features, but he assured me that it was "accessible enough" and that there were bigger issues that needed attention. I shyly nodded my head and asked him to try using the feature without a mouse at least once before closing the issue. He mumbled something and went back to his office.

A few days went by and other testers began to report similar issues, but the lead still had not tried using the feature without a mouse. I decided it was time to try a different tactic, so before I went home that night, I bravely walked into the lead's office, unplugged his mouse, and left a note stating I would give the mouse back once we had agreed on the accessibility goals for the project.

I came in early the next morning, just in case the lead didn't share my sense of humor. A few of us peeked into his office and were happy to see him smile when he saw the note. We went back to work and waited. Less than an hour later, I met with the lead to rediscuss accessibility and walk through the application without a mouse. Because of the discussion, we ended up fixing most of the keyboard accessibility issues and produced a better quality product.

Testing for Accessibility

Using personas is an important approach and something that Microsoft capitalizes on for numerous facets of testing. Some approaches of accessibility testing are common to most applications and should be part of any testing approach. Some of these test lines of attack are as follows:

- **Respect system-wide accessibility settings**   Verify that the application does not use any custom settings for window colors, text sizes, or other elements customizable by global accessibility settings.

- **Support high-contrast mode**   Verify that the application can be used in high-contrast mode.

- **Realize size matters**   Fixed font sizes or small mouse targets are both potential accessibility issues.

- **Note audio features**   If an application uses audio to signal an event (for example, that a new e-mail message has arrived), the application should also allow a nonaudio notification such as a cursor change. If the application includes an audio tutorial or video presentation, also provide a text transcription.

- **Enable programmatic access to UI elements and text**   Although this sounds like a testability feature (enable automation tools), programmatic access through Active Accessibility or the .NET UIAutomation class is the primary way that screen readers and similar accessibility features work.

Testing Tools for Microsoft Active Accessibility

The Active Accessibility software development kit (SDK) includes several worthwhile tools for testing accessibility in an application, particularly applications or controls that implement Microsoft Active Accessibility (MSAA).

- With the Accessible Explorer program, you can examine the IAccessible properties of objects and observe relationships between different controls.

- With the Accessible Event Watcher (AccEvent) tool, developers and testers can validate that the user interface (UI) elements of an application raise proper Active Accessibility events when the UI changes. Changes in the UI occur when a UI element is invoked, selected, has a state change, or when the focus changes.

- With the Inspect Objects tool, developers and testers can examine the IAccessible property values of the UI items of an application and navigate to other objects.

- The MsaaVerify tool verifies whether properties and methods of a control's IAccessible interface meet the guidelines outlined in the specification for MSAA.[1] MsaaVerify is available in binary and source code forms at CodePlex (http://www.codeplex.com).

Whether you are satisfying government regulations or just trying to make your software appeal to more users, accessibility testing is crucial.

---

[1]   *http://msdn.microsoft.com/library/en-us/msaa/msaapndx_2a05.asp*

Usability Testing

Usability and accessibility are quite similar, but there is a significant difference between the two terms to consider. Accessibility is the ability of anyone to use the user interface, whereas usability refers to how easy it is for the user to understand and interact with the UI. Accessibility features can enable higher degrees of usability, but usability can mean a lot more. Helpful documentation, tooltips, easy-to-discover features, and numerous other criteria all contribute to highly usable software.

When testing the user interface of an application, usability testing includes verifying that the features of the application are discoverable and work as a user expects them to. Similarly, when testing an API or object model, usability testing includes verifying that programming tasks using the exposed functions are intuitive and that they perform the expected functionality. Usability testing also includes verifying that documentation is correct and relevant.

Usability Labs

Many product teams at Microsoft take advantage of usability labs. Testers are usually not directly involved in conducting the study, but they do use the data from the study to influence their approach to usability testing. For example, although the study might reveal design issues to be addressed by Program Management or Development engineers, testers often use the data on how the application is used to build scenarios or to weight testing in specific areas based on usage patterns. Of course, many other factors lead to determining the modeling of how customers use an application. (Some of those techniques and tools are covered in Chapter 13, "Customer Feedback Systems.")

The formal usability studies at Microsoft are conducted in a lab with a layout similar to the one shown in Figure 11-8. Participants spend approximately two hours using an application and are usually asked to accomplish a few targeted tasks.

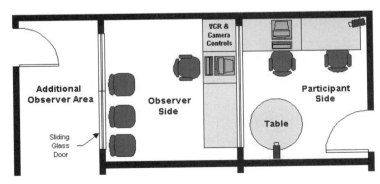

FIGURE 11-8 Usability lab layout.

The goals of these sessions vary, but common questions that these studies seek to answer include the following:

- What are the users' needs?
- What design with solve the users' problems?
- What tasks will users need to perform, and how well are users able to solve them?
- How do users learn, and then retain their skills with the software?
- Is the software fun to use?

When we talk to teams about usability testing, we consistently share one bit of advice: Usability testing will always occur . . . eventually. It's your choice whether you do it as part of your testing effort or leave it for the customer. Early usability testing makes the product more successful in the eyes of the user community and has a huge impact on reducing the number of support calls for your product.

> **Note** Microsoft has more than 50 usability labs worldwide, and more than 8,000 people a year participate in Microsoft usability studies.

Usability testing continues to grow and advance at Microsoft. New techniques used more often include eye tracking, remote usability testing over the Internet, and advances in playtest usability testing for games.

Security Testing

Security testing has become an integral part of Microsoft's culture in recent years. Reactions to malicious software and spyware have given all engineers at Microsoft a security mindset. Security testing is such a major subject that it is more worthy of an entire book than a section of this single chapter. In fact, a quick browse on an online bookstore shows me no less than half a dozen books on security testing, including books written by Microsoft employees such as Hunting Security Bugs by Gallagher, Landauer, and Jeffries, as well two security books in the How to Break . . . series by James Whittaker (who is also a noted software security expert). Additionally, Writing Secure Code by Howard and LeBlanc is on many testers' bookshelves at Microsoft. Any of these books or others on the subject will be beneficial if you desire depth or breadth in this area.

The tester's role in security testing is not just to find the bugs, but to determine whether and how the bug can be exploited. A few of the key approaches and techniques for security testing are discussed in the following subsections.

Threat Modeling

Threat modeling is a structured activity that reviews application architecture to identify potential security threats and vulnerabilities. Threat modeling is in wide use at Microsoft, and testers are highly active participants in the threat model process. The familiarity testers typically have with input validation, data handling, and session management drives them toward being key contributors when examining applications for potential security issues.

Threat models—as do many other concepts discussed in this chapter—work best when carried out during program design. A threat model is a specification just like a functional specification or design document. The big difference is that the intention of a threat model is to identify all possible ways that an application can be attacked, and then to prioritize the attacks based on probability and potential harm. Good threat modeling requires skills in analysis and investigation—two skills that make Test a well-suited participant in the process. More information about threat modeling, including examples, can be found in Threat Modeling by Frank Swiderski and Window Snyder (Microsoft Press, 2004).

Fuzz Testing

Fuzz testing is a technique used to determine how a program reacts to invalid input data. A simple approach would be to use a hex editor to change the file format of a data file used by a program—for example, modifying the bits in a .doc file used by Microsoft Word. In practice, the process is nearly always much more methodical. Rather than randomly changing data, fuzz tests usually involve manipulating the data in a manner that exposes a potential security issue such as an exploitable buffer overrun. Fuzz testing is equally applicable to database testing, protocol testing, or any other situation where part of a system or application must read and interpret data.

Finding fuzzing holes

During Windows Vista development, I oversaw the file fuzzing tests on the Microsoft Windows Shell (user interface). The most difficult part of this problem was not creating and executing the fuzz tests, but identifying all of the different ways that the Shell can parse files. The Shell is extensible by nature, and many teams across Windows extend it to improve the user experience of dealing with files in Windows Explorer. The sheer quantity of file parsers and cross-organizational code ownership creates a high likelihood of test holes. We realized this, and to address it we authored a very detailed test plan based on categories of parsers (that is, property handlers, shell folders, thumbnail extractors, and so forth) and compiled lists of things to test based on a meticulous hand audit of the code.

Even though we reviewed our data with architects and test leaders across the organization, we fully expected to miss things. Thus, we began watching the bug database for any crashes, hangs, or memory spikes in the Shell that originated from malformed files. Late in the Windows Vista cycle, we discovered a bug that had come out of ad hoc testing with corrupted files. Of course, we immediately researched this issue to understand why our extensive fuzzing effort had not flushed this out. We discovered a fuzzing hole in one of our cross-team-owned property handlers!

The root cause was an instance of incorrect assumptions: The owning feature team assumed the API-based file fuzz testing they had done provided full coverage of their property handler, but in fact, they had some small amount of code that was not covered by fuzzing of the underlying APIs. Alarmed at the prospect of more serious security issues lurking in this unfuzzed code, we quickly spun up a cross-team effort to provide the fuzzing coverage we had missed. This particular component parsed several unique file types. Two of us used a lab of computers and spent a week doing execution tests to close this hole completely. The fuzzing of this component eventually yielded six crashing bugs, all of which were fixed before release. Eric Douglas, Senior Test Lead

Summary

Functional testing is extremely important—as are many of the techniques and methods used to carry out functional testing effectively. The point that teams sometimes forget is that customers don't care about the number of bugs found or the number of tests that failed or code coverage rates. These are all important and valued ingredients of the testing recipe, but in the end, customers care about the non-functional aspects of the product. They want secure, reliable software that easily does what they want to do. They want software with easily discoverable features that responds to their actions quickly.

Non-functional testing is an integral complement to functional testing and is critical to establishing whether a product is of high quality and ready to ship. A dilemma with non-functional attributes is that most aspects require significant thought early in the development process; but measurement of many attributes cannot happen until the customers use the software. The key to solving this dilemma is to keep the customer voice—through personas or other similar mechanisms—at the forefront of all testing efforts.

Chapter 12
Other Tools

Alan Page

Every professional employs a trusted set of tools. A good carpenter needs and uses dozens of tools and knows how to use each of these tools best to accomplish a specific task effectively. The detectives I see on television rely on an endless supply of tools, each used for just the right situation to solve crimes (nearly always within 60 minutes, too). I have always considered testing similar to many other lines of work in the use of tools. To be successful in almost any endeavor, you need substantial knowledge of the area as well as tools that can assist with complex tasks.

A tester's tools are applications to help testers do some part of their job more efficiently or more effectively. Testers at Microsoft use countless numbers of test tools throughout the testing process. Tools run tests, probe the system, track progress, and assist in dozens of other situations. Previous chapters have mentioned a few of the tools used by testers at Microsoft, but there are others that many testers consider essential. This chapter discusses a few more of the tools that testers at Microsoft find to be effective and beneficial.

Code Churn

Churn is a term used to describe the amount of changes that happen in a file or module over a selected period. Several measurements can be used to calculate code churn. The most common include the following:

- **Count of Changes**   The number of times a file has been changed
- **Lines Added**   The number of lines added to a file after a specified point
- **Lines Deleted**   Total number of lines deleted over a selected period
- **Lines Modified**   Total number of lines modified over a selected period

Microsoft Visual Studio Team System calculates a *Total Churn* metric by summing the total of Lines Added, Lines Deleted, and Lines Modified, as shown in Table 12-1.

TABLE 12-1 Sample Churn Metrics from Visual Studio Team System

Submission number	Total churn	Lines Modified	Lines Deleted	Lines Added	Total Churn
857	161	0	0	161	161
899	359	3	178	178	161
932	72	2	35	35	161
946	16	0	0	16	177
Grand Total	**608**	**5**	**213**	**390**	**177**

Similar to the complexity metrics discussed in Chapter 7, "Analyzing Risk with Code Complexity," code churn measurements can be indicative of where more bugs are likely to be located. In a sense, this is an intuitive metric. Other than writing new code to add features, the reason for code changing (churning) is most often a result of fixing a known bug. Significant percentages of bug fixes either don't actually fix the problem or cause another error to occur. Both of these situations require additional code changes (churn) to fix the new (or remaining) failures. Often, this scenario repeats; if the code is particularly complex, the cycle can continue for several iterations until all known bugs are fixed, and no new failures are *found* (odds are, however, that highly churned code will have even *more* bugs remaining).

Keep in mind that churn is another metric that falls into the "smoke-alarm" category; excessive churn doesn't always mean that there are dozens of new bugs to be found, but it is an indicator that you might need to take a closer look at the area of the product that is changing.

Research on code churn

Microsoft Research has investigated the relationship of churn and bug density using several different churn metrics, including churned (changed) lines of code, deleted lines, and numbers of files changed. The researchers generated churn metrics for the Microsoft Windows Server 2003 source code and bug data from the bug management system and found a correlation between the two.

Next, the researchers created a model using these metrics and used a randomly selected set containing two-thirds of the binaries to build a prediction model. The resulting model was successful in predicting the bug density of the remaining one-third with high statistical significance. Finally, the model was used to try to split the binaries into sets that could be considered "fault prone" or "non–fault prone." Again, the binaries were randomly split where two-thirds went into building a prediction model and one-third into the testing group. The binaries in the testing group were correctly classified into the fault-prone and nonfault sets with 90 percent accuracy.[1]

Because of this study, many Microsoft teams now monitor code churn and use it to determine when to redesign a component or to assess risk when evaluating the need to make a change late in the product cycle.

Keeping It Under Control

Source control, the ability to track changes in source code, is as important an asset to testers at Microsoft as it is to developers. Almost all development teams in the software industry use a source code management (SCM) system, and Microsoft development teams certainly aren't an exception. Every test team at Microsoft uses source control to some extent—both for traditional uses as well as for specific testing tasks.

Tracking Changes

Similar to typical SCM usage, the primary use of source control on test teams is for tracking changes to code written for test tools and test automation. Entire teams, and sometimes teams spanning all of Microsoft, share test tools. When more teams adopt a tool, it becomes more important to track changes so that any bugs or unexpected behavior caused by the change can be more easily identified. This usage is equivalent to SCM usage in development environments, with the fundamental difference being that the "customer" of the tool is another tester or test team in the company.

It is also beneficial to track changes in test automation or test cases. In addition to tracking changes in tests over the lifetime of a product, with SCM systems teams can create and recreate the state of the entire body of source code and related documents at any arbitrarily selected point in time. The most common use of this is to generate snapshots of the system from key milestones in the product life cycle. A common example is creating a snapshot of all product code *and test code* at the moment the product was released to manufacturing. By having a copy of the tests used to ship the product, sustained engineering teams can make changes to the product code with confidence. This is the same concept adopted by developers who use a suite of unit tests to help ensure that any changes they make to a module do not cause a regression. Sustained engineering teams use the tests to help them assess risk of a code change causing an unforeseen bug in another part of the system.

---

[1] Nachiappan Nagappan and Thomas Ball, *Use of Relative Code Churn Measures to Predict System Defect Density* (Association for Computing Machinery, 2005), *http://research.microsoft.com/~tball/papers/ICSE05Churn.pdf.*

What Changed?

The *Hocus-Focus* comic strip by Henry Boltinoff ran in the newspaper my family received while I was growing up. If you're not familiar with the comic, it was a simple two-panel strip where the two panels *looked* identical, but the text in between the panels asked the reader to "Find at least six differences in details between panels." It usually took me only a few minutes to find all six differences, but my strategy was consistent. I cycled through each object or feature in the first picture and compared its shape, size, and other attributes with the same object in the second picture. Sometimes the difference was in *part* of the object, and sometimes I had to look at an entire area at once to see the difference. Over time, I got better and better (faster and more accurate) until I reached a point where I could spot all six in a few seconds every time.

Similarly, as a software tester, I use a SCM system and *diff tools* (utilities that show the differences between two files) to isolate coding errors. Figure 12-1 shows the comparison of two files using a diff tool. Because the SCM system records every change made to the product source code, when a tester discovers a bug while testing a scenario that previously worked, he often turns to the SCM system to help isolate the problem. Source control can show all changes made to a file, module, feature, or entire application between any points in time. If a tester discovers a bug that didn't occur on a test pass two weeks earlier, she can easily identify all source code changes and examine the differences to investigate which change might have caused the error. Note that on some teams, developers can be the team members who go through this process. (See the sidebar titled "Who Wears What Hat?" that follows for more information on this topic.)

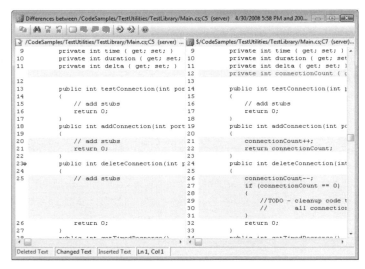

FIGURE 12-1 Comparing files in Visual Studio.

Monitoring changes isn't unique to source code. It is also important to track changes made to specifications and other documents. Many applications can track the changes made to a document. The chapters in this book, for example, pass from authors to reviewers to editors and back again. At each stage, a reviewer might make several edits and suggestions. All changes are tracked within Microsoft Office Word so that each of the authors can track progress as well as document and refer to the discussions leading up to wording or content decisions.

Word can also compare two documents even if the reviewer forgets to activate the Track Changes feature, as shown in Figure 12-2. This is convenient for checking the changes made between two versions of a document and for reviewing the changes, for example, when reviewing edits made simultaneously by several reviewers.

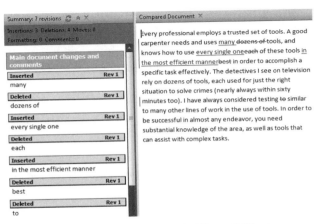

FIGURE 12-2 Comparing documents in Microsoft Word.

Who wears what hat?

A question I hear often from testers when teaching introductory testing and debugging courses at Microsoft is "How far should I debug?" Developers, interestingly enough, often ask, "How far should I expect testers to debug?" The answer to both questions is, of course, "It depends."

Debugging is detective work. Examining states of variables in a live debugging session, examining log files, and examining changes in source code are all methods of debugging, that is, attempting to find the cause of an error. The challenge for many new testers (and developers) is to understand at what point between "find a bug" and "fix a bug" does their work stop. Many testers are as good as (and sometimes better than) the developers they work with on investigating and isolating the cause of a bug. On some Microsoft teams, testers routinely debug errors to the point of isolating the file, line number, and check-in that caused the bug, while on other teams, testers might do little investigative work beyond reporting the bug. Nearly all testers at Microsoft are capable of debugging to a deep extent, so the decision comes down to time constraints and expectations.

Time investment can be a factor if a test team is understaffed, behind schedule, or bound on some other critical resource. In other words, sometimes a test team just doesn't have time to debug errors completely. Expectations, however, are the much more important aspect of this dilemma. I've known developers who didn't *want* testers debugging their code, and I've known testers who didn't *want* to debug someone else's code. I personally don't like either of these scenarios. When I face questions about who should debug what, I encourage a conversation between tester and developer (or test team and development team) that answers two key questions for each party: "What can I expect from you?" and "What do you expect from me?" This conversation topic works well for any discussion on relationships, but in the case of the tester and developer, it clears the air on many important topics ranging from unit tests to test strategies—and, of course, what's expected by whom on bug reports and in debugging sessions.

Why Did It Change?

Sometimes when I'm playing hocus focus with source code changes I can *see* the change, but I have no idea *why* the change was made.

```
===================================================================
--- math.cs;8  (server)     5/2/2008 5:24 PM
+++ math.cs;9  (server)     5/6/2008 7:25 PM
****************
*** 20,26 ****
                }
                else
                {
!                       return value;
                }
--- 20,26 ----
                }
                else
                {
!                       return value * 2;
                }
===================================================================
```

In the preceding code, it is obvious what this change does—it changes the returned value by a factor of 2! But *why* was this change made? Source control systems give testers a few key pieces of information in their detective work. One useful type of information is access to the names of each developer who has changed the code along with exact descriptions and records of the code the individual has changed. If you know who made a change that you don't understand, you can walk down the hall, call, or e-mail that person and ask him or her about it.

Tracking down a developer for quick communication is often a great solution for understanding recent changes or changes made to a current version of a product, but what do you do if the developer has gone home, has left the group, or has left the company? The source control system often houses many points of highly relevant data, including developer comments and a bug number or link to the issue fixed by the change in the bug management system. When code is *committed* (a working copy is merged into the master source control system), the author of the change is generally required to fill in several fields in a submission form including the bug fixed by the change (or in the case of new code, an ID associated with the particular feature). Other fields might include such items as the name of the code reviewer and a short description of the details of the change, as shown in Figure 12-3. All of these items are clues that aid testers and developers alike in bug investigations.

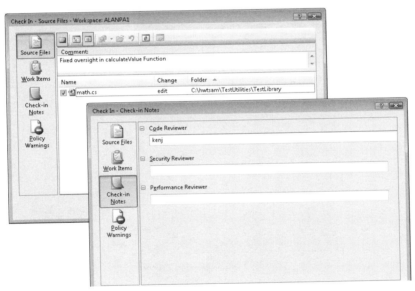

FIGURE 12-3 Check-in forms in Visual Studio Team System.

A Home for Source Control

The use of source control among test teams at Microsoft has evolved and grown with the company. In my early days at Microsoft, source control for the test teams I worked on was quite informal to say the least! Most of the test teams used source control for their test code or data files, but each part of the team used a separate source control server. The fact that we used source control on managed servers ensured that the test source code was backed up and revisions were tracked.

As long as you didn't want to share or view source from another team, there were no problems with this system. On my team, it was the tester's responsibility to compile the test source code, and then copy the resulting binaries to a common share where other testers or the automation system could find them when they were needed. This system worked *most* of the time, but errors occurred occasionally when a copy failed or someone accidentally deleted a file.

Over time, more teams began to consolidate test source into single servers and systems for their entire team. The structure and layout became more formal and far less ad hoc. These days, most teams store test source code next to product source code on the same servers and systems, as shown in Figure 12-4. Then, a *build lab* (a single person or small team dedicated to creating daily builds for the team) builds product code and test code daily and propagates the test binaries to servers automatically.

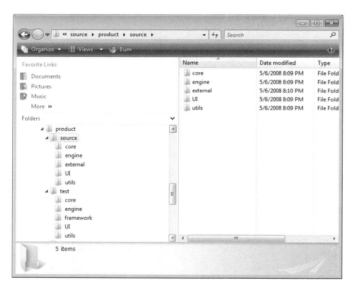

FIGURE 12-4 Typical layout of product and test code in source control.

A source control layout such as the one shown in the figure has several advantages. One of the most important features is that code is easy to find. If a developer wants to run some of the test team's tests, he knows where to go. Similarly, if a tester wants to understand a bit more about the implementation of the code she is testing, she can find the product code easily. It also makes it much easier for the build team to investigate any build errors caused by inconsistencies between product and test code. Finally, if the build team is building both product and test code as part of the same process, it is simpler for the team to add consistent version information to the test code and product code. Consistent versioning allows for easier management of test binaries and product binaries, and can facilitate better regression analysis.

Build It

The build, along with the many related activities that stem from the build process, is an integral part of the daily work of every team at Microsoft. Source control, bug management, and test passes all stem from the build process:

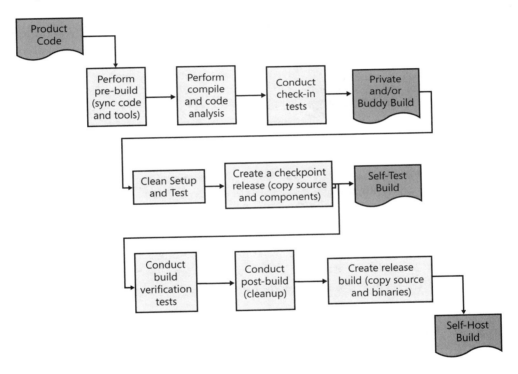

The Daily Build

For most teams, the entire product is compiled from source code *at least* once a day. Microsoft has performed daily builds for years, and *continuous integration* (continuous builds along with frequent code check-in) is strongly supported by the Agile community. The build process includes *compiling* the source (transforming the source code to binary format), *linking* (the act of combining binaries), and any other steps required to make the application usable by the team such as building the setup program and deploying the build to a release server.

Note The Windows Live build lab creates more than 6,000 builds every week.

A day in the life of a build lab

A typical 24 hours in the life of a build lab.

Sometime around 15:00, the build process starts. Automated scripts prepare individual computers for the build process. All remnants of old builds are removed, and source code is synchronized to the latest "good" changes. For a midsize product, the build takes between one and four hours (larger products such as Microsoft Windows or Office can take much longer).

The initial build process turns the source code into the binaries that make up the product. For the next several hours, more automated scripts take these binaries and create dozens or more of installable products known as SKUs (stock keeping units)—variations of the product such as "Professional," "Ultimate," or a variety of localized versions. Although this is an automated process, someone on the build team could be designated as the "build watcher" for the evening. The build watcher might be responsible for periodically checking the status of the builds to ensure that they are progressing, but in many cases, the build system is self-monitoring and can send a page, e-mail, or text message to the build watcher if an error is encountered.

Sometimes an error occurs early on, sometimes errors show up late, and from time to time random things happen such as an unexpected shutdown of a critical computer or network issues. During the build period, all errors are either tracked as bugs and sent to the product team or otherwise tagged and resolved by the build watcher.

Early in the morning, the build team members begin arriving at work and review any outstanding issues from the previous night in a nightly summary created by the previous night's build watcher. If any blocking issues remain, the build team tracks down the product owner and reminds him or her to provide a fix immediately. Once the build is ready, build verification tests (BVTs) begin. If bugs are found, product owners are contacted immediately and bugs are filed.

The goal is to release the build to the team for testing around noon. If there are still outstanding bugs at this time, a decision needs to be made to determine whether to release the build late, or not release that day. A daily build is so much part of the flow at Microsoft that *not* releasing a build is something that is not taken lightly. If the decision is made to try to release the build, the build remains on hold until the necessary fixes are made and tested. When the build is ready for release, files are copied from the build computers to distribution servers, and an e-mail message with the build information and all known issues is sent to the entire team.

More often than not, the daily build process also includes a suite of *smoke tests*. A smoke test is a brief test to make sure the basic functionality of the application works. It's similar to driving a borrowed car around the block to check for obvious faults before driving all the way across town. Test teams usually run a suite of smoke tests. Most often, these are known as *build acceptance tests* (BATs) or *build verification tests* (BVTs). Some definitions of these terms denote BATs to be a smaller suite of tests than BVTs, but in most cases, the terms are interchangeable. A good set of BVTs ensures that the daily build is usable for testing. Table 12-2 lists several BVT attributes.

TABLE 12-2 BVT Attributes

BVT attribute	Explanation
Automate Everything	BVTs run on every single build, and then need to run the same every time. If you have only one automated suite of tests for your entire product, it should be your BVTs.
Test a Little	BVTs are non-all-encompassing functional tests. They are simple tests intended to verify *basic* functionality. The goal of the BVT is to ensure that the build is usable for testing.
Test Fast	The entire BVT suite should execute in minutes, not hours. A short feedback loop tells you immediately whether your build has problems.
Fail Perfectly	If a BVT fails, it should mean that the build is not suitable for further testing, and that the cause of the failure must be fixed immediately. In some cases, there can be a workaround for a BVT failure, but all BVT failures should indicate serious problems with the latest build.
Test Broadly—Not Deeply	BVTs should cover the product broadly. They definitely should not cover every nook and cranny, but should touch on every significant bit of functionality. They do not (and should not) cover a broad set of inputs or configurations, and should focus as much as possible on covering the primary usage scenarios for key functionality.
Debuggable and Maintainable	In a perfect world, BVTs would never fail. But if and when they do fail, it is imperative that the underlying error can be isolated as soon as possible. The turnaround time from finding the failure to implementing a fix for the cause of the failure must be as quick as possible. The test code for BVTs needs to be some of the most debuggable and maintainable code in the entire product to be most effective.
	Good BVTs are self-diagnosing and often list the exact cause of error in their output. Great BVTs couple this with an automatic source control lookup that identifies the code change with the highest probability of causing the error.
Trustworthy	You must be able to trust your BVTs. If the BVTs pass, the build must be suitable for testing, and if the BVTs fail, it should indicate a serious problem. Any compromises on the meaning of pass or fail for BVTs also compromises the trust the team has in these tests.
Critical	Your best, most reliable, and most trustworthy testers and developers create most reliable and most trustworthy BVTs. Good BVTs are not easy to write and require time and careful thought to adequately satisfy the other criteria in this table.

An example of a BVT suite for a simple text editor such as Windows Notepad could include the following:

1. Create a text file.

2. Write some text.

3. Verify basic functionality such as cut, copy, and paste work.

4. Test file operations such as save, open, and delete.

A daily (or more frequent) build and BVT process reduces the chance of errors caused by large integrations or sweeping changes. Keeping the product in a state where it will build and where it will run every day is critical to a healthy software organization. Test teams at Microsoft have the same need for daily builds as product teams. For this reason, source code for automated tests and test tools are also built daily, typically as part of the same process used to build the product code.

Breaking the Build

The most minimum effect of a daily build is ensuring that compilation errors (also known as build errors) are caught within 24 hours of check-in. Compilation errors are rare but can stop the engineering flow if the test team is waiting for the daily build to begin testing. The most common reason for a compilation error is also the most preventable: syntax errors by the developer. Anyone who has ever compiled any code or run a script has made a syntax error. A missing semicolon, a mistyped keyword, or an errant keystroke can cause an error when the program is compiled or when the script is run. These sorts of errors are inevitable, but they only cause a problem if the broken code is checked into source control. I don't know any programmers who deliberately check in broken code, but some still make these mistakes through carelessness. Usually it's "just a little change" that the developer forgets to double check by recompiling the local source code. A simple prevention method could be to require developers to build before checking in source code, but this might be difficult to enforce, and some mistakes could potentially still slip through.

You broke the build!

Throughout the software industry, there has been a long tradition of punishing those who break the build by making them wear a silly hat, putting a sign on their office door, making them buy donuts for the entire team, or otherwise calling attention to their mistake. I've known teams that called developers at home in the middle of the night to announce that they broke the build and need to come in—pronto! This process can work in cases where people just need to be a bit more careful and think about what they are doing before they check in code, but sometimes people just make honest mistakes.

Fortunately, many teams are beginning to realize that humans do make mistakes, and that some build breaks are inevitable. Instead of focusing on the punishment, these teams choose to do what they can to prevent any build breaks that do happen from adversely affecting the team.

Build breaks are often caused by reasons other than syntax errors. "Forgetting to check in a file" is one of the most common reasons I have seen that triggers a build break. When working with large, complex systems, it is also quite common to see build errors caused by a dependency changing in another part of the system. Think of the core Windows SDK header files (the files containing definitions of Windows data types and functions). A small change to one of these files can often cause build errors in far-reaching components. On a smaller scale, changing an interface name in a COM library or other shared components can just as easily cause compilation errors in dependent components.

Testing with compilation

On large platforms such as Windows, Windows CE, and Office, the test code frequently uses the available exported functions more than the supported applications. When I was on the Windows CE team, our daily build process would build the operating system, and then build all of our tests.

From time to time, the compilation of our test code would cause a *break* (compilation error) because of a change to a function prototype or definition. It's hard to be *happy* about build breaks, but it was nice to catch these bugs long before a customer would have a chance to do so. Having the test code built at the same time as the product code enabled us to find these bugs.

Stopping the Breaks

I don't know anyone who has worked with daily builds who hasn't experienced a build break on their team. At Microsoft, we use several techniques to minimize the number and impact of build errors. Two of the most popular and effective techniques are *rolling builds* and *check-in systems*.

In its simplest form, a rolling build is an automatic continuous build of the product based on the most current source code. Several builds might occur in one day, and build errors are discovered sooner. The fundamental steps in a rolling build system include these:

- A clean build environment
- Automatic synchronization to the most current source

- Full build of system

- Automatic notification of errors (or success)

The easiest way to implement a rolling build is with a simple Windows command script (cmd) file. Scripting tools such as Sed, Awk, and Perl are also commonly used. An example of what a rolling build script might look like is in Listing 12-1.

Listing 12-1 Simple Rolling Build Windows Command Script

```
rem RollingBuild.cmd
rem sync, build, and report errors

rem The following two commands record the latest change number
rem and obtain the latest source changes

:BEGINBUILD
rem clean up the build environment
call cleanbuild.cmd

changes -latest
sync -all

rem build.cmd is the wrapper script used for building the entire product
call build.cmd

rem if ANY part of the build fails, a build.err file will exist
rem notify the team of the rolling build status
IF EXIST "build.err" (
  call reporterror.cmd
) ELSE (
  call reportsuccess.cmd
)

goto BEGINBUILD
```

Some Microsoft teams also include some or all BVTs in a rolling build and automatically report the results to the team. Teams that conduct several rolling builds each day often pick one—for example, the last successful build before 13:00—and conduct additional testing and configuration on that build before releasing it to the team as the daily build.

Another method of preventing build breaks and increasing code quality is the use of a *check-in system.* Years ago, when developers had changes to check in to SCM, they would check the code directly into the main source tree. Any mistakes they made—either syntax errors or bugs—would immediately affect every build. You can get away with a system like this for small projects, but for larger software projects, a staged check-in can be quite beneficial.

Figure 12-5 shows the basic architecture of a check-in system. Instead of checking the code directly into the main SCM, when programmers are ready to submit changes, they submit them to an interim system. At a minimum, the interim computer verifies that the code builds correctly on at least one platform, and then submits the code on behalf of the programmer to the main source control system. Most such systems build for multiple configurations and targets—something that is nearly impossible for a single developer to do on her own.

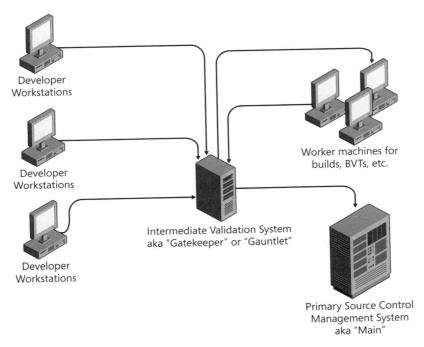

FIGURE 12-5 Check-in system architecture.

The interim system (sometimes referred to as a *gauntlet* or *gatekeeper*) will also typically run a selection of automated tests against the change to watch for regressions. Depending on the implementation of the system, the set of tests can be static, can be selectable by the programmer at the time of submission, or is created dynamically based on which parts of the code are changed.

Any selection of pre- or postbuild tests can be added at any time to the system. To the developer, it *feels* the same as checking directly into *main* (the main source tree), but a substantial number of bugs are found before they ever get a chance to cause problems for the entire team.

Static Analysis

When a test team begins *writing* software to *test* software, a funny question comes up: "Who tests the tests?" The question is easy to ignore, but it pays to answer it. A tremendous amount of coding effort goes into writing test code, and that code is susceptible to the same sorts of mistakes that occur in product code. In a number of ways, running the tests and examining failures are a test for the tests, but that approach can still miss many bugs in test code. One effective method for finding bugs in test code (or any code, for that matter) is to use tools for automatic *static analysis*. Static analysis tools examine the source code or binary and identify many classes of errors without actually executing the code.

Native Code Analysis

A number of different tools are available for analysis of *native code* (that is, code written in C or C++). Traditional tools include commercial products such as PC-Lint,[2] KlocWork,[3] and Coverity,[4] as well as the static Code Analyzer included with Visual Studio Team System.

Every team at Microsoft uses code analysis tools. Since 2001, the primary tool used at Microsoft for native code analysis is a tool named *PREfast*. This is the same tool available for native code analysis in Visual Studio Team System.

PREfast scans source code, one function at a time, and looks for coding patterns and incorrect code usage that can indicate a programming error. When PREfast finds an error, it displays a defect warning and provides the line number of the offending source code, as shown in Figure 12-6.

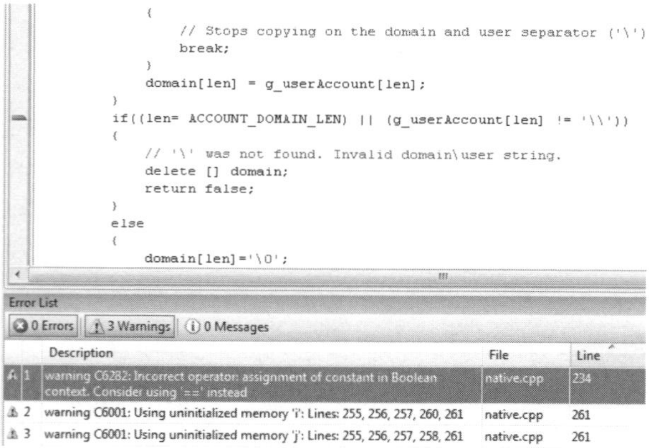

FIGURE 12-6 Static analysis warnings in Visual Studio using PREfast.

---

[2]   See *http://www.gimpel.com*.

[3]   See *http://www.klocwork.com*.

[4]   See *http://www.coverity.com*.

Watching out for broken windows

In the classic book *The Pragmatic Programmer*, the authors discuss the broken window theory[5] and its relation to a concept of software entropy where small errors left unfixed breed additional errors.[6] When a team first begins running code analysis tools, they are inevitably overwhelmed with the number of potential issues they need to investigate. A giant challenge facing teams is that even the best of these tools report some amount of false positives. As mentioned in Chapter 10, "Test Automation," false positives are errors reported by a tool or test that are not the result of a problem in the program or code. When the code analysis tools are reporting hundreds or thousands of errors, these false reports only muddy the water.

A few years ago, I was in charge of deploying our static analysis toolset and reporting results. The code base was huge, so I left the decisions on which reported defects to investigate up to the various development managers on the team. We knew that, eventually, we wanted to investigate and fix all of the errors reported by our analysis tools, but the short-term strategy was up to management. We fixed all of the critical errors (ignoring the false positives) and released a new version of the product later that year.

A few months later, one of the developers was investigating an issue reported by a customer. The issue required some unique conditions and ended up taking nearly an entire day to debug. I remember the developer walking into my office early that evening and saying, "I have some good news, and some bad news. The good news is that I found the bug and know how to fix it. The bad news is that our static analysis tools *also* found the bug, and discovered it three months ago."

We brought in a few other developers to talk about the issue and discovered that our tools found dozens of errors in this particular component. They weren't ignored completely, but the developer had looked at a few of the errors, recognized them as false positives, and ignored the rest of the errors in the component.

We learned some lessons from this experience. We made sure that developers knew how to safely suppress false alarm warnings, and then we required that at least two developers review all suppressed false positives before concluding that the error should be suppressed. We fixed (or suppressed) all of the reported issues and added additional verification to our check-in system to ensure that the code base stayed clean. It's hard to tell how many potential customer issues we prevented, but we were all confident that fixing our broken windows was a good investment.

---

5 James Q. Wilson and George L. Kelling. "Broken Windows: The Police and Neighborhood Safety," *Atlantic Monthly,* 1992.

6 Andrew Hunt and David Thomas, *The Pragmatic Programmer* (Boston, MA: Addison-Wesley Professional, 1999).

Managed Code Analysis

FxCop is an application that analyzes managed code and reports a variety of information such as possible design, localization, performance, and security improvements, as shown in Figure 12-7. In addition to detecting many common coding errors, FxCop detects many violations of programming and design rules (as described in the Microsoft Design Guidelines for Class Library Developers). Anyone creating applications in managed code will find the tool beneficial.

FxCop is available as a stand-alone tool or integrated into Visual Studio. Testers can use the stand-alone tool to examine a managed binary for errors, but most testers and developers use the integrated version of the tool for analysis.

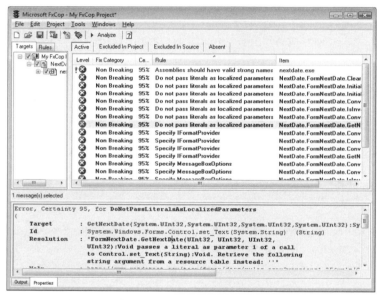

FIGURE 12-7 FxCop analysis tool.

Note The Code Analysis Team Blog at *http://blogs.msdn.com/fxcop* contains a wealth of information on analysis tools in Visual Studio Team System.

Code analysis overload

The most difficult challenge in using code analysis tools is getting started. In a brand new project where code analysis tools are used in the early stages, the "extra" work to detect and fix code errors is barely noticeable. However, when starting to use analysis tools in established products, the initial overload of potential errors can scare a team into turning off the tool.

A few years ago, I was in charge of supporting, maintaining, and implementing static analysis tools across a large code base. My initial reports indicated that there were thousands of errors that needed to be investigated before our next release. Although everyone knew that the errors were coming, in a team of about 100 developers, I knew I would take some heat if I gave everyone 10 to 20 new bugs to investigate.

So, I explained to everyone that I was going to start logging bugs for errors found by our static analysis tools in our legacy code. I went on to explain that, initially, I would log bugs only for the most critical errors (potential crashes and security issues), but over time I would be adding additional rules and checks. I logged a small number of bugs initially, and a few more every week after that while I added a more strict set of rules. Sometimes there was some grumbling, but within a few months, we had fixed thousands of analysis errors—including many beyond what were used in my initial report.

This is a classic application of the Boiled Frog parable[7]: people don't notice gradual changes as much as drastic changes. Over time, the team more than caught up on their backlog of code analysis bugs, but an even more impressive feat is that many members of the team frequently approached me and asked me to turn on *more* code analysis rules.

Just Another Tool

FxCop and PREfast are both powerful tools that should be used by every software team. Static analysis tools are great for finding certain classes of errors well before the test team sees the code, but they do not *replace* testing. It is certainly possible (and probable) to write code that is free of code analysis–detected defects that is still filled with bugs. However, fixing these bugs earlier does give the test team more time—and a much better chance—to find a huge number of more critical bugs throughout the entire product cycle.

---

[7]   See *http://en.wikipedia.org/wiki/Boiled_frog*.

Test Code Analysis

Many types of errors are specific to test automation. One such area is *environmental sensitivity*. This refers to the reliance of tests on noninvariant environmental factors. This issue can reveal itself in a variety of forms, which are best represented by example. Consider a test of a user control called a *FileSaveWidget*, which accepts an input file path and saves data to the specified file. A simple test of this component is listed in sample code for a *FileSaveWidget* test here.

```
 1 void TestFileSaveWidget()
 2 {
 3    // this file contains the expected output of the file save widget
 4    string baselineFilePath = @"\\test-server\TestData\baseline.txt";
 5
 6    // the local path for the save file
 7    string outputFilePath = @"D:\datafile.txt";
 8
 9    FileSaveWidget widget = new FileSaveWidget();
10    widget.SetDataFile(outputFilePath);
11    widget.Save();
12    try
13    {
14        VerifyDataFile(baselineFilePath, outputFilePath);
15        WriteTestResult("PASS");
16    }
17    catch (Exception e)
18    {
19        String errorMessage = e.Message;
20        if (errorMessage.Contains("File not found"))
21        {
22            WriteTestResult("FAIL");
23        }
24    }
25 }
```

The code looks straightforward enough, but there are at least three issues in this example. On line 4, notice the use of a remote file share on a computer called test-server. There is no guarantee that this server will be visible when the test runs on a network or user account different from the one the tester originally intended. Line 7 contains a hard-coded reference to drive D. Perhaps all computers that this tester has encountered so far have writeable partitions on D, but this assumption will likely lead to failures later on (D could be a CD-ROM drive or simply nonexistent).

Line 19 hides a more subtle but important issue. The expected error message in the case that the save operation fails might indeed be "File not found"—if the test is running on an English-language operating system or English-language build of the product. However, a Spanish localized build might return "Archivo no encontró" in this case, which would not be caught by this test. Many test teams at Microsoft use scanning tools to find issues that can cause problems with test code. Sample output from a test code–scanning tool is in Table 12-3.

TABLE 12-3 Test Code Analysis Results

Issue	Location	Owner	Details
Hard-coded share path	Test.cs:4	Chris Preston	A hard-coded share path was found in a test source file. Hard-coded paths to specific file shares can make the test unportable.
Hard-coded local path	Test.cs:7	Michael Pfeiffer	A hard-coded local path was found in a test source file. Hard-coded local paths can make tests unportable. Consider putting any hard-coded paths into a configuration file.
Hard-coded string	Test.cs:19	Michael Pfeiffer	Hard-coded exception string "File not found"; please use ResourceLibrary to comply with localization testing.
Invalid user name	Test Case ID 31337	(N/A)	Test case assigned to invalid user "Nobody"; please assign to a current team member.

Analysis tools often go beyond analyzing code and look for errors in the test cases or almost anyplace else where testers might make errors. Some examples of the biggest improvements to test code as a result of analysis such as this include the following:

- Improved success running localized test passes as a result of proactively catching and reporting usages of hard-coded English strings

- Improved test reliability resulting from checking for potential race conditions (usage of *Thread.Sleep*), invalid configuration files, and so on

- Improved completeness of test coverage by checking for "orphaned" tests (code that was checked in but not enabled in automated runs, incorrectly marked in the TCM, and so on)

The bigger value added by analysis is that it preempts issues from occurring by flagging them on a daily basis. Every day, testers get feedback on the quality of their tests and test cases, and they use the feedback to improve the quality of their tests and, ultimately, the quality of the product.

Test Code Is Product Code

These errors might not be important for production code, but they are critical for test code reliability and maintainability. Error-prone test code is one of the biggest concerns I hear from test managers throughout the industry. Even at Microsoft, where many of our SDETs are top-notch programmers, we rely on these tools to help us create tests that can run reliably and report accurate results for a decade or more and through thousands of executions.

By now it should be clear that testers at Microsoft commonly use many traditional development tools. What this really means is that at Microsoft, source code is treated the same as product code regardless of whether the code ships or not.

Even More Tools

There is no end to the number of tools testers use. Microsoft employees consistently take advantage of any efficiency or effectiveness gains achieved through the aid of software, and they are careful to ensure that using a tool rather than a manual process doesn't affect the final output. Continuing the toolbox analogy used at the beginning of this chapter, using software to aid testing is similar to using a power tool rather than a hand tool. In many cases, the power tool is faster and achieves better results, but some jobs still make sense to complete by hand.

Tools for Unique Problems

Most of the previously discussed tools are ones that almost every tester uses. Countless others solve big problems for smaller groups of people. Screen recorders, file parsers, add-ons for automation tools, and even the font display tool shown in Chapter 10 are all examples of software programs written to solve specific testing problems.

In addition to tools, testers customarily share *libraries* (reusable functionality that can be added to any application) in their team so that everyone on the team can solve similar problems using a consistent, well-tested solution. For example, the Office team has shared libraries that are used to help automated tests access the window controls common to all Office applications, and the Windows Mobile team has shared libraries to simulate cellular data. These are both areas where a common solution helps the entire test team do their jobs better.

Tools for Everyone

Microsoft employees love to create tools. Thousands of tools ranging from test helper libraries to Outlook add-ins to productivity enhancers are available in an easy-to-access repository. Engineers love to use software that helps them do their job better, and many employees share their applications with their teams across the entire company.

> **Note** The Microsoft internal tool repository contains nearly 5,000 different tools written by Microsoft employees.

Employees can search the tools in this repository (the ToolBox), as shown in Figure 12-8, and they can subscribe to RSS feeds to notify them of new tool submissions. Each tool entry lists information about the tool and the name of the tool owner in case more information is needed. Finally, every tool can be rated and comments can be added to aid future toolbox browsers in their tool-choosing decisions.

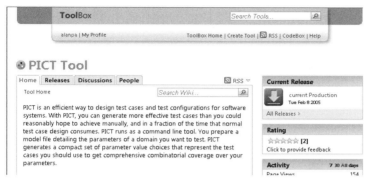

FIGURE 12-8 The Microsoft ToolBox.

Summary

One of the qualities I've noticed in great testers is that they are extremely efficient in their testing. They are not hurried in their testing activities; rather they all seem to know exactly the point where software can help solve their current testing problem faster than their brain can. When software is a potential solution for their current situation, they are able to find or repurpose an existing tool to their needs or, when necessary, create a new tool to solve a problem.

Testers need to use new tools when appropriate and reexamine their current toolbox periodically to be most effective. As is the case with source code management, testers should also examine their toolset and determine whether existing tools can be used in a different way. An adequately filled toolbox, along with the skill and knowledge to use those tools, is one of the biggest assets a tester can have.

Chapter 13
Customer Feedback Systems

Alan Page

A big piece of the quality puzzle is the customer. Software companies such as Microsoft write software for people—software that can help people be more productive or accomplish tasks they wouldn't be able to do otherwise. This chapter discusses the tools and techniques Microsoft uses to gather data from our customers and partners to help us improve the quality of our products and to influence our testing.

Testing and Quality

I hope this isn't a shock, but customers don't really care about testing. At some level, I suppose they care that some effort went into testing the product before they spent money on it, but they're not at all concerned with most of the actual work that testers do.

Imagine that you are browsing for software at a store and pick up a box to read the bullet points on the side describing its features:

- Ran more than 9,000 test cases with a 98 percent pass rate.

- Code coverage numbers over 85 percent!

- Stress tested nightly.

- Nearly 5,000 bugs found.

- More than 3,000 bugs fixed!

- Tested with both a black box and white box approach.

- And much, much more...

Those bullet points are all interesting to the engineering team, but the customer doesn't care about any of them. Customers only care if the product solves a problem for them and works in the way they expect. If you consider software quality to be the value it provides to the user, most test activities don't directly improve software quality. Despite this, testing is indeed valuable (or I wouldn't be writing this book). So, what does testing do?

Testing Provides Information

The bullet points mentioned previously provide information about the testing activity and, in some cases, the status of the product. This information is critical in assessing progress and identifying risk. For example, if the latest report from the test team says that they have run half of their tests and have found 40 critical "severity 1" bugs, that relates a different risk metric than if test tells you they've run all of their tests and found only 1 critical bug. Of course, this is not enough information either—you would want to know what types of tests were done, which scenarios were tested, which areas of the product they had tested, how many noncritical bugs were found, and dozens of other points of data. I've never liked the idea of test being the gatekeepers of quality. Rather, I like to think that the information that testing provides helps the product's decision makers make the right decisions regarding schedule and risks.

Quality Perception

If everything goes perfectly, the work that the test team does *increases* quality by *decreasing* risk. In reality, this doesn't always happen. Too often, the information provided by the test team is not reflective of the way customers will actually use the product.

You can think of test data and customer-perceived quality (I like to call this *experience quality*) as two related but distinct spheres of data relating to quality:

If our test information were perfect, we would be able to predict the experience quality that our customers will have—that is, at the time of release, we would know within a few points what the customer satisfaction numbers would be when we survey customers six months later. Our two spheres of quality would nearly overlap:

Most of the time, these circles intersect, but rarely quite as much as we hope:

Microsoft is working hard to get experience quality and test data to match—by finding more measurements that can *predict* how customers will perceive quality. Data that shows how the customers are using a product, where it is failing them, and what they like and dislike about the product is invaluable in developing quality software.

One of the big problems many of Microsoft's large software projects face when gathering customer data is processing all of the diverse sets of data in a way that accurately reflects the diversity of needs of the customer base. Product support data, e-mail, customer surveys, and usability studies all provide valuable information, but it can be difficult to prioritize the feedback and understand the scenarios surrounding these data points, as depicted in Figure 13-1. Moreover, we discovered that often the data from various sources didn't agree, was subjective, and we frequently couldn't process and comprehend all of the data.

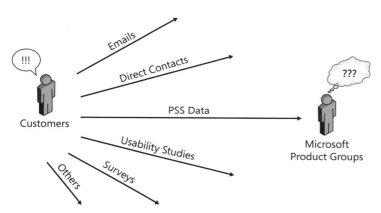

FIGURE 13-1 Customer feedback.

There are many ways to find and collect information and feedback from customers. This chapter discusses four methods in use across most product teams: Customer Experience Improvement Program (CEIP), Windows Error Reporting (WER), Send a Smile, and Connect. Many of these tools are available to our partners and Microsoft corporate customers.

Customers to the Rescue

The best way to find out how customers use your software is to watch them. When you have only a few users, and know when they will be using your software, and if they agree to let you watch them, this is a great solution. Knowing how the customers use your software goes beyond what can be discovered by a usability study. Knowing how the customers use your software means that you know how they *learn* to use the program, which tasks they perform most often, and which tasks they never use.

When you install certain Microsoft applications, the dialog box shown in Figure 13-2 opens asking if you would like to help make the application better by providing feedback on your use of the product. If interested, you can enroll in the Customer Experience Improvement Program (CEIP). When you opt in to this program, anonymous data about how you use the application is occasionally uploaded to Microsoft when your computer is idle. At Microsoft, we know that to make great products, we need to understand as much as we can about how the products are used. Millions of people use Microsoft products, so it is impossible for us to contact even a fraction of the customer base for some of our larger products. CEIP data provides a massive amount of information that helps us understand how customers use our products—I like to think of CEIP as being just like one of those Nielsen Ratings boxes used for collecting TV ratings, except for software.

FIGURE 13-2 CEIP option in Windows Live Messenger.

When a customer agrees to participate in the program, we collect anonymous, nontraceable data points detailing how the software is used, what hardware the software is installed on, and a variety of other bits of information to aid in understanding customer usage (confidential or personally identifiable data is never collected). The initial consumers of this data are often designers or user experience engineers. The data, collected from millions of customers, provides a unique insight into how they use our products. Some examples of the types of data collected are as follows:

- Application usage
  - ❏ How often are different commands used?
  - ❏ Which keyboard shortcuts are used most often?
  - ❏ How long are applications run?
  - ❏ How often is a specific feature used?
- Quality metrics
  - ❏ How long does an application run without crashing (mean time to failure)?
  - ❏ Which error dialog boxes are commonly displayed?
  - ❏ How many customers experience errors trying to open a document?
  - ❏ How long does it take to complete an operation?
  - ❏ What percentage of users is unable to sign in to an Internet service?
- Configuration
  - ❏ How many people run in high-contrast color mode?
  - ❏ What is the most common processor speed?

❑ How much space is available on the average person's hard disk?

❑ What operating system versions do most people run the application on?

The data points can influence many aspects of product development. Figure 13-3 and Table 13-1 show example CEIP data measuring the amount of time users spend running an application. In this case, the product team initially assumed that users of the software ran the program constantly in the background, and that they would switch tasks to activate the application from time to time. Based on this assumption, a significant portion of their test scenarios and development efforts concentrated on measuring resource usage over time and in detecting other issues that might occur while running the application for long periods. The CEIP data supported this assumption and showed that one-quarter of the users ran the product for 8 hours or more, and that nearly half the users ran the program for sessions lasting at least 2 hours.

TABLE 13-1 Sample Data from Customer Experience Improvement Program (CEIP)

Time spent running application in 24-hour period	Sessions	Percentage of total	Active session time (in seconds)	Average minutes in session	Percentage of time active
Less than 5 minutes	2,496,181	24%	17,811,873	—	—
6–30 minutes	1,596,963	15%	8,572,986	18	31%
31–60 minutes	691,377	7%	4,997,432	45	16%
1 hr	757,504	7%	6,957,789	90	10%
2 hrs	487,616	5%	5,645,785	150	8%
3 hrs	395,007	4%	5,514,112	210	7%
4 hrs	347,705	3%	5,593,810	270	6%
5 hrs	331,561	3%	6,135,420	330	6%
6 hrs	355,017	3%	7,785,188	390	6%
7 hrs	457,104	4%	12,357,653	450	6%
8 hrs and up	2,636,023	25%	68,692,969	960	3%

The unanticipated piece of data that the product team discovered was that nearly one-quarter of the users ran the application for 5 minutes or less, and that another 15 percent ran the program for less than 30 minutes. Instead of leaving the application running in the background for quick access, a significant percentage of the users started the application to view updated data, and then closed the application shortly after. After analyzing this data, the test team reprioritized a portion of their test scenarios and performance work around improving application start-up and shutdown time to improve the experience for people using the application in this manner.

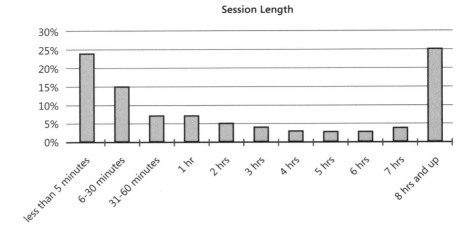

FIGURE 13-3 Application session length data from CEIP.

The CEIP data drives many design decisions but is also quite beneficial to test teams. Data from released products can influence the testing approach and strategy used for future versions of the product, as well as to aid in root cause analysis of significant issues found after release. During the product cycle, frequent analysis of this data from beta users and key partners makes it possible for the test team to consistently update test scenarios and priorities as the team gains a greater understanding of customer usage patterns and pain points.

Note The top three most-used commands in Microsoft Office Word 2003 are Paste, Save, and Copy (courtesy of CEIP data).

Through my years at Microsoft, I have analyzed many bugs found by customers after product release to identify how our team could improve testing in subsequent product work. Somewhat surprisingly, I discovered that only a few of the customer errors were in areas that we "missed," such as areas where we didn't have test coverage or scenarios. Most of the errors were right in the middle of areas where we had defined test scenarios or high code coverage—but the errors were apparent only when the customer scenario differed from *our* scenario. In recent years, CEIP data has helped many test teams begin to bridge this gap.

More Info For more information about CEIP, see the Microsoft Customer Experience Improvement Program page at *http://www.microsoft.com/products/ceip*.

Customer-driven testing

Our group built a bridge between the CEIP data that we were receiving and incoming data from Microsoft Windows Error Reporting (WER) from our beta customers. We monitored the data frequently and used the customer data to help us understand which errors customers were seeing and how they correlated with what our testing was finding. We put high priority on finding and fixing the top 10 issues found every week. Some of these were new issues our testing missed, and some were things we had found but were unable to reproduce consistently. Analyzing the data enabled us to increase our test coverage and to expose bugs in customer scenarios that we might not have found otherwise.

—*Chris Lester, Senior SDET*

 Note An early pilot of an MSN subscription service timed out the sign-up process at 20 minutes. CEIP data revealed that many users took longer than 20 minutes to complete the sign-up process and were disconnected before they could finish!

Games, Too!

Inspired by CEIP, the Microsoft Games Systems team created an application instrumentation tool named VINCE (Verification of Initial Consumer Experience), also named after *Voodoo Vince*, the first game instrumented with the toolset. Today, whereas CEIP can run on all versions of the Windows and Windows CE operating systems, VINCE can run on Xbox and Xbox 360, as well as the PC platform, and supports issues specific to games. For example, beta users can provide feedback on how difficult they thought a certain portion of the game was by completing a short customer survey designed to be answered quickly using the game controller.

One of the most successful instrumentations to date is with *Halo 2*. The single-player campaign of *Halo 2* consists of 14 levels, and each level consists of dozens of encounters (there are 211 total encounters in the game, ranging from 2 minutes to 30 minutes in length). Using instrumentation, the team was able to get consumer feedback on each of the encounters at least three times. Overall, they collected more than 2,300 hours of gameplay feedback from more than 400 participants—something that would have been impossible without instrumentation.

One example of how this data was used is on a *Halo 2* level called *Gravemind*, which is about two-thirds of the way through the game. The encounter takes place in a room filled with enemies, including the vicious Brutes. This is the first time the player fights Brutes, and this room is particularly lethal.

By looking at the instrumentation reports, the Halo team was quickly able to identify this encounter as being especially difficult immediately after the testing session. Further analysis of the encounter showed that a high number of deaths occurred as a result of plasma grenades, needlers, and Brute attacks. One valuable feature of VINCE is that it can capture video of areas requiring additional investigation. Watching the associated video revealed that the arc of the plasma grenades was too flat (not giving players enough time to dodge the grenades), that Brutes were killing players from behind (players were dying immediately, without knowing why), and that people were incurring a lot of damage from the needler weapon (because some enemy characters were holding two needler weapons, making them extremely deadly).

The Halo team made several changes based on this feedback: a global change about how grenades are thrown (removing the instance of flat-arc grenades in that encounter), the location of enemies in the room (all enemies appear from one location instead of several to reduce the chance of the player being killed from behind), and an overall reduction in waves of enemies the player has to battle through. Other minor changes were made as well. Through iterative testing, they found that the design changes dramatically reduced the number of deaths in this room while improving the attitudinal feedback (a.k.a. the fun factor) about this encounter. In other words, they were able to reduce the difficulty and number of deaths without making the encounter too easy for players.

Customer usage data is an important technique for influencing product and test design for any software application. The data can be used to define missing scenarios or to modify existing testing scenarios and configurations. It is certainly not the only way to influence design, and it isn't helpful at all if the appropriate instrumentation to supply feedback does not exist in the product code. It is one significant technique that teams at Microsoft use to aid in designing, creating, and testing programs that recognize and support key user scenarios and areas of customer pain and frustration.

Windows Error Reporting

One thing that's been amazing at Microsoft is the impact that our monitoring data has had on how we prioritize our software work. I'm sure you've all seen in Windows that whenever an application or the system malfunctions, you get the ability to send a report back to Microsoft.

We get a lot of those reports, and we've created very good data-management systems to go in and look at those things, and therefore understand what drivers aren't reliable.

We allow anyone who has an application that runs on Windows to sign up and get the reports that relate to their application, and we've got winqual.microsoft.com where people can do that.

*Today we've seen a lot of that activity from the driver manufacturers, but we want
to see even more at the application level so it gets us working together on anything
where a user is not having a great experience.*

—*Bill Gates, 2003 Professional Developers Conference*

Just about every Microsoft customer has seen the Windows Error Reporting dialog box
shown in Figure 13-4.

FIGURE 13-4 Windows Error Reporting dialog box.

Most users of Windows see a similar dialog box each time an application crashes. Although
I, for one, would like to see far fewer appearances of this dialog box, it has one advantage:
Every time it appears, in the background it is generating data points that Microsoft uses to
increase product quality. The dialog box shown in the figure is a part of the Windows Error
Reporting (WER) infrastructure. Note that on the Windows Vista operating system, errors
can be configured to be automatically sent to Microsoft without the need to interact with an
error reporting dialog box.

The Way We WER

WER is a flexible event-based feedback infrastructure designed to gather information
about the hardware and software problems with applications or the operating system that
Windows can detect, report the information to Microsoft, and provide users with any available solutions. WER is a simple and secure method for users to provide information about
application crashes and provides a database that categorizes and prioritizes reports for
Microsoft and partner software vendors. It also provides a means for Microsoft and vendors
to respond with status reports, requests for additional information, or links to other information about a specific issue.

On Windows Vista, Problem Reports and Solutions in Control Panel, shown in Figure 13-5,
keeps a record of all system and application issues reported through WER and gives you

more information about the errors, including a list of all existing possible solutions for these problems.

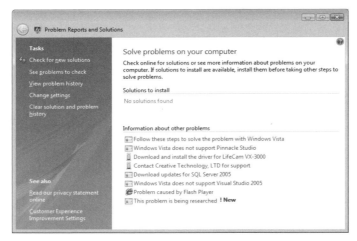

FIGURE 13-5 Windows Vista Problem Reports and Solutions.

WER works a lot like a just-in-time (JIT) debugger. If an application causes an error that is not caught by any of its own error handlers, the Windows error system catches the error. In addition to displaying the error reporting dialog box, the system captures data at the point of failure, including the process name and version, loaded modules, and call stack information. The entire process looks something like this:

1. The error event occurs.

2. Windows activates the WER service.

3. WER collects basic crash information. If additional information is needed, the user might be prompted for consent.

4. The data is uploaded to Microsoft (if the user is not connected to the Internet, the upload is deferred).

5. If an application is registered for automatic restart (using the *RegisterApplicationRestart* function available on Windows Vista), WER restarts the application.

6. If a solution or additional information is available, the user is notified.

Although WER automatically provides error reporting for crash, hang, and kernel faults, applications can also use the WER API to obtain information for custom problems not covered by the existing error reporting. In addition to the application restart feature mentioned previously, Windows Vista extends WER to support many types of noncritical events such as performance issues.

Corporate Error Reporting

Corporate Error Reporting (CER) is a version of WER that companies can use to capture crash information from applications and forward the reports to Microsoft when they occur.

CER provides companies with several benefits. Many companies do not want their users to automatically forward crash data to Microsoft because of concerns of forwarding company confidential information. (Microsoft places strict confidentiality restrictions on the crash information it receives.)

The primary benefit companies that implement CER receive is the ability to track crash errors in the environment. By recording hard data of when corporate users experience crash events, companies can prioritize which updates to their production environment will have the most positive impact. This information is also a valuable metric for the IT department to measure the effect it has on improving user productivity.

Filling the Buckets

You might wonder who the poor soul is who is responsible for looking at millions and millions of crash reports from WER. Fortunately, this job is a great task for a computer to help accomplish, and the backend error reporting system does a fantastic job of processing an enormous number of error reports.

The crashing process name, version, call stack, processor registers, and other collected data are automatically analyzed and sorted into *buckets*. A bucket is a categorization of all instances of a specific error associated with a particular version of a driver, application, Windows feature, or other component. By using buckets, the product teams can appropriately prioritize how they will address WER reported issues. In other words, product teams sort WER issues by number of hits in each bucket. To ensure that they address the issues causing the most customer pain, all issues that exceed a team-designated threshold for number of occurrences are automatically entered as bugs in the product bug tracking systems so that teams can focus on the issues causing the most customer frustration.

Emptying the Buckets

As more error reporting data becomes available, trends inevitably develop. Analysis of data shows that across all reported issues fixing 20 percent of the top-reported bugs can solve 80 percent of customer issues, and that addressing 1 percent of the bugs would fix 50 percent of customer issues, as shown in Figure 13-6. Simply put, of the total number of crashing errors experienced by customers, most are caused by a small number of actual errors. The same analysis results are generally true regardless of the application. The goal of the product team is to look first at those defects that are causing the most crashes. Focusing on them will produce the biggest return for the smallest relative effort.

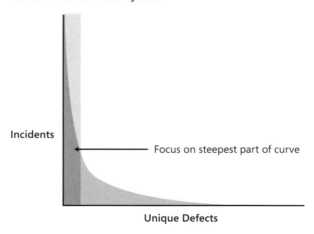

Incidents

Focus on steepest part of curve

Unique Defects

FIGURE 13-6 WER incidents bucket report.

Like other feedback data, WER information is always beneficial but is critically effective when collected and analyzed during beta releases. Table 13-2 contains typical crash data for the top 10 issues found in an application. Many product teams set goals regarding WER data collected during product development. Common goals include the following:

- **Coverage method**   When using the coverage method, groups target to investigate *N* percent (usually 50 percent) of the total hits for the application.

- **Threshold method**   Groups can use the threshold method if their crash curves (one is shown in Figure 13-6) are very steep or very flat. With flat or steep crash curves, using the previously described coverage method can be inappropriate because it can require too many or too few buckets to be investigated. A reasonable percentage of total hits for the threshold method is between 1 percent and 0.5 percent.

- **Fix number method**   The fix number method involves targeting to fix *N* number of defects instead of basing goals on percentages.

TABLE 13-2 Example WER Data

Bucket ID	App name	Version	Module name	Module version	Symbol	Hits	Type
231387	app.exe	1.0.0.1	appsupp.dll	6.1.0.0	appsupp.dll!Erase	1,511,546	Crash
309986	app.exe	1.0.0.1	app.exe	1.0.0.1	app.exe!Release	405,982	Crash
195749	app.exe	1.0.0.1	appsup.dll	6.1.0.0	appsupp.dll!Draw	394,517	Hang
214031	app.exe	1.0.0.1	appsup2.dll	6.1.0.2	appsup2.dll!Reset	137,638	Crash
485404	app.exe	1.0.0.1	app.exe	1.0.0.1	app.exe!SetObject	100,630	Crash
390064	app.exe	1.0.0.1	appsup2.dll	6.1.0.2	appsup2.dll!Display	95,604	Hang
208980	app.exe	1.0.0.1	appsup3.dll	1.0.0.1	appsup3.dll!AppPrint	74,997	Crash

Bucket ID	App name	Version	Module name	Module version	Symbol	Hits	Type
204973	app.exe	1.0.0.1	app.exe	1.0.0.1	app.exe!Release	55,434	Crash
407857	app.exe	1.0.0.1	app.exe	1.0.0.1	app.exe!MainLoop	54,886	Crash
229981	app.exe	1.0.0.1	appsupp.dll	6.1.0.0	appsupp.dll!function	51,982	Crash

Test and WER

At a minimum, test should be responsible for monitoring the aggregated crash data and measuring the progress against fix goals. A wealth of additional information can be mined when you know all the different ways customers have found to crash an application.

It is vital to *fix* the issues causing the most customer pain, but big improvements come from investigating the root cause of the issues customers are experiencing most often. Often, understanding how an error was created or how code analysis tools, testing, or another process missed detection of the bug can lead to implementation of a solution that prevents similar types of issues from ever occurring again. Fixing the bug alone is great for the customer, but being able to prevent a class of bugs from ever seeing the light of day is a fantastic opportunity.

Analysis of the root problem can also lead to identification of *crash patterns*. In the world of software, *design patterns* are common solutions to recurring problems. In this light, you can think of a crash pattern as a common, transferable method for crashing a perfectly good program. Analysis of common crashing problems often reveals other areas of the product that might crash in the same way. Patterns can be (and are!) applied to many other types of bugs as well.

> **More Info**   For more information about WER, see the Windows Error Reporting topic on Microsoft MSDN at *http://msdn.microsoft.com/en-us/library/bb513641.aspx*.

Smile and Microsoft Smiles with You

Start every day off with a smile and get it over with.

—W. C. Fields

I often wonder what's going through the mind of someone using a piece of software I've worked on. Which parts do they like? Which parts do they despise? How can I find out more about their experience? CEIP and WER give me the data to find out *which* features customers are using and whether the application is crashing or locking up, but I know that for every crashing bug, someone might run into at least a hundred other issues while using any software program. We want users to feel good about and enjoy the experience of using our products. Despite our best efforts during the design and development process, we know that users often feel frustrated while using our products. But what specifically about our products is frustrating—and, conversely, what do users love about our products?

Emotional response is difficult to measure: Usability lab studies measure user performance on a set of tasks, but given their structured nature, these studies do not reliably reproduce the right context to elicit emotional responses from users. Surveys measure usage and satisfaction but rarely capture how users feel about our products. Site visits and focus groups produce retrospective accounts of users' experiences, but users are notoriously poor at recalling enough context to relate the details of those experiences.

Emotional responses have always been a challenge to capture because of the difficulty of reproducing the exact context that triggered the reaction. As a result, traditionally little data has been collected in this area. One solution is to ship each software release with a set of electrodes and hardware to monitor pulse rate and a variety of chemical and electrical signals to gauge emotional reaction to using the software. Unfortunately, what I'd expect that we would find is that human emotion is difficult to measure (not to mention that most users probably wouldn't properly configure the measurement devices).

An alternate method for collecting customer feedback is the Send a Smile program. Send a Smile is a simple tool that beta and other early-adoption customers can use to submit feedback about Microsoft products. After installing the client application, little *smiley* and *frowny* icons appear in the notification area, as shown in Figure 13-7. When users have a negative experience with the application that they want to share with Microsoft, they click the frowny icon. The tool captures a screen shot of the entire desktop, and users enter a text message to describe what they didn't like. The screen shot and comment are sent to a database where members of the product team can analyze them.

FIGURE 13-7 Send a Smile smiley and frowny icons.

External customers who have participated in Send a Smile studies have come to love the tool. They find great pleasure in clicking the frowny icon when something bothers them and are pleased with the fact that they have to do nothing more than click an icon, type a comment in the text area shown in Figure 13-8, click Send, and the feedback forwards to Microsoft. Participants in this program have a direct connection with the feedback program administrator and find out later how much of their feedback influenced a new or changed product design.

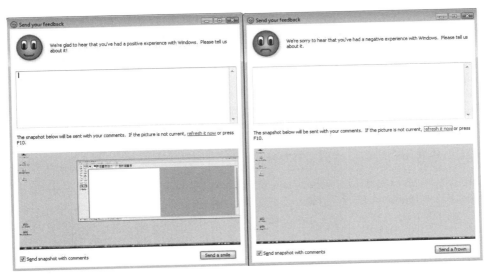

FIGURE 13-8 Send a Smile user interface.

The Send a Smile program is relatively new, and not all Microsoft groups are using it at this time. The system does have an enormous amount of potential for gathering customer input. It encourages customers to provide quick, spontaneous feedback at any time. Think about all of the times you have been frustrated with an application and couldn't do anything but groan about the problem—or the times you were using a new piece of software and were a bit surprised how *well* it worked for you. Programs like Send a Smile provide users an opportunity to provide this feedback immediately.

Send a Smile Impact

Although Send a Smile is a relatively new program, the initial benefits have been significant. Some of the top benefits include the following:

- **The contribution of unique bugs**   The Windows and Office teams rely heavily on Send a Smile to capture unique bugs that affect real consumers that were not found through any other test or feedback method. For example, during the Windows Vista Beta 1 milestone, 176 unique bugs in 13 different areas of the product were filed as a direct result of Send a Smile feedback from customers in the early adopter program. During Office 12 Beta 1, 169 unique bugs were filed as a result of feedback from customers in the Office early adopter program.

- **Increased customer awareness**   Send a Smile helps increase team awareness of the pain and joy that users experience with our products.

- **Bug priorities driven by real customer issues**   Customer feedback collected through Send a Smile helps teams prioritize the incoming bug load.

- **Insight into how users are using our products**   Teams often wonder which features users are finding and using, and whether users notice the "little things" that they put into the product. Send a Smile makes it easy for team members to see comments.

- **Enhancing other customer feedback**   Screen shots and comments from Send a Smile have been used to illustrate specific customer issues collected though other methods such as CEIP instrumentation, newsgroups, usability lab studies, and surveys.

Connecting with Customers

In my early years as a software tester, I used a beta version of a product called Microsoft Test that came with my company's MSDN subscription (this product later became Microsoft Visual Test). For a prerelease application, it worked surprisingly well, but I did run into a few roadblocks and had a few questions that I couldn't answer. As the only tester at my company, my options for feedback were limited, but our CEO had one option for me. Armed with his CompuServe[1] account name and password, I logged on and found a Microsoft forum where I could ask my questions. I had never even called a product support line before and had no idea when (or whether) I would get any answers. I checked in the next day and was surprised to see that I not only had a response, but that I had reasonable answers for my questions and that my suggestions would be considered by the product team. I asked a few more questions over the next few months, and each time someone from the product team responded similarly. Over time, I also learned a lot from reading other testers' questions and the posted answers. I even remember answering a few!

Today, newsgroups and forums remain a method for customers and Microsoft product team engineers to communicate. The hierarchy under microsoft.public.* contains hundreds of newsgroups with active participation from Microsoft engineers and their customers. Hundreds of other active discussions take place in the online forums at *forums.microsoft. com*. Nearly another thousand Microsoft employees blog about their products and jobs on *http://blogs.msdn.com*. Customer feedback received through any of these means is taken seriously and is used to help weigh decisions on fixing bugs and adding or changing features or functionality.

Microsoft Connect (*http://connect.microsoft.com*) is yet another way for Microsoft employees and customers to communicate, but Connect adds unique and valuable information to the conversation. The goal of Connect is to create a community around product feedback and provide customers with a channel for communication with the engineering teams working on Microsoft products. Customers can report bugs, ask questions, and even make suggestions for new features. The "fun" part of using Connect is that bugs and suggestions can be *voted* on by members of the community. When a user makes a suggestion or enters a bug report, other people who think the suggested feature would be valuable, or who are also

---

[1]   CompuServe was the first major commercial online service.

experiencing some pain from the specific bug, can add a "me too" to the feedback report. Over time, the most popular suggestions (and most *un*popular bugs) rise to the top and help the product team make quick and accurate decisions on what work to do next. All of the bugs and suggestions are searchable, and community members (or Microsoft employees) can offer workarounds or alternate suggestions if appropriate. Figure 13-9 shows the Microsoft Connect user interface for Microsoft Visual Studio and the .NET Framework.

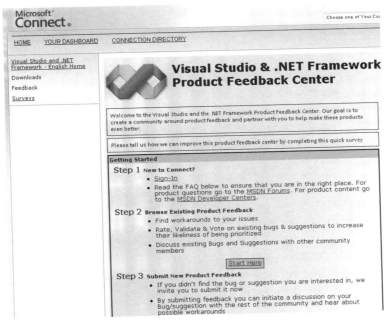

FIGURE 13-9 Microsoft Connect.

Microsoft Connect offers a few other worthwhile features for customers. Software (including prerelease software for early adopters), white papers, and other information are available for download. Surveys—a great way to ensure that the customer voice is heard—are available and help Microsoft gather input to improve our software.

More Info For more information about Microsoft Connect, see the Microsoft Connect Web site at *http://connect.microsoft.com*.

Customer connections—regardless of the method—are much more than just a good thing. They are one of the most critical building blocks of quality software.

OneNote customer connection

During the Office 2007 cycle, the OneNote test team explored and engaged in numerous customer connection activities. The team worked closely with product planning and usability engineers to engage on 24 customer visits across 7 different personas. This allowed the test team to interact with real customers, gather feedback, and better understand real-world usage. The process informed our test strategy, test cases, configurations, and real-world projects. It also created more empathy, which is important to understanding the potential pain that customers experience using our products.

Each tester went on two or three customer visits and took notes about the job, examined notebook structures, asked for feedback, and so forth. This data was used to inform personas, feature decisions, and ultimately our testing and real-world projects. An additional benefit customer visits provided was a great sense of job satisfaction for the test team, and many team members commented that customer visits were one of the high points of the release.

The test team used blog search engines to find out what early adoption customers were saying about the product. The team found a blog titled "I hate OneNote and SharePoint." We contacted the blogger by using comments and started an e-mail thread trying to track down the issue. We were able to track down a complex WEBDAV configuration that a customer was using and getting OneNote sync failures on. The test team had been seeing this bug randomly but could never reproduce it internally. By working with the blogger, we tracked down the issue and found the fix, which was installing a specific Windows Server QFE.[2] Additionally, the test team now had a better WSS/Windows Server configuration to test, and we better understood the overall issue. We added this information to our set of test collateral.

OneNote also took full advantage of Microsoft Connect. The site was used extensively during the beta phases, and we were able to engage the community to gather bugs, better understand configurations, and collect large amount of real-world files that we now have in a repository. Some examples from our Connect site include these:

18,000 members.

More than 475 product bugs logged, with 146 marked as fixed.

Best example bugs from the community: During the final phase of the OneNote 2007 cycle, we had two separate OneNote corruption files submitted and fixed through our Connect site. We also had ink bugs that were submitted and fixed, as well as a few basic missed test cases that were obvious bugs.

Customer surveys issues with more than 2,000 responses.

---

[2]   QFE stands for Quick Fix Engineering. In other words, a software update.

Another significant effort initiated toward the end of Office 2007 was a large-scale set of cross-division real-world projects. More than 50 testers and PMs from almost 30 teams across the division created eight different projects that focused on fully flexing the integrated Office 2007 System software by building real-world projects as diverse as a small construction company site to a MySpace site. The project was successful and there were many recall class and security bugs logged and fixed before release.

Through this new push into customer connection, the test team was able to help ship a product that customers use and love, with high quality and high customer satisfaction.

—*Mike Tholfsen, Test Manager, Office*

Numerous other efforts exist to help Microsoft engineers understand more about how customers use our products. One other significant example is *scenario voting*. Scenario voting presents to users a description of a scenario and asks them to provide a rating or opinion of the scenario, and optionally offer their opinions on satisfaction and relative importance of the scenario. The engineering team can use the data to capture some of the perceptions of the scenarios in a prioritized fashion and to identify areas where users might be having difficulty and areas that are working well. The scenario voting concept is discussed in detail in *The Practical Guide to Defect Prevention* (Microsoft Press, 2007).

Summary

Testers regularly refer to themselves as the folks that wear the customer hat, but despite this claim, many testers do not have the opportunity to engage as deeply in customer connection activities as is necessary. One aspect of the test role is that it should provide a natural closeness to the customer and lend unique insight into how customers use and feel about our products. It is vital that test takes a proactive role in customer-related activities.

By using the feedback mechanisms discussed in this chapter, testers at Microsoft can identify missing test scenarios, discover holes in their tests, and create scenario tests deeply based on customer usage patterns. Balancing customer feedback approaches with deep technical analysis through functional testing and code coverage analysis is a critical aspect of creating quality software.

Chapter 14
Testing Software Plus Services

Ken Johnston

Father's Day 2007, for a gift I was presented with the hardback edition of *The Dangerous Book for Boys*.[1] I let my son hold the book and he ran his fingers over the muted red fabric that covered the book. He began to trace the big gold letters of the word *dangerous* and I saw his eyes open wide and a big grin envelop his face. The book seemed to be calling out, "Read me and the secrets will be revealed."

The first chapter on essential gear for handling and getting into danger was critically important for us as we assembled our ultimate adventurers' backpacks. The chapters on knots, fossils, and dinosaurs were all big hits. The chapter I wasn't too sure about was the one on tripwires, but my son thought this topic was just the coolest ever. I relented, and we went through the material but I was very clear that he was not to set up a tripwire anywhere in the house or his father's tool shed.

Young boys and danger just seem to be a natural fit. They will find each other no matter what. Having a book like *The Dangerous Book for Boys* is a valuable tool to help any young boy learn to differentiate between the little dangers and the big ones.

Software Plus Services (S+S) and Microsoft seem to be a natural fit as well. Microsoft has tens of millions of lines of code written for application and server products. These products run successfully on millions of computers and devices around the world. It makes sense to use these products and all the computing power of these devices in an integrated S+S system.

Many books on services-oriented architecture (SOA) and software as a service (SaaS) have been published. I hope you have read at least one book from this category of technology. It is vitally important for anyone working with services to learn the fundamentals from one of these resources.

There is, however, a very big gap in the available reference material for services. No book describes the dangers and risks of developing and shipping an S+S solution. What this category needs is a book with a big red cover and golden letters warning us of the dangers and providing survival tips when testing Software Plus Services.

---

1   Conn Iggulden and Hal Iggulden, *The Dangerous Book for Boys* (New York: Harper Collins, 2006).

Two Parts: About Services and Test Techniques

Although this chapter is about testing S+S, it just isn't possible to dive straight into the testing elements without first covering some background. To make it easier for you, the chapter is broken into two very distinct parts.

Part 1 covers Microsoft's services history and our services strategy, and then contrasts S+S with traditional packaged products and SaaS. This section also shows just how much Microsoft invests in services in terms of our datacenters and the number of servers we use to run all the Microsoft services.

Part 2 is all about testing services. In this section, I focus on some of the variables that can affect a test approach, and then dive deep into some of the new techniques used to test services in an S+S environment. At the end of Part 2 are some additional thoughts on bugs that I have seen make it into production and some points on how to drive quality improvement even after a service has gone live.

Part 1: About Services

In this section, I review some of the major turning points in Microsoft's Internet and services strategy. Next, we look briefly at the architecture elements of services. This section helps those new to services to understand some of the basic differences between traditional packaged software and what Microsoft is working to deliver with S+S.

The Microsoft Services Strategy

Software Plus Services is the term Microsoft coined to demonstrate our belief that there is great value in distributed software that integrates the centralization and collaboration of online services while using the processing power and offline capabilities of the more than 800 million computers and billions of smart devices consumers, knowledge workers, and gamers already own.

In a very brief period, services have become a major component of the software ecosystem and many believe they will represent the majority of software usage in the near future. Given this, it might seem odd to have a chapter about services testing near the end of the book and under a section about the future of testing. At Microsoft, we are rapidly evolving our approaches to services testing, and at this level of continuing advancement and innovation, it seemed that the topic fit better with future trends than with the more proven practices covered in the previous chapters.

Shifting to Internet Services as the Focus

In 1995, Bill Gates released a memo that called for Microsoft to embrace the Internet as the top priority for the company. Inside Microsoft, this is often referred to as the "Internet memo," an excerpt of which follows. With clear marching orders, the engineers of Microsoft turned their eyes toward competing full force with Netscape, America Online, and several other companies ahead of us on the Internet bandwagon.

The Internet tidal wave

I have gone through several stages of increasing my views of its importance. Now I assign the Internet the highest level of importance. In this memo I want to make clear that our focus on the Internet is crucial to every part of our business. The Internet is the most important single development to come along since the IBM PC was introduced in 1981.
—Bill Gates, May 26, 1995

Within months of the Internet memo, the Internet started showing up in all sorts of products, for example, the Microsoft Office Word HTML add-in that helped the user author and save HTML to the Internet development tool Visual Interdev. For some time, the most popular Internet tool in Microsoft was Notepad simply because it let you quickly read and edit raw HTML.

Ten years later, a new memo rose to the forefront. The "Services memo," which follows, was sent to all employees in October 2005 by Ray Ozzie, our new Chief Software Architect. Microsoft had been in the Internet services business since the launch of MSN a decade earlier, but this new memo talked of a world of seamless integration and harnessing the power of services over the Internet. From this memo, we have refined the strategy to be Software Plus Services, and it represents our strategy around desktop applications and the Microsoft Windows operating system working seamlessly with online services as well as our use of SaaS and Web 2.0 technologies.

> ## The Internet services disruption
>
> Today there are three key tenets that are driving fundamental shifts in the landscape—all of which are related in some way to services. It's key to embrace these tenets within the context of our products and services.
>
> 1. The power of the advertising-supported economic model.
>
> 2. The effectiveness of a new delivery and adoption model.
>
> 3. The demand for compelling, integrated user experiences that "just work."
>
> —Ray Ozzie, October 28, 2005

In an S+S strategy, the Internet is at the center of all implementations, but the list of supported clients is much longer than a pure online-only SaaS approach. S+S uses computing power on PCs and mobile devices that are already at the user's fingertips.

Around the time this book is released and for several quarters after that, Microsoft will be launching waves of cloud services. A cloud service is any service on the Internet that another service builds on top of. Recently, we announced the launch of our new cloud infrastructure platform under the new product name Azure Services Platform. (See *www.microsoft.com/ azure* for more information.) Azure (or RedDog, as it is known among bloggers) will be a cloud service for developers to use for basic functions such as computer power through virtual machines and cloud storage. Live Mesh is a component of the Azure live services that helps users synchronize data across multiple computers and devices such as smart phones.

These advanced cloud services are changing the way developers write and run services and will further change how we test services. Companies such as Smug Mug and Twitter report massive cost savings by using the Amazon Simple Storage Service (S3). They have also had to deal with service outages when S3 goes down.[2]

Growing from Large Scale to Mega Scale

In 1994, Microsoft launched the Microsoft Network (MSN). MSN grew rapidly, becoming the second largest dial-up service in the United States. We even had an advertising campaign that marketed MSN as the Internet without training wheels. This was of course a jab at our much larger rival service AOL.

Even as the second largest service of its kind, MSN was big with thousands of production servers. We had outgrown our first datacenter, named Canyon Park, and were rapidly filling

---

[2] Jon Brodkin, "More Outages Hit Amazon's S3 Storage Service," *Network World*, July 21, 2008, *http://www.networkworld.com/news/2008/072108-amazon-outages.html*.

our second datacenter, called Tuk1. The MSN teams had a lot of top-notch best practices for developing and shipping a dial-up client, services such as e-mail and Internet connectivity. There was still a lot to learn outside of our areas of expertise. The breadth of just how much there was left to learn was brought home when, in 1997, we acquired both WebTV and Hotmail. In my opinion, these acquisitions accelerated our move from being a large-scale dial-up service to being a mega-scale provider of Internet services.

I had the great fortune of being one of many engineers that flew down to Silicon Valley to learn from WebTV and Hotmail. These companies brought with them many brilliant engineers and introduced us to all sorts of innovative concepts for running large-scale services. From those meetings I took two key concepts.

The first from WebTV was the concept of *service groups*. Service groups are units of production that function largely independently of each other. A service group is a unit of production scale as well as a unit of deployment for the next upgrade. Service groups also provide buffers from site-wide outages. If a single service group goes down for some reason, it should in theory not affect the other service groups.

The second concept was *field replaceable units* (FRUs) from Hotmail. They would brag, and justifiably so, about the number of computers they had in production and how cheap they were. These computers quite literally were motherboards with a hard drive and power stuck on a flat tray. Computers ran much cooler and at lower power back then, so the central air-conditioning of the datacenter was sufficient to keep the machines cool without any cases to cover or direct the airflow.

Inside Microsoft, the concept of service groups evolved into the scale group concept that retains the notion of service segmentation but also includes purchasing increased capacity as a single large order. Field replaceable units have become known as commodity hardware to emphasize buying large numbers of inexpensive servers.

Although these concepts are still in use, they are being challenged by a vastly higher rate of growth than we have ever seen before. Microsoft now adds an average of 10,000 computers a month to our datacenters just to meet the growing demands of the users of our services. Even scale units and commodity hardware are insufficient to deal with that level of purchasing and production installation.

A few years ago, we started purchasing servers in what we called rack units or rack SKUs. These were tall racks fully loaded with servers. Roll the rack off the delivery truck into the datacenter, hook up all the cables on the back side, power it up, and off you went. That innovation dramatically improved the efficiency of our procurement and installation pipeline. Unbelievably, rack units are no longer fast enough.

Walking the Talk: Microsoft Builds First Major Container-Based Datacenter

Containers filled with preconfigured, ready-to-run servers are being touted as a quicker, more modular way to expand datacenters on the fly

Microsoft and Sun Microsystems both may claim to have pioneered the 'datacenter in a box' concept, but Microsoft appears to be the first company that is rolling out container-er-based systems in a major way inside one of its datacenters."[3]

Recently, we built out an entire datacenter based upon the concept of the container. A container SKU is a fully loaded and production-ready cargo container that can be shipped on a truck or a train, as shown in Figure 14-1, hoisted off the flatbed with a crane, and positioned on the floor of the datacenter. A few massive cable bundles come out of various panels; when they are plugged in, suddenly there are hundreds of servers ready for production use. Years later when the servers are starting to fail at a high rate, the container is taken out of production, shipped back to the manufacturer, recycled, and updated with new equipment.

Photo courtesy of Rackable Systems, Inc.

FIGURE 14-1 Rackable.com produces a container SKU called the ICE Cube.

Just getting all the hardware in place to support our Software Plus Services strategy forced Microsoft to develop world-class logistical planning. Product engineers are constantly interacting with the procurement specialists to ensure that the right equipment is in place at the right time. The overhead of managing orders is decreasing and will eventually be fully eliminated.

The numbers in Table 14-1 are based upon recent history and projections for the near future. We are constantly dealing with the growth that comes through acquisitions. At the time of

---

3 Eric Lai, "Microsoft Builds First Major Container-Based Datacenter," *Computerworld*, April 8, 2008, *http://www. infoworld.com/article/08/04/08/Microsoft-builds-first-major-container-based-datacenter_1.html.*

this writing, Microsoft is *not* going to buy Yahoo, but if we do a major acquisition like that later, expect these numbers to change dramatically.

TABLE 14-1 Microsoft Services Factoids

Number of servers	On average, Microsoft adds 10,000 servers to its infrastructure every month.
Datacenters	On average, the new datacenters Microsoft is building to support Software Plus Services cost about $500 million (USD) and are the size of five football fields.
Windows Live ID	WLID (formerly Microsoft Passport) processes more than 1 *billion* authentications per day.
Performance	Microsoft services infrastructure receives more than 1 trillion rows of performance data every day through System Center (80,000 performance counters collected and 1 million events collected).
Number of services	Microsoft has more than 200 named services and will soon have more than 300 named services. Even this is not an accurate count of services because some, such as Office Online, include distinct services such as Clip Art, Templates, and the Thesaurus feature.

Power Is the Bottleneck to Growth

The average datacenter costs about $500 million to construct. What we have found over the years is that Moore's law still applies to computers: Approximately every 18 months the processing power doubles. The amount of effort it takes to run and cool a single server has also continued to climb.

The power needs of the newer production servers start to draw power unevenly. Major power upgrade projects need to be implemented until the infrastructure reaches its maximum capacity. At that stage, the only option is to redesign the infrastructure and plan a window of time to literally rip out and rebuild the majority of the power infrastructure.

Power is so critical to the operation of our services that we work closely with Intel and various original equipment manufacturers (OEMs) to design servers that are better optimized between power consumption and performance. For example, an OEM, which is optimizing for a lower cost server, might pick a standard power supply that uses more power than is actually needed. This makes the cost to build the server lower, but the long-term cost of running the server in one of our datacenters is higher. We strive to ensure that we use more low-power components in the servers and that the system is well tuned so that we do not waste power.

Producing higher efficiency light bulbs is a fine way to reduce power consumption, but learning to see in the dark is much better...

The entire construction and day-to-day operating expense for a datacenter can be thought of as an investment toward delivering power to the equipment housed in the datacenter. Under this model, the role of the concrete floor is to deliver power, the role of the HVAC system is to deliver power, and the role of the security personnel is to deliver power. Visualize all expenses within the facility as being tracked and delivered by kilowatt inside the datacenter. That's how Microsoft thinks about the costs of operating large-scale datacenters, and we spend our time focused on innovation that brings down cost in each generation of datacenter we construct.

Now think about the work done by any particular technology using that kilowatt-hour of datacenter capacity. The main cost efficiency metric at Microsoft considers the cost of a workload per kilowatt-hour. We ask ourselves, are we becoming more cost efficient over time with how we turn power into an online scenario—a query, an e-mail message, a page view, a video stream?

Metaphorically, we ask developers and testers to build higher and higher efficiency light bulbs while those building our facilities make them cost efficient at delivering power.

But how do you destroy the demand entirely?

People do things based on different motivations. Although we support developers and testers factoring cost into their design, we recognize different people are motivated by different things. One interesting program recently put in place calculates and allocates the carbon produced by the various online services at Microsoft and allocates the carbon footprint to the technology team that developed the online service. Developers and testers now see the carbon produced by their technology each month. This Carbon Allocation Model (CarBAM) is available to all employees on the Microsoft intranet and the metric is put on cost reports. If this simple awareness uniquely motivates a developer or tester to conserve power by deploying less equipment in the datacenter, we accomplish pure demand destruction. This approach now complements the constant search for higher efficiency code.

We've found that producing higher efficiency light bulbs is a fine way to reduce power consumption. Creative motivation that compels our engineers to see without them is much better.

> —*Eric Hautala, General Manager*

Services vs. Packaged Product

Packaged product is essentially any software product that can be purchased on CD or DVD. Inside Microsoft, we tend to refer to these products as *shrink-wrap* software. For Microsoft, shrink-wrap also includes product versions you can have preinstalled on a computer or downloadable versions that you run on your computer.

> **Note** Shrink-wrap, also shrinkwrap or shrink film, is commonly used as an overwrap on many types of packaging: CDs, DVDs, software. It is polymer plastic, and when heat is applied to this material it shrinks tightly over whatever it is covering.

In recent years, the notion that all products are either services or shrink-wrap has blurred. Some Xbox games are bought in a store, but users can play against each other on Xbox Live and download extra levels. Microsoft Office Outlook is a very popular e-mail client for the Windows Live Mail (WLM) service. Microsoft Expression is a product that can be purchased in a store or over the Internet and is a tool that helps Web site owners rapidly develop rich content-driven Web sites, but it was also built in anticipation of users being connected to the Internet so that they can download additional content and add-ins. Even though all of these products have service components they are usually purchased through a retailer or PC manufacturer, so we consider them to be part of the shrink-wrap group.

> **Note** In 2005, several of Microsoft's major online services such as Hotmail and Passport were renamed to include the Windows Live brand. Hotmail is now Windows Live Mail (WLM), and Passport is now Windows Live ID (WLID). Users with a Hotmail account do keep the @hotmail. com address despite the change in the name we call the service.

There are many different names for a Web service. Some common terms are *Web service*, *Web site*, *Web property*, and *online service*. Generally, inside Microsoft we call our services by the team names such as Xbox Live, Search, Windows Live ID (WLID), Spaces, Sky Drive, and Office Live Small Business (OLSB). In some cases, such as for OLSB or Xbox Live, it would be better to call them a collection of services. OLSB offers public Web sites, private Web sites, Web site management, short message bridge to cell phones, business e-mail, and other services such as contact manager and ad manager as add-ons. Each subservice can be consumed by another service; for example, OLSB is sold with Dynamics Live or CRM Online. Xbox Live has its own on-demand video download services as well as tournament services.

In the February 11, 2004, notes of the W3 working group for Web Services Architecture Requirements, *web service* was defined as follows: "A Web service is a software system identified by a URI [RFC 2396], whose public interfaces and bindings are defined and described using XML. Its definition can be discovered by other software systems. These systems may then interact with the Web service in a manner prescribed by its definition, using XML based messages conveyed by Internet protocols."

This is a fine definition, but some Web sites that many consider to be Web services have little to no XML. For the latest notes and changes to definitions, visit *http://www.w3.org/TR/wsa-reqs/*.

S+S Example

Consider the Windows Live Mail service as an example. WLM is by far the largest e-mail service in the world with hundreds of millions of active users. Part of the appeal of WLM is its reliability but also its support for multiple client experiences. WLM works with many different Web browsers, the Microsoft Office Outlook client, the Windows Live Email client, Mobile smart phones, and desktop applets that alert users when new mail arrives in their inbox.

The down-level browser experience is more like a SaaS experience. SaaS is largely about using a service while connected to the Internet. It does not have an offline capability. In SaaS, a large portion of the processing takes place on the servers in the cloud with the client usually providing just rendering of the user experience.

> **Note** *Down-level* (downlevel) *browser* is a term used in Microsoft as well as on Web development sites. One strict definition of down-level browser is a browser that supports only HTML 3.2 or earlier versions. Often the term is used more generically for older browser versions that are missing key features such as cascading style sheets or JavaScript and that do not present the best user experience on a Web site.

Web 2.0 tends to rely upon newer browsers, Flash, or Microsoft SilverLight for a rich browser experience where the processing is largely shifted from the servers in the cloud to the desktop computer. A Web 2.0 client might also have offline capabilities.

S+S moves the processing to the place that makes the most sense for the user and the user experience. For rich clients such as Outlook, the majority of the processing happens on the user's computer. Similarly, with smart phone e-mail clients, the phone handles the majority of the processing. S+S also emphasizes the ability to work offline as well as the capability to have clients that bridge internal and cloud services as we see with the Outlook Connector that can read corporate email and a personal account in one integrated experience. In the near future, servers will run in a hybrid mode, seamlessly integrating corporate servers with cloud servers and extranet services.

In the WLM example, down-level browsers are examples of SaaS, and Outlook, Outlook Mobile, and the WLM rich e-mail client are examples of S+S. The last element of this example shows how services are no longer stand-alone. For example, in the case of WLM, authentication (when a user enters a valid user name and password) is provided by the Windows Live ID service. This concept is discussed later in the section titled "Moving from Stand-Alone to Layered Services."

With S+S, compatibility goes far beyond just various browser versions and may include dozens of different clients, as shown in Figure 14-2. Additionally, high availability, scalability, strong security, and trusted policies and procedures for maintaining privacy are more critical than they are even in enterprise scenarios. From a test perspective, this means that quality is deeply tied to features, architecture, and most uniquely with services and the procedures for running and maintaining them. At Microsoft, test plays a big role in driving these issues deep into the product and ensuring proper implementation. Test even evaluates and in many cases directly tests the underlying policies for running a service.

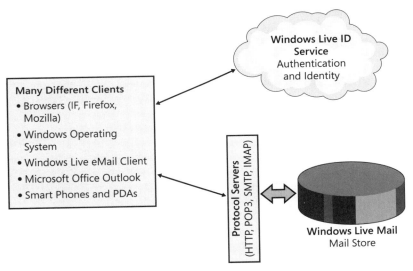

FIGURE 14-2 Simplified diagram of the Windows Live Mail S+S.

Moving from Stand-Alone to Layered Services

In the very early days of the Internet, many online sites were mostly self-contained. One exception might be credit card processing services that from the very outset had multiple retail and online endpoints. Beyond that, most other services were developed and run as independent services. In many respects, every online property was like a complete single-family home: It had floors, walls, roof, electrical wiring, and plumbing. Each service had to build every component to include mechanisms for signup, authentication, customization/personalization, storage, deployment, and reporting.

With layered services, building a new service is now much easier than, say, building a complete dwelling, but it is still challenging. By comparison, launching a new service in today's world is probably comparable to remodeling a bathroom. Platform services from Microsoft and competitors will continue to expand and provide more of the infrastructure for new services. A service can even mix and match across infrastructure services from multiple companies for best of breed solutions. As platform services evolve, developing and launching a new service should become as simple as painting an empty bedroom.

Currently, most consumers perceive online sites such as Amazon.com and eBay.com to be stand-alone services, but these sites do contain modules and layers. In the case of eBay, the PayPal service was an acquisition that was then deeply integrated with the eBay auction service while still allowing other services to use it. In the case of Amazon, on rare occasions some services such as customer reviews or the section showing what other customers have purchased don't populate, but the product you click still comes up for purchase. This happens because each of these features is a separate module running on separate servers. If they do not respond in time, the page loads anyway. Through layering, these services can ensure that the main user experience is functioning even if some subcomponents might not be working properly. It also allows for each layer to innovate on its own schedule without creating dependencies on other teams and their features. Figure 14-3 shows a simplified view of how services can be layered.

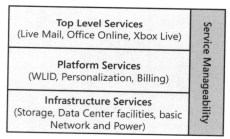

FIGURE 14-3 Simplified view of a layered services model.

In many respects, the strategy for testing a stand-alone service is easy: Test every part of the service and its subcomponents, test every integration point between all those parts, and test end-to-end scenarios that run through the system. It might sound silly, but when you own it all, you can control what changes and when it changes. Managing risk caused by change is therefore more easily controlled.

It took many years to migrate Window Live Mail (formerly Hotmail) from its homegrown authentication service to one shared across all Microsoft services, but it did happen. All (well, actually almost all) services, including WLM, now use the WLID service for authentication.

Layering and integration are adding significant complexity to building and running services. As we move further and further down the S+S path, the number of clients and how they interact with multiple services increase the compatibility testing matrix. Add to this dozens of mashups developed by third parties that interface with public APIs of multiple services to create a new user experience, and the integration map becomes massive.

> **Note** A *mashup* is a Web application that can combine data or user interface (UI) from more than one source into a single integrated service or application. For example, Zillow.com is a service that combines data from the Multiple Listing Service (MLS) for real estate sales, its own data generated by users, and the Microsoft Live Earth service for mapping the data.

Layering is the approach Microsoft takes for developing all its services. Many new start-up services are using infrastructure services from Microsoft and other companies. In Part 2 of this chapter, I discuss techniques for testing Software Plus Services with special emphasis on services testing in a layered multiservices ecosystem.

Part 2 Testing Software Plus Services

Part 1 of this chapter covers a great deal of information about services including Microsoft's history with services, how big a bet services are for us, what S+S is, and how it differs from other paradigms we have used previously.

In this part, I provide a general overview of some test techniques for services, and then describe a handful of very specific but different approaches to testing services and clients with services.

Like many of the examples in the earlier chapters, the examples in this part are from Microsoft and tend to be about big software projects or, in this case, big services. Even though the examples are drawn from Microsoft, the techniques can and should be applied to projects of all sizes.

Waves of Innovation

In researching this chapter, I found several articles that talked about waves of innovation in PC computing history. Here is a list of innovation waves through which Microsoft has lived and competed:

1. Desktop computing and networked resources
2. Client/server
3. Enterprise computing
4. Software as a Service (SaaS) or Web 1.0 development
5. Software Plus Services (S+S) or Web 2.0 development

We are clearly just beginning this newest S+S wave of innovation. With each of these waves, software testing has had to evolve to meet new challenges. Most of these challenges have been around the growth in the number of users and user scenarios along with the number of different clients and supported environments, as shown in Figure 14-4. With each wave, complexity has increased and the overall test matrix has grown. The challenge for testing is that the matrix never shrinks. With each wave, most old tests carry forward and many new tests are added.

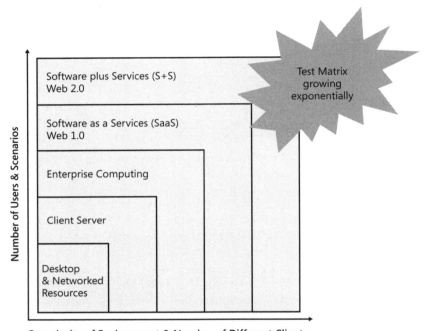

FIGURE 14-4 Each new wave of innovation adds more to the software testing matrix.

Microsoft started with the desktop wave with MS-DOS and the Basic programming language. We built Windows on top of DOS and moved into the networked PC realm. With each wave, we have evolved our testing. We have developed many new processes to help us better deal with the exploding test matrix of both SaaS and S+S testing.

Designing the Right S+S and Services Test Approach

It would be fun to write the *Dangerous Book for Software Plus Services*. I see it coming bound in black leather with silver lettering and would have a lock on it but no key. Readers would have to figure out how to pick the lock if they want to read the secrets within. The reason for the security is that if I wrote it, I would have to share all the mistakes I have made while developing, testing, and shipping services.

They key to success in testing services is to be fully aware of the dangers and craft your test approach to mitigate those dangers. This section discusses several factors that affect the design of a good services test approach.

Client Support

For many years, testers at Microsoft have had to update their list of browsers to be used in testing for every release. These matrices usually include the most recent version of every major browser and previous versions of those browsers that still have sizable market share.

In an S+S environment, you don't just have a browser matrix for testing but also a long list of client applications. For example, for Windows Live Mail we have all the browsers for the Web interface but we also have versions of Outlook, Outlook Express, the new Windows Live Mail client, and various mobile devices. Additionally, we have all the other matrixed complexities around operating system version, language, and regional settings that come with any shrink-wrap test project.

The key to keeping the test permutations for clients under control is not quite the same as a straightforward equivalence class exercise, but it is close. Review market share for supported browsers and clients, compare that to business goals by markets, and add in some operating system market penetration. A product team should then choose which combinations to officially cut from their supported list, and then prioritize among the remaining list. The highest priority combinations are candidates for much deeper and frequent testing whereas the remainder can be covered with a tightly controlled set of basic compatibility tests.

Built on a Server

The great opportunity for Microsoft in our S+S strategy is to use our rich desktop clients and our enterprise servers in the services world. In some cases, a service is built from the ground up using a much stripped down version of the Windows Server operating system and in some cases a simplified Web server. Many of our enterprise server products such as Microsoft Office SharePoint Server and Microsoft SQL Server provide the core technology for a service.

When a service is built on a server product, there has already been a lot of testing on that product, so we don't need to retest core functionality. However, two areas in particular do need substantial focus.

The first (and most obvious) is the integration of the new code written on top of the server and the interaction between the service and the server. The majority of the early bugs will be around basic functionality and in the public APIs of the server product. As the code stabilizes, we often start to find issues around performance and diagnosability between the new Web service components and the underlying enterprise server product. One example is when a lock occurs on an object that wasn't designed to deal with multiple simultaneous reads or writes. Scenarios like this are often considered by design for an enterprise offering, and the cryptic error messages presented when something like this happens can often be difficult to use in diagnosing the root cause.

The second area is testing the server product itself for manageability and scalability in a large-scale datacenter environment. In many cases, we deploy and configure the enterprise server product so that it functions at Internet scale. Often additional work is needed to make the remote maintenance of the server fully automated so that no person needs to enter the datacenter and touch the actual computer. Improvements in these areas can lower operational expenses and help a service become profitable. In these scenarios, test focuses on not just finding bugs but finding improvements to drive into the server product for future releases.

Platform Services vs. Top-Level Services

In Part 1, Figure 14-4 shows how Microsoft's services are becoming more and more layered. We know this is also true of many of our major competitors. This approach of building services on top of each other is not unlike that used in building the layers of an operating system or even the Open Systems Interconnection Basic Reference Model (OSI model) for networking. Lower down in the stack is where you will find critical platform services such as WLID. The branded services such as Office Live that directly generate revenue are much higher in the stack. Behind the Virtual Earth service (*maps.live.com*) is a series of infrastructure services that take all the satellite and low-level flyover photos and turn them into tiles.

Figure 14-5 shows a conceptual example of the AutionCloud.com mashup that integrates eBay with Zillow. Zillow is itself a mashup of several other services. As the stack becomes deeper and ownership is spread across multiple organizations and companies, debugging problems in a service can become ever more complex. .

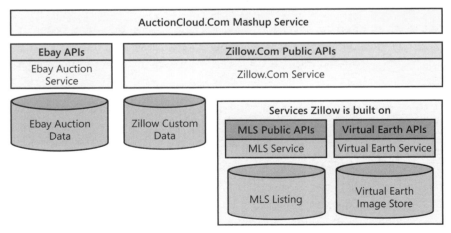

FIGURE 14-5 AuctionCloud.com mashup built on Zillow and eBay; Zillow mashup built on MLS and Virtual Earth.

Deep down in the stack we eventually get to platform (sometimes called foundation) services. PayPal and credit card processing are common platform services for e-commerce sites. Authentication services such as WLID are also platform services. Testing of a platform service requires an internal focus. It can be a lot like having a public API: You know many developers will write to the API and use nearly every feature in the API, you just don't know exactly *how* they will use it. The test effort for a platform service focuses on the entry points to the service. After verifying an API's internals, a good test approach is to have the API tested in some number of real-world integration scenarios but not all of them because that would be impractical if not outright impossible.

In the case of platform services, the focus is also on internal consistency testing over integration testing. In higher level services, integration testing can become the primary focus.

In the case of a service higher up in the stack, the test effort for that service would spend a great deal of time focused on testing specific integration scenarios with all platform services but not the platform service itself. The degree to which a higher level service must test against a platform service depends upon the level of coupling between the two services.

Loosely Coupled vs. Tightly Coupled Services

This section could easily have been titled "Loose Dependencies or Tight Dependencies" except that coupling for services combines the elements of good object-oriented design with organizational coupling. Doug Kay addresses this topic in his book *Loosely Coupled: The Missing Pieces of Web Services* (Rds Associates, 2003). In this book, he covers many of the project management dependency elements of coupling across services.

The reason coupling is both a project management and a design element for services is directly related to the rate of shipping. Layered services are constantly taking on new dependencies and changing existing dependencies with every release.

> **Note** In computer science, *coupling* or *dependency* is the degree to which each one program relies upon another. Loosely coupled systems are best when either the source or the destination program is subject to frequent change.

Ideally, services should be *loosely coupled*. *Loose coupling* is a term used often in software design to describe an interface, component, or system that makes minimal assumptions about the dependent systems. The lighter weight the dependencies between services are, the more each can independently innovate and ship. In this sense, coupling affects a software project as a dependency management challenge. The tighter services are coupled, the more project management overhead needs to be applied to ensure that the resulting user experience is high quality and valued. The following sidebars are two examples, both of which come from Windows Live ID.

Example 1: Loosely coupled: Windows Live ID authenticated user

In the case of Office Online, a user can come to the Web site (*office.microsoft.com*) and get a lot of value as an anonymous user. Tasks such as finding and downloading a template do not require any authentication. There are other features such as signing up for some notifications that require the user be *known*.

A known user for Office Online is one who has been authenticated through WLID and has a valid cookie. Office Online checks the encrypted cookie to ensure that the user is valid and trusts that to be the user's identity. This lack of a hard dependency on WLID for exposing functionality and the use of WLID only for authentication make the relationship between Office Online and WLID very loose. WLID can make many changes to its service and the Office Online team need only validate that the core functionality of reading the encrypted cookie still works for them. With a properly designed cookie data structure, even an extension to that data structure is of minimal concern as long as the base data elements do not change.

Example 2: Tightly coupled: Microsoft Passport (WLID) parental controls

When we were shipping MSN 9, we were enabling parental controls in the MSN client. To be able to set this up, we had to have the concept of a hierarchy of accounts in Microsoft Passport. Additionally, this feature crossed into another platform service for personalization.

The MSN client, Passport, and the personalization teams had to work closely on this new feature set. They had to decide who would do what work, how to call each service, and what format the response would come in. After deciding which team would deliver each component, they then had to integrate their schedules and plan for enough time for each team to complete integration testing.

The MSN client team was able to work on the UI for parental controls but could not actually write all the code to integrate or test until the Passport team had made significant progress. In terms of testing, this was a major challenge because the test team had to ensure that they were using the right build of the client for the right version of the services when testing.

Of these two scenarios, loosely coupled clearly provides more flexibility and self-determination for both services. Even in Microsoft, tightly coupled, co-development scenarios are hard to manage. Doing a project like this with multiple companies over the Internet is even more challenging.

Many of our sites integrate with external companies. One example is credit card processing. We take credit cards that are processed through services on the Internet, we also take PayPal for payment, and we might integrate with many retailers' extranet Web services. The loosely coupled projects, the ones that have well-defined interfaces, shipped on time. The very tightly coupled projects often bogged down and seemed as if they would never ship.

Every one of these non-Microsoft organizations is continuing to evolve their service in parallel with our own development efforts. Tightly coupled services have a hard time testing without a current instance of the platform service. A loosely coupled service can often stub out calls to other services or use emulators. (See the section titled "Integration Testing vs. Test Flags and Emulation" later in this chapter.) This allows testing to continue without an instance of the other service. Integration testing is still done, but the testing of the core functionality of the service is not blocked.

Stateless to Stateful

Stateless services are those with very simple, fast transactions that do not need any data stored. The less state a service has to maintain, the more failures it can experience with any component while continuing to provide a good user experience. An example of this in software might be Outlook sending an e-mail message. If the message fails to go out on the first try, Outlook tries again later. The user rarely notices.

When a service takes a long time to complete a transaction and needs to store unique user or business-critical data, it is considered to be more stateful and thus less resilient to failure. Compare stateful to working on a Microsoft Word document for hours, and then experiencing a crash just as you are trying to save the file. It might be a single crash, but the impact on the user is dramatic.

Stateless Services

A basic Internet search is a great example of a relatively stateless service. Each search query completes and renders results usually with subsecond responses. For any large sized search engine, the index that powers the service is updated every hour of every day and is replicated across multiple datacenters. Even though the index might be stateful, losing a single instance of the index is not going to cause irreparable harm to a user. At most, a few search queries will fail to return results until the bad index is pulled out of rotation.

Stateful Services

CRM Online and Salesforce.com are examples of services that are very stateful. These services help small to midsized businesses automate their sales process and customer support over the Internet and allow them to interact directly with their customers. They usually store business-critical data such as a company's contact list, copies of quotes, and copies of final contracts. A user of the service can open a quote template and spend an hour filling it in before saving and sharing it with a customer. A marketing campaign might run for months. In these types of services, user activities and transactions cover a greater period of time. The data in the system lives on for a long time. Resiliency down to the smallest component as well as disaster recovery take on much more critical roles in determining quality.

Time to Market or Features and Quality

For any software product or IT project, quality and features must be balanced against time to market. The challenge in the commercial services space is that the first mover (the first company in a category of service) can become the de facto standard in a very short period of time. Services for e-commerce, auctions, posting videos, and social networking are dominated by a handful of early successes. The list is short and we can all name them: Amazon. com, YouTube, eBay, Facebook, and MySpace have all benefited from early releases and rapid follow-up. Unseating an incumbent service can be much harder than developing and launching the next big breakfast cereal.

Friendster launched in March 2002 and is considered the first major social networking site. MySpace and Facebook came along several years later, but when they launched, they changed the game. Self-promotion in social networking became acceptable. These services were able to leap frog the first-mover advantage of Friendster and move dramatically ahead.

Testing strategy needs to consider the state of the market and be crisp and very clear about the quality bar for launch. Sometimes faster time to market is the right call, but I must say that in my experience it can take years to get operability, manageability, and overall high quality back into a low-quality service after it has launched. If possible, I push for as many features in these areas as I can get while still helping to find ways to get the service launched and into the market quickly.

Release Frequency and Naming

Hand in hand with time to market for a major release is what happens after that release. Often a service will launch with *beta* attached to its name. One prominent example was the GMail service that spent three years in beta. This allowed the service to weather the discovery of many major bugs without losing much customer loyalty.

> **Note** A service with beta in the title is clearly indicating to users that there are bugs in the service, but that there is enough functionality to start allowing users access.

Another technique teams use is to plan releases to follow quickly on the heels of a major release. The monthly or quarterly release process means that any bug found but not fixed in the current release will not wait too long before it is fixed. As a tester, it can be OK to allow a bug in an edge case to ship into production as long as you know a fix is coming. If the bug is known and so bad that it should be fixed within hours of a release to Web (what we typically call a hotfix), I recommend holding the release until the fix is made in the main source sent to production.

Testing Techniques for S+S

After careful consideration of all the design, naming, and business factors that influence your test approach, it is time to pull together the right set of techniques to drive the testing process. This section digs deeper into the different techniques that services require and gives some solutions to the dangers raised in the *Dangerous Book for Software Plus Services*.

Fully Automated Deployments

For just about every product Microsoft develops, we have a daily build. (See Chapter 11, "Non-functional Testing.") The moment the build drops (finishes compiling and is propped to a share on a server), automated scripts take over, install the software on test computers, and then run thousands of tests. This is true for games, servers, mobile devices, and desktop applications. This is not always true for our services, though.

Many Microsoft services test teams have started to measure time from build complete to first deployment complete. This is covered in more detail in the section titled "Performance Test Metrics for Services" later in this chapter.

If you've ever had a private build from a developer with release notes saying, "Copy this file here, add this to the configuration file, and register this .dll," you know this takes extra time and is very error prone. A complete setup routine is the key to unlocking the ability of test to install a product quickly and run tests. Deployment is the same way for services and needs to include fully automated deployments from a one-box to a multiserver test configuration and to full production. (See the section titled "The One Box" later in this chapter.) The code for deployment to these various environments must be the same and the variations driven by the input XML.

The sad reality for services is that many product engineering teams see deployment as something that needs to happen just once, for the final build deployed to the production servers. When teams make this mistake they delay writing any code for deployment until late in the product cycle. This code is not data driven, it won't be complete, and it won't get tested. Deployment needs to be staffed and tested like a first-class feature.

Operations engineers tend to love these next three tips. As testers, we should try to file the bugs first.

> **Tip** If operations has to do anything more than double-click an icon and wait for the green light to come back saying the deployment completed successfully, there are still bugs in the deployment code. They might be design bugs, but they are still bugs.

Tip If the deployment guide to operations has any instructions other than, "Go here and double-click this file," there are bugs in the deployment guide.

Tip If there needs to be more than two engineers in the room to ensure that the deployment is successful, there are design flaws in the deployment code and the deployment guide.

Fully automated, data-driven deployments are the foundation that unblocks all other testing, and they must be the top priority.

Great deployment is critical to operational excellence

For a new service I have typically had at least one developer and one tester dedicated to deployment coding and testing. If done correctly, this level of investment can be trimmed back significantly in future releases.

Deployments in jargonese: The key features of a good deployment are zero downtime, zero data loss, partial production upgrades (or running in mixed mode), rolling upgrades, and fast rollback.

- Initially Web services had downtime during upgrades, and some even had weekly maintenance windows. Today most services look to complete upgrades without any (zero) downtime for users.

- Zero data loss is really for the highly stateful services with a lot of unique user data. Upgrades to these services are particularly challenging when the service is undergoing significant schema changes.

- *Partial production upgrade* means that a service might upgrade a small percentage of what is considered the production servers to the new version of the code. This could be anything from 50 percent down to 10 or even 5 percent.

- *Mixed mode* means that a service might upgrade a portion of production to a new version, but that users can get the same high-quality experience whether using the old or new version of the service. Although mixed mode might show up during an upgrade deployment, it is really a design point for the service. In the case of significant user interface (UI) changes, mixed mode ensures that users who are exposed to the new experience continue to get that experience each time they access the service.

- *Rolling upgrade* means that a service can have portions of the live production servers upgraded automatically without any user-experienced downtime. Literally, the deployment just rolls along on a schedule whether it is hours or days long and completes automatically.

- Fast roll back is the safety net used if anything goes wrong. Whether a service is at 10 percent completion or 90 percent completion, if a recall class bug is identified, the service should quickly roll back to the last known good version.

I often tell my operations team that for a large service they should insist on the deployment taking no less than three days. The reason for this is to manage risk to the full production service. On more than one occasion, we have started the deployment of a "small low-risk update" to a service, and before we were even 10 percent finished upgrading the computers, we'd identified a recall class bug and had to roll back.

Partial production upgrades that allow a service to run in a mixed mode of the next version alongside the current version allow the service to manage risk. Rolling upgrades are similar to partial production upgrades but emphasize full automation of the deployment. When a recall class bug is identified during deployment, fast rollback allows the service to get back to a last known good state quickly. Many of our services have this process so well automated that they can run multiple overlapping upgrades on a single day. In fact, some also have the ability to propagate all the new code (copy the code to all the production servers) with a go-live date (the date the user should see the new version). This allows the server to hold both the current and the previous version on the computer at the same time and allows a very rapid process for moving forward (read from the new directory) and moving back (read from the old directory) between versions.

Note With the release of the Windows Server 2008 operating system, the performance of virtualization has been significantly improved. Virtualization, or virtual machines, is quite literally running another completely separate instance of the Windows operating system in the operating system that loads when a computer is turned on. We are starting to see significant increases in the use of virtual machines as the way to deploy and run many Microsoft services. In the next few years, this will likely become the most common method for rapid and fully automated deployments.

Test Environments

Whether the testing is focused on services, clients, or the integration of clients and services, getting the test environment just right is a critical element. A test environment that is too different from the configuration that will be run in final production can miss many bugs. A test environment that is so exactly like production that it is production can cost too much to build; if built, it will funnel all testing to a single environment.

Most services test teams in Microsoft run many different types of test environments, and each helps facilitate effective testing for different classes of defects. The key to defining and using different test environments effectively is understanding the service architecture and integration dependencies. By defining and mapping test processes in the early stages of a project, a test team can maximize their test hardware and mitigate risk with proper testing in the optimal environment.

The One Box

Sometimes the one-box test platform is called a single box, a single OS, or the one OS test environment. Mostly, it is just known as the one box. When working to integrate with another team's service, the new team often asks whether the platform team has a one box that they could use in their testing.

To my knowledge, at Microsoft, the term *one box* started with the MSN Billing 2.0 team back in 2002. When the team deployed the 2.0 billing system it was to a new set of computers and the data in the version 1.0 system was to be migrated to the new computers. It was a big project with an absolute cannot-slip schedule or MSN would have missed the holiday shopping season. Deployment was one of the last features coded. Many of the deployment steps were never automated, so the team produced a massive deployment guide with step-by-step instructions. This document was called "the paper deployment wizard."

I will say this much about the wonderful idea of the paper deployment wizard: The words *paper* and *wizard* should be eternally banned from use together.

Days and hundreds of hand-scrawled notes on the printed copy of the deployment guide later, the deployment finished. There was no major ah-ha moment for one person or even a keen insight that just a few individuals had. In this case, it was blatantly obvious to every single person on the project that deployment had to be a first-class feature that was tested every single day along with all the other feature tests.

The Billing 2.0 team dedicated resources to developing an XML-based tool that developers, testers, and operations engineers could use to run deployment quickly and easily in multiple environments. With this data-driven tool, they were able to define deployments that would install and configure sizable amounts of service functionality on a single computer. This configuration became known as the billing one box, and the term has grown from there.

With the increasing popularity of using virtual machines (VMs) on Windows-based systems, I constantly have to point out that the one box test environment is not so much about a single computer as it is about a single operating system test environment. Developers have often said to me that they have a one box in their office running a 10-VM topology. That is not a one box; that is a test cluster on a single computer.

For Microsoft testers, a one box is a single operating system instance of a major amount of service functionality that can be used to execute tests against. We have a one box instance of WLID and a one box of our internal subscription billing system. Each of these services runs on hundreds of servers in production, but we can also make it all run on a single computer, even a laptop.

The one box is critical to allow developers to run unit and pre-check-in tests. It is vital for running BVTs and massive automation suites in parallel. The one box allows for increased agility simply because it is quick and easy to build out, tear down, and build again. An environment like this is essential for rapid turnaround scenarios such as the regression of a simple string change bug.

Next to fully automated deployments, the one box is the most vital test requirement of any service.

The Test Cluster

Fully automated deployments that are data driven are the first requirement for testing. By taking advantage of the data-driven aspect, we can have production deployments scaled down to a one box. The next step is to have those deployments automated for scaled-down versions of production known as *test clusters*. A test cluster is usually a scaled-down version of production with an instance of each server by role, as shown in Figure 14-6.

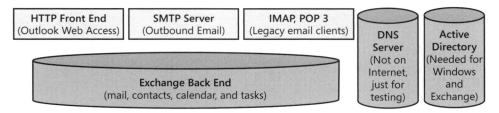

FIGURE 14-6 Example of a test cluster for a service built on Microsoft Exchange Server.

The term *machine role* refers to the purpose the computer fulfills in a service. A simple service such as search could have machine roles such as crawlers that go out and crawl the Internet for content to index, indexers that build key word indexes off the content, and query servers that take the search request from users and pull results from the index servers.

In a test cluster, we are not looking to find bugs in the core logic of the service but instead focus on finding bugs in cross-server transaction. Quite often, a service such as Microsoft Internet Information Server (IIS) will be able to query a local Microsoft SQL Server because they are both using the same account with administrative-level permissions. When services are split across computers, we can find performance, permissions, and other configuration bugs that would not show up in any other environments. The key is to use the one box for everything you can, and then use test clusters for those specific tests a one box would hide.

Heavily shared test clusters just don't make sense to me

This is my one chance to tilt at a windmill, so please bear with me. When I interview someone to be an SDET, I look for that thing that makes testers different from developers. Deep down in the DNA of every great tester is the desire to find the bugs the developer left in the code, to break software, and to break it good. I love to break software and that is why I think testing is the best job ever.

What I don't understand is why a team would build out a big shared test cluster and invest as much as 60 percent to 70 percent of their testing effort in that environment. They take a great team of testers all wanting to break software and point them to a shared environment. Suddenly, the testers are constrained by rules, rules for what you can and can't do on the cluster all because we don't want the cluster to go down. If the cluster goes down, everyone is blocked and the team loses vital test time.

The litmus test to know whether you have too much testing effort invested in a shared test cluster is to unplug it for a day and see whether the project slips by a day. If you slip by a day, the test approach needs more varied test environments.

Even if a team has a diversified approach, testers need to be able to test off the shared environment. All testers need to be let loose on code so that they can run wild and develop their tester instincts. I would much rather find a way for testers to run their tests in an environment they control and let them be mean and nasty to the code than to push those testers to use a shared cluster. Use a shared cluster for finding integration bugs and encourage all other testing to be conducted on independent test environments. Be careful not to turn predatory testers into docile bug loggers, fundamentally changing the DNA of testers.

The Perf and Scale Cluster

Simple environments such as the one box can be used to conduct performance profiling tests and even page load time tests (covered later in this chapter). The perf and scale cluster is used for conducting a different type of system-level test. In the services world, when components are spread out across computers, various components become bogged down before others do. Performance testing for services is often about finding the right balance of hardware to produce an efficient and performant system.

Another challenge with services is that they can become bottlenecked as they are scaled up or out. The term *scale up* is commonly used to refer to an increased amount of data in the system. An e-mail inbox with 10 e-mail messages will behave very differently from an inbox with thousands of messages in it. Many services will either begin to perform slowly or will just stop working altogether because the amount of data grew beyond what was expected or tested for.

Scale out refers to a service being able to increase capacity by adding additional computers. The scale unit approach discussed earlier in this chapter helps create logical purchasing and production units for a service so that it can continue to scale out. The goal of scale out is really about identifying how best to configure the number of servers of each type, the configuration of the hardware, and the configuration of the operating system to maximize the output of the whole system at the lowest cost. This testing is useful in producing early capacity models.

Both performance testing and scale testing are hardware-intensive activities. Other tests such as load tests analyzing mean time between failures (MTBF) can benefit from being run on production-grade hardware configurations. (See Chapter 11 for more information about MTBF testing.) Because these types of tests have many similarities and all benefit from execution on a large production-like test environment, most teams run them on a single set of shared hardware.

The Integrated Services Test Environment

In a world of layered services, there are always bugs to find during integration testing. The timing and approach to this testing depend upon the degree of coupling between two services. The more loosely coupled two services are, the less need there is to do real-world integration testing.

Let's build INT

Back when MSN was competing with AOL, we kept losing reviews because the MSN service just wasn't as well integrated as the AOL experience. Our major goal for the next release was to pull this ragtag collection of services together into a very smooth and high-quality client.

The MSN test managers meeting was always held in the conference room just behind the Service Operations Center (SOC). Through the glass windows of the room you could see the projected images of network traffic, alerts, and tickets. The SOC room was set up with workstations on a series of tiered rings much like a college lecture room. All the workstations were facing the wall with the three big projections of network traffic, alerts, and tickets.

Inside the conference room, we were debating how to handle this mandate of getting our services to integrate better. We had some major new features related to parental controls and sharing contacts that ran across every service and client. Friedbert and Monte were the most senior test managers in the meeting, and they were both pitching the idea of an *integrated test environment* (INT). This INT environment would require each of us to put a test cluster on a common shared network so that we could test against the latest build of each other's services.

It was very painful, but we eventually made INT work, and MSN did beat AOL in most product reviews that year.

TellMe, which joined Microsoft in 2006, also used the concept of the integrated test environment so that their integration partners could develop and test against the TellMe service. They called it the green zone, and it was very successful in the early days of the service when things were changing rapidly and many features were in co-development.

Although INT is a great tool for testing multiple-service integration early in a project, it does come with two key risks.

The first problem with INT testing is that it is not and never will be exactly like production. Many testers say they need to get their code into INT so that they can test it in a production-like environment. That's just the point—it is production-like, but it is not production, so bugs will be missed.

The second problem with INT testing comes when the shared test cluster (covered earlier in this chapter) is brought into the INT environment. In this case, a shared test cluster is pointed toward INT and all the testers run their tests there. The challenge arises when INT goes down. By definition, INT is not the final build of any service, so it will be more unstable and will experience greater downtime than production. If a team puts too much emphasis on testing against INT, they will find themselves being constantly blocked and falling behind schedule.

If the project is one of multiple tightly coupled and highly integrated services or even one with deep integration with client applications, an INT test environment is needed. The key to success is to make sure the INT environment has a well-established, reasonable quality bar and that all test teams have an option to run tests even when INT has a major outage.

Testing in INT is a powerful testing option. The key to successfully using INT for testing is to ensure you can complete a substantial amount of your services testing without an INT environment.

The Deployment Test Cluster

I have already discussed the importance of fully automated deployments as a key feature to unblock testing. The one box helps developers and testers work independently and is usually part of pre-check-in tests for any service. Those tests, however, do not ensure that the deployment code will work on a multimachine test environment. That is where the deployment test cluster comes in.

A *deployment test cluster* is similar to production in terms of the number of computers found in a scale unit. Because deployment testing is not about tuning for hardware, the tests can be run on a set of very inexpensive computers (commodity hardware) or as a set of virtual machines. I recommend the virtual machines for maximum flexibility.

Deployment tests focus on two areas:

- Ensure that the deployment code and any new features are working as expected for a production deployment. In this case, the software is either connected to the INT test environment or to the live production site of a service. In some cases, emulation or test flags (covered next in this chapter) are used but are not preferred. These tests ensure that not only the deployment of the service code is automated, but the connectivity to platform services is also automated.

■   The deployment test environment is ideal for working on service hardening. With a default installation of Windows Server (or any enterprise server), often many services are installed that won't be needed in production. A deployment environment can be used to turn off and uninstall unneeded components systematically. This is often considered a type of security testing, but it is still best conducted in a deployment test cluster.

If the deployment test cluster is built with commodity hardware or through virtual machines, it should not be a very expensive test environment. The value of having a place to run deployments over and over again while experimenting with configurations is very beneficial in testing any service.

Test Environments Summary

Different types of tests are best run in optimized environments. The goal of splitting up all these tests and test environments, as shown in Table 14-2, is to find the right set of bugs in the simplest test environment as quickly as possible. Most testing will occur on the one box or in a test cluster, but all the environments serve a critical purpose in testing and releasing a new service or a major upgrade to an existing service.

TABLE 14-2 Table of Test Environments

Test environment	Primary test focus
One box	Pre-check-in test
	Basic functionality tests
	Test automation authoring
	Large automated test suite parallel execution
	Quick deployment validation
	Page load time
Test cluster	Full functional test passes
	Full automation test suites
	Validates service components interoperating across the network
	Failover testing
Perf and scale cluster	Core performance testing across the network
	Scale-out and scale-up limitations
	Early capacity planning verification
INT environment	Multiservices end-to-end integration testing
Deployment test cluster	Large cluster of computers or VMs dedicated to running and improving deployment code and validation tests

Integration Testing vs. Test Flags and Emulation

As mentioned earlier, services no longer stand alone; they are usually built on platform services and need those services in place to be fully functional. With all these dependencies, the integration points of services must be tested in a manner that allows each service or layer of a service to maintain its own ability to innovate independently. Integration testing and test flags and emulation are techniques to help with this challenge. The selection of the right technique is driven by the degree to which the services are coupled, as shown in Figure 14-7.

	Emulation/ Test Flags	Integration Testing
Loosely Coupled	**Primary** Feature development and most testing	**Secondary** Late in product cycle for integration testing
Tightly Coupled	**Secondary** Used mostly for simple regressions	**Primary** Feature develoment and most testing

FIGURE 14-7 Two-by-two matrix for selecting integration testing versus test flags or emulation.

Test Flags and Emulation Provide Agility

By using *test flags* and *emulation,* you can test a service without any platform services. To really make the one box or test cluster work for rapid testing and regression of internal bugs, a service needs to have the ability to remove the dependency on these platform services. Test flags and emulation do this in different ways.

Test Flags

Test flags internally stub out calls to a platform service. A global setting in a configuration file or the Windows registry turns the test flags on or off. When the test flag is set to *true,* any calls to a platform service follow a new code path designed to allow the test to complete.

The test flag code path usually returns a positive response with simple static well-formed data. Some test code is written to return errors and variable data, but this is less common. Test flags are a great way for a tester to quickly take a new build and regress simple bugs such as changes to an error message string or UI navigation, essentially bugs that have nothing to do with integration. Test flags can also be used during stress tests.

Stress test newsgroups

The Office Online (soon to be rebranded Office Live) Web site is one of the most popular on the Internet. Microsoft Office users go to this site for help, clip art, templates, training, and user forums.

The Office Online Web site needed to integrate content from newsgroups while maintaining the Office Online user interface. This feature is called MSCOM threaded discussion service and is a set of APIs that allows the Office Online service to read and post to newsgroups without users leaving the Office Online experience. For functional testing, a fake newsgroup was created. This met the needs of most test scenarios.

When the feature needed to undergo performance and load testing, it was clear that flooding live newsgroups or even the fake newsgroup was not a viable option. The team created test flags that would allow them to do manual tests as well as perf testing against a local .xml file.

The addition of test flags unblocked the perf testing but also allowed for greater agility in running simple manual tests of core functionality. The following code sample shows one method we used to turn the test on or off by simply having the text file in the correct location. In many environments, we used a shared service, named Jukebox, to turn test flags on and off globally.

```
///<summary>
   ///return thread messages for the given asset.  if file exists.
This is a test so use file.  if not, use service
///</summary>

  Private string GetThreadMessages(string strAssetId)

  {
    string strPath = Path Combine(Path.Combine(m_strDataPath,
strAssetId), "ThreadMessage.txt";
    if (!File.Exists(strPath))
      return null;
    return ProcessFile(strPath);
  }

  /// <summary>
  /// Get message bodies for the given asset.
  /// </summary>

  private string GetMessageBodies(string strAssetId)
```

```
{
    string strPath = Path.Combine(Path.Combine(m_strDataPath,
  strAssetId), "MessageBody.txt");
    if (!File.Exists(strPath))
        return null;
    return processFile (strPath);
}
```

—*Marty Riley, Senior Test Lead, Office Online*

Emulation

Emulation is the preferred method for testing a service with the ability to find integration bugs and still maintain agility. Since the platform services are being emulated, bugs with malformed xml can often be caught in this environment before moving to full integration testing.

A typical emulation solution will have an emulation service running on a machine other than the service under tests. For a One-Box test scenario in which the service does not have test flags the emulation service may run locally. The emulation service should have a pluggable architecture to allow the addition of other services as needed. Each plug-in can be coded to receive a well formed request and generate a response. The response can be static or driven from test data. The approach to using test data allows for greater variations in the response and can allow for more boundary and edge case testing.

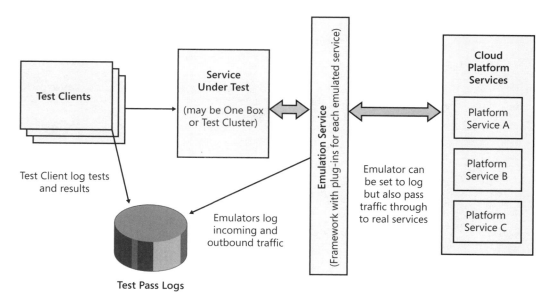

FIGURE 14-8 Example of an emulation framework with logging and pluggable emulators for multiple services

Logging of test cases and results is a common feature of test automation frameworks. A good emulation service will log incoming and outbound traffic as well. With this approach, a test that passes can check to see if the correct data was sent to and from the service. I once had a bug where a SQL Stored procedure would make two calls to a remote service but would write only one row of data in the database. Without logging from the emulator, we would not have caught this bug.

Some of the better emulation solutions allow the test environment to be set up to call into the emulator but have flags to allow for the request to pass through. In this approach, the emulator still logs all traffic but the request can go to a real instance of the service.

Emulation is ideal for load testing. The use of logs and simplified logic in the emulators allows them to scale much higher than trying to test against a test instance of a platform service. Emulators can also simulate varying latency no matter what the true load is.

Testing Against Production

To operations engineers and many product teams, the thought of allowing another service to test its new code against your live site seems ridiculous. Who would want all those mean testers doing horrible things to the code and trying to break your service? The thought of letting testers bang away at production sends chills down the spine of most operations managers.

Over the years, I have developed a few arguments to help everyone realize that testing against production is a good thing and to explain that it is happening whether you like it or not.

The first example I use is to ask anyone to go out and try to create a WLID account starting with the term *test* or *test account*. You will have to try a lot of combinations of letters and numbers after these words to find an available name. Something tells me that the individuals who created these accounts are doing some sort of testing and that there is very little WLID can do to stop them.

All services run some level of transaction monitoring as a way to alert the SOC when something goes wrong. After every upgrade, the operations engineers often run a battery of tests called *smoke tests* to ensure that all major functionality is still working. Well, these are tests just like the ones run against a one box and other test environments. This means that operations is testing in production already.

Hackers are constantly looking for vulnerabilities in production services. If a service must be robust enough to withstand a hacker's attempt to break in, it should be able to survive a few automated tests.

Mashups is the last example I use. Many mashups are developed by small teams of developers and use public APIs. Some even go so far as to screen scrape to build their application.

The point is that they must develop their mashup over the Internet against production. In this case, they are not only testing their solution against production, they are developing against production.

> **Note** *Screen scraping* is a technique for taking a fully rendered UI—for a mashup this is a Web page—ignoring the binary information such as pictures, and pulling out and parsing the data from it. This is not an optimal method because a fully rendered UI rarely has data presented with delimiters for easy parsing.

Once a team is convinced that they can test against production, you do need to establish some guidelines. Simple rules such as "no load tests against production" and "no direct access to backend services" are the most important. Architecturally, there is another challenge: the need to isolate test traffic from real users. With so many services being ad funded, advertisers won't want to pay for impressions or click-throughs generated by test automation.

Production Dogfood, Now with More Big Iron

Dogfood, first covered in Chapter 11, is still a major component in how we test S+S. Services dogfood is about setting up a full-fledged instance of the production service built out with the same hardware as the rest of production. Users of dogfood clusters, sometimes called beta clusters, are usually employees, family members of employees, partners, and occasionally technology reviewers. Users of dogfood realize that they are on an environment where things will occasionally break. The benefit to users is access to the newer code before it goes into broad use.

Dogfood clusters are upgraded more frequently than production. Users on a dogfood cluster get the benefit of using the newer code before anyone else. They also are expected to give quality feedback to the development team throughout the process.

Other uses of dogfood clusters include running full suites of automated tests to help catch regressions and usability tests. Public demonstrations of the next big release are often run from the dogfood cluster.

Production Data, so Tempting but Risky Too

To test Microsoft Office, we have a library of thousands and thousands of documents our customers have given us to use. These are real-world documents with all sorts of macros and Microsoft Visual Basic for Applications (VBA) code and crazy custom styles. We use this library to test for backward compatibility and the number of calls from a client to a service (round tripping). Round trips add to performance degradation.

In services that are very stateful, there is always a large real-world data set. A service needs to clearly state in the privacy statement whether this data will ever be used for purposes outside of the production environment. This is especially true if the data contains any personally identifiable information (PII).

Using production data in testing is a great asset to test. We find that the shape of the production data changes over time as the use of certain data elements extends and other elements are forgotten and left as legacy.

Whether the production data contains any PII or not, it must be sanitized before testing. I have seen teams forget to scrub live site end points from their production data and accidently send a flood of test traffic over the Internet against the production site. Therefore, the first rule in using production data is to sanitize it.

> **Note** Data masking, usually referred to as *data sanitization* in Microsoft, is a process of obscuring specific data within database tables to ensure sensitive production data is not accidently leaked. Scrubbing algorithms are used to generate random substitute but fully functional data in place of the original.

The second key to using production data is to analyze it. Too often teams take the data, sanitize it, and use it for testing By analyzing the data, we can look for boundary conditions. If you want to know the longest city name from a dump of personalization data, analyze it and pull that out. It could be a valuable piece of information in producing tests that can run without production data.

Performance Test Metrics for Services

Throughout this book, we have discussed many different metrics used to drive quality into Microsoft products. All of the metrics covered so far apply to S+S testing. Fortunately, this chapter presents new metrics to measure and track for S+S testing, as presented in Table 14-3.

Most of these metrics come from design best practices. The great thing about a best practice is that there is quite often a test needed to verify that it was applied optimally.

TABLE 14-3 Test Metrics for Browser-Based Services

Metric title	Definition
Page Load Time 1 (PLT1)	Measures the amount of time it takes for a browser to load a new page from the first request to the final bit of data. A new page is any Web page the browser has never been to before and for which it has no content cached.
Page Load Time 2 (PLT2)	Measures the amount of time it takes for a page to load on every visit after the first. This should always be faster than PLT1 because the browser should have some content cached.

Metric title	Definition
Page weight	The size of a Web page in bytes. A page consisting of more bytes of data will typically load more slowly than a lighter weight page will.
Compressibility	Measures the compression potential of files and images.
Expiration date set	Test validates that relatively static content has an expiration date greater than today.
Round trip analysis	Evaluates number of round trips for any request and identifies ways to reduce them.

Certainly, many other metrics are unique to services and some are unique to specific types of services. For example, in the search space one of the most critical measurements is relevance. This is a measure of how likely the content of a Web page will meet the user's needs based upon the search criteria.

In this section, I pared the list of potential metrics down to a small subset focused on performance. These metrics are common to any online service. I also picked metrics that reference good-quality freely available test tools to use in running the tests:

- Visual Round Trip Analyzer (VRTA) will be available on the Microsoft Developer Network (*http://msdn.microsoft.com*) by the time this book is published.

- Fiddler is already available at *http://www.fiddler2.com* and there are a number of articles about it posted on MSDN.

Page Load Time 1 and Page Load Time 2

Page Load Time 1 (PLT1) and Page Load Time 2 (PLT2) are the key measures for user satisfaction. Research has shown that Web pages that take longer than just a few seconds to load rate lower than a similar page that loads much quicker. Some search engines even use PLT measurements in weighting of search results. A slower page will fall farther down in the list of returned pages even if the content is as good a match as another faster page.

In Microsoft, we focus heavily on measuring our own services' PLTs as well as those of our competition. This analysis is done for PLT1 and PLT2 but also by country, as shown in Figure 14-9. PLT for a country is often affected by the bandwidth to the country and the distance the data must travel to reach the user. Network engineers are fond of saying that they are limited by the speed of light.

In some respects, it's like watching one of those cable news channels when the field reporter is halfway around the world and the anchor is asking a question. The field reporter stands there nodding as the question is asked. When the anchor is done asking, we all see the reporter continue to nod for another second before starting to answer. In the same way, data sent from a server to a browser is limited by the speed of light.

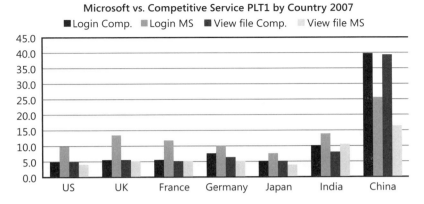

FIGURE 14-9 Analysis of two user transactions, login and view file, for Microsoft service versus a competitor. In most cases, except for China, Microsoft is slower.

Network impact on PLT is just one element. The biggest improvements to PLT can be made through various optimization techniques. The rest of the metrics covered in this section are ones that we use to improve the quality of the code and content for optimized page load times.

Page Weight

Page weight is simply the number of bytes that make up a single Web page. Because Web pages often are dynamic and composed of many elements such as script files, images, and even ActiveX controls, most page weight tests are conducted in lab scenarios where the variable elements are fixed.

For pages with a high page weight, bugs are filed and developers work to reduce the total number of bytes. Goals for maximum page weight vary by product and frequency of access.

Compressibility

Compressibility analyzes the degree to which any file, whether XML, HTML, image, cascading style sheets (CSS), or JavaScript (JS), can be compressed. A lot of JavaScript is posted with white space and comments. These won't affect how the script runs, but they affect file size and thus page load times. VRTA3 is an ideal tool to use to analyze compressibility.

Many elements of a Web pages such as JavaScript or cascading style sheets (CSS) can be compressed by four or more times their original size. This saves on the amount of data that needs to be sent between a Web server and the browser. Decompressing on the client computer is negligible. Removing white space such as spaces and comments can yield another 20 percent reduction in the size of a Web page. VRTA3 analyzes files for all these elements and identifies top candidates for compression and how much will be saved.

Table 14-4 shows the data from a compression report. A compressibility measure of 1.0 indicates that the file is already optimally compressed. A measure of 4.1 indicates that the file could be compressed to be 4.1 times smaller than it currently is.

TABLE 14-4 Compressibility analysis of several JavaScript scripts for a Microsoft Web site

URI	Length	Compres-sability	What if compress'd	Duration
http://www.abcxyz123.com/	52,771	4.1	12,871	2.766
http://abcxyz123.move.com/fah/hp.js	16,981	3.2	5,307	1.35
http://abcxyz123.move.com/fah/common.js	163,201	3.1	52,645	5.447
http://abcxyz123.move.com/fah/Tracking.js	15,851	3.0	5,284	1.292
http://abcxyz123.move.com/cbrdc/org.js	13,657	2.7	5,058	1.207
http://abcxyz123.move.com//cbrdc/org.css	2,297	2.4	957	1.176
http://static.move.com/abcxyz123/js/nc/s.js	24,407	2.2	11,094	1.145
	289,165	3.1	93,216	

Expiration Date

A common mistake in Web page design is not setting the maximum expiration date on relatively static content. This is vital for reducing PLT2 (the second time a user visits a site). If the file has no cache setting, the browser will request an updated version of the file from the server. Even if the file has not changed and is not redownloaded to the browser, time is wasted making the request to the server.

Fiddler is a tool developed by Eric Lawrence of Microsoft and is available on the Internet at *http://www.fiddler2.com*. It is used largely by security testers in Microsoft but also has a number of performance features, as shown in Figure 14-10.

In the detailed results tab of a performance test, Fiddler shows all the files that were loaded with a Web page and the cache setting for them. It is an easy way to find files that could be cached. With the tool, you can also see what percentage of time the page takes to load various bits of content.

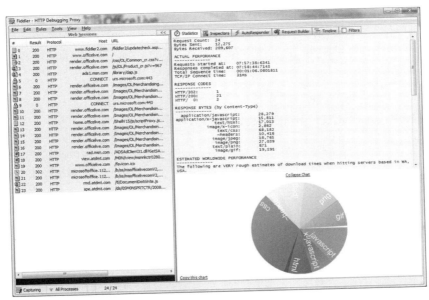

FIGURE 14-10 Fiddler loading www.officelive.com.

Round Trip Analysis

The biggest impact to page load time is the network. As the distance from the source to the client increases, the network becomes an increasingly influential component of page load time. Reducing page weight reduces the amount of data, but it is really the number of round trips that most affects PLT.

VRTA3 and Fiddler can help with this analysis, and VRTA3 does have some nice graphical representations that help.

VRTA used to find bugs in Internet Explorer

VRTA was designed to help engineers visualize the download of a Web page. I have been using this technique inside of Microsoft for the past four years. Presenting this process in a very visual way so that the engineers can see what items are serialized behind each other has helped improve page load times for many services.

The tool has also helped to identify some of the more difficult to diagnose issues in browsers. One problem we found in Microsoft Internet Explorer 7 was the JavaScript blocking behavior, which restricted the number of files loading simultaneously. The effect was that parallel TCP ports were limited to only two. VRTA is also in active use for testing our new Internet Explorer 8 browser, but as of the writing of this book, that product hasn't shipped and I can't really share those bugs just yet.

—*Jim Pierson, Perf Architect, MSN and Windows Live*

The Microsoft Office Live team sets a threshold for the maximum number of round trips (un-cached) that each Web page can have. When the developer makes a check-in to the source control system, a suite of tests for performance run and any page exceeding the round trip threshold is flagged.

Several Other Critical Thoughts on S+S

In this section, I want to share a bit more on testing in an S+S world. Although these points didn't really fit well under test techniques, each contains information that any tester on a service should champion.

Continuous Quality Improvement Program

In Chapter 3, "Engineering Life Cycles," we discussed the concept of Milestone Q (a.k.a. MQ or M0). For larger projects, this milestone is typically about clearing the decks and getting ready for the next major release. Teams invest in infrastructure improvements to help the process of developing and shipping to be smoother and faster. Developers often investigate new technologies and develop new prototypes. In the services world, where teams might go years shipping monthly or quarterly, we don't often take time for an MQ. In the services world, we focus on continuous improvement.

All of our production services are very data driven and most use a very Six Sigma–like process we call quality of service (QoS) to drive continuous improvement. This QoS should not be confused with the computer networking concept that gives certain applications priority network access over others. Our version of QoS is about finding the unique insights that will help us to improve customer satisfaction.

A successful QoS program must have data from three major categories. It can include other data, but in many cases that can distract from the very clear goal of improving customer satisfaction. The three major categories of data are voice of the customer, product quality, and operational quality, as shown in Figure 14-11.

FIGURE 14-11 Three key data sources for QoS.

Voice of the customer can be gathered from multiple sources. Direct surveys of customer satisfaction are the most common. Many services teams have shifted from using direct surveys of customer satisfaction to the Net Promoter score. Blog and Twitter mining is another way to see what customers are saying about your product or service.

The Net Promoter score is a management tool that can be used to gauge the loyalty of a firm's customer relationships. It serves as an alternative to traditional customer satisfaction research.

For services with direct support, call center data is a vital component of voice of the customer. Whether through actual phone calls or online chat help, user requests are categorized. By mining this data, a service team can identify the top customer escalations and prioritize those to improve customer satisfaction but also drive down the support costs.

Product quality focuses on bugs and performance. In many cases, bugs might already be known, but how important they are to fix relative to other bugs is often hard to determine. A major area of product quality is the continual measurement and improvement of page load time relative to competitors. What is good performance today is not necessarily a customer satisfaction driver in the future.

Operational quality is the same set of data operations that you would use to look for internal efficiencies, but in a QoS approach it is used to identify potential dissatisfaction (DSat) drivers. I often like to kid with the operations engineers, saying that there is little they can do to drive up customer satisfaction but a lot they can do to drive it down. This fact doesn't put operations in a very fun position, which is why it can be a challenging role. Here are a few key operational metrics and how they can be used to improve QoS:

- *Root cause analysis (RCA)* on any production outage can identify either a process problem or an underlying bug or architecture flaw.

- A high *time to detection* for a production issue can show holes in monitoring.

- A high *time to resolution* can indicate inadequate logging or diagnostic tools.

- *Percentage of tickets resolved through Tier 1 or a self-healing system* can show efficiency of handling simple, high-volume production issues. Resolving at Tier 1 or in an automated self-healing system also brings down time to resolution.

- *Percentage of false alarms* can show errors in monitoring or alert thresholds.

- The richest area for finding product improvements is *tickets by bucket*. This is very similar to the call center coding but is the operational view instead of the customer perspective. Any area that has a high count is rich for product improvement or self-healing automation.

When all three data sources are brought together, the team can better prioritize the right fixes to maximize improvements to customer satisfaction. Here is an example of how this could work in a very layered service: The call center team has a high number of complaints from users that could not process PayPal payments on the evening of June 23. When enough calls about a common problem have come into the call center an alert is sent to the live site operations team. Upon investigation they discover that PayPal has updated a certificate on their service that requires any other service trying to connect to them to also update to the new version. Certificates are essentially private keys services use to identify trusted partners. Upon review of this incident the call center, operations team, and product engineering team identify a gap in the service monitoring and agree to implement a PayPal monitoring solution and an alert system for when certificates need to be updated. The solution to add an alert will warn the operations team when the certificate is due to expire and thus prevent a future outage. On the off chance that this does happen again, the enhanced monitoring will reduce the time to detection and time to resolution.

The key to the successful use of this approach is to bring all the data and all the stakeholders together to identify root cause and optimal improvements.

Just run it once a week, the customers won't mind . . . oops!

My own passion for QoS started many years ago after we launched the new version of the billing platform. It is a very embarrassing story, but it happened quite a long time ago and many names have been changed to protect the involved but innocent.

The new billing platform was a major internal service that let us track all the users of the subscription services and allowed us to bill them correctly and be paid by the credit card companies. One element of the system was the nightly billing batch job. We ran it at night more out of history than for any design reason.

A couple of weeks after launch, we were all in the war room triaging bugs. Operations joined us a bit late and started to share the issues they'd seen with the new system. Zach informed us that the nightly billing batch job was taking about five days to complete. They had only had two successful runs so far.

We were all shocked—we knew that the credit card number encryption would add some overhead, but not to this degree. Fixing this bug would mean a complete rewrite of the batch job that would certainly cause us to slip out the next major release by several weeks.

Just then someone, and I really can't remember who, said, "Why don't we just charge customers once a week. I mean if they were supposed to pay us on June 1st and we wait until June 6th, who's going to care? I know we'll lose interest for Microsoft, but at least the customers will be happy."

This really did seem like a brilliant idea. We were only nine months away from the next major release, so the batch job could wait until then. We did decide to add a metric to our QoS scorecard for billing batch job time to completion with a goal of less than 168 hours because that would be more than seven days and that was just unacceptable.

Two months later, we all got together for the monthly QoS review. We had Dev, Test, PM, and Operations in the room. The call center team was on the speakerphone; they always seemed more comfortable on the phone than actually being in the room for a meeting. Each team began by going over their section of the scorecard.

The product team called out that they'd fixed 15 bugs this month and that page load time for the signup pages had improved by 200 percent. We all felt that would surely have a positive impact on customer satisfaction.

Next, operations presented. Zach went through the numbers on availability and ticket volume. He got to his last metric, which was billing batch job completion time. "The batch job is starting to take longer, but we are still under 130 hours. At the rate customers are being added to the system, we could exceed our one week max in about a year."

Everyone was actually pleased by this news because we were well on track to have the next major version out long before we ran out of buffer time.

The call center team started their presentation by going over call volume and time to resolution. When they got to call by category, we had a new number one category with the temporary name of "you bounced my check." The call center team didn't know quite what to do because customers were calling in and blaming us for overdraft charges on their bank accounts.

"This doesn't make sense," Chris said. "We only take credit cards, so we can't cause checks to bounce."

Bharat leaned forward and spoke up so that those on the phone could hear him, "I could see us impacting bank accounts. I don't know about all of you, but when I signed up for my test account I used the credit card number from my bank ATM card."

Bharat was right. People were just starting to use ATM cards as substitutes for credit cards. This still didn't explain why they were blaming us for overdraft charges.

Brett asked, "Are they saying we're overcharging them?"

"No," said the voice on the phone, "they are saying we are taking money out of their accounts and either causing them to bounce checks, or when we do take the money, they don't have the funds in the account."

Most of us in the room were starting to realize what was going on, but it was Ben that first said, "It's the batch job!" Yes, many of our customers had grown used to us taking payments on a specific day of the month. After that, any remaining funds they could spend as they liked. We realized we could not wait to fix the batch job.

If not for the QoS process, we would not have had all of these teams and data in the room and would not have been able to realize how a bad design and a bad decision were leading to customer dissatisfaction.

Within a few weeks the new job was put into production and completed in just a few hours. It was a major rewrite with a substantial amount of parallel processing and dedicated equipment for the decryption process. We also changed the metric on the QoS scorecard to be "Days in a row the billing job finished in under 5 hours."

I left the team shortly after this, but last I heard they had topped a thousand days and were closing in on two thousand.

Common Bugs I've Seen Missed

Inside Microsoft, I have a video blog series called "War Stories—Bugs in Production." The series is dedicated to wallowing in the bugs that got past everyone and into production. These are not just little bugs that would have been nice to have fixed. These horrible nasty bugs have caused more than one outage.

Some testers are reluctant to share the story of the one that got away. It's as if they feel responsible for the bug. I like to point out that they didn't make the bug; either a developer wrote the bug or a PM designed the bug. As testers, they found hundreds or thousands of other bugs, and eventually a bug gets past everyone. I like to believe one of the best tools a tester has for learning is to hear about the bugs others have missed.

Legacy clients can bring your service to its knees. After a service has been around a while, it might have a dozen or more older clients still in active use. There are still versions of the MSN client that shipped in the mid-1990s in use to this day. One bug I've seen a few times occurs when the service is upgraded and it causes a new behavior in a legacy client. The new behavior is often related to some retry logic that has never really been hit before. This could be caused by a new data structure for a query response being recognized by the client as malformed and tossed out, or it could simply be a slow response from the server that triggers a new request. The problem occurs when the client does not have a retry logic throttle so that it keeps increasing the number of requests until the production site is brought down as if by a denial of service (DoS) attack.

The "disallow server cascading" failure is another one I like. In this scenario, a service that is built on top of a platform service can become influenced by the reliability of those underlying components. Some higher level services develop the disallow or block this server list feature: If a server in a platform component is not responding in a timely enough fashion, it is put on the disallow list. This allows the higher level service the opportunity to reissue the query to another server in the platform cloud. The problem occurs when the platform service is under high load and is simply not responsive within the time expected so that the query is reissued to another server. The overload now spreads as servers are added to the disallow list and other servers get ever increasing loads. When the service is down to just a few servers that are not on the disallow list, it grinds to a halt and all higher lever services fail.

The last example I have is the tsunami or tidal wave. I first started talking about the tsunami effect back in 1995 after we had an outage in the MSN authentication service. For a few hours, the authentication service behind our dial-up connection was down. It wasn't down long, but the timing happened to be just near the end of the workday on the East Coast. Users were unable to log on, but they still wrote e-mail messages to friends while in the offline mode. In the background, the client kept trying to connect. When the service came back online all those users connected and a torrent of e-mail was sent out over the Internet. A lot of it went to AOL. Within a few hours, our e-mail servers were knocked offline by a flood of e-mail coming back from AOL.

The tsunami effect still exists on the open Internet. We had a recent occurrence when the intercontinental network connections from North America to Japan went down for just a few hours. When the network came back up, the very popular MSN Messenger service was flooded by authentication requests that were routed to the WLID service. This sudden surge in authentication requests slowed WLID for several hours.

Bugs in production are great to study and learn from. Truly, most of the worst ones are design flaws rather than simple coding mistakes. Either way, wallowing in a production bug is a great way for team members to learn.

Summary

Services are a big bet for Microsoft. We've been building products and services for the Internet since the early 1990s. Both Bill Gates's memo "The Internet Tidal Wave" and Ray Ozzie's memo "The Internet Services Disruption" have reinforced the importance of the Internet and services to our long-term success. Microsoft invests billions of dollars a year in capital to support our services growth, and while doing this we work closely with industry to find ways to improve power consumption and resource utilization.

Traditional software products for desktop computers and servers have a lot in common with services. This commonality allows us to bring all the test techniques we used to ship those shrink-wrap products to bear on services testing.

There are still many differences between shrink-wrap and services, however. These differences have required Microsoft SDETs to develop many new test techniques. Fully automated deployments and the one box are key to unblocking testing. Test clusters using test flags, emulation, or services integration help find bugs in service-to-service transactions. By moving closer to production with testing, we can start to test new services against live production instances of platform services and even pull sanitized production data into test labs.

All the metrics used to measure traditional software apply to services and S+S, but services need to pay special attention to page load times. Customers do not like to wait for a Web page to load. There are many simple improvements, such as reducing page weight, setting cache on files, and reducing round trips, that should be constantly measured during testing to improve PLT.

The key to services is not to think shipping is done when the service goes live. In many respects, that's when the final test pass begins. A test environment will never be exactly like production, so some bugs will be missed. Keeping an eye on production also means implementing a robust continuous improvement process that should integrate data from the voice of the customer, product quality, and operational quality. High production quality also means learning from our mistakes and wallowing in the bugs that got past us and into production.

Part IV

About the Future

Chapter 15
Solving Tomorrow's Problems Today

Alan Page

Software testing is a growing field that will continue to mature for many years. Many of the innovations and new approaches in test have been *reactions* to the problems test teams have run into. The creation of software testing jobs occurred after programmers discovered that they couldn't find all of their own bugs. Implementation of many test automation solutions occurred after management discovered that testing would require either more testers or a more efficient method of conducting some segments of testing.

It seems that there is always another obstacle to overcome in software testing. For the most part, testers wait until the problem is big enough so that a solution for the problem is imperative. For the art, craft, and science of testing to continue to advance and expand, we need to be able to anticipate some of these problems before their burden becomes overwhelming. This chapter covers some of the testing problems that Microsoft is currently facing and the direction we are taking in solving those problems.

Automatic Failure Analysis

If a tester runs 100 test cases and 98 percent of them pass, the tester might need only a few minutes to investigate the two failures and either enter the bugs into the bug tracking system or correct the errors in the test. Now, consider the case where the tester has 1,000 different tests that run across 10 different configurations and 5 different languages. That same 98 percent pass rate on an "exploded" test matrix of 50,000 test points[1] results in 1,000 failures for investigation. With an increasing number of product configurations available, it is becoming common for small teams to have a million test points, where even a tiny percentage of failures can result in enough needed investigation to cause "analysis paralysis"—a situation where the test team spends as much time investigating test failures as they do testing.

Overcoming Analysis Paralysis

Just as automated testing is one solution for testing a countless number of different product configurations, *automatic failure analysis* (AFA) is a solution for dealing with a large number of test failures. The most effective way to avoid paralysis is to anticipate it—in other words, don't wait until you have an overwhelming number of failures to investigate before

---

[1] As mentioned in Chapter 9, "Managing Bugs and Test Cases," a *test point* is an instantiation of that test case in a unique environment.

considering the impact the investigation will have on the test team. It is easy for a test team to become stuck in an infinite loop between creating automation and investigating failures (or, as I have sometimes heard it said, creating failures and investigating automation). Living in this loop rarely results in well-tested software.

In the best circumstances, analyzing hundreds or thousands of failures merely takes time. In other scenarios, much worse things can happen. Consider this conversation between a manager and his employee John:

> **Manager**: John, how far did you get investigating those test failures?
>
> **John**: I investigated some of the results and identified these four bugs in the product. I haven't had time to get to the rest, but I recognize several tests among those that have been failing because of known issues that won't be fixed until the next release.
>
> **Manager**: OK, I want you to get back to work on automating tests for our next new feature.
>
> . . . two months pass . . .
>
> **Manager**: John, we have a serious problem with the release. Customers are reporting serious issues.
>
> **John**: Yeah . . . it turns out that the failures I didn't investigate failed in a different way than they had before and there was actually a serious issue. It's unfortunate, but I don't have time to look at every single failure, and it made sense at the time not to look further. . . .

In this example, John didn't finish the analysis for a few reasons. He skipped some of the investigation because in his mind the failures were already understood. Furthermore, even his manager thought that the best investment of John's time was to move on to creating new automated tests.

If you run a test twice and it fails twice, you cannot assume that it failed the same way both times. Similarly, if you run the same test on five different configurations of the software and it fails all five times, you don't know that the configurations all failed in the same way unless you investigate all five failures. Performing this analysis manually is tedious, error prone, and keeps testers from doing what they need to be doing—*testing software*!

Successful AFA requires several critical components. Figure 15-1 shows a basic architecture of an AFA implementation.

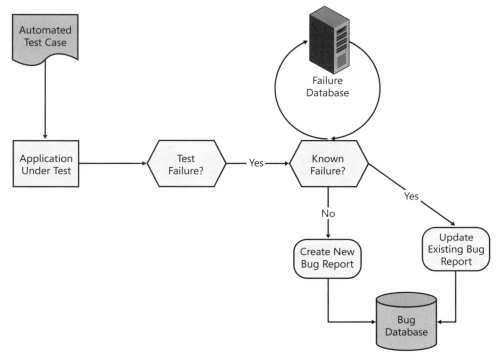

FIGURE 15-1 Failure analysis architecture.

The Match Game

The most critical piece of an AFA system is failure matching. If I'm running a manual test (scripted or exploratory) and it fails, I log a bug containing specific information on the environment and scenario that led me to the bug. Poorly constructed automated tests might merely report that a "failure occurred in test case 1234" and move on to test case 1235. For AFA to work, the automated tests need to report consistent information about the environment, scenario, and steps that lead to the error occurring. Good logging practices (discussed in the following section) are the backbone of reliable failure analysis. If the test logs are unstructured or contain insufficient information, there is no way failure matching will work.

On the back end, a *failure database* contains information about every known test failure. When a test fails, a comparison against known failures occurs, and the system either creates a new bug report or updates an existing report. Implementation of the analysis engine can be complex. At a minimum, it would compare log files or stack traces or both. A more extensive and reliable implementation should include a sophisticated matching algorithm to allow for flexibility and growth. For example, the two logs in Listing 15-1 should match as being the same failure despite the minor differences, and should not show up as two distinct failures.

Listing 15-1 Log File Matching Example

```
Log file 1
Test Case 1234:
SysInfo(MyDevBox)
DateTime.Now
Test Input Boundaries [int foobits(int)]
Testing lower boundary [0]
Testing lower boundary passed.
Testing upper boundary [32768]
Expected result -1
Actual result 0
Result:  Test Failed.

Log file 2
Test Case 1234:
SysInfo(MyTestBox)
DateTime.Then
Test Input Boundaries [INT FOOBITS(INT)]
Testing lower boundary [0]
Testing lower boundary passed.
Testing Upper Boundary [32768]
Expected -1
Actual 0
Result:  Test Upper Boundary Failed.
```

A smart and flexible failure-matching algorithm allows for minor changes in the logging information as well as the changes commonly introduced by data-driven variations or test generation techniques.

Good Logging Practices

Good logging is essential for analyzing and matching failures. Logging is too often an ad hoc and unreliable "tax" that testers add to their automation. As trivial as it might sound, high-quality and consistent logging practices can be the difference between "throw-away" automated tests and those that run reliably for 10 years or more. Table 15-1 lists some things to consider when writing log files.

TABLE 15-1 Logging Best Practices

Logging practice	Description
Logs should be terse on success and verbose on failure.	In practice, "noisy" tests are often poorly written tests. Each piece of information recorded to the log should have some purpose in diagnosing an eventual test failure. When a test fails, the test should trace sufficient information to diagnose the cause of that failure.

Logging practice	Description
When a test fails, trace the successful operation(s) prior to the observed failure.	Knowing the state of the last good operation helps diagnose where the failure path began.
Logs should trace product information.	Logs should trace information about the product, not information about the test. It is still a good idea to embed trace statements in automated tests that can aid in debugging, but these statements do not belong in the test results log.

Trace sufficient and helpful failure context.	Knowing more about how the failure occurred will assist in diagnosis of the underlying defect. Instead of logging:
	
	`Test Failed`
	
	Log something like:
	
	`Test Failed`
	
	`Win32BoolAPI with arguments Arg1, Arg2, Arg3 returned 0, expected 1.`
	
	Or:
	
	`Test Failed`
	
	`Win32BoolAPI with arguments Arg1, Arg2, Arg3 returned 0 and set the last error to 0x57, expected 1 and 0x0`

Avoid logging unnecessary information.	Log files do not need to list every single action executed in the test and underlying application. Remember the first rule above and save the verbose logging for the failure scenarios. Note: For debugging purposes, it can be beneficial to have a user-specified logging level that can allow minimal or maximal trace logging.
Each test point should record a result when a result has been verified or validated.	Tests that aggregate failures often mask defects. If a test is in a fail and continue mode, it is important to know where each failure occurred to diagnose which subsequent failures were dependent and which were independent of the previous failures.
Follow team standards on naming.	Standards can help ensure consistency in reading the log files. All object, test, and procedure names should make sense and be nondegenerate (one name for one thing).

Anatomy of a Log File

What information is beneficial in a log file? Table 15-2 breaks down the log file from Listing 15-1.

TABLE 15-2 Log File Annotations

Log entry	Purpose
Test Case 1234	Unique name
SysInfo(MyDevBox)	Placeholder for environment data
DateTime.Now	Contextual data (this will never match another test)
Test Input Boundaries [*int foobits(int)*]	Identifies what is being tested
Testing lower boundary [0]	What was the value? If a crash occurs, we'll never get to trace it later
Testing lower boundary passed	(Last) Known good execution
Testing upper boundary [32768]	Record the current input value
Expected result –1	What did we want to observe?
Actual result 0	What did we observe? (fail state observation)
Result: Test Failed	Formal summary of test case status

Getting started with AFA

Technical debt led me to automated failure analysis.

Our existing automation was unmaintainable and poorly constructed. We were spending three days a week analyzing the weekly single platform test pass. We were unable to tackle new work because of the overhead of our legacy of automation. We'd reached analysis paralysis through chasing shortsighted objectives and directives (like 100 percent automation—without regard for the kind or suitability of that automation).

AFA goes to the base assumptions of how we test, how we report our results and analyze those results. Without a voice from above, each team will happily speak its own dialect and be incomprehensible to its neighbors.

AFA deals with the back end of the technical debt we build up writing weak automation. High-quality AFA demands cleaning up the entire process and is never the quick solution that most teams are looking for. We're finding it difficult to bite the bullet and spend three months implementing a solution that will pay off our technical debt. If you've done it right all along you can get up and going with AFA in a couple weeks. If you've been close to right, you can get it going in a month; if you've done it wrong all along, it can take several months, but only because AFA can require your balloon payment on technical debt before you get started.

—*Geoff Staneff, SDET*

Integrating AFA

An excellent return on investment for large-scale test automation requires integration in all stages of the automation, check-in, and bug tracking systems. A successful solution greatly reduces the need for manual intervention analyzing test results and failures. Another use of AFA is in analyzing trends in test failures. For example, analysis can indicate that parameter validation errors contributed to 12 percent of the test pass failures over the last six months, or that UI timing issues contributed to 38 percent of the test pass failures over the last six months. This data can be used effectively to understand and target risk areas of the product.

AFA in action: Three short stories

Use of an AFA system delivers numerous additional benefits. The following scenarios describe some of the possibilities that occur in such a system.

Bob the Developer has just checked in the fix for bug ID 4321. When checking in the code to the source code management (SCM) system, bug 4321 was automatically re-solved in the bug database. The failure analysis system notes that the bug is marked as fixed and automatically moves all of the tests that were failing because of this bug to the front of the automation queue so that the verification of the fix can occur early in the test run.

Several test cases have been failing for the past few weeks because of bug 7734. On today's automated test pass, the tests failed again, but the failure analysis system noted that two of the tests failed differently from how they had in the past. A new bug is au-tomatically created. The bug contains information about the failure as well as a link to bug 7734. Finally, an automatic scan of recent code changes takes place, and the bug is assigned to the developer who most likely caused the new failure to occur.

This morning Jane the Test Manager saw that the latest test pass had 48 new failures. The AFA system identified the same root cause for all 48 of the failures and noted the failure pattern in the bug report.

With AFA, the team can focus on new issues as they occur. Much of the risk in analysis of test results is in losing important variations in the noise of expected variations. When investigat-ing a series of failures it is natural (and common) to make evaluations such as "This test point failed last week; this week's failure is probably the same as last week's." An AFA system is capable of removing the tedium from test pass analysis and removing avoidable analysis er-rors by using rules of analysis when deciding whether a failure has been previously observed. Furthermore, these rules are not relaxed because of familiarity with the tests or frequency of the observed test point failure.

Machine Virtualization

Microsoft test teams use massive labs filled with desktop computers and walls of rack-mounted systems. The computers are a finite resource and are in demand for use as build machines or for nightly or weekly manual and automated test passes. Microsoft Hyper-V (formerly known as Windows Server Virtualization) is quickly gaining ground as an alternative that is allowing test teams to use virtual machines. (The most simple definition of a virtual machine, or VM, is an implementation of a computer that runs as a program on a host system.) Hypervisor-based virtualization (like Hyper-V) has much better performance and security than does hosted virtualization (where the VM runs as a program inside the host operating system).

Virtualization Benefits

Virtual machine usage for testing is rapidly being adopted. One of the main benefits for the individual tester is convenience—maintenance of one physical computer and a library of virtual machines is much simpler than maintaining several physical computers. Another big benefit is that a whole set of virtual machines can be easily run by one tester on a single computer, whereas traditionally, testers might need several computers in their office or access to a large lab. Cost savings is another benefit that virtual machines provide. Costs are reduced by using fewer computers and by getting better usage out of the existing hardware as a result of the parallelization benefits of VMs. These savings are beneficial in a tester's or developer's individual office as well as in a test lab.

In the Office

Testers and developers often need multiple computers in their office. For example, they might need to test on different hardware architectures or on multiple computers at once. Rather than fill their office with computers (in my career as a tester, I have had as many as 10 physical test computers in my office), each office can have one Hyper-V server with several different VMs running on it. By using virtualization, testers and developers can create VMs with various specifications at the same time, and configuration is relatively fast and simple. This flexibility allows testers and developers to get much greater test coverage without adding additional hardware to their offices.

Test Lab Savings

Test lab managers can use the server consolidation application of Hyper-V to make their existing hardware more efficient and get the most out of new investments. Most test groups at Microsoft have large labs full of computers responsible for automated tests, stress tests, performance tests, and builds; these labs are prime candidates for consolidation. Test labs rarely run anywhere near full capacity. By using virtual machines, lab administrators can get the same work done on far fewer computers. This saves valuable lab space as well as power costs.

Reducing server machine count also saves time for lab managers. Every lab computer has a time cost that results from the work that must be done to install, rack, and configure it. Management overhead is also associated with a server, including tasks such as upgrading and troubleshooting hardware. Some overhead will always exist, but VM usage greatly reduces this overhead. Virtualization reduces the number of physical computers that need this time commitment. Although many of these same tasks are still necessary on virtual machines, the work is easier because of the potential for automation. It is impossible to automate some aspects of the physical setup of a computer, but scripting through the Windows Management Instrumentation (WMI) can perform the equivalent work for a virtual machine. For example, virtual networks allow lab managers to dynamically modify the network topology programmatically rather than by manually unplugging cables.

Because Hyper-V allows virtual machines of different types to run on the same physical computer, it is no longer necessary to have a wide variety of servers in a lab. Of course, it is still valuable to have computers to represent esoteric hardware, and for this reason, we would never recommend that VM testing replace physical testing entirely. But virtual machines can easily represent simple differences such as processor or core count, 32- versus 64-bit, and memory configurations.

Test Machine Configuration Savings

Virtualization use is saving more than money, power, and space. Development time is an enormously valuable resource, and virtualization can make developers and testers more efficient by reducing two major engineering time sinks: test machine setup time and test recovery time.

Testers and developers both spend a great deal of time setting up computers to test and validate their code. By using virtualization solutions, users can create test images once, and then deploy them multiple times. For example, a tester could create a virtual machine and store it on a file server. When it is time to run a test, testers just copy the VM to a host server and execute the test, rather than take the time to install the operating system and other software. Testers and administrators often create entire libraries of virtual machines with different configurations that serve this purpose. Testers and developers can then choose the exact virtual machine they need instead of setting up a machine manually. Need to run a test on the German build of the Windows Vista operating system with Microsoft Office XP preinstalled? The environment to run this test is only a file copy away.

Test computers often enter an unrecoverable state during testing. After all, the point of most tests is to find bugs, and bugs in complex applications and system software can cause a computer to fail. Virtual machines provide two different solutions to this problem. The first, and simplest, is the fact that a VM is not a physical computer. When a VM fails, the physical hardware is not compromised, data in the parent partition is not lost, and other VMs are unaffected. The impact of a catastrophic failure is greatly reduced.

The other time-saving benefit and the second recovery solution provided by virtualization is the ability to take snapshots of the system. (*Snapshot* is the term used by Microsoft Hyper-V. Other virtualization methods might use a different name for this feature.) A snapshot is a static "frozen" image of the VM that can be taken at any time. After taking a snapshot, the VM continues to run, but the state at the time of the snapshot is saved. Snapshots can help developers and testers quickly recover from errors. By taking a snapshot before the test, testers can quickly and easily roll back the VM to a point before it failed. They can then run the test again or move on with other tests without the need to re-create the VM or reinstall its operating system.

There are a few things to keep in mind before going too wild with snapshots. Although it might seem perfectly logical to create a massive number of snapshots to have a "repro case" for every bug imaginable, this would lead to poor performance in Hyper-V. Each snapshot adds a level of indirection to the VM's disk access, so it would get very slow after several hours of frequent snapshots. It is also worth noting that snapshots are not a portable copy but a set of differences between the original VM and the snapshot—meaning that snapshots cannot be used outside of the VM they belong to.

Virtual Machine Test Scenarios

Virtual machine use is advantageous in a variety of testing scenarios. Discussions of some of the more common scenarios are in the following section, but the usage scenarios are limitless, and many additional test scenarios can benefit from virtual machines, such as API tests, security tests, and setup and uninstall scenarios.

Daily Build Testing

Many testers are responsible for testing an assortment of service packs, updates, and new versions of products. For example, consider an application that can run on various releases of the Windows operating system. The first version of the product has shipped, and the test team is beginning to test version 2. Table 15-3 lists a typical hardware/operating system matrix for such a product.

TABLE 15-3 Host Operating System Test Matrix[2]

	32-bit		64-bit	
	Single-proc	Dual-proc	Single-proc	Dual-proc
Windows XP SP2	To be tested			
Windows Server 2003 SP2	To be tested	To be tested	To be tested	To be tested
Windows Vista SP1	To be tested			
Windows Server 2008	To be tested		To be tested	

Typically, a tester would have three or more test computers to support this matrix (depending on the number of test cases). It is certainly possible for a tester to test the variations with one computer by testing one operating system after another; however, this would be much less efficient and consume substantial time in installing and configuring the test environments. Installations of the operating system and updates, as well as the associated restarts, are extremely time-consuming tasks. Because three or more virtual machines can run on a single physical computer, virtualization can transform three test computers into nine or more virtual test machines while cutting test machine setup time in half. This is possible by using features such as snapshots and the scripting interface exposed by Hyper-V.

In the preceding matrix, the tester would usually install eight different versions of the Windows operating system across the physical computers throughout the test pass. By using a virtualized solution, testers can install all eight versions in virtual machines using three (or fewer) physical computers. The setup time for an automated test pass completes in a fraction of the time, and manual test coverage increases because the tester can stay focused on testing the product instead of setting up environments to get to the next test case. Compatibility and upgrade testing also benefit immensely from this approach of using virtual machines.

Network Topology Testing

Hyper-V facilitates creating complex networking topologies without the hassle of configuring masses of wires and physical switches.

The diagrams in Figures 15-2 and 15-3 illustrate how machine virtualization can be used to create a complex networking environment. The entire network topology in the diagram can be created on one physical server.

---

[2] Because the Windows Server 2008 operating system adjusts the kernel between multi-proc and single-proc, a reinstall of the operating system for multi-proc is unnecessary. It is necessary for operating systems prior to and including Windows Vista.

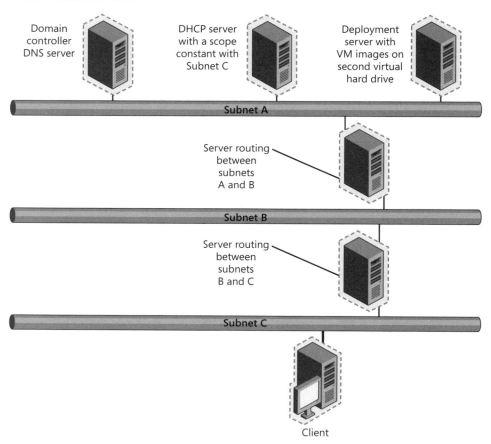

FIGURE 15-2 Virtualized network topology.

In this scenario, three subnets are created and bridged together by two servers acting as routers. Subnet A contains all the typical infrastructure people rely on to get onto the network. Subnet A also holds a deployment server that deploys windows images. The client on subnet C represents a computer that is expected to start from the network and install the latest release of the Windows Vista operating system.

In Figure 15-3, three virtual servers are behind a fourth that is acting as a firewall. The firewall VM is connected to the host's physical network interface through a virtual switch, but the other three servers are not. They are connected to the firewall server through a second virtual switch that does not provide direct connectivity to the outside network.

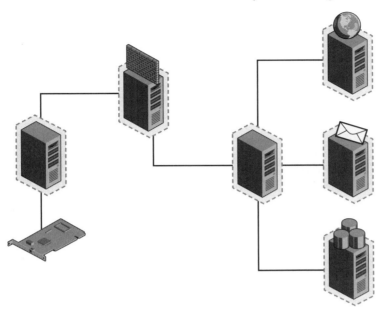

FIGURE 15-3 Firewall topology.

The exciting part of this scenario is that creation of all these machines, switches, and subnets can take place through automation and run on a single physical computer. Prior to virtualization, test beds like these would have required several physical computers and all the wires and routers necessary to create the network topology—not to mention the human resources to actually do all of the work!

When a Failure Occurs During Testing

Failures found during testing can be a time-consuming road block for testers. Time is often lost waiting for a developer to debug the issue or answer a question about the error. This can delay testers from getting more testing done if they need to hold a computer for hours or days waiting for a response.

Some failures are so uncommon that they can take several hours or even days to reproduce. This takes time from testers as well as developers, especially if the developers want to observe state on the computer before the failure actually occurs.

The following two examples are common occurrences in a test organization. Virtualization has the potential to help an engineering team be more efficient by utilizing export and import and snapshots.

Export and Import

When using virtual machines, the tester does not need to wait for a developer to debug a failure. Instead, the tester can save the virtual machine and export it to a network share. Saving the virtual machine causes the entire state of the virtual machine to be saved to disk. Export packages up the virtual machine's configuration and stores it in a specified location.

A developer can then import that virtual machine at her convenience. Because the virtual machine was paused before it was exported, the virtual machine will then be opened in the paused state. All that a developer needs to do is resume the virtual machine and debug the failure just as if she were sitting in front of a physical computer. This allows the tester to regain control of his test computers faster than if he had been executing a test on the host. It also allows the developer to prioritize the investigation of the issue correctly, and the tester can create and save multiple snapshots of difficult-to-reproduce errors for additional debugging.

Snapshots

Snapshots can help reduce the time it takes to reproduce bugs that only seem to happen after running for several hours or even days. For example, a tester could write a script that takes a snapshot of the virtual machine every hour. As that script is running, test would execute in the virtual machine. After a failure occurs, the tester can investigate and find the snapshot that occurred prior to the failure. Then, the tester can revert to the snapshot, start the virtual machine from that point, and hit the bug in no more than 60 minutes. Snapshots make it possible for the tester to do this repeatedly without having to wait hours and even days for the bug to reproduce. Some nondeterministic bugs might not be immediately reproducible by this method, but this method can work for bugs that appear after a known period of running time.

Snapshots to the rescue

In testing Hyper-V, snapshots have become an important feature for us. We use snapshots so that we do not have to reinstall the guest operating system in a virtual machine every time a new build is available to test. What we do is install the guest operating system in each virtual machine, and then we copy any tools that do not change from build to build. Once the virtual machine is prepped and ready to go, we turn the virtual machine off and create a snapshot of the virtual machine. It is at this point that we start the virtual machine backup, install the daily build, and begin our testing. The reason we do this is that we want to be able to put the virtual machine back to a clean state quickly. We do this by reapplying the snapshot, and then installing the next build of our application right away. This way, on a day-to-day basis the only cost to us is installing the daily build—which takes only five minutes rather than the hours of setup time needed previously.

I do wish I had snapshots back in the day of testing service packs. I remember times of having to install the RTM operating system and then installing a service pack and testing. I would have to do this on a daily basis. If I had snapshots, I would only need to install the RTM operating system once and take a snapshot, and then install the service pack. When I was done testing the service pack, I would reapply the snapshot and have a guaranteed clean RTM operating system on which to install the next build of the service pack. This truly would've saved me hours.

—*Shawn McFarland, Senior SDET*

Test Scenarios Not Recommended

Despite all the advantages of virtualization, there are some cases where it is not advisable. If host computers are going to be used for hosting only one or two virtual machines, the cost benefit will be much less because this setup does not provide a significant efficiency gain in hardware usage. However, in some cases benefits such as rapid deployment and snapshots outweigh the overhead introduced by virtualization.

Because Hyper-V provides its own device drivers to the guest operating system, it is not possible to test device drivers inside virtual machines. Likewise, tests that require specific hardware or chipsets will not have access to hardware installed on the host. The Hyper-V video driver is designed for compatibility and is optimized for remote desktop usage. Therefore, high-performance video and 3-D rendering will not work on VMs. Hyper-V dynamically allocates processor resources to VMs as needed, so low-level power-management software will not have any effect inside a VM.

 More Info For more information about virtualization and Microsoft Hyper-V technology, see the Microsoft Virtualization page at *http://www.microsoft.com/virtualization*.

Code Reviews and Inspections

Code reviews are an integral part of the engineering process. After I finish a draft of the chapter you are reading, I will ask several colleagues and subject matter experts to review what I've written before I submit the chapter to the editors for further review. This is one of the best ways to get the "bugs" out of the prose and unearth any errors in my data or samples. Code reviews provide the same service for code and can be extremely effective in finding bugs early.

Code reviews are part of the development process for every team at Microsoft but remain an area where improvements and increases in effectiveness are under way.

Types of Code Reviews

Code reviews range from lightweight ("can you take a quick look at my code") to formal (team meeting with assigned roles and goals). *Pair programming,* an Agile approach where two developers share one workstation, is another form of code review. Different approaches vary in their effectiveness, as well as in the comfort of participation of those involved. Many testers at Microsoft are actively involved in reviewing product code, and many teams have the same code review requirements for test code as they do for product code.

Formal Reviews

The most formal type of inspection is the *Fagan* inspection (named after the inventor of the process, Michael Fagan). Fagan inspections are group reviews with strict roles and process. Reviewers are assigned roles such as *reader or moderator.* (The author of the code attends the session but does not take on any of the other roles.) The moderator's job is to ensure that everyone attending the review session is prepared and to schedule and run the meeting. There is an expectation that reviewers have spent a considerable amount of time prereviewing the code before the meeting, and they often use checklists or guidelines to focus their review efforts.

Fagan inspections require a large time investment but are extremely effective in finding bugs in code. One team at Microsoft using Fagan inspections was able to reduce the number of bugs found by the test team and customers from 10 bugs per thousand lines of code (KLOC) to less than 1 bug per KLOC. Despite the potential for finding errors, the biggest obstacle blocking teams from using Fagan inspections is how much time they take (inspection rate is approximately 200 lines per hour) followed closely by the fact that most developers don't *like* to spend 25 percent to 30 percent of their time in formal inspection meetings. For these reasons, despite the effectiveness, Fagan-style inspections are not widely used at Microsoft.

Informal Reviews

The challenge in developing a solution for effective code reviews is identifying a level of formality that is both time-efficient and effective in finding critical issues during the coding phase. "Over the shoulder" reviews are fast but usually find only minor errors. The "e-mail pass-around" review has the benefit of multiple reviewers, but results vary depending on who reads the e-mail message, how much time reviewers spend reviewing, and how closely they look at the changes.

The best solution appears to be to find a process that is both collaborative and time efficient. Programmers need the benefit of multiple peer reviews with assigned roles but without the overhead of a formal meeting. Companies such as Smart Bear Software have conducted and published case studies[3] with these same premises in mind and have shown success in creating a lightweight review process that is nearly as effective as a formal inspection. Studies internal to Microsoft have shown similar results, and many teams are experimenting to find the perfect balance between formality and effectiveness when conducting code reviews.

Checklists

I think it's fair to say that most people do better work when they know what to do. When an employee arrives at work, she probably accomplishes more if she has a list of tasks to address (regardless of whether she created the list herself or a superior created it for her) rather than if she is simply told "go do some work." Yet many code reviews start with a request to "please look at my code." Some reviewers can do a fine job reviewing code without any guidelines, but for most, a checklist or guideline can be highly beneficial.

Checklists guide the reviewer toward finding the types of bugs that are easiest to detect during code review and the bugs that are most critical to find during the review phase. An example checklist might look like this:

- Functionality Check (Correctness)
- Testability
- Check Errors and Handle Errors Correctly
- Resources Management
- Thread Safe (Sync, Reentry, Timing)
- Simplicity/Maintainability
- Security (INT Overflow, Buffer Overruns, Type Mismatches)
- Run-Time Performance
- Input Validation

Other types of checklists might focus entirely on a single area such as performance or security so that multiple reviewers can focus on different aspects of the code under review.

Other Considerations

The funny thing about code reviews is that relatively few teams directly monitor the effectiveness of reviews. This might seem silly—why would you put effort into something without knowing what the return on the investment was? An indirect measure of effectiveness is to

---

3   Jason Cohen, ed., *Best Kept Secrets of Peer Code Review*, *http://www.smartbearsoftware.com*.

monitor the bugs that *are* tracked; that is, if, after implementing a new code review policy, there are fewer bugs found by the test team and customers, you *could* say that the code reviews were effective . . . but *how* effective were they? If you really want to know, you, of course, need to measure the effort and effect. An accurate ROI measurement of code reviews, or any improvement process for that matter, requires that the time investment is measured and that the bugs found during review are tracked in some manner.

Activities

Table 15-4 lists two hypothetical products of similar size and scope. In Product A, only bugs found by the test team or bugs found post release (by the customer) are tracked. Product B also tracks bugs found through developer testing and code reviews.

TABLE 15-4 Bugs Found by Activity

Product A		Product B	
Bugs found through developer testing	?	Bugs or rework found through developer testing	150
Bugs found through code review	?	Bugs or rework found through code review	100
Bugs found by test team	175	Bugs found by test team	90
Bugs found by customer	25	Bugs found by customer	10
Total bugs found	**200**	**Total bugs found**	**350**

Product A has 200 known bugs, and Product B has 350. Product B also has fewer bugs found by the customer—but there isn't really enough data here to say that one product is "buggier" than the other is. What we do know about Product B, however, is which types of *activities* are finding bugs. Coupled with data from planning or any tracking of time spent on these tasks, we can begin to know which early detection techniques are most effective, or where improvements might need to be made.

Taking Action

In addition to the number of issues found by activity, it can be beneficial to know what *kinds* of issues code reviews are finding. For example, a simple lightweight root-cause analysis of the bugs found by the customer or test team might reveal that detection of a significant portion of those bugs could have occurred through code review and indicate an action of updating checklists or stricter policy enforcement.

Furthermore, classifying issues by the type of rework necessary to fix the issue identifies where additional early detection techniques might be implemented. Table 15-5 lists a sample of some common rework items found during code review, along with an example technique that could be used to detect that issue *before* code review.

TABLE 15-5 **Code Review Issues and Associated Prevention Techniques**

Issue type	Detection/prevention technique(s)
Duplicate code, for example, reimplementing code that is available in a common library	Educate development team on available libraries and their use; hold weekly discussions or presentations demonstrating capabilities of libraries.
Design issue, for example, the *design* of the implementation is suboptimal or does not solve the coding problem as efficiently as necessary	Group code reviews can catch these types of errors while educating all review participants on good design principles.
Functional issue, for example, the implementation contains a bug or is missing part of the functionality (omission error)	Functional bugs can lead to implementation of new guidelines or techniques to be applied in developer testing.
Spelling errors	Implement spell checking in the integrated development environment (IDE).

Time Is on My Side

An accurate measurement of code review effectiveness requires accurate knowledge of the time spent on reviews. You could just ask the team how much time they spent reviewing code, but the answers, as you'd guess, would be highly inaccurate. This is one of the reasons teams that want to measure the value of code reviews use some type of code review tool for all of their code reviews. If the reviews are conducted in the framework of a review tool, time spent on the review task can be tracked more easily. There are, of course, some difficulties in measuring time spent on review as part of application usage. One mostly accurate solution is to monitor interaction with the application (keystrokes, mouse movements, and focus) to determine whether the reviewer is actively reviewing code or merely has the code review window open.

Time spent on code reviews can be an interesting metric in the context of other metrics and can answer the following questions:

- What percentage of our time did we spend on code review versus code implementation?

- How much time do we spend reviewing per thousand lines of code (KLOC)?

- What percentage of our time was spent on code reviews this release versus the last release?

- What is the ratio of time spent to errors discovered (issues per review hour)?

- What is the ratio of issues per review hour to bugs found by test or customer?

- And so on . . .

The preceding questions are samples. To determine the right answers for a particular situation, you need to ask yourself what the goals of code review are for your team. If the goals are to spot-check code before check-in, the time on task measurement might not be very interesting. But if you are interested in improving effectiveness or efficiency, some of these questions might help you determine whether you are reaching your goals.

More Review Collateral

Much more happens in a code review other than identifying rework. An important part of the process that is often lost over time is the conversations and comments about a piece of code. For example, when I have some code ready for review, I don't say, "Here's my code—take a look." Instead, I put together an introductory e-mail message with a few sentences or a paragraph describing what the code is doing (for example, fixing a bug or adding a feature), and I might describe some of my implementation decisions. This information helps the reviewers do a better job, but when the review is over, that information is lost. The loss gets worse when considering that the follow-up conversations—whether they are in e-mail, in a team review, or face to face—are also lost. Over time, this lost information can lead to difficulties in knowledge transfer and maintainability issues.

Another way a review tool can aid with code reviews is by tracking some of this collateral data. A code review tool can contain questions, comments, conversations, and other metadata and link them with the code. Anyone on the team can look at a source file and view the changes along with explanations and conversations regarding any change. If someone on the team needs to ramp up quickly on the background pertaining to a single file or component (for example, a new developer on the team), a tool could queue up all of the changes and related review comments and play them back in a movie or slide show. This movie wouldn't win an Oscar, but it would have phenomenal potential for preparing new team members (or existing team members taking on new responsibilities) quickly.

Two Faces of Review

For most people, the primary benefit of review is detecting bugs early. Reviews are, in fact, quite good at this, but they provide another benefit to any team that takes them seriously. Reviews are a fantastic teaching tool for everyone on the team. Developers and testers alike can use the review process to learn about techniques for improving code quality, better design skills, and writing more maintainable code. Conducting code reviews on a regular basis provides an opportunity for everyone involved to learn about diverse and potentially superior methods of coding.

Tools, Tools, Everywhere

A big advantage of working at a company with so many programmers is the number of software tools written by employees that are available to help solve any problem you might be facing.

A big disadvantage of working at a company with so many programmers is the number of software tools written by employees that you have to sort through to solve the problem you might be facing.

Microsoft's internal portal for engineering and productivity tools has been a tremendous asset for many years, and the number of tools available has grown substantially every year. One drawback to the growth has been the number of disparate tools that solve a single problem, albeit all in slightly different manners. Searches on the portal for "test harness" and "test framework" return 25 and 51 results, respectively. Although many of these tools have unique features or purposes, there is a considerable amount of duplication in functionality.

Reduce, Reuse, Recycle

The concept of *code reuse* (reusing sections of code or components) has always been a topic in software engineering. A software library, such as the common dialog library shipped with Windows, is a good example of code reuse. This library (comdlg32.dll) contains all of the dialog boxes and related functions used for opening and saving files, printing, choosing colors, and other common user interaction tasks. Programmers don't need to write their own functions or create their own UI to open or save files; they can just use the functions in the common dialog library.

Several years ago, when Office made the shift from being merely a group of applications geared toward people who needed spreadsheet and word processing functionality to a unified suite of applications for the business user, the team discovered that many functions were duplicated across the different applications. Because of this, mso.dll, the shared Office library, was born. With the shared library, programmers on the Office team can easily access common functions and implement consistent functionality and user interface across applications. A bigger benefit is that the test team needs to test these functions only in one place—everyone benefits.

Shared libraries work well in Windows and Office mainly because they are development platforms; that is, they are designed with the intent that programmers will use the exposed functionality to add to or enhance the baseline platform architecture. Code reuse also works well in Office because it's one product line. The challenge in taking better advantage of code reuse in tools and utilities is that most divisions or product lines have their own solution developed without knowledge of the other solutions. For the most part, there's no motivation and little benefit to share code.

What's the Problem?

On many levels, there is no problem. There are far worse problems a company can have than having too many lightweight XML parsers in the library. Additionally, the tools are shared in a central repository where everyone in the company can search for utilities and download whatever is appealing to them. More choices *should* lead to a better selection for everyone, but the opposite is generally true. In *The Paradox of Choice*,[4] Barry Schwartz discusses how having too many options to consider makes the ultimate decision much more difficult; that is part of the problem, but there's more to it.

One of the great things about Microsoft is that every product group sets their own goals, their own vision, and they determine their own way to solve the engineering problems they face from day to day. There's not much motivation other than saving time to adopt or reuse code for tools and utilities.

But still, there is a prevalent worry that code reuse isn't used as much as it should be, and that duplication of efforts and the not-invented-here (NIH) syndrome are prime targets as areas of improvement. To make tool adoption work across groups in a company the size of Microsoft, it is not enough to share just the tool—the code needs to be shared as well.

Open Development

Sharing code and tools between teams relies on meeting the unique needs of each team. If an individual or team cannot customize code or a tool themselves, or if the owner of the code cannot make the needed changes for them, their only remedy is to create their own copy or start from scratch. Unless, of course, the code is available for anyone to contribute to or modify.

In 2007, Microsoft launched a new internal portal named CodeBox, which is shown in Figure 15-4. With CodeBox, Microsoft engineers can create, host, and manage collaborative projects. Built by the Engineering Excellence team, CodeBox is an internally shared application with a look and feel similar to CodePlex (*http://www.codeplex.com*). CodeBox includes support for source control, which enables anyone to make additions and enhancements to any of the projects. The owners of the projects have complete control over which changes they accept, while those who are making changes remain free to work in a *branch* or *fork* (a branch or fork is a distinct copy of the original source that retains the same history) in case they need to retail special features that have not yet been accepted.

---

4   Barry Schwartz, *The Paradox of Choice* (New York: Harper Perennial, 2005).

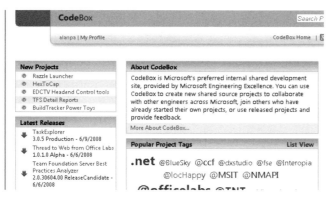

FIGURE 15-4 Microsoft CodeBox.

CodeBox use is growing quickly. Many of the popular tools from the previous tool portal have already been migrated to the shared source model on CodeBox. From January 2007 to March 2008, contributions grew from 50 to 400 per week. In addition to the shared tools and utilities, larger groups are using CodeBox as a workspace for developing applications that will someday grow to be new Microsoft products.

It's too early to tell the long-term benefit CodeBox is going to have on increasing code reuse, but the initial prognosis is good. As adoption and usage grow, shared code and tools will benefit the entire company in terms of reduced development costs, higher quality tools, and replacement of constant reinvention with building on the knowledge and experience of an entire engineering community.

Summary

Software engineering continues to grow in advancements as well as in complexity. With this advancement and complexity, new and bigger challenges consistently appear. To many software engineers, these challenges are a big part of the excitement and draw of the profession. Keeping one eye on the problems of today while anticipating and acting on the emerging problems of the future is a crucial attribute of great technical leaders at Microsoft and in the software industry. Improvements in failure analysis, code reviews, virtual machine usage, and code reuse are only four of the dozens of big challenges Microsoft engineers are confronting. These challenges, along with a continuing effort to improve software engineering, are an exciting part of the Microsoft culture.

Chapter 16
Building the Future

Alan Page

Software testing is still a relatively new discipline when compared with software development. Companies such as the Computer Usage Corporation (CUC) and Applied Data Research (ADR) started business in the 1950s and provided systems software and applications for computer manufacturers and business users. At that time, testing and debugging were synonymous, and both activities were entirely the programmer's job. In later years, testing became a separate activity, transforming roles from the acts of "bug finding" and verifying that the software satisfied the requirements to activities of finding errors and measuring quality.

For the most part, software testing is still an act of verifying software functionality and an attempt to find the most critical errors before the product finds its way into the hands of the customer. Software programs today are bigger, more complex, used in more varying scenarios, and have massive numbers of users. Although more testing occurs earlier in the product cycle in software companies and IT departments, it's unclear whether the investment is making headway against the growing complexity of today's software.

Even with our advances in techniques and improvement in software quality despite increases in complexity, we have to ask the obvious question: Where does testing go from here?

The Need for Forward Thinking

In *The Art of Software Testing*, Glenford Myers first stated the progression of testing from debugging to verification.[1] In 1988, Gelperin and Hetzel elaborated on the progression and growth of software testing,[2] and stated that the testing activity was moving toward a prevention activity. Twenty years later, testing is *still* moving toward becoming a prevention activity. There will always be a need for verification and analysis, but the biggest gains in software quality will likely come through preventative techniques.

Thinking Forward by Moving Backward

As the story goes, one day a villager was walking by the river that ran next to his village and saw a man drowning in the river. He swam into the river and brought the man to safety. Before he could get his breath, he saw another man drowning, so he yelled for help and went

---

[1] Glenford J. Myers, *The Art of Software Testing* (New York: John Wiley, 1979).

[2] D. Gelperin and B. Hetzel, "The Growth of Software Testing," *Communications of the ACM* 31, no. 6 (June 1988).

back into the river for another rescue mission. More and more drowning men appeared in the river, and more and more villagers were called upon to come help in the rescue efforts. In the midst of the chaos, one man began walking away along a trail up the river. One of the villagers called to him and asked, "Where are you going? We need your help." He said, "I'm going to find out who is throwing all of these people into the river."

Moving quality upstream is a commonly heard term in software testing circles, yet it's not done enough in the majority of contexts. Most software used today is too complex, too big, and too expensive to improve quality from testing alone. Almost every computer science book I own shows a graph illustrating the cost of a bug over time, yet the software industry still relies on one of the final stages of software engineering—testing—for a substantial portion of product quality. Table 16-1, taken from *Code Complete*,[3] is one such example of cost increase estimates dependent on the phase the bug was introduced.

TABLE 16-1 Average Cost of Fixing Defects Based on Introduction and Detection Phase

Time detected					
Time introduced	Requirements	Architecture	Construction	System test	Post-Release
Requirements	1	3	5–10	10	10–100
Architecture	—	1	10	15	25–100
Construction	—	—	1	1	10–25

The data presented by McConnell in this table explains that a bug introduced in the requirements phase that might cost $100 dollars to fix if found immediately will cost 10 times as much to fix if not discovered until the system test phase, or as much as 100 times as much if detected post-release. Bugs fixed close to when they are introduced are generally easier to fix. As bugs age in the system, the cost can increase as the developers have to reacquaint themselves with the code to fix the bug or as dependencies to the code in the area surrounding the bug introduce additional complexity and risk to the fix.

Striving for a Quality Culture

Joseph Juran, who is widely known for his contributions to quality thinking, was recognized for adding a human dimension to quality issues. Juran felt that cultural resistance was the root cause of quality issues.

A culture is shared beliefs, values, attitudes, institutions, and behavior patterns that characterize the members of a community or organization. A quality culture is one in which members of the community share values, attitudes, and beliefs regarding quality and take on their

---

[3] Steve McConnell, *Code Complete: A Practical Handbook of Software Construction* (Redmond, WA: Microsoft Press, 2004).

daily work with these attributes as a driving force. If quality is not ingrained into the culture in this way, quality practices will be viewed as pieces of the engineering puzzle that can be done "later."

Unfortunately, there is no such thing as "just-in-time" quality, and expecting quality to happen at the end of the product cycle is foolish. If quality is not at the forefront of engineering processes, it is impossible to reach acceptable levels of quality in the end. At a recent conference, Watts Humphrey rephrased this long-standing problem as, "If you want to get a high quality product out of test, you have to put a high quality product into test." The hard problem that we often avoid is, how can we get higher quality products into test?

Testing and Quality Assurance

Machiavelli wrote, "In the beginning of a malady it is easy to cure but difficult to detect, but in the course of time, not having been either detected or treated in the beginning, it becomes easy to detect, but difficult to cure."[4] The parallels of this statement in software are obvious: Early detection and prevention are the keys to avoiding problems that might be difficult to "cure" later.

The most common method for improving quality at Microsoft (and in the rest of the software industry as well) is testing. Testing is the means to unearth defects in software before customers can find them. In fact, with some of the best software testers in the industry, and the common practice of involving test early in the product cycle, Microsoft is extremely effective at finding bugs early in the product cycle. As good as that is, the prevailing approach is still to *test quality into the product*.

The word *testing* is often synonymous with quality assurance; however, these are two different acts of engineering. Testing is a *reactive* approach—finding defects that are latent in the product using various detection and investigative techniques, whereas quality assurance is a *proactive* approach—building an environment where bug prevention and a quality culture are inherent in the development life cycle. Aspects of quality assurance are present in all disciplines but are most prevalent in the test discipline.

The Engineering Excellence group at Microsoft designed and regularly delivers a course for senior testers at Microsoft where a large amount of the material covers quality assurance techniques rather than testing techniques. In many cases, a senior test role at Microsoft is much more like a quality assurance role than a test role, where the primary role is to improve quality practices affecting all engineering disciplines across a group or division.

---

4   Nicolo Machiavelli, *The Prince* (1513).

Who Owns Quality?

Many years ago, when I would ask the question, "Who owns quality?" the answer would nearly always be, "The test team owns quality." Today, when I ask this question, the answer is customarily "Everyone owns quality." Although this might be a better answer to some, W. Mark Manduke of SEI has written: "When quality is declared to be everyone's responsibility, no one is truly designated to be responsible for it, and quality issues fade into the chaos of the crisis du jour." He concludes that "when management truly commits to a quality culture, everyone will, indeed, be responsible for quality."[5]

A system where everyone truly owns quality requires a *culture* of quality. Without such a culture, all teams will make sacrifices against quality. Development teams might skip code reviews to save time, program management might cut corners on a specification or fudge a definition of "done," and test teams might change their goals on test pass or coverage rates deep in the product cycle. Despite many efforts to put quality assurance processes in place, it is a common practice among engineering teams to make exceptions in quality practices to meet deadlines or other goals. Although it's certainly important to be flexible to meet ship dates or other deadlines, quality often suffers because of a lack of a true quality owner.

Entire test teams might own facets of quality assurance, but they are rarely in the best position to champion or influence the adoption of a quality culture. Senior managers could be the quality champion, but their focus is justly on the business of managing the team, shipping the product, and running a successful business. Although they might have quality goals in mind, they are rarely the champion for a culture of quality. Management leadership teams (typically the organization leaders of Development, Test, and Program Management) bear the weight of quality ownership for most teams. These leaders own and drive the engineering processes for the team and are in the prime organizational position for evaluating, assessing, and implementing quality-based engineering practices. Unfortunately, it seems that quality software and quality software engineering practices are rarely their chief concerns throughout any product engineering cycle.

Senior management support for a quality culture isn't entirely enough. In a quality culture, every employee can have an impact on quality. Many of the most important quality improvements in manufacturing have come from suggestions by the workers. In the auto industry, for example, the average Japanese autoworker provides 28 suggestions per year, and 80 percent of those suggestions are implemented.[6]

Ideally, Microsoft engineers from all disciplines are making suggestions for improvement. Where a team does not have a culture of quality, the suggestions are few and precious few of those suggestions are implemented. Cultural apathy for quality will then lead to other challenges with passion and commitment among team members.

---

5   W. Mark Manduke, "Let SQA Be Your Guide," *STQE Magazine* 5, no. 6 (November/December 2003).

6   R. Wall, R. Solum, and M. Sobol, *The Visionary Leader* (Roseville, CA: Prima Lifestyles, 1992).

The Cost of Quality

Cost of quality is a term that is widely used but just as widely misunderstood. The cost of quality isn't the price of creating a quality product or service. It's the cost of *not* creating a quality product or service.

Every time work must be redone, the cost of quality increases. Obvious examples include the following:

- Rewriting or redesigning a component or feature

- Retesting as a result of test failure or code regression

- Rebuilding a tool used as part of the engineering process

- Reworking a service or process, such as a check-in system, build system, or review policy

In other words, any cost that would not have happened if quality were perfect contributes to the cost of quality. This is also known as cost of poor quality (COPQ).

In *Quality Is Free*, Phillip Crosby divides quality costs into three categories: appraisal, preventative, and failure. Appraisal costs include salaries (including the cost of paying testers) and costs to release. Preventative costs are expenditures associated with implementing and maintaining preventative techniques. Failure costs are the cost of rework (or the COPQ as stated previously). We rarely measure preventative costs, and we even more rarely reward them. Instead, we prefer to concentrate on heroics—working all night to fix the last few bugs, or investigating a workaround for a serious issue at the last minute.

Consider this quote from *The Persistence of Firefighting in Product Development*[7]:

> *Occasionally there is a superstar of an engineer or a manager that can take one of these late changes and run through the gauntlet of all the possible ways that it could screw up and make it a success. And then we make a hero out of that person. And everybody else who wants to be a hero says "Oh, that is what is valued around here." It is not valued to do the routine work months in advance and do the testing and eliminate all the problems before they become problems. What is valued is being able to make a change in the last minute and ramrod it through.*

This quote might seem familiar to many readers. We don't need heroics; we need to prevent the need for them.

---

[7] Nelson P. Repenning, Paulo Gonçalves, and Laura J. Black, *Past the Tipping Point: The Persistence of Firefighting in Product Development* (Cambridge, MA: Sloan School of Management, Massachusetts Institute of Technology, n.d.), *http://web.mit.edu/nelsonr/www/TippingV2_0-sub_doc.pdf*.

A New Role for Test

Some might ask if quality becomes deeply integrated in the design, and developers create far fewer bugs, what will the test team do? The truth is that finding bugs today might be *too* easy. In an organization where quality is inherent in the habits of everyone, the emphasis on the role of test moves away from finding massive numbers of defects to concentrating on emulating customer scenarios, peer review, and validation. There will still be bugs to find, but finding them will be a much bigger challenge than it is today. Testers will have the time to investigate complex integration scenarios and, unblocked by basic functionality issues, find a great number of the bugs that our customers find after release, removing much of the tremendous cost of hotfixes, updates, and service packs.

Others from the test role (as well as from other disciplines) can begin to function in a quality assurance role. These individuals will analyze and implement process improvement, defect prevention techniques, and infrastructure, and be the ambassadors for quality thinking and a quality culture in their organization. Growth and development of this role could be a key part of building and evangelizing a quality culture that spans the company.

More ideas on bug prevention, including root cause analysis and the need for a quality culture, are found in *The Practical Guide to Defect Prevention* (Microsoft Press, 2007), a book written by some of our testing colleagues at Microsoft.

Test Leadership

With more than 9,000 full-time testers at Microsoft at the time of this writing, there is tremendous need for a way to connect, share, and grow the capabilities of the discipline. This is a huge challenge in an organization of a hundred testers, but with a massive number of testers spread throughout the world, the challenge at Microsoft is monumental. Leadership is the key to developing a vibrant test engineering discipline, and leadership is how Microsoft addresses this issue.

The Microsoft Test Leadership Team

Leadership teams exist for every engineering discipline at Microsoft, and the Microsoft Test Leadership Team (MSTLT) is one of the most active and successful of these leadership teams. The principal goal of this team is to support sharing of testing knowledge and practices between all testers across the company. This goal is reflected in the MSTLT's mission (see the following sidebar) and in their accomplishments to date.

> ## The Microsoft Test Leadership Team vision
>
> The mission of the Microsoft Test Leadership Team (MSTLT) is to create a cross–business group forum to support elevating and resolving *common* challenges and issues in the test discipline. The MSTLT will drive education and best practice adoption back to the business group test teams that solve *common* challenges. Where appropriate the MSTLT will distinguish and bless business group *differences* that require local best practice optimization or deviation.

The MSTLT is made up of about 25 of the most senior test managers, directors, general managers, and VPs representing every product line at Microsoft. The selection process for representation for leadership team membership is critical to ensure its success. Membership selection is based on level of seniority, as well as nomination or approval from the TLT chair and the product line vice president. (See Chapter 2, "Software Test Engineers at Microsoft.") Without the proper makeup, leadership teams cannot speak for their community at large in a balanced and representative way. Additionally, they need the support of their organizational leadership to represent their organizations adequately and fairly.

Test Leadership Team Chair

Grant George was (and remains) the first chair of the test leadership team. He took on the role of chair of the MSTLT in August of 2003 and fostered growth of the team through its initial period. In 2004, the Engineering Excellence organization began to support these virtual teams, and as such, the MSTLT chair became a close partner for engineering excellence. This virtual merger also allowed the MSTLT to have a very active role in reviewing and proving feedback on tester training, engineering excellence awards, and the career development road map for testers (developed jointly by the MSTLT and HR).

> ## Kicking off the Microsoft Test Leadership Team
>
> **From:** Grant George
> **Sent:** Friday, October 17, 2003, 13:11
> **Subject:** Microsoft Test Leadership Team
> **When:** Wednesday, December 17, 2003, 12:00–14:00 (GMT-08:00) Pacific Time (US and Canada)
> **Where:** 17/3002
>
> As you may know, there is collective effort to form "professional discipline leadership teams" across our product groups at Microsoft to create community and collaborative solving of some of the biggest challenges facing each discipline in our businesses. There are a number of complex and challenging product cycles ahead of us in the

"Wave 12" (next 2–3 years) time frame and we should meet with more regularity to tackle those challenges and leverage and coordinate the leadership and approaches we must deliver on across test teams at Microsoft for high quality product delivery—if not also agree on how we will measure continued growth, increased impact, and higher efficiency in test engineering at Microsoft.

Our kickoff meeting as this newly formed leadership team will be on Wednesday, November 12, from noon to 2 p.m. in 17/3002.

At that first meeting we will discuss meeting frequency and mechanics, how we want to work as a leadership team, what our collective responsibilities need to be in how we channel/represent the constituent test teams in the business groups we will each represent, and prioritize the set of issues facing our test businesses over the coming product cycles (again, next 2 to 3 years). We will review specific proposals for this in the first meeting along with a number of other issues on our collective test engineering radars. There is much we can and should coordinate, improve, and lead our businesses on— test tools, test automation environment approaches and strategies, cross-group testing and technology delivery, people growth and performance management practices in Test, among many others topics.

Thanks in advance for your help and participation in this new forum.

—*Grant*

Test Leadership in Action

Every year, the Microsoft Test Leadership Team (MSTLT), in conjunction with the Engineering Excellence team, selects three to six areas where significant research or investigation related to the growth or improvement of testing at Microsoft is necessary. Past examples have included work on career paths for senior testers, automation sharing, lab management, and career stage profiles for testers.

The MSTLT meets monthly. The meeting agendas vary from month to month but focus on a few main areas. These include the following:

- **Updates on yearly initiatives** At least one MSTLT member is responsible for every MSTLT initiative and for presenting to the group on its progress at least four times throughout the year.

- **Reports from human resources** The MSTLT has a strong relationship with the corporate human resources department. This meeting provides an opportunity for HR to disseminate information to test leadership as well as take representative feedback from the MSTLT membership.

- **Other topics for leadership review**   Changes in engineering mandates or in other corporate policies that affect engineering are presented to the leadership team before circulation to the full test population. With this background information available, MSTLT members can distribute the information to their respective divisions with accurate facts and proper context.

The Test Architect Group

The Test Architect Group (TAG) is composed of senior nonmanagement leaders from the test discipline. When Soma Somasegar, then a Director of Test in the Windows division, created the Test Architect title, he encouraged the initial Test Architects to meet regularly and discuss the challenges and successes they were having on their respective teams. The group started with only six Test Architects, mostly from the Windows division, but has since grown to more than 40 Test Architects spanning every major division at Microsoft. Originally, only testers with the Test Architect title were members of the group, but as Microsoft has moved more toward standard titles (for example, SDET, Senior SDET, and Principal SDET, as discussed in Chapter 2), the group now includes all senior testers who are functioning in a test architect *role* regardless of their address book title.

TAG—You're it!

From: S. Somasegar
Sent: Thursday, January 11, 2001, 10:46
Subject: Test Architect

We are creating a new position called Test Architect. There are a lot of opportunities for us to apply some strong technical leadership to how we test and what we test to ensure that we continuously move quality upstream into our development process, be smart about our test automation so that we are very efficient in testing, build testability hooks in the product, etc. We need to make some big investments in solving the scalability issues related to testing/validating increasingly complex products across an expanding hardware base.

The Test Architect position provides an opportunity for us to invest in senior, individual technical contributors in the test organization to focus on some of these key issues.

The primary goals for creating the Test Architect position are:

- To apply a critical mass of senior, individual contributors on difficult/global testing problems facing Windows development teams

- To create a technical career path for individual contributors in the test teams

---

Some of the key things that Test Architects would focus on include:

- Continue to evolve our development process by moving quality upstream
- Increase the throughput of our testing process through automation, smart practices, consolidation, and leadership

The profile of a Test Architect:

- Motivated to solve the most challenging problems faced by our testing teams
- Senior-level individual contributor
- Has a solid understanding of Microsoft testing practices and the product development process
- Ability to work both independently and cross group developing and deploying testing solutions

Test Architects will be nominated by VPs and would remain in their current teams. They will be focused on solving key problems and issues facing the test teams across the board. The Test Architects will form a virtual team and meet regularly to collaborate with each other and other Microsoft groups including Research. Each Test Architect will be responsible for representing unique problems faced by their teams and own implementing and driving key initiatives within their organizations in addition to working on cross-group issues.

Nearly 10 years after the establishment of the group, the TAG members still meet nearly every week. Test architects are primarily dedicated to addressing technical issues on their own teams, but this group has found numerous benefits in meeting regularly to share ideas and best practices on testing and quality issues at Microsoft. In fact, many of the meeting agendas center on the original mission of sharing current challenges and success stories.

The value of having Microsoft's most senior testers regularly review, brainstorm, and dissect solutions for complex test problems is immeasurable. In recent years, TAG has become something of a sounding board for new thinking, new methods, or new tools in testing. Presentations and demonstrations of ideas and implementations from test groups spanning every Microsoft division fill many of the meeting agendas. The value and depth of the feedback that the TAG provides is respected and sought after. A few meetings a year are reserved for "TAG business," which includes discussions about company-wide initiatives driven by TAG and other projects where TAG is a significant contributor (such as the MSDN Tester Center).

Perhaps the largest benefit of the regular meetings is in the value of networking. The extensive peer discussions and the view into the variety of work done across the company that is presented give TAG members much of the knowledge and information they need to make strategic decisions that affect the entire company.

Another way that the Test Architect Group provides value to Microsoft is by being open and available for informal discussions on any topic with anyone. E-mail discussions and ad hoc meeting requests are a start, but one of the most successful initiatives in this area is the "Have Lunch with a Test Architect" program. Every month, Test Architects across the company have dozens of lunch chats with testers of all levels of seniority and in a variety of product groups.

Have lunch with a Test Architect

The announcement on the internal Test Architect Web site reads:

One of the greatest benefits we've seen from the Test Architect Group is the power of networking. Since the group is comprised of members from all over Microsoft, it has been really great for us to hear the different viewpoints, share techniques, and reduce the Six Degrees of Separation that make it hard to work across groups. We wanted to find a way to scale up this benefit for all testers, make our group more accessible, and make more connections throughout the company to share the best test efforts and raise the bar for everyone. To that end, we'd like to talk with you. Do you want to talk about technical problems you are facing with a tester from another group? Would you like to brainstorm on a solution you are considering? Want to learn more about what a Test Architect does? Want to have a casual conversation about careers?

So do we! We'd love to grab a lunch, share information about hard problems, better understand the problems your group is facing to see if we can help (or know someone who can), and grow our list of contacts to advance the test community at Microsoft. If you're interested in sitting down with one of us, feel free to contact anyone in the list below.

Our calendars are up to date, and our interests and experience are available below. Just send any of us a meeting request for lunch—you don't even have to come to the cafeteria in our building! We look forward to talking to you.

Note   Microsoft Research has an entire group that studies software testing and verification (along with program analysis and other software measurement). Descriptions of their projects can be found at *http://research.microsoft.com/srr*.

Test Excellence

In 2003, Microsoft created the Engineering Excellence (EE) team. In addition to technical training (the core of the group was the previous technical education group), the mission of the group is to discover and share best practices in engineering across the company. The group as a whole encompasses all engineering disciplines, with the test discipline represented by the Test Excellence team. This team considers their customers to be every tester at Microsoft. From new hire to vice president, success of the overall test community is what drives this group. The primary tasks of the Test Excellence team can be summarized as *sharing*, *helping*, and *communicating*.

Sharing

Sharing aligns with the EE goal of sharing best practices. In the case of Test Excellence, sharing incorporates practices, tools, and experiences.

- **Practices**   The Test Excellence team identifies practices or approaches that have potential for use across different teams or divisions at Microsoft. The goal is not to make everyone work the same way, but to identify good work that is adoptable by others.

- **Tools**   The approach with tools is similar to practices. For the most part, the core training provided by the Test Excellence team is tool-agnostic, that is, the training focuses on techniques and methods but doesn't promote one tool over another. However, when a specific tool is identified as being the best solution for solving a specific problem or application of a specific technique, it can be used and evangelized in a core technical training class. An example of this is the PICT tool discussed in Chapter 5, "Functional Testing Techniques." This is a perfect tool for pairwise analysis and is universally used when teaching this particular technique.

- **Experiences**   Microsoft teams work in numerous different ways—often isolated from those whose experiences they could potentially learn from. Test Excellence attempts to gather those experiences through case studies, presentations ("Test Talks"), and interviews, and then share those experiences with disparate teams.

 Note More than 20 Test Talks (presentations on effective test practices) are held every year. Test Talks are open to all testers at Microsoft (including live Webcasts and recordings for testers outside of Redmond).

The Engineering Excellence Forum

One of the most visible ways the Test Excellence team and all of Engineering Excellence help share practices with all engineers at Microsoft is through the Engineering Excellence Forum. The forum is an annual event, held over five days every June. The forum is packed with presentations, panel discussions, demonstrations, and of course, free lunch and snacks. The EE Forum is much like one of the huge software development or testing conferences that occur every year, but targeted at, and attended exclusively by, Microsoft employees. Hundreds of employees take part in the planning, preparation, and presentations, while thousands more attend every year. It's a prime opportunity for employees to learn about practices and tools used by other teams at Microsoft.

Helping

The Test Excellence team functions as facilitators and experts for the overall test community. They use these roles to establish and maintain connections with testers. In fact, the tagline for the Test Excellence team is *We connect the dots . . . to quality*, and this brand statement drives much of their work. Some of the ways this team helps testers are *facilitation, answers,* and *connections*:

- **Facilitation**   Test Excellence team members often assist in facilitating executive briefings, product line strategy meetings, and team postmortem discussions. Their strategic insight and view from a position outside the product groups are sought out and valued.

- **Answers**   Engineers at Microsoft expect the Test Excellence team to know about testing and aren't afraid to ask them. In many cases, team members do know the answer, but when they do not, their connections enable them to find answers quickly. Sometimes, team members refer to themselves as *test therapists* and meet individually with testers to discuss questions about career growth, management challenges, or work–life balance.

- **Connections**   Probably the biggest value of Test Excellence is connections—their interaction with the TLT, TAG, Microsoft Research, and product line leadership ensures that they can reduce the degrees of separation between any engineers at Microsoft and help them solve their problems quickly and efficiently.

Communicating

Another key value of Test Excellence is simply in communicating what they know and discover. There is tremendous value in sharing relevant information in a large community. Some of the communication coming from the Test Excellence team includes the following:

- A monthly test newsletter for all testers at Microsoft includes information on upcoming events, status of MSTLT initiatives, and announcements relevant to the test discipline.

- University relationships are discussed, including reviews on test and engineering curriculum as well as general communications with department chairs and professors who teach quality and testing courses in their programs.

- The Microsoft Tester Center (*http://www.msdn.com/testercenter*)—much like this book—intends to provide an inside view into the testing practices and approaches used by Microsoft testers. This site, launched in late 2007, is growing quickly. Microsoft employees currently create most of the content, but industry testers provide a growing portion of the overall site content and are expected to become larger contributors in the future.

Working together

The Engineering Excellence group recently remodeled their office space to include team rooms for each of the discipline-focused "Excellence" groups. Microsoft's policy of supplying individual offices to engineers is well known, and *Peopleware*,[8] DeMarco and Lister's seminal text on productivity among software engineers, explains how and why private offices for engineers increase productivity.

Why would Microsoft change their ways and make a "cube farm"? In the case of Engineering Excellence, the decision was almost purely experimental. Agile software development practitioners talk about the necessity for collaboration that a team room provides, but I've also met many people who would rather work in a treehouse than in a shared office. The work that our team performs does have some collaborative aspects, but certainly can't be considered as collaborative as a software product. Nevertheless, in May of 2006, just a few days before the remodel was to begin, we packed and moved to a temporary office; then, moved back into our new team room a few months later.

I don't know if any of us knew completely what to expect, but overall, I think we were all pleasantly surprised. I think the biggest benefit is that we have nearly 1,000 square feet of space dispersed between six of us. Given the nature of our jobs, it seems even bigger because, outside of team meetings, it's extremely rare that we are all in the office at the same time. We also have flexibility—if we were to add one more person

---

8 Timothy Lister and Tom DeMarco, *Peopleware: Productive Projects and Teams* (New York: Dorset House, 1987).

to the team, we could make some small modifications and find room for that person easily. We have couches, chairs, a ceiling-mounted projector, an Xbox, and an espresso machine. Almost every wall is usable as a whiteboard, and we've hung whiteboards on most of those that aren't. Most of the workspaces sit along a wall of windows. Figure 16-1 shows the current configuration of our room.

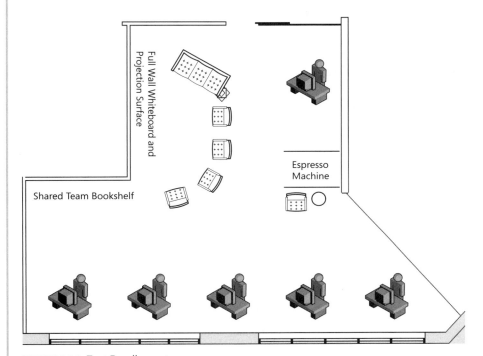

FIGURE 16-1 Test Excellence team room.

The room can get "busy" sometimes, and we all have had to resort to headphones occasionally to cut down on the distractions, but most of the time we are all happy with the room. We have our own spaces, but we can talk face to face when we need to. Our arrangement is a bit of a compromise between a "cube farm" and an individual office.

We have six in the room now, and it would probably work with a few more, but I think the team room concept would fail as team size approached double digits. The biggest benefit of the shared space is that we are all more aware than ever of the work that our teammates are doing—and we have a fun, modern place to work.

Perhaps the most prevalent indicator of the success of our new room was when I took over the leadership of the Test Excellence team. I chose to keep my desk in the team room. I also have an office that we all use for 1:1 (pronounced one-on-one) meetings, interviews, and other private meetings, but I enjoy spending most of my time working in what we have come to call our "test lounge."

Keeping an Eye on the Future

Perhaps the most critical role of the Test Excellence team is anticipating the future needs of testers at Microsoft and being proactive in defining the future vision of software testing. This vision is the basis for yearly planning and Test Excellence initiatives. The purpose of the vision, like most good visions, is to give direction on the discipline and to guide the work to be done.

Microsoft Director of Test Excellence

One of the most unique roles at Microsoft is that of the Director of Test Excellence. In some ways, the role is simply to be the manager in charge of the Test Excellence team, but it also has a tremendous amount of scope and opportunity to influence testers across the entire company.

Not surprisingly, it's a role that all three authors of this book have held. Currently, the Director of Test role is tied to the Director of Test Excellence role, but originally it was just a senior test position responsible for advancement of the testing profession at Microsoft.

The following people have all held the Director of Test position:

- Dave Moore (Director of Development and Test), 1991–1994
- Roger Sherman (Director of Test), 1994–1997
- James Tierney (Director of Test), 1997–2000
- Barry Preppernau (Director of Test), 2000–2002
- William Rollison (Director of Test), 2002–2004
- Ken Johnston (Director of Test Excellence), 2004–2006
- James Rodrigues (Director of Test Excellence), 2006–2007
- Alan Page (Director of Test Excellence), 2007–present

Because this is a full-time position managing a small strategy team the role also functions as the connection between the TLT and the TAG with an emphasis on working closely with the chairs of the two organizations.

The Leadership Triad

The Microsoft Test Leadership Team, Test Architect Group, and Test Excellence organizations fill a vital role in the development and maintenance of the test culture at Microsoft, as shown in Figure 16-2. In each of these organizations is a leadership position chartered to work for the discipline and across the teams. In the case of the TLT chair and the TAG chair, these are virtual teams and the chairmanship is an extra duty for the individual in that role. For the Director of Test Excellence it is a full-time position.

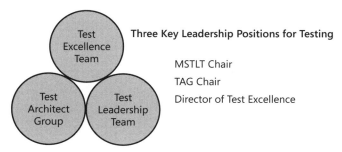

Three Key Leadership Positions for Testing

MSTLT Chair

TAG Chair

Director of Test Excellence

FIGURE 16-2 Three key leadership positions in the three test support organizations.

Innovating for the Future

All new Microsoft employees attend the New Employee Orientation (NEO). New Microsoft hires spend most of their first two days learning about policies, organizations, and other top-ics that we feel all new employees should know about. I frequently present on the topic of innovation. Microsoft will certainly continue to innovate in our new products, as well as in new areas such as Zune and tabletop computing, but the big message I try to convey is that innovation might be more important in the *way* we make our products and in how we enable customers to innovate on our technologies.

When I think of software in the future, or when I see software depicted in a science fiction movie, two things always jump out at me. The first is that *software will be everywhere*. As prevalent as software is today, in the future, software will interact with nearly every aspect of our lives. The second thing that I see is that *software just works*. I can't think of a single time when I watched a detective or scientist in the future use software to help them solve a case or a problem and the system didn't work perfectly for them, and I most certainly have never seen the software they were using crash. That is my vision of software—software everywhere that just works.

Getting there, as you've realized by reading this far in the book, is a difficult process, and it's more than we testers can do on our own. If we're going to achieve this vision, we, as a soft-ware engineering industry, need to continue to challenge ourselves and innovate in the pro-cesses and tools we use to make software. It's a challenge that I embrace and look forward to, and I hope all readers of this book will join me.

If you have questions or comments for the authors of this book (or would like to report bugs) or would like to keep track of our continuing thoughts on any of the subjects in this book, please visit *http://www.hwtsam.com*. We would all love to hear what you have to say.

—*Alan, Ken, and Bj*

Index

A

closed (bug status), 193
cloud services, 320
CLR (Common Language Runtime), 179
CMMI (Capability Maturity Model Integrated), 53
code analysis. *See* static analysis
code churn, 273–275
code complexity
 in automated tests, 247
 cyclomatic complexity, 133
  measuring, 63, 149–152, 155
 estimating (code smell), 147
 estimating test time, 65
 Halstead metrics, 152–153
 how to use metrics for, 157
 lines of code (LOC), 147–148
 object-oriented metrics, 153
 quantifying, 146–148
 risk from, 145–158
code coverage
 analysis tools for, 293
 behavioral and exploratory testing, 117
 combinatorial analysis and, 112
 with functional testing, 77
 milestone criteria, 46
 quality gates, 49
 scripted tests, 117
 statement vs. block coverage, 118
code reuse, 385–387
code reviews, 379–384
 collateral data with, 384
 measuring effectiveness of, 381–384
code smell, 147
code snapshots, 275, 374, 378
CodeBox portal, 386
Cole, David, 261
collaboration. *See* communication
collecting data from customers. *See* CEIP
 (Customer Experience Improvement Plan)
combination tests, 102
combinatorial analysis
 effectiveness of, 111
 tools for, in practice, 104–111
communication, 380
 cross-boundary collaboration (competency), 28
company values at Microsoft, 4
comparing documents, 276
compatibility testing, 261–263
 dogfooding (being users), 264, 350

competencies, 27
compilation errors, 284, 285
complexity of code
 in automated tests, 247
 cyclomatic complexity, 133
  measuring, 63, 149–152, 155
 estimating (code smell), 147
 estimating test time, 65
 Halstead metrics, 152–153
 how to use metrics for, 157
 lines of code (LOC), 147–148
 object-oriented metrics, 153
 quantifying, 146–148
 risk from, 145–158
complexity of test automation, 221
compound conditional clauses, testing, 129
compressibility (metric), 352, 353
computer-assisted testing, 230
computing innovations, waves of, 329
condition testing, 129–132
conditional clauses, testing. *See* condition
 testing; decision testing
conditions (test case attribute), 212
confidence (competency), 28
 with functional testing, 77
configurability of bug tracking system, 191
configuration data, collecting, 300
configurations (test case attribute), 212
conformance, in test time estimation, 65
Connect site, 312
container-based datacenters (container SKUs), 322
Content discipline, 15
context, bug, 194
continuous improvement. *See* process
 improvement
contrast, display, 268
control flow diagrams (CFDs), 122
control flow graphs, 149
control flow modeling, 118, 122
control flow testing. *See* structural testing
control testability, 67
Corporate Error Reporting (CER), 307
cost of quality, 369
cost of test automation, 220
count of changes (churn metric), 273
counters (performance), 254
counting bugs, 200, 204
counting test cases, 215–216, 217
coupling, services, 333–335, 346

Best Practices for Software Engineering

Software Estimation:
Demystifying the Black Art
Steve McConnell
ISBN 9780735605350

Code Complete,
Second Edition
Steve McConnell
ISBN 9780735619678

Amazon.com's pick for "Best Computer Book of 2006"! Generating accurate software estimates is fairly straight-forward—once you understand the art of creating them. Acclaimed author Steve McConnell demystifies the process—illuminating the practical procedures, formulas, and heuristics you can apply right away.

Widely considered one of the best practical guides to programming—fully updated. Drawing from research, academia, and everyday commercial practice, McConnell synthesizes must-know principles and techniques into clear, pragmatic guidance. Rethink your approach—and deliver the highest quality code.

Agile Portfolio Management
Jochen Krebs
ISBN 9780735625679

Simple Architectures for
Complex Enterprises
Roger Sessions
ISBN 9780735625785

Agile processes foster better collaboration, innovation, and results. So why limit their use to software projects—when you can transform your entire business? This book illuminates the opportunities—and rewards—of applying agile processes to your overall IT portfolio, with best practices for optimizing results.

Why do so many IT projects fail? Enterprise consultant Roger Sessions believes complex problems require simple solutions. And in this book, he shows how to make simplicity a core architectural requirement—as critical as performance, reliability, or security—to achieve better, more reliable results for your organization.

The Enterprise and Scrum
Ken Schwaber
ISBN 9780735623378

ALSO SEE

Software Requirements, Second Edition
Karl E. Wiegers
ISBN 9780735618794

More About Software Requirements:
Thorny Issues and Practical Advice
Karl E. Wiegers
ISBN 9780735622678

Software Requirement Patterns
Stephen Withall
ISBN 9780735623989

Agile Project Management with Scrum
Ken Schwaber
ISBN 9780735619937

Extend Scrum's benefits—greater agility, higher-quality products, and lower costs—beyond individual teams to the entire enterprise. Scrum cofounder Ken Schwaber describes proven practices for adopting Scrum principles across your organization, including that all-critical component—managing change.

microsoft.com/mspress

Collaborative Technologies—
Resources for Developers

**Inside Microsoft® Windows®
SharePoint® Services 3.0**
Ted Pattison, Daniel Larson
ISBN 9780735623200

**Inside Microsoft Office
SharePoint Server 2007**
Patrick Tisseghem
ISBN 9780735623682

Get the in-depth architectural insights, task-oriented guidance, and extensive code samples you need to build robust, enterprise content-management solutions.

Led by an expert in collaboration technologies, you'll plumb the internals of SharePoint Server 2007—and master the intricacies of developing intranets, extranets, and Web-based applications.

**Inside the Index and Search
Engines: Microsoft Office
SharePoint Server 2007**
Patrick Tisseghem, Lars Fastrup
ISBN 9780735625358

**Working with Microsoft
Dynamics® CRM 4.0,**
Second Edition
Mike Snyder, Jim Steger
ISBN 9780735623781

Customize and extend the enterprise search capabilities in SharePoint Server 2007—and optimize the user experience—with guidance from two recognized SharePoint experts.

Whether you're an IT professional, a developer, or a power user, get real-world guidance on how to make Microsoft Dynamics CRM work the way you do—with or without programming.

**Programming Microsoft
Dynamics CRM 4.0**
Jim Steger *et al.*
ISBN 9780735625945

ALSO SEE

Inside Microsoft Dynamics AX 2009
ISBN 9780735626454

**6 Microsoft Office Business Applications
for Office SharePoint Server 2007**
ISBN 9780735622760

Apply the design and coding practices that leading CRM consultants use to customize, integrate, and extend Microsoft Dynamics CRM 4.0 for specific business needs.

**Programming Microsoft Office
Business Applications**
ISBN 9780735625365

**Inside Microsoft Exchange Server 2007
Web Services**
ISBN 9780735623927

microsoft.com/mspress

About the Authors

Alan Page began his software testing career in 1993 and joined Microsoft in 1995. In Alan's career at Microsoft, he has worked on various versions of Windows, Internet Explorer, and Windows CE. While a member of the Windows CE team, Alan became one of Microsoft's first Test Architects in 2001. Alan joined the Engineering Excellence team in 2005 and is currently the Director of Test Excellence at Microsoft, where he and his team provide technical training and consulting for testers at Microsoft

Ken Johnston is the Group Manager for the Microsoft Office Internet Platform & Operations team. This team develops manageability features for server products and services as well as provides live site operations support for Office Online, Office Live, CRM Online and several other services. Since joining Microsoft in 1998 Johnston has filled many other roles, including test lead on Site Server and MCIS and test manager on Hosted Exchange, Knowledge Worker Services, Net Docs, and the Microsoft Billing and Subscription Platform service. For two and a half years (2004-2006) he served as the Microsoft Director of Test Excellence.

Bj Rollison is a Test Architect in the Engineering Excellence team. He began his Microsoft career in 1994, working on Windows 95. He also worked on various releases of Internet Explorer, Outlook 98, and several smaller projects until becoming the Director of Test in 1999. Prior to Microsoft, Bj worked for a small OEM company in Japan building hardware and software solutions for small business-es. Bj is a frequent speaker at international conferences, contrib-utes regularly to professional trade journals, and also teaches courses in software testing and test automation for the University of Washington Extension Program.

What do you think of this book?

We want to hear from you!

Do you have a few minutes to participate in a brief online survey?

Microsoft is interested in hearing your feedback so we can continually improve our books and learning resources for you.

To participate in our survey, please visit:

www.microsoft.com/learning/booksurvey/

...and enter this book's ISBN-10 or ISBN-13 number (located above barcode on back cover*). As a thank-you to survey participants in the United States and Canada, each month we'll randomly select five respondents to win one of five $100 gift certificates from a leading online merchant. At the conclusion of the survey, you can enter the drawing by providing your e-mail address, which will be used for prize notification only.

Thanks in advance for your input. Your opinion counts!

* Where to find the ISBN on back cover

ISBN-13: 000-0-0000-0000-0
ISBN-10: 0-0000-0000-0

Example only. Each book has unique ISBN.

Microsoft® Press

www.microsoft.com/learning/booksurvey/